Bold Resilient Women

Bold Resilient Women

Women in a Global Arena

Eleni Palivos Bousis

© 2025, All rights reserved. No portion of this book may be reproduced, stored in a retrieval system, or transmitted in any form or by any means—electronic, mechanical, photocopy, recording, scanning, or otherwise—except for brief quotations used in critical reviews or articles, without the prior written permission of the author.

First published in Athens, October 2024

Book pagination/design by Michalis Sideris Publications

Andrea Metaxa 28 & Themistokleous, Exarchia, 106 81 Athens, Greece

Tel: +30 210 3301161-2-3 • Fax: +30 210 3301164

Email: info@siderisbooks.gr • www.siderisbooks.gr

Global Edition Published in 2025 by Game Changer Publishing

Paperback ISBN: 978-1-969372-55-1

Hardcover ISBN: 978-1-969372-56-8

Digital ISBN: 978-1-969372-57-5

www.GameChangerPublishing.com

This is an inspirational and powerful book of personal stories, family tragedies and the enduring emotional and physical pain of war, poverty, illness and death. But it's also filled with hope, perseverance and motivation.

Bold Resilient Women

Women in a Global Arena

Eleni Palivos Bousis

Table of Contents

Preface	xi

Part One: The Old Country

Chapter 1: Courage	3
Chapter 2: Grandmother's Family	13
Chapter 3: Faith	23
Chapter 4: Love of a Strong Woman	27
Chapter 5: War and Eruption of Corpses	35
Chapter 6: Dad's Pain	39

Part Two: A Modern Woman in a Modern World

Chapter 7: Innocent Eyes	45
Chapter 8: Immigrants	47
Chapter 9: Inspirational Mentors	53
Chapter 10: Chicago, a Big City	61
Chapter 11: Laughter	67
Chapter 12: Satisfaction	69
Chapter 13: Committed Parents	73
Chapter 14: An Explosion	79
Chapter 15: A Holy Woman	89
Chapter 16: Stages of Life	91
Chapter 17: Finding My Passion	97
Chapter 18: Young Innocent Love	105
Chapter 19: Challenges at Childbirth	121
Chapter 20: More Challenges	127
Chapter 21: Second Pregnancy	131
Chapter 22: Adolescence	139
Chapter 23: Losing Control of My Life	143
Chapter 24: Reunited as a Changed Woman	151
Chapter 25: My Third Child, a New Beginning	155
Chapter 26: An Exceptional, Beautiful Child	159
Chapter 27: Another Change	165
Chapter 28: Strong Women Never Give Up	169
Chapter 29: Fourth Pregnancy	173
Chapter 30: What's Missing	177

Chapter 31: Staying With My Baby	181
Chapter 32: Being Open-Minded	185
Chapter 33: Neglect	189
Chapter 34: Changing the World in His Eyes	193
Chapter 35: Conquering the World	197
Chapter 36: Monumental Objects	201
Chapter 37: Without Entitlement	203
Chapter 38: A New Home	207
Chapter 39: People in Your Path	211
Chapter 40: Cancer Hits Home	217
Chapter 41: Unconditional Love	225
Chapter 42: India, Kathmandu, Nepal, Fish Island	229
Chapter 43: Success	233

Part Three: Everyone Has a Story

Chapter 44: A Mother Losing Hope	239
Chapter 45: Eye Openers	243
Chapter 46: Carole, a Dear Mentor	249
Chapter 47: Zoe	257
Chapter 48: Losing a Young Child	261
Chapter 49: Connection of Pain	265
Chapter 50: Dorothy	271
Chapter 51: Irene, a Dynamic Woman	275
Chapter 52: Andrea	281
Chapter 53: Friends Losing Faith	287
Chapter 54: Innocent Girls Left Behind	291
Chapter 55: Laura	295
Chapter 56: Marie	299
Chapter 57: Susan and Charlene	303
Chapter 58: Claire's Nightmare	309
Chapter 59: Not Seen as Beautiful	313
Chapter 60: Anna	315
Chapter 61: Resentment	319
Chapter 62: Mary Kay	321
Chapter 63: Mr. Bouras, a Man of Steel	327
Chapter 64: Lost Love	333
Chapter 65: Marianne, a Woman of Strength and Courage	337
Chapter 66: Riches to Rags	345

Part Four: The World Today

Chapter 67: My Calling	353
Chapter 68: Strong Women Among Us	355
Chapter 69: Love Conquers	359
Chapter 70: The Elderly	363
Chapter 71: Life and Learning	367
Chapter 72: Learning the Facts of Life Violence	371
Chapter 73: Children Without a Choice	381
Chapter 74: Tough Decisions	385
Chapter 75: Children in a Challenging World	389
Chapter 76: Today's Challenges	395
Chapter 77: Women Helping Women	399
Chapter 78: Making Choices	403
Chapter 79: Teach Children the Meaning of Love	409
Chapter 80: Yesterday and Today's Women	415
Acknowledgments	421

Preface

My book is inspired by life's difficulties, my children, and the strain of the daily challenges my husband and I faced as a young married couple. If I didn't have inspiring, strong, secure, and powerful women in my life, I could not have become the woman I am today. My success is a tribute to the remarkable women and men who became my role models and motivation in life.

Most of my life involved balancing marriage and motherhood and working to raise four successful and talented children. Meanwhile, I took college courses while simultaneously working. I wanted to stay connected to family, friends, and my spiritual life, which at times was very difficult. Life became vigorous and complicated. I didn't want to lose my interest and passion for public service. Philanthropy has always been part of my life, even when I was a young girl. I could not allow any obstacles or challenges to stand in the way. I needed to do it all. I thought I was indestructible and nothing could break me.

Serving on numerous boards and organizations while raising a young family and working to support our family was chaotic and complicated. I didn't have the time or energy to concentrate on my identity. Who was I? What did I want to achieve? What was my life's purpose? What did I want my legacy to be?

Meeting and working with a variety of women globally from different paths, backgrounds, cultures and faiths inspired me to see the gift of a woman's perspective and her role in society.

I noticed that women react differently to certain situations and comments from different people. I witnessed how different cultural backgrounds and

Preface

environments affected women. Individuals felt energized, enlightened, and blessed by the fact that they simply existed, while some women wished they had never been born. Others wanted to be advocates for humanity, saving women and children from abusive situations. Others wanted to explore certain parts of the world.

In monitoring and observing young women for numerous years, I noticed a dramatic change in their attitudes and empathy when surrounded by men from their culture. Women seemed to be under intense stress levels and anxiety when they engaged within their own cultural environment. Women's confidence, self-esteem, and behavior changed when men walked into a room. Women were expected to behave in particular ways that were permitted by their culture.

What has become a concerning and disturbing trend is that young women don't acknowledge their strength and their ability to love themselves more than others. Throughout my life, I have realized again and again what *agape* means. Unless you love yourself by taking care of your health and wellness first, it's impossible to assist others with their needs. You cannot provide unconditional love to someone else without first building your inner self and confidence.

It took many years of challenges, struggles, pain, and countless tears to understand the theory of selfishness and the idea of focusing only on myself and what will satisfy my ego.

As time, moments, and years drifted quickly in front of my eyes like a wild river, I acquired knowledge, confidence, and unwavering love for my true self and identity. I wanted to take responsibility for my own actions, whether they were good or bad. The viability of my internal world and my ability to look deep into my soul to witness strength and power helped me become a stable individual with confidence. I came to love myself unconditionally without judging my external looks or body.

Years came and went, and many individuals entered and departed my life like a drifting wind. Some of them were prominent citizens who infiltrated my life during times of distress and need. As each one came and left my life, I wanted to emulate them in many inspiring ways. I wanted to follow in their footsteps and succeed by becoming a motivated individual for others to follow. I gained wisdom and an understanding of life's sacrifices. I witnessed true integrity and compassion. My friend and mentor, Carole, always said, "Money and power are useless unless you have a good and honorable name in society. To be intelligent and kind is an inner quality and gift one can offer to many others without any reciprocation."

Getting to know family members and dear friends has been a lesson in

Preface

patience. Comprehending and sympathizing with their needs and afflictions was a challenge, so I became an attentive listener. Many acquaintances, employees, board members, and friends began to see me as a positive and energetic individual. My reputation excelled in every community due to my empathetic support and love for others. I was fortunate to receive a positive reception from the organizations I chaired by earning their trust and soliciting feedback.

Associates within various organizations inspired me with positive words and helped build my confidence to support those facing many painful struggles. They engraved in my heart pride for my upbringing as well as my values and morals, which eventually made me a stronger and more productive person. I gained the wisdom and intellectual confidence to be able to initiate and maintain a discussion by helping others through their struggles and sufferings.

Throughout my journey, I have learned to gain respect for individuals who supported my mission to care for those who had lost hope. Every person carried a different load of pain and sorrow, regardless of their background or financial security and stability.

Individuals who didn't come to terms with their suffering became resistant to change as they fought against the unbearable outcome. People struggling are left hopeless and distressed by hitting a dead end.

Watching many individuals hit rock bottom, seeing them disoriented and lost, made me aware of the importance of communication with those around me. People in my life have witnessed the power of God and His spirit through prayer and faith, lifting them up when all hope was lost.

No one needs to be apologetic, remorseful, ashamed, or disrespectful when it comes to situations beyond their control. We cannot judge anyone without knowing the secrets of their past and present. People only show us what they want us to see.

Listening to so many stories of heartache, breakups, and distress has made me realize that nothing in life is consequential. God has the ultimate plan for everyone. He is in control, and we are simply the passengers along for the ride. In God's plan, we experience things that teach us discipline, patience, obedience, and tolerance. I started to view and assess my own situations with a completely different perspective than what I had planned and imagined for my future.

Becoming an empty nester, with my four children off pursuing their own dreams and aspirations, left me feeling lonely, depressed, estranged, and useless. I didn't know my purpose in life. Although I remained involved with many foundations, I felt a huge void in my life. I saw my choice clearly. I could

Preface

attend school full-time, get a job, or concentrate on becoming more active with all my foundations.

I have been asked repeatedly to be an inspirational and motivational speaker for families and children, sharing the attributes and life experiences that allowed me to change and grow.

Friends from different parts of the world were amazed. I had accomplished multitasking, raising four children, and been married for numerous years to a successful man. Sometimes, years seemed like a short day, while many times, twenty-four hours felt like a lifetime.

I found out at an early age that true love either happens when you're in your teenage years or later on in life, when you have experienced knowledge, success, failure, and heartbreak. My desire to love unconditionally came in my teenage years when I married my high school friend. When you are a teenager, you focus only on loving someone with all your heart. Without realizing it, you give up your dreams, aspirations, and ambitions. You give away your youth, your heart, and your soul to someone else, leaving nothing to protect yourself. As a wife and mother in my teenage years, I became selfish, living only for today and never thinking of the future. At a young age, you don't realize the intensity of supporting a family. The task of creating and nurturing a family was bigger and greater than I ever imagined.

I was an aggressive and assertive person who believed in defending and telling the truth, no matter how awkward the situations were. I always believed in being yourself and doing things your way. It can be difficult to ignore the chaos of the world, but we must listen to our calling and inner voice. For so long, I didn't know the impact I had on many individuals and my family's lives. I never realized the importance of a kind word or a simple smile, which helped many depressed friends. You can give someone a purpose to live and not lose

Preface

hope. You can become a beacon of love and kindness. Everyone needs a good listener. Everyone wants to be heard. Everyone wants to be loved.

It's my hope that this book—and the stories of my grandmother, mother, friends, family, and me—inspire you to become a bold, resilient woman. I want to show readers that you, too, can make a difference in your own life as well as the lives of others. Change can never be accomplished until you put in the effort to change yourself first. Only then can you proceed and inspire others to follow. We are stronger than we know, smarter than we think, more resilient than we can imagine, and have a larger capacity for love and compassion than we can even comprehend. We just have to know how to use our gifts and our talents.

Part One
The Old Country

Courage

I became a mother at seventeen. It was a constant challenge. I didn't know anything, and had no idea what to expect. All I knew was that I loved my husband, but the moment I laid eyes on each of my children, I fell massively in love all over again. I was overcome with love and devotion for them. I immersed myself deeply in monitoring my baby's every movement. I wanted to care for them and protect their innocence. I wanted to protect my own, too; I was a child, having a child.

I never felt anxiety or pressure in having to multitask, because I wasn't forced to choose between motherhood, going to school, working, and hustling for survival. Deep down in my heart, I knew I was not a victim. I made a choice to face consequences, bad or good, and I had to work things out on my own. Sometimes this process was strenuous and exhausting, but, at the end, there was always a resolution.

Even when I was young, I was compassionate and wanted to make a difference in someone's life. I wanted to be active in the church and other organizations. I came from capable and strong women, wise descendants who had made a difference for their communities and people's lives, forces of nature who never gave up. These women knew me; they had molded me to be strong and bold. I wanted to continue their legacy.

My grandmother Eleni would say, "I didn't give birth to women or raise girls to take up space in the world. I gave birth to strong, intelligent, honorable, and incredible women to become leaders, machines who never stop for anything." Even when I was young and didn't fully understand what she was saying, I saw the resolve on her face.

"Mom," I asked one day, while we were walking down the street. I was a thoughtful child, and I often had a lot of questions about how the world works. Sometimes I felt like I saw everything. "Why do the women of your village show you so much love, respect, and admiration?"

"I have helped many young women, even when I had nothing myself. The girls in my village trusted me with their deepest secrets, their loves, their heartbreak. I was always there to pick up the pieces, my darling daughter. I was in love with your father from a young age, and I could feel their pain and sorrow. I could never bear it if your father tarnished my name and humiliated my family. When I was young, girls could not speak to their mothers about their deepest secrets—they would get beaten, and disowned, and forbidden to ever leave their homes. They were punished in horrible ways if they ever disgraced the family name."

Even as I heard this, I knew it to be true. Mom shared with me many frightening and painful stories. She wanted me to know every challenge she had faced. It was her way of teaching me to protect myself as a young girl. These were real stories about a small village with many young, beautiful girls, and young men from different parts of Arkadia who saw an opportunity to come and pursue them.

"Every Saturday night, all the village girls from all parts would gather at the south end," my mom told me. "They had worked hard all week and were ready to dance and sing the night away. The girls dressed up in the customary village dress for an evening out, all trying to outdo one another. Young men from different villages and towns would come to join them in the celebration.

"The young men would surround the young women in a circle and clap while they danced. This was how they would evaluate the girls and seek the one they would pursue. Then they would come every weekend to see the girl they had fallen for. They were flirting in this pure, innocent way."

"Mom," I asked her one day as we walked to the market. I can still see her now as we walked next to each other, strong and confident, her blue eyes shining and determined as we accomplished another item on her never-ending list. "How did you meet Dad?"

"Your father would see me selling vegetables in the streets of Tripoli," she said, smiling as she remembered. "He knew my brother, Peter, from the *platea*

Bold Resilient Women

(town square or public plaza), where all the boys would gather to play soccer after school. Dad was working while the boys were releasing stress by playing sports. They knew sooner or later that they would have to leave their loved ones to travel to an unknown world to help support their family. One day, he realized I was Peter's sister when he saw me walk over to hand him the money I had made selling endives. I was a young girl, not more than fifteen years old. This was a year or two before my brother departed for the United States at the young age of fourteen. Your dad began coming to the celebrations every Saturday evening to see how I danced and how I looked cleaned and dressed up."

My father always told me that he fell for her instantly. "I fell in love with her big blue eyes," he would say.

I knew the stories of their courtship well, and to this day, I hold them tightly in my heart. My father was a handsome young man and every girl was trying to pursue him. My dad only had eyes for Mom.

One day, a wealthy man asked my dad if he would marry his daughter. He knew Dad from the tailoring shop and had seen him work hard since he was a child to support himself. He wanted him for a son-in-law. Word spread that Frango wanted my father for his daughter. My mom said she was devastated; she was falling in love with this charming young man.

When Dad went to the celebration the following Saturday, he took my mom's hand to dance with her. It was the equivalent of declaring his love, but she was so upset she threw his hand aside and left the dance. She started to run toward her house, but he ran after her, asking, "What did I do?" He told her he didn't mean to embarrass her in front of the villagers.

Mom told him he had no right to insult or humiliate her in front of everyone. They were not a couple; there was nothing between them. She wished him luck with his bride. She told him she knew he was poor and had struggled all his life, and now he had a chance to marry someone wealthy. She told him she understood; she didn't have a dowry to give him, just herself. Peter, her older brother who had traveled to America, would send money if she ever got married. He had made this commitment to his mom, since she had worked so hard to help him through school.

Dad was shocked, and hurt, and worried that he had lost my mom. He rode his bike back to Tripoli, a good 15 kilometers. By the time he got back to Tripoli, he was furious. Didn't she see how much he cared for her? He rode his bike back and forth only to see her!

Meanwhile, Mom was hurting, too. She was sixteen and had fallen hard for this charming and handsome eighteen-year-old man. Though girls didn't confide in their mothers at this time, she told her mother she had fallen for the young orphan who was her brother's friend. My grandma saw my mother's heartache. The following Saturday, my dad's cousin told him they would go to the celebration together, and after some pressure, finally convinced him. The two boys planned for my dad to go to the dance circle and hold my mom's hand. He did it, and she accepted.

After the dance, they hid behind a tree, and Dad told her that all the money in the world couldn't keep him from her. "I don't want money," he told her passionately. "I want someone to love and start a family with, and that someone is you."

They married shortly after. They were young and poor and innocent and sought as much work as possible to support a family. Dad opened a little store in the village, where he sold many products, similar to a dollar store. He also had a small shop on the side of the store where he had several people working, making brooms. They didn't have an education, but they knew how to work endless days and nights.

Soon after my parents' wedding, Mom's entire family immigrated to the United States. My mom's older brother sent Dad some money to help him out. Dad had told him he wanted to purchase a three-wheel motorcycle to start selling crops to the surrounding villages. My mom ran the store with a crib positioned next to her behind the counter. A couple of years later, Dad was able to buy a truck, allowing him to sell more crops and cover more territory. He would come home and start his tailoring and broom work. There wasn't any time for sleep.

Mom would tell me we wouldn't have left Greece if Dad hadn't had his accident.

One day, he fell asleep while driving on the cursed mountain. This was one of the most dangerous mountains in the Peloponnese, where if you go off the cliff, no one can find you. The accident kept my dad in the hospital for months, and the truck was a total loss. Though he thankfully recovered, he had lost everything. He and Mom decided to immigrate to the States. He had suffered enough in Greece, and he didn't have the willpower to start over again. While he created a new life in the U.S., he had scars up and down his arms and legs to remind him of the accident.

My mother did many jobs, and she also worked as a midwife in her village. She was so compassionate to the whole family, but especially the mothers, whom she cared for as though they were her own relation. She often was in charge of stitching up girls, too, after they had lost their virginity. In this role, she saw the joys and hardships of life firsthand. She shared so many stories with me as I grew up. When there was time in the cleaners and shoe repair shop we owned in Chicago, or as we walked together near Lake Michigan with the hot dog cart we owned, she would share what she remembered from this former life.

She wanted me to understand that life was a chess game. It was not simple. It was complicated, and filled with pain, and happiness, and sorrow, and many obstacles and challenges.

She told me there was a seventeen-year-old who was madly in love with a young man a few years older than her. She was impregnated by him, and she was too far along in her pregnancy to abort the baby.

"The girls were innocent," Mom told me. "They didn't realize that if they had missed a period, there was something wrong. No one ever told them what pregnancy symptoms were." My mom took her to her aunt in Tripoli. They told her parents she was going to work as a cleaning girl and would reside in the house as a live-in.

When the time came to give birth, my mom was the midwife, and she helped bring a beautiful little girl into the world. My mom's aunt had arranged for a young, educated couple to take the child, and they loved and cared for her better than if she had been their own. This baby grew up in a loving, upscale neighborhood in a secure and solid environment. She was educated at some of the finest schools, and became a distinguished woman and a prominent lawyer. Until her last breath, Mom believed abortion should not be a political decision. She would say a woman's body belongs to her, and no one but her, her doctor, and her connection with God can decide whether to terminate her pregnancy or not. Women are intensely devoted to their families and children, and if a woman is fearful of having a dangerous pregnancy or delivery, she should not have to risk her life.

The most startling story happened to one of her neighbors. This young girl had met a handsome, educated, young man who had come from one of the big cities to join in a village celebration. He had heard that there were many beautiful and hardworking young women, so he came and he lured my mother's friend into a relationship. He visited her for months. One day, she confided to her two close friends that she had been sleeping with him and she was not feeling well.

The next day, when Mom went to work selling vegetables, she saw a nurse who worked at the local hospital and told her what symptoms her friend had. The nurse said, "Are you sure she is not pregnant?" Mom started to shake, knowing the implications of such a situation. When she told her friend what the nurse suspected, the girl broke down crying hysterically. She could not believe this was happening to her. How was he going to react? Was her family going to kill her for disgracing the family?

She kept the news from her parents until she could tell her lover. At the next celebration, she was excited. She thought he was going to marry her and they would live happily ever after. But when she pulled him aside and told him she was carrying his child, he stood up instantly and told her he didn't want the child and wasn't going to marry her. He said he was leaving and never coming back. He belittled her, wondering how she ever thought a wealthy, intelligent, and handsome man like him was ever going to marry a peasant girl. He walked out and never returned.

The next few weeks, she waited with my mom and her friends for him to return to the celebration, but he never came. He had vanished, as if he never existed.

One evening, as my mom and her friends helped her finish up her work, she told them she wasn't feeling well. They had her lie down and finished the picking and selling of vegetables for her. Mom told her to tell her parents that there were a lot of vegetables, and she got extremely tired.

Later, my mom and her friends went to visit her at the house. The girl's mother told them she had gone to the well for water. The girls instantly knew that was a lie—she was going to throw herself in and drown. The girls raced there and arrived just in time, as she was readying herself to jump in. Mom grabbed her and they all started to cry, hugging each other. My mother brought her back to her home, where my grandmother decided she would help the girl tell her family. Her mother and grandmother could take her to Tripoli, where she could give birth and find a family to adopt the child. No one would ever know—especially since in the village in those days, women wore huge pleated dresses or skirts with a vested top and a scarf. Her pregnancy would remain unnoticed.

These unique and gorgeous dresses were works of art. They were made with rhinestones, sequins, needlepoint, and other decorations. You could not identify if a woman was pregnant or not.

Grandma walked into the girl's parents' home with my mom and their daughter and asked to speak to them in private. Grandma, being a wise and loving woman with four daughters of her own, knew how to talk to another mother and make her aware of difficult situations. She explained with a lot of compassion and fear that their daughter had fallen in love with a liar, she was carrying his child, and he had left her, never to return. The parents were devastated. They were poor, and their daughter's reputation would be destroyed; they had no money to give to someone to marry her.

Grandma told them that their daughter had tried to drown herself to save their reputation, and the girl's mother was shattered. My grandmother kept reminding them that everyone falls in love, and we can never know if that individual loves us back or will betray us with no regrets.

They appreciated Grandma's love and friendship. They promised no harm would come to their daughter, and said they didn't want to lose her. They would go to the city the following day to find a childless family who wanted to adopt. Mom and Grandma were happy and satisfied. They agreed to wake up at dawn and travel with the horses to Tripoli. No one would ever find out what this horrible young man did to her, and someday she could find happiness with someone else.

During the night, things progressed faster than expected. The young girl was going into labor and they heard someone crying and yelling from the house next door. By the time Grandma and Mom got up to get dressed and see what was happening, they heard a baby's cries. The baby had arrived. Halfway to the house, they heard silence. There was no more crying.

Grandma knocked on the door while Mom stood behind her, crying. The girl's mother answered. Behind her, they saw the baby dead, wrapped in a blanket. They asked what happened and were told the baby died instantly. Mom and Grandma didn't dare question what really happened. They stayed to clean and comfort the young girl, while the father went out to the fields to bury the child. They were all devastated. The young girl recovered, and no one ever spoke of the incident.

A few months later, the girl received her visa and immigration papers to leave for Australia. She departed without saying goodbye to anyone, and they never heard from her again.

Bold Resilient Women

Occasionally, Mom would ask her mother how she was, and she would say she was happy in the new world. Years later, Mom found out she had gotten married to a wonderful man and had a beautiful family.

"What do you think happened, Mom?" I asked her when she told me this story. I was transfixed. I had never heard anything so tragic, and my heart was shattered for the girl.

"God forgive me, because I didn't see anything. But I think the father strangled the baby," she said. "My friend should never have suffered like this. It was so unfair. She was one of the purest and most meticulous young women in the village." She looked at me and said, "Make sure you find a nice man who's suitable for a good and ethical girl. A girl who has been around the block knows the tricks, and will end up with the best."

One day, while folding sheets together, Mom stopped and held them close to her chest. "Honey, when a young girl gets married in the village, after their first night together as newlyweds, the sheets are hung outside the balcony."

I started to laugh. "But what does that mean?" I asked curiously.

"When men marry girls, they have to be virgins," she explained. "The first night together was the honeymoon night, and after their first sexual intercourse, the man would hang the sheet outside on the balcony, with blood stains on it, to prove to everyone he had taken her virginity. If the girl wasn't a virgin, they would send her back to her parents or ask for an obscene amount of dowry to keep her."

She told me that this young woman had an affair with a young man who had left for America. He was supposed to get his green card and come back to take her, but as time went by, he never came back. After many years, another young man fell in love with her, but she didn't tell him about her affair. Because my mom was a nurse and a midwife, and a trusted confidante, she went to her for help.

My mom knew all the girls in the village were naive and innocent, and she had witnessed firsthand the way men from different places came and took advantage of them. Mom told her she was going to take care of her. She had heard from a nurse what to do if the girl wasn't a virgin. She gave her a glass of cognac to drink to numb her from the pain, then she proceeded to sew up her uterus. The girl acted sick for a couple of days, and my mom explained that she was tired from all the preparations. There is a lot to do before a Greek wedding. The bride and her family have to prepare her dowry, consisting of various cultural crocheted tablecloths, blankets, machine-woven rugs, sheets

Bold Resilient Women

and everything needed to set up the couple's home. Preparing the items and readying for the celebration and greeting all of the families was enough to cause anxiety.

In Greek villages, the tradition of a wedding takes place for an entire week. The Thursday before the wedding, the girl and her family set up her new bedroom with all brand-new furniture. The bed has to be fixed with new sheets and blankets, and both the bride's and groom's families come and sing and throw money on the bed, so that the new couple will have a healthy and successful life together. At the end, they take a little baby boy and toss him on the bed, so that their firstborn can be a boy who will carry the family name.

When the wedding day arrived, my mom gave her specific instructions: Do not dance at the celebration. Pretend you are dizzy and sit down. At that point, Mom would run to her rescue and tell the groom not to let her dance, telling him that after the bride witnessed the slaughtering of the lambs, she hadn't been feeling well.

When the groom saw how pale and tired she was, he didn't bother to continue dancing and entertaining their guests. Everyone knew she was overtired and needed rest. This young woman went on to live a beautiful life with her husband, and they had five healthy and successful children.

Years later, when my mom passed away, many people attended her funeral, including hundreds of people from all over Greece. People told us remarkable stories about how she was their lifesaver, how she had helped them during difficult years. Many ladies would say, "Your mom was the most decent individual in the world." They told us how she saved children and supported the young orphan girls in Chrystovoulio, an orphanage just for girls. Mom and Dad would visit them a few times a year, and on Easter and Christmas, they would deposit money in bank accounts, which they had opened for each one of them.

This amount was designed to help the girls get a start when they left the orphanage, after they had finished college, or any other skill school they attended. My mom and dad would travel to poor areas and feed the poor. They were both compelled to help others in need.

Before her funeral, my brothers and I only had a small glimpse of how my mother had impacted people's lives. But at her funeral, I fully understood my mom's great legacy. My brothers and I didn't understand where all these people came from and how Mom affected their lives. Now I understood who these people were, how they saw my mom, and what she had done to save them. I appreciated my mom more after she had passed away. Never in my wildest dreams did I think so many people would be so grateful for my mother's compassionate heart.

Bold Resilient Women

On the eve of my beloved Mom's passing, she called me three times. I was departing for Greece the following day to visit her.

"Did you forget to ask me to bring something?" I said.

"My love, come." She said, "I just want to tell you I love you so much. I am proud of you as my daughter. Your kids are so lucky to have you as a great role model. How I wish God had given me four daughters just like you. You four would have conquered the world."

"Thank you, Mommy, but why are you telling me this when I will see you tomorrow?" I asked. "We will be together to discuss everything, like we always do."

She responded, "Yes, but I love you so much and I am proud to call you my daughter."

"I am the luckiest girl in this world to have had you, a peasant girl, as a mother," I said, my voice overflowing with love.

These were the last words I shared with my beloved Mom. We never had closure; we never finished our conversation. She died the next day.

I underestimated the courage my mother had. Hearing these true stories, I learned to discipline myself as much as I could. I feared getting hurt; I didn't want to lose faith or trust in God and my instinct. As I was learning a hard lesson in life, I was encouraging my beloved friends and other girls to be cautious and never trust anyone but their moms. I didn't want young women to lose trust in themselves and make mistakes. They had to have faith in facing situations and the courage to make a difference.

Grandmother's Family

The first time I met my grandmother's sister, Katerina, I was mesmerized by her beautiful light blue eyes, which sparkled like the blue sky. My grandmother always spoke about her in such a loving way, so I was excited to meet her. My grandmother was excited to give her gifts from America, knit sweaters and wool nightgowns.

"We are going to the monastery tomorrow," Grandma told her. But before she could even completely finish her sentence, Katerina's face turned dark, and she started cursing the nuns and the monastery. I had never heard someone talk so angrily and disparage the church so intensely. I was turned off by her anger. It occurred to me that her sister was completely the opposite of my grandmother and her two brothers, whom I had known since I was young. She seemed distant and distracted by her surroundings, and uninterested in the visitors who had come from America. I could not understand what was making her so angry.

That's when my grandmother took me aside and told me we would talk on the way to the monastery about Katerina's tragedy. She told me how Katerina's son and nephew were caught in an explosion during the war, and how she brought their torn-apart bodies back to the village. She had never fully recovered from the trauma of all of it. How she never set foot in a church or stopped cursing God. After Grandma finished explaining this story in detail, I felt so much pain and grief for her. As a young child, I was always asking questions and wanting to know more, but this time, I had nothing to ask. My *Yiayia* (grandmother) had told me everything, and I didn't want to know any more.

Bold Resilient Women

The following day, we visited the monastery again. My parents and Yiayia were making their donation for a few icons to honor our saints. They wanted to show gratitude and appreciation to the Lord, the Virgin Mary and all of the saints for protecting our family from harm and illness. They wanted to show gratitude for all the blessings they were bestowed with.

My family started writing the names of the deceased on one page and the living on another. It was a long list, and when they finished, they gave it to the head nun in an envelope with money for holy bread, oil, and flour. We sat for a service, and after, the nuns took us to the dining area where they had coffee and *koulouri*—a Greek cookie—prepared.

Yiayia was talking with the nuns, arranging her upcoming three-month stay at the monastery to help the nuns sew their garments. I was devastated that she was not coming back to the States with us.

"This is what I do every year, sweetheart," she said gently. I stay and sew all their garments for the following year." I was astonished and fascinated by my Yiayia's love, dedication, and commitment to the monastery.

The following day, we visited the cemetery to light all the family candles and to clean the dry grass around the tombs. The cemetery was a peaceful place on the side of the mountain, which is visible as you travel from our village to Athens. As you travel to and from, you can greet or say farewell to your loved ones.

Beneath the cemetery is the tunnel of Poseidon, the Greek god of the sea. Scientists have come from different parts of the world to investigate and see if this mythology was true or if it was made up for publicity. They injected a special iodine to see where the iodine would travel to, and to everyone's shock, the iodine came out by the sea of Nafplion, proving this was not a myth.

Bold Resilient Women

As Yiayia told me more stories of her childhood, my mom's difficult upbringing, and her family's pain and sorrows, we approached her family's burial site. I glanced and saw a huge statue with the names of many soldiers who had served our country. I turned to my right, where Grandma was standing and crying, and saw a photo staring at us from inside the closed window. It was an attractive, blue-eyed, young soldier wearing a hat with the seal of the king. I didn't have a chance to ask Yiayia who he was before she started speaking to the picture, telling him how much she loved him, how she missed him, and how he was deprived of his family. As I started to read the names, I noticed his name was Evangelo Virvilos.

My God, this is my grandmother's name. I thought. *Who was he?* My legs were numb—I could not move. While my grandmother always shared stories with me, I realized there was so much I didn't know about her.

She kept talking to him, looking up at his face in a picture as she spoke. She was crying and calling him brother. She talked of his wife and children. Her face looked more like her sister's at this moment, shades of grief and anger —but why? I knew I should wait until we got home to ask her, but I couldn't.

"Yiayia," I said as we walked away. She was still crying, wiping tears from her cheeks. "Who was he? His name is Evangelo Virvilos?"

She looked at me with red eyes filled with tears. "My younger brother, Vageli." She said.

I didn't know about a younger brother. I knew only about her two brothers in the States. We were quiet the rest of the way home.

Finally, we arrived at the house. Yiayia sat at the kitchen table. I gave her some water and started to cut some fresh grapes. My mom walked in laughing, "Where did my two Elenis go today?" She started to say, and then she stopped. She saw Grandmother wiping tears and me cutting grapes, a startled look on my face.

"What's going on?" she asked.

"We visited the cemetery and saw grandmother's younger brother from the burial picture on top of the tomb," I said. I didn't have to say more. Mom knew it all.

"Let's go outside," my mom suggested. The three of us pulled chairs onto the balcony, and I settled in. The sun was shining outside, and we sat close to each other while a warm breeze floated through the air.

My grandma steeled herself. "I will tell you of the death of my thirty-four-year-old brother, Vageli. I am so proud of his courage. He never betrayed his country or the king, and he sacrificed his life to save four other soldiers."

She told me that Vageli was a very tall, handsome, young man with striking light blue eyes and an irresistible charisma. He was drafted to serve as a soldier of the king in the city of Tripoli. The guerrillas were fighting each other, and they had abducted young boys and girls and enlisted them in the Communist Party. Vageli was married to a beautiful village girl, Magdalina. She gave birth to their first child when she was twenty-three, and fifteen months later, she gave birth to another little boy.

When Vageli learned of his son's birth, he asked his commander for a leave of absence to go meet him. He was excited and anxious. He had married his wife out of love, and nothing and no one could stop him from being with her and their two little baby boys.

The village was twelve kilometers from Tripoli, and during that time, the only transportation poor people had was a bicycle or tricycle. Cars were for the wealthy. Vageli hopped on his bike joyfully at nightfall, believing it was safer to travel after dark than during the day. But the Communist guerrillas were ahead of him. As he was halfway to the village, the Greek *militia* caught him and demanded that he renounce democracy and the king and join them. They also asked him to give the names of the other soldiers who were serving the king.

He resisted, telling them he would serve the monarchy and democracy and would never tell the names of the rest of the soldiers serving the king. They captured and tortured him. They cut his entire body into pieces, put it in a wooden box, and sent it, on a horse, to Magdalina's house.

She was waiting impatiently with joy to show her love to his little family. She stood outside their house, which was near the *platea*, ready to greet him with the two babies. But instead of her husband on a bike, she saw a horse with a huge box. Neighbors were coming out of their houses to see what was happening. As her family and neighbors surrounded her, they heard horses leaving the village, and people saw guerrillas, guns in one hand, the horse's reins in another, riding fast away from the village.

One of the guerrillas—who was from a nearby village—approached a villager, asking for information about the soldier's wife: which house she lived in, and whether she had two children, one of them a newborn. Back then, everyone knew everyone's business, family life, tragedies, and whereabouts. Everyone looked out for each other and their families.

They informed them that Vageli's wife was the one with the two babies.

Bold Resilient Women

One of the leaders led the horse carrying her husband's remains to the door and gave them to her.

Yiayia said that everyone lost their minds. His wife had to be confined to a hospital because of her grief; she didn't care to live. Both families took care of the babies until she was released from the hospital.

"My sweet girl," Yiayia continued. "Her tragedy didn't end there." She explained that five years later, her younger son died. Her sister-in-law was never the same. She became a widow in her late twenties and stayed that way. She dedicated her life to her only child, Jimmy, and her daily visits to the cemetery.

Yiayia and her entire family were very supportive. They brought her to the United States to be near family, and to get away from the painful memories and suffering she had witnessed and endured. And they all wanted my uncle, Jimmy, to achieve the American dream of success to support his widow mother who had endured so much suffering.

Jimmy established a pizza business, and everyone loved the homemade pizzas as well as the young man who was providing quality food. Eventually, Uncle Jimmy got married. He had three amazing children and a life partner who was also a beautiful mother.

Things were finally going smoothly for their family, but that would soon change. While his mom babysat the three children, pain again struck the family.

My little cousins were playing outside while their grandma kept an eye on them. There was a car riding around the quiet neighborhood they lived in, which stood out because everyone knew each other and kept an eye on each other's homes. My uncle had fired one of his employees, and this man knew what my uncle was worth, and where the safe was. In this car were three men dressed as women, and they pulled up so quickly outside, grabbed the two-and-a-half-year-old, and sped away—right in front of their grandma's eyes. She started screaming, and the entire neighborhood came outside.

The police, Secret Service, and FBI were called immediately. Everyone was terrified, especially because a young girl had been abducted the previous month and was found dead. Because this was a heated topic, and no one wanted a second abduction and murder, the authorities were immediately on the case. They closed all of the borders leading to Wisconsin, Indiana, and all surrounding areas. When the kidnappers sent the ransom letter, my uncle recognized the writing, so they knew who they were looking for. The abductors saw no way out and left my little cousin in the cornfields before the border of Wisconsin, where she was found by a Black couple who heard her cries. They called the police, and my little cousin was reunited with her family.

Bold Resilient Women

Today, I believe in my heart that if the police hadn't had a previous murder on their hands, my little cousin might not be with us. To this day, she remembers the abduction, the way the abductors were dressed, and being left alone in a field. I want to kiss and hug her, and tell her God and her grandfather saved her. She is a very special person with a great heart of kindness, love, and spirituality. The family reunited, but the fear and agony remained in my uncle's home for the rest of his life. Grandma could not forget that someone had abducted her granddaughter in front of her eyes. She blamed herself until she passed away. No one could make her understand this was not her fault.

After his mother's death, Uncle Jimmy was opening another pizza location. They were constructing and cleaning the surrounding area by cutting down dead trees and bushes. My uncle, an entrepreneur and hard-working man, wanted to finish the place fast and open it for business. While the landscapers went for lunch, Uncle Jimmy decided to assist them by setting up a ladder and cutting the branches with a chainsaw.

Although my aunt was against it, Jimmy insisted. He told her he would be finished by the time the landscapers came back. My aunt assisted him by holding the ladder tight against the tree. But while cutting, he must have gotten dizzy. Without warning, he suddenly fell off the ladder, landing in front of my aunt's feet. They called an ambulance, but as he was being transported to the hospital, he passed away. He was in his forties.

"The cycle of pain had ended," Yiayia finished, tears still in her eyes. "Thank God Magdalina died before her son. She would not have survived another tragedy."

My Yiayia must have seen the shock and pain on my face after hearing such a tragic family tale. She looked at me and continued.

"Sweetheart, we have faced many difficult times. The years were challenging in our country, and all of Europe, and the world. The painful times seemed to go on forever. We didn't know if we would live to the next moment.

"My lovely granddaughter, I pray and hope none of you witness what we saw and lived. We went through bloody wars. Entire villages were wiped out by the Germans. People would hide beneath the ground. Girls were sent to the mountains to hide from the guerrillas so they would not be abused, raped, or killed.

"We didn't have food on our table. We would share a loaf of bread with fifteen people. Children would die from malnutrition and undetected medical illnesses in their parents' arms. We faced so much pain and sorrow; everyone was in it together.

"We worked hard and were tortured as slaves one more time. We lived and breathed every moment suffering. There were times my eyes were dry, and no more tears would come down my cheeks. We lived seeing our loved ones killed, and dying in front of our eyes, and we could not scream, because we were hiding, and if they caught us, they would kill us and the entire family. We lived in fear and agony for many years. War brings suffering and devastation. But we never lost our faith in God."

As I grew up, Grandmother would watch people walk through the world and be shocked at what we thought we knew. "Young women and men think they have it rough," she would say. "But they don't know the meaning of rough, of pain, and suffering. Therefore, *agapimou* (my love), I smile, laugh, and take care of the vulnerable. I do great things for nursing homes because I have seen elderly people thrown away, so they didn't impose on the young people who were fleeing to the mountains. I take care of monasteries and churches because we were all saved by hiding in the churches. Our faith and prayers became our comfort. I lived in poverty and neglect, so I can understand people who live in a complicated and complex world.

"I pray for worldly love and peace. I want you to try to enjoy every moment of life. I am giving you this advice because I have seen and lived everything." During that summer holiday with both Grandma and Mama, I had the opportunity to learn more about these amazing, dominant, resilient, and powerful women and their family members. I was proud and privileged to be born into their life. As the stories penetrated my heart and mind, I realized I was born from these dynamic and inspiring women; there wasn't anything that could take them down. I was living and hearing real-life lessons that could never be taught from any textbooks.

Almost every day, Yiayia, Mom, and I sat outside on the balcony, and I would ask for more stories. I was frantic. I needed to know more. I couldn't believe this was my family.

"Whether we were pregnant or not, it did not matter; we had to work in the fields to provide for our family," my grandmother told me one day. "Mothers would go into labor on their own or with the support of the other village girls, and they would wrap the newborn baby in sack linen material to serve as a baby blanket. When the baby was born, mother and newborn had to start their journey back to the village, despite the unbearable pain. Riding on the horse with a newborn, we didn't have time to think about pain or cramping. All we wanted was to reach the village to relax after traveling for hours.

"Some new mothers lost their lives.

"Others ran a high fever and were confined in bed for many days, while others lost their babies by the time they arrived home. This is what happened to all of us; we all did what we had to do, we had no other choice. We didn't have the care of a doctor or hospital."

Bold Resilient Women

"How many children did you give birth to by yourself?" I asked her, my voice tentative but insistent.

"Honey, thirteen." She said, "Six lived, and seven died." I was horrified. What woman would suffer today by having a self-taught midwife cut her open, as she helped in desperation, while in excruciating pain? Who would have the courage to help the midwife cut open their belly with a knife used to cut grass, because the baby was breech? Many of my grandmother's relatives and other village women were faced with this terrifying decision.

This is when Grandma could not control her tears. She waved her hand to indicate she was finished talking. She wasn't interested in continuing.

This unforgettable trip with both of them was traumatic, bonding, and healing. I learned so much about my ancestors and living relatives. It was going to take a long time to comprehend and digest so much pain and suffering. Without thinking, I had opened up old wounds for Grandma and Mom.

A month after arriving back home, I went to visit Grandma. I loved and cared for her very much, and I wanted to make sure she wasn't hurting from sharing the past during our trip together to the village. After all, we could not change what had transpired. I walked into the house and she called me to go to her bedroom. As she was getting dressed, I approached and gave her a big kiss and started to help her, when I saw something that brought back memories of our discussion at the village.

My grandma's belly was cut up with wounds all over. It didn't look right; it was all chopped up. I was shaken, but summoned the courage to ask what happened.

"Grandma, is this what you were telling me in the village?" I asked. "Eleni, remember how I told you women gave birth to children in the fields by themselves and brought them to the village in potato sacks?" I nodded.

She told me of the children she had given birth to in the fields by herself. Due to complications or the extreme heat during the summer or the cold in the winter, by the time she arrived at the village, they had died. Out of the thirteen pregnancies, Grandma had brought into life only six children. As much as I tried, I couldn't hold my tears back. I felt the hurt and pain of my Grandma so powerfully that I wanted to let out a scream. I wanted to hold my grandma and tell her I was sorry for the suffering she had endured. This was the first time I left her in a hurry. I was choking, and I had to leave the house.

My God, what did my sweet Yiayia and many of her family members and friends go through? How did they keep going? How did they focus on providing for their families? These questions repeated through my mind as I drove home, tears running down my face.

I felt ashamed and repentant for complaining about little, meaningless things in life. All I kept saying to myself was, *If Grandma and Mom can have impeccable and beautiful smiles everyday of their lives, there isn't any reason for any of us to complain about life.*

"There is a purpose for all of us in this world," they both told me. "We need to be givers, not takers. Those who have love in their hearts and have seen death, suffering, and pain know nothing is ours. We can all fall fast and relive the painful past."

Faith

My Yiayia, Eleni, lived through World War I, World War II, Communism, and the Greek Civil War, in which many of her family members and friends were massacred and killed. She would tell me stories of living through these horrors, of the people she had loved and lost, the terror, and the difficulty rebuilding after a war.

When she was dying, I visited her often. I loved, admired, and respected her more than anything, and I wanted to know all of her stories so I could not only better understand where I came from, but also so I could share them with my own children.

"Yiayia, tell me. What is your advice for living a beautiful and fulfilled life?" I asked, sitting next to her bedside. I held her soft and fragile hand.

"My beautiful *Elenitsa mou* (dear Elini), I lived one big, long day," she said. Tears were running down her cheeks, but I thought maybe she had lost it. This comment didn't make sense to me.

"Your life, too, will be one long day as you reflect back," she continued. I realized hers was one long day of war, death, tears, suffering, pain, poverty, killings, torture, hunger, journeys, marriage, divorces, sacrifices, unending work, tolerance, faith, happiness, tears, joy, laughter, and sorrow. "You wake up in the morning and open your eyes, energized for the new day, without realizing that night comes, and you go to sleep. Everything will feel like a couple of hours. That's why, my love, I am telling you, laugh and don't let things worry you.

"As we say, when the sun comes out, we are glorious and filled with joy; when the clouds come, fear strikes and we hide beneath the clouds." My parents, grandparents, older relatives, and many of the elderly people I have known speak in parables. They are poetic, but also take a bit of thought. Their meaning is not always apparent when you first hear them.

"Yiayia, I don't understand." I was leaning closer now, eager to hear every word. Her voice had gotten softer, but it was still clear, especially when sharing wisdom with people.

"When you wake up and proceed with your daily work, you are filled with joy and happiness. But unpredictable and unforeseen issues arise and ruin your day. As a strong woman, in that moment, you have to say, 'And this too shall pass.' Never be fearful and cower behind anyone's shadow."

The image of moving sunshine and clouds brought to mind a memory. My mind had been filled with them, the memories of my Yiayia coming in sharp and clear as this strong, powerful woman spent time in bed, waiting with open arms to travel to her creator. Not too long after, I had to leave for Egypt, and she passed. I had lost my sweet grandma without being by her side.

I remembered several years earlier, when I had traveled to Greece with my Yiayia. We went to our village, Nestani, Tripoli, in Arkadia, south of Athens. I asked her to tell me the history of this remarkable and beautiful village, filled with monasteries, culture, faith, traditional costumes, and so much history. Nestani is a village surrounded by large mountains covered in pine trees. There's a breathtaking monastery overlooking the village at the peak of Goula Mountain. This monastery was the meeting place for the beginning of the 1821 revolution. Private meetings were held beneath the monastery, as heroes planned the Greek revolution. They strategized how they would fight the Ottoman Empire, gain independence, and liberate our country, setting it free after four hundred years of slavery. They could no longer sit back and let destruction continue to take place.

The monastery is 960 years old and is dedicated to the Virgin Mary of Gorgopikou. Here, the Holy Mother rushes to assist those who ask and pray for help and guidance. It's happened before. Many years ago, the village stood on the sides of the mountain. A huge earthquake occurred, and the top of the mountain broke off, rolling down toward the village. All of the villagers came out and started to pray to our Holy Mother, whom we also call the *Theotokos*. Suddenly, the Virgin Mary appeared from the clouds and reached down toward the falling rock. She grabbed the rock by the sides, holding it to a stopping point, and protecting the village.

Today, after hundreds of years, the rock still stands on a thin stone without any support. Visiting the monastery, one can witness a true miracle. Although many scientists have come from all over the world to investigate this phenomenon, they have not been able to understand or assess how or why this rock is still standing.

But we don't need an explanation. Walking around the rock, you get an overwhelming sensation. A power consumes you. An internal voice dares you to contradict what has transpired and what is in front of your eyes at this moment, but you can't. You stand in awe at this miracle.

My village is rooted in this faith; it's a part of who we are. My grandmother carried it with her and passed it along to her family, and now that I was here, at the end of her life, hearing of all she survived, I realized that it was her faith that got her through. It was her belief that God would be with her whatever she endured.

When she finished talking, she rested her eyes, and I held her hand, rubbing it. I admired not only her physical and emotional strength but also her spiritual strength. Holding fast to something you can't see takes enormous power.

Love of a Strong Woman

My paternal grandmother was a stunning woman, with long, dark black hair, and a tall, slim figure. She was a village girl who endured much suffering in her life.

She also played a role in my healing process when I was ill. Though she was dead, she came to a spiritual man to pray to the Lord to heal me from my pain and suffering.

My grandmother was one of five sisters living in a beautiful historical village, Langadia, in the Peloponnese. She came from a very poor family and worked day and night to support them. She would go to the center of the village early in the morning with all the young girls to get water from the well for their homes. This water was for cooking, drinking, taking showers, and for chores. Then she would go to perform her daily responsibilities with the animals or in the fields.

Early one morning, a handsome young man came riding into the village on a white horse and asked the young girls for one of them to give him a cup of water, since he had traveled far and was thirsty. All the girls were shy and afraid to give a stranger water. But my grandmother, who was feisty, reached

Bold Resilient Women

into her barrel. She was a young and beautiful fourteen-year-old. She looked up at this young man.

"Since you are traveling far and are thirsty, I will offer you water," she said. She handed him a cup and gave him water to drink. Many villagers sitting at the square were wondering why this *archonda* (a wealthy aristocratic man of the area) would accept water from a peasant girl?

The man on the horse was my nineteen-year-old grandfather, Louis; he instantly fell in love with my grandmother's kind heart and beauty. He went back to his village and told his parents he was going to take a wife.

His father was delighted. "That's wonderful news! And what family does she come from?" he asked.

"The Kouris family," my young grandfather answered.

His father was outraged. "Absolutely not. They are the poorest of the poor. They have five daughters and no dowry to give for the marriage. If you dishonor me, I will disown you." This meant he would not be able to claim any land.

My grandfather was infuriated. He had fallen in love with this beautiful and kind girl, and he didn't care that she was from the poorest family. He got on his horse and left home. He went to my grandmother's village, Lagadia, and abducted her. But they didn't stay in her village, nor did he bring her back to his own. He went seeking an unknown place to create a family. He loved a small place called Bouliari, because it oversaw the Eleonas River, which gave electricity to most of Arkadia. It was a peaceful village with twenty-five homes, a chapel, and many loving and caring neighbors. My grandmother's cousin lived there, creating her family life after she got married. Therefore, she would not be lonely without any immediate family.

My grandparents settled down and started a family immediately. They didn't want anyone coming between them. They were very happy together. Many villagers used to tell stories of how much love they had between them, and how they used sweet nicknames for each other.

My grandfather was a skilled man. He knew how to hunt and was a pro in shooting, so he was constantly getting called to war. He could not stay long enough at home to enjoy his wife and family. In between wars, he had six children—five boys and one daughter. My father was the last baby to be born.

My grandmother was twenty-eight, and my grandfather was thirty-three, when my father was born. They lived in an era of war, poverty, suffering, and an unknown future. They were surrounded by many conflicts.

My grandfather was off fighting when he heard my grandmother had a little boy. He asked permission from the general for a sabbatical to visit his newborn son, who was already six months old.

As he was riding through the mountains to the village, he felt an excruciating pain in his back and chest. He thought it was a severe cold, the aftereffects of World War I, and the fight between the liberals and the populists. At the time, the military supported Venizelos due to his difficulties in securing the foreign economic debt of our country. My grandfather supported democracy and not the movement of the coup, which was destroying our country.

When he arrived home, all the children ran over, entangling themselves around his legs and body. They were all under the age of thirteen and had missed their father, who they hardly knew since they kept calling him to serve in different wars to protect our country from the political instability and from being taken over.

He asked my grandmother to make him mountain tea to help warm up since the pain persisted. He was so excited to see the new baby, and while he looked at his newborn, the other little children surrounded him around the fireplace.

Suddenly, my grandmother heard screams from the children. She ran out and saw my grandfather collapsed on the floor. She screamed for help; all the neighbors came and saw my grandfather lying dead on the floor. Here was a six-foot-four handsome man who had so much to live for, surrounded by his grieving children. My grandmother was devastated. She could not handle the grief and pain.

They sent horsemen to notify my father's brother of the passing of his brother. My dad's grandparents had passed away, and all the family he had left was one brother, Evangelo. Upon hearing of this tragedy, Evangelo came riding on his black stallion as a tribute to his dead brother. (Those who were wealthy and owned lots of land rode on lavish white or black stallions).

As Evangelo walked into the house, his devastated sister-in-law leaned on him, crying desperately, while his brother's dead body lay on the floor of the living room with six little children crying hysterically. The villagers and my dad used to tell us that even the newborn felt the loss of his father; he kept sobbing for days. Evangelo was hurt, devastated, and bitter. So many years had gone by without any contact with his brother, and now he had to say goodbye forever. He was shattered, feeling so much heartache.

In our part of Greece, if a parent died and a baby wasn't baptized, immediately after the funeral, the child would get baptized and take the name of the deceased parent to carry on his or her legacy. Dad's uncle didn't have a family, so he asked my grandmother if he could baptize the baby and give him his name instead of his father's, Louis (Elia).

He kept apologizing to my grandmother for not having any contact with them, since his father's wishes were to denounce his brother. He told Grandma and her family that because my grandfather was denied his wealth, he would go back to his birth city and sign a will to leave everything to my dad and the kids.

There were many people who came from all parts of Gortinia, in the state of Arkadia, to bid my grandfather farewell. He was loved by many for being very kind and generous. They buried him with his many medals for serving his country. Funeral songs were played by a clarinet.

Immediately after the funeral, they baptized my dad, calling him Evangelo, or Vageli for short. After everyone visited the house and had coffee and cognac, our traditional farewell to the dead, Evangelo got on his horse to go back and take care of the proper documents of the will.

On his way to the city, he died of a massive heart attack. The horse went by itself into the village. When the villagers saw the horse alone without its master, they went out seeking my grandfather's brother, Evangelo. They saw him lying helpless on the road.

Many people from across Gortinia heard of the Palivos tragedy. They could not imagine how all this was going to unravel. My grandmother's uncle, Papou Houndi, was considered one of the best stonecutters in Peloponnese. He worked for all the aristocrats in Athens fixing their stone homes, and was notified of this tragedy.

He came to comfort his niece, advising her on what they must do. There were so many witnesses who heard her brother-in-law's wishes. She was entitled to everything before the extended family got a grip on everything.

My grandmother, an honorable and religious woman, said in front of the village, "God meant for me to lose my love, Elia, and to be a widow with six little children. I will roam the streets of Arkadia to raise my children, and I will serve the church in our village, St. Anna, to protect and guide me and my family."

Her response is still engraved in all Gortinia. "I never had anything, and nothing was mine; therefore, I don't accept or want anything from the Palivos family."

Bold Resilient Women

My grandmother suffered day and night to raise her children. Those were difficult years not only in Greece, but in every country across the world. People were starving. My dad said they had one cow that grandma would milk, mixing the milk with flour to make soup. That was their daily meal, along with noodles she made from flour, milk, and eggs from her six chickens.

Having five boys and one girl during the Greek Civil War was dangerous. The guerrillas were recruiting young men, persuading them to become heroes by fighting the conservative government. They would recruit girls to cook and clean for them.

In 1940, when my grandmother heard this was happening, she decided to start sending her boys away. She was dedicated to the Greek monarchy and King George II. She didn't want her sons deviating from their late father's beliefs and his service to the monarchy and to democracy.

She had extended family in Australia, and at that time, the country was accepting young men to immigrate there for work. With grief and immense pain in her heart, but feeling she had no choice, she shipped two of her young sons overseas. Fortunately, her oldest son, John, lived in another part of Gortinia. He had fallen in love and married a widow with a young girl, so he would be kept out of harm's way. They didn't recruit men with families; they wanted strong young guerrillas. Her second oldest, Nikola, was her protector; therefore, he had to serve the Greek army and his family. The only child left was my father, who was ten years old.

My grandmother could not fathom having someone take her little boy. Her uncle told her about a wealthy and influential couple whose summer home he was building, and mentioned they needed a charcoal carrier. He suggested she send my father to Tripoli. Grandma was torn to pieces. It was so far, in the center of the Peloponnese. But she realized she had no option. She prepared my father with two little pieces of clothing and a bucket of soup made from milk and flour, and sent him away with her uncle. They had to ride across many mountains without getting caught by the Germans or guerrillas.

Finally, after riding for three days, they reached Tripoli. My father was introduced to his master and his wife. They took a liking to him, but they treated him like a servant. They were authoritative with their demands and expectations. My father was a hard worker, and he was endlessly curious. He didn't have any schooling so he would finish his errands and sit outside of the courtroom to listen to how lawyers and judges spoke so he could learn how to speak intelligently.

After stopping in front of the tailor's storefront window one day, my father became curious about the craft. He would finish his chores by late afternoon and run to stand outside a tailor's store. He was fascinated just watching him cut patterns to make suits. My dad grabbed newspapers from the garbage to quickly draw the designs that he saw. When he went home to his bunk in the evening, he would try to make a suit out of newspaper. He thought, if I can learn to design and cut patterns when I grow up, I can be a tailor since I don't have an education.

One day, the housekeeper forgot to iron the master's shirt before leaving. He asked my eleven-year-old dad to iron it. Dad thought it was easy and he had no choice, since it was demanded by his master. Dad filled the metal iron with charcoal. He let it get hot and started to iron the shirt, but he was soon frantic—the shirt was getting burned. The master saw this, ran over, grabbed the burned shirt and smacked my father across the face. My dad said that his face was on fire with the force that he hit him. My poor dad ran out into the rainy streets, crying hysterically, and cursing God and the day he was born. There was so much thunder and rain, he went for safety beneath the stairs of the theater at the center of the *platea*.

Dad was hurt and angry. He said it was the first time he cursed God for taking his father. As he sat outside, he thought to himself, if I had a father, I would not have been a charcoal carrier, nor would anyone have the courage to strike me.

The master realized what he had done to an innocent orphan child and went out with his driver to find my dad in the streets. Finally, they found him at the *platea*, wet, sad, hungry, and upset. The master took him hom,e and his wife gave him a hot bath and a hot meal.

"Although I was so hungry, I had no appetite," my dad told me when he remembered the moment. "I could not eat for two days. I was too hurt for comfort."

From that day forward, his master never complained or told Dad what to do. He was humiliated that he had hit an orphan child. What did he know about housework and ironing? The couple treated my dad as their own child, but my dad was too hurt to accept any kind of gesture.

Every Sunday, the Germans would bring Greek citizens to the main *platea* and execute them. My father was always going there, watching from a hiding place to see if any relatives were getting killed. He hated what he was witnessing. He learned, lived, and witnessed so much suffering at such a young age.

After a few weeks, a villager went to see my grandmother. He had heard what the master had done to my dad, and when he told my grandmother, she was infuriated. She wanted to make sure her little boy was okay.

Bold Resilient Women

Grandma got up and started making soup for my dad. When the soup was finished, she put on warm clothes and put her things in a bundle of cloth, which she tied on a piece of wood. She hung it over her shoulder. When the sun went down and it got dark, she left for her journey. She was a lonely woman traveling across the mountains to see her child. She didn't think of herself and the suffering she was going to endure; she only thought of her little boy. She needed to see for herself that he was fine.

Grandma's legs and hands were bleeding as she traveled through thorny woods and mountains, trying to get to her son. On the second day, as the sun was coming out, before she could hide, a German soldier caught her.

When the commander, who spoke Greek, saw her bleeding hands and legs and her clothing ripped from the thorns, he asked where she was going. My grandmother was terrified, but he assured her no harm would come to her. He asked again who she was, what she was doing, and what was in the bag she carried. While he interrogated her, he had a soldier bring her hot cocoa to drink. Grandma was horrified. She thought they were drugging her to rape her.

The commander again told her it was warm cocoa and reassured her that nothing was going to happen to her.

Grandma was a very smart woman. She knew if she told the truth of what had transpired with her son and the master, he might get executed. So, she decided to tell him her side of the story in her own way.

"Dear commander," she said, "I was a widow at twenty-eight years old and was left with six orphans. I could not support all my children and had to send them to family and friends to help me. My uncle thought it would be a great idea if my ten-year-old son went to work as a coal carrier in Tripoli. I was informed that my little boy is very sick, and I am taking him soup to get better."

The commander was distraught hearing my grandmother's sincere story as he saw tears streaming down her cheeks. He kissed her bleeding hands and ordered his driver to take her to Tripoli. He told them no one is to lay hands on her or else they will be executed.

My grandmother had a ride to Tripoli, and sat on the edge of the car seat, anxiously waiting to see my dad. Dad was hiding beneath the theater to see who the Germans were executing.

When he saw his mother, his heart stopped. But she winked at him, telling him she was fine. The commander's driver treated her with respect and compassion.

Grandma's tears were rolling down her cheeks as she was hugging and kissing her little boy. She assured him she was going to handle everything.

Bold Resilient Women

She took my dad by the hand and marched into his master's home. She told him he had no right to lay his hands on her son. She told him she was left a widow but not a woman without guts, dignity, and honor.

The couple felt horrible, and they promised my grandmother that her son would be treated as their own. Grandma decided to get a job in Tripoli, just to make sure her son saw her every day to help him gain strength and feel safe and secure. Grandma lived half of the year in Tripoli and half of the year in the village, as she had to uphold her promise to take care of the church of Saint Anna, her family's guide and protector.

My beautiful, loving, faithful, and vivacious grandma died at just sixty-seven years old. I believe she was tired of life and wanted to go home to her Elia. During her final days, Dad came to Greece and stayed with her until her passing. She told him how much she loved her baby. (Grandma, all the village, and the entirety of Gortinia never called my dad by his name—they only called him Baby.) Grandma was glad her kids were all healthy and well.

I hardly knew my grandmother, but she would eventually become my savior. She wanted to save her beloved son, Evangelo—my father—from the pain and suffering of losing a child. She knew how death had torn her family apart.

This is when I realized that the dead are around us in spirit. Physically, we don't see them, but there is presence when we need them. We feel their energy and support. They carry us when we can't carry ourselves and our pain.

War and Eruption of Corpses

My mother felt an urgency to share her family stories with us. She wanted us to know where we came from, the strength and power of our ancestors. She also wanted us to know the sacrifices that had been made for generations to get me here, to a safe home in Chicago.

One day, when we were working in the kitchen together, she turned to me. She was wearing a scarf over her hair, which was the style in the old country, and her kind blue eyes looked right into mine. "Have I ever told you about my Aunt Katerina?" she asked.

"No," I said, "but Grandma told me a bit about her when I asked her why she spoke with so much anger and hate for God." Mom motioned for me to sit down, and I did. She pulled out a chair and sat across from me, looking relieved to rest.

"My grandmother's sister had to pack her son and nephew's body parts into a cloth sack after a hand grenade erupted in their hands." She told me. "They were two young boys, helping Katerina pick, cut, and fold wheat in the fields. They found a rubber oval with a circle and a string. It was unfamiliar to them and, being kids, they started to play with it. Suddenly, a loud noise echoed across the mountains, spreading throughout the fields, reaching the village.

"My aunt panicked and sprinted toward the smoke. She kept calling their names, but there wasn't a response. As the smoke cleared, she saw children's body parts scattered across the entire area. Her screams were heard across the mountains to the village, forcing the villagers to run toward the fields. They were panicked, wondering if the Germans had executed villagers, and that's why they were hearing all the screaming.

"As they approached Katerina, they saw her walking beside a horse. A sack was hanging down on each side of the animal, and blood dripped down the horse's sides. She also carried a bloodied bag and was screaming. The mountains echoed with her cries. They were horrified. What was she carrying? Whose corpses did she find? Her husband asked her where the children were, and between screams, she showed them the sacks filled with blood and howled in pain that these were the remaining pieces of their children. The entire village mourned for many years.

"Katerina was taken to a hospital. The trauma was too severe for her; she was losing her mind, and she was never the same again. At this moment, her life had ended, and she blamed herself for taking the children to work with her in the fields. She said she was responsible for their deaths, and no one could convince her that it was an act of the war that killed the two innocent children. She was a walking  dead person, roaming the village and streets, crying and blaming God and herself for this tragedy. God gave her another baby in her mid-fifties, but she was heartbroken until her last breath. Everyone considered this a miracle at her late age. She cared for and loved the baby, who brought joy into the entire family, especially to his older sister. But Katerina couldn't stop dreaming and thinking of the pain and cost of the war. As she would walk through the village, she would scream. 'You don't understand how war rips families to pieces! You are never the same! You wait for death to take you!'"

My great-aunt's family ended up spreading their wings to different countries. Her daughter, Dimitra, and younger son grew up, got married, and immigrated to other countries, where they, too, found survival and success. But when you asked my aunt Dimitra why she returned to the mountain to rebuild her parents' home, she said, "My mother brought back on her horse the bodies of my brother and cousin. This is the least I can do for their memory."

They always spoke of their mother's pain and suffering. This is the reason I had a special place in my heart for her.

"Everything in life can be corrected and rectified but death," my mom added. "Once someone dies, words for comfort are lost."

My mother was always there to remind me that no one is truly satisfied with their lives; everyone wants what other people have. But often what you

Bold Resilient Women

see is superficial and fake, and you never know what's hidden behind closed doors. She often heard from friends about their big houses, or about the homes that her brothers had, while six of us lived in a two-room apartment.

"Sometimes the biggest, most elegant homes are hollow inside. They might have problems, illness, or pain and suffering. A person's family and their surroundings are what mold someone into becoming a decent and moral citizen." Mom was never impressed with what others had. She never forgot that she came from a poor, humble family, and she had to work from a young age. She never had big dreams or hopes. All she wanted was to educate her children and make sure they felt loved and supported by family, and she worked day and night for this.

"When you love your children, you protect them by not arguing or yelling in front of them," she would tell me. "You try to spare them from choosing sides. Lock yourself in the bedroom and resolve your issues in your bed. You will be surprised how many things can be solved in bed when there is still love and respect in a couple's lives."

One day, on a visit back to Greece, my mom and I were driving to the village at the outskirts of Argos. She pointed at a mountain and started to cry. "What is it, Mom?" I asked. She asked me to pull over at the next exit, where our coffee stop always was. She wanted to tell me a story from when she was twelve years old, which traumatized her to this day.

We sat outside at a small table, and my heart began to pound. What traumatic experience had my beautiful mom faced? What had happened to her at such a young age? Why was she in so much pain and agony?

"Every year from October to March, all the girls from the village would come to Argos to work picking oranges," she said. "There wasn't any transportation to where we were going, or if there was, it would cost too much. We had to walk, crossing the mountains for two days to get there. World War II was coming to an end, and our biggest fear was from the Communists and the guerrillas. We had heard so many horror stories about girls abducted and taken to the mountains to be raped and become their property.

We were warned to protect ourselves and be aware."

She explained that as she started out, she fell ill. She had gotten her period. She didn't want to tell the girls to stop and take care of her, because time was of the essence. So, she cut leaves from the trees and put them in her underwear to serve as a sanitary pad. But as she walked, she felt a burning sensation. Again, she said nothing.

When they arrived at the house for the employees, and the boss came out to meet the girls, my mom collapsed with a high fever. They rushed her to the hospital. Mom had a severe infection from the leaves. The master's wife was terrified, not knowing what the outcome would be, so she sent a horseman to the village to bring her mother, my grandmother, to see her.

When the horseman arrived, my grandma started crying before he even spoke a word. She thought someone had abducted my mom because she was the most beautiful girl in the village with the biggest light blue eyes. The horseman told her that Mom was in the hospital in Argos.

My grandma got on a neighbor's horse and followed the horseman across the mountain to get to mom. When Grandmother arrived, she was horrified. My mom was naked from the waist down, her lower half covered with red blisters. She was covered in creams and had been given antibiotics. Grandmother cried hysterically and began praying. She couldn't stop.

For three months, my mom suffered. No one thought she was going to survive, but somehow, she was spared by God.

As we sat outside at the café next to the road, the mountains looming overhead, my mom ended the story, tears still in her eyes. I grabbed and kissed her, gaining even more love and respect for her through the struggles she faced as a small child. I finally understood why my grandmother would always say, "I love your mom more than all my children because she has been tormented from a young age." Everything made sense now.

From that moment, every time I went back to my village, I would look up at that mountain, *Goula*, and pray. God healed my mom and because of that, I had the honor and privilege to be raised by this incredible woman. I was proud to come from her and to have a great role model and idol.

It was from both her family history and her own history that she would tell me, you should not pass judgment on other individuals' suffering or make comments. We don't know or recognize their personal stories.

Dad's Pain

"My children, never bite the hand that feeds you, or you will be cursed and the food you eat will be stuck in your throat."

My dad would deliver his words of wisdom to us wherever he could. Whether he was sitting at the table as we ate dinner together, walking our family to church, or sitting down on a kitchen chair, exhausted from a long day, my father never missed an opportunity to share his stories. He wanted us to know his pain, so we never took anything for granted. He wanted us to really see people; to know that everyone has a story.

My dad was a strict and dominant man, tall and thin with black hair and dark eyes. When he spoke to us, he would put his right hand under his chin, resting his head. We knew his story by heart, yet whenever he shared it, it always felt like we were hearing it for the first time.

"I was working in the streets of Tripoli, Arkadia, when I was ten years old," he would tell us. "I was physically and mentally abused and kicked around. I was cold and didn't have a coat on my back. I didn't have heat to warm my skinny body.

"Look at my toes, how messed up they are. I didn't have socks to wear, and the rain and snow would penetrate my shoes into my skinny toes." Now, I understand why when I cut his nails, they were deformed. "Many nights, I would sleep by the fireplace to warm my feet and they were purple from the cold. I slept many nights without food. I was starving, eating leftover breadcrumbs from the tables of the restaurants. The aristocrats would waste food, while many of us didn't eat for days.

"When I was eleven years old, I was slapped by my master," he continued. "He gave me his shirt to iron for his meeting. I didn't know how to iron with a charcoal iron, so as I started to iron the shirt, it was too hot and burned it. My master stormed in when he smelled the burning and slapped me so hard that I can still feel it to this day." When he told us this, he would move his hand from his chin to his cheek, as though the pain was fresh. "I fled the house. It was a cold, rainy day. I ran to the *platea* and sat beneath the awnings of the movie theater, crying and cursing God. I was yelling, 'Why God didn't you take me? Why did you leave me to be tormented? Why did you take my father?' My mother had so many kids, and she was young; he was needed more than me."

These memories always sparked Dad to remind us how their pasts had inspired them to create a new future. "Your mother and I came to this country with nothing so that our children could live with respect and dignity. We are smart, but we had the disadvantage of not being educated. You must be educated so you have the tools to succeed, but don't ever take our love, sweat, and commitment for granted. Remember to give everyone who crosses your path love, kindness, and respect, and God will grant all of your wishes."

My brothers and I would stare at my father wide-eyed, taking in his words. We lived with a leg in each country: America and Greece. My parents made sure we were closely connected to our roots, yet also allowed us to grow in this new country.

"Always respect your birth country, Greece," he would say. "It gave you your birth, your foundation, and your identity. Always honor, love, and respect your country, America, for fulfilling your dream of education and prosperity."

My father was very strict about family, faith, and country. Many in his family had sacrificed and given their lives serving Greece and America, and he had witnessed many horrors, especially during World War II. This experience molded and changed him for life. He was never shy about sharing his stories with us; he wanted us to know.

"Wars took away my brothers, uncles, aunts, and my father," he would tell us. "People don't understand the impact war has on children. Every Sunday, I would hear the bells of the church ringing out, saying it was time to hide. Cities and villages all over were being burned by the Germans. The German soldiers would make an announcement at the *platea*: If you cooperate with us, and don't kill a German soldier, no one will die. If you don't cooperate, and if you kill one German, we will wipe out your village. They were brutal to our people. Villagers would be brought to the *platea* and executed. We would hide from the Germans for days with only a piece of bread. We lived in fear of being captured and executed." Sometimes, when he told us this, his face would take on a faraway look, as though he was right back in that hiding place, starving and scared.

"All around me, people were being killed or running for shelter. Beautiful buildings were being destroyed. Villages and cities were ghost-like. Many individuals who cooperated with the Germans by becoming their spies became very wealthy, while others starved to death.

"War claims many innocent lives, and families like mine are never the same again. The whole family feels the impact of the war for generations, and countries develop an eternal instability. Living during the war left a huge void in my heart. Many evenings, when I close my eyes to sleep, I remember the beloved family members I lost. I relive the pain and suffering I witnessed. That's why, my children, I never want to hear about war. I have too many painful memories. I hope and pray you never live or witness what my eyes did."

But it wasn't always about the past. My father loved to share his hopes and dreams for our futures. He would sit, sipping mountain tea from our village in Greece, and share what he wanted for us. He wanted us to take everything he had seen and learned and make sure it helped us to become responsible and ethical people. He wanted us to learn what he had without having to see what he did.

"My children," he would say. "Never forget the friends who helped you along the way. They will become more important as you become older. You will love your family and children, you will be busy, but you will always need a dear friend. They will give you wise advice without wanting anything in return. Friends will be the backbone of your life, the way they were a shield in mine."

He was a confidante to all of us as we grew up, too. When I married, became a new mother, and as my kids grew up and developed their own lives, he was right there, sharing his experience with me, whether I was celebrating their joys or missing them terribly. In his older age, his advice became deeper and more existential.

"As you get older, your children will grow up, get married, live their lives,"

Bold Resilient Women

he would tell me. "They will become independent, just like you kids did. Their friends will matter more than you. You will become their neighbor.

"This will break your heart, but your children will cut the cord—they have to, in order to create their own legacy. Families will grow, and desires, ambitions, attractions, weaknesses, and strengths will

become a part of their, and your, daily life. But it will change. You, too, will see what you once could do at a young age, and you won't be able to do when you get older. "We, your parents, will someday pass away, the way you, too, will depart from this world. But life will keep moving on. It's an adventure of joys, sorrows, and incredible mysteries, and challenges. Happiness is loving your family and friends. Love them with their faults and don't impose your own desires or criteria on them."

I've lived my life with my father's advice tucked into my heart. His experience has shaped my worldview, and his words have provided a compass for how I exist as a partner, parent, and friend. I've learned not only the importance of giving back, but the way it has a ripple effect on those around you.

"You can only teach understanding and empathy if you become the role model for your children and friends to follow," he would always say. It's how he lived his life, and it's how I try to live mine, too.

Part Two
A Modern Woman in a Modern World

Innocent Eyes

Traveling with my family across the Atlantic as we immigrated to America, I saw in my imagination different scenarios that terrified and scared my tiny body. Immigrating to America at six years old, away from everything I knew. I looked out the airplane window and saw the blue water below. It was the first time I had ever seen a body of water, and it was vast and unending, with no land in sight. Even from up high, I could see the waves, wild, roiling, and unpredictable. The entire experience was simultaneously exciting but also frightening, the two emotions flowing in and out of each other—just like the water below. America was so far from our small Greek village, where everyone not only knew each other, but helped care for each other's families. It was a village in every sense of the word. What did we know about the American Dream?

Now, we had landed in a new country that seemed beautiful, but was also bewildering. When we arrived in our new city, Chicago, the sheer size of the buildings made our jaws drop. Miles of skyscrapers seemed to actually touch the sky, and we marveled at how they could have been built. Towers, monuments, ecclesiastical buildings, museums, and parks—all of it took our breath away. The streets were large. Big, colorful cars sped along in different directions. At night, rather than being swallowed in darkness, the city was lit by big, colorful lights, illuminating my innocent face and eyes as I took it all in. It was unimaginably beautiful.

I was most fascinated by the people. While in Greece, our friends and family had worn long dresses with scarves over their hair. Here in Chicago, people were dressed in their own unique and modern way, wearing colorful dresses, bellbottom pants, fur coats and incredible hats.

Everyone greeted us with kindness—which my parents weren't expecting—and were so willing to help us adjust to our new home. The adjustment wasn't easy. We felt so strange, and it was difficult to assimilate, even in America, a melting pot of diverse cultures and ethnicities. The most unnerving part, though, was that we could sense our parents' fear. They were perfectionists and desperately wanted to succeed in this strange world. We watched them agonize over every decision, needing to make good choices for their children and the future of their family. They wanted so badly for us to understand why they left everything they had ever known and jumped at the chance to immigrate to America. They were energized by the American Dream and ready to conquer this new life, all the while making sure we understood why they had brought us here. They wanted to write their own success story filled with education and prosperity.

But it came at a great cost. My mother and father faced severe pain, suffering, and a life filled with immeasurable challenges. What got them through was a laser focus on our education. They wanted us to gain the power of knowledge, which they believed would be our stepping stone to a fulfilling life—and they were right. Both my mother and father carried with them every single day the burden of not being educated and not understanding the culture and the English language, and they wanted better for us.

My fear of water remains even today. If I can't have my feet on the ground when I'm in the water, I will have a panic attack. But when I see the ocean, no matter where I am, my thoughts immediately go to my parents. What encouraged them to cross the Atlantic with four young children? As a young woman, I had to wonder, but now that I am a mother, and my children have had even more opportunities than I have, I fully understand.

Immigrants

From when I was a young girl, confidence and perseverance were instilled in my life from incredible mentors and role models who impacted and inspired me. These amazing and dynamic women were my grandmothers, Eleni and Georgia, my mom, Bessie, and my dear father, Angelo. I learned from a young age the meaning of selfless *agape,* which is to love everyone and everything more than myself. There was never a question of caring for myself. I always came last.

Bold Resilient Women

I learned the lesson of love and tenderness at the age of seven. I was a skinny, fragile, little girl who cared for two younger brothers, Peter and George. My hard-working, affectionate parents left for work at sunrise, and I had to wake up the boys, get them cleaned, dressed, and fed, and walk them four blocks to my grandmother's home. Keeping the boys on track was tough. Louis would take off and go to school by himself, and Peter wanted to play and throw stones. He didn't understand that time was of the essence, as I had to go to school. These walks every morning seemed to last hours. I was tired before the day had started.

Louis was always tired. He would bribe me to do his chores, saying, "If you don't do what I ask, I will tell our parents you stayed up late reading romances and movie magazines."

One early morning in the middle of winter, I tied my little brother, who overpowered my fragile and skinny frame, with a sheet around my waist to walk to my grandmother's home. I don't understand what possessed me to walk across the little park instead of down the sidewalk. As a young child, I didn't know that the weight of the snow would pull me down, and I would get sucked into the snow. I was stuck. I was terrified. I could not get up from the snow, and my brother was on my back, making the weight even heavier. I yelled to my brother, Peter, to scream for help so someone would hear us and come to our rescue. A lady came and lifted me and the baby and walked us to the sidewalk.

She made sure we arrived safely at grandmother's home. When I got there, I broke down crying. I was freezing, I was cold and soaking wet. I was late for school, and I didn't have dry clothes to change into. My grandmother went into her bedroom and got a pair of pants and a pullover shirt, which belonged to grandfather. I was horrified. I could not attend school and have everyone make fun of my looks. I just kept saying to myself, "What's grandmother thinking? I look like a homeless gypsy! Why did she dress me like this?!"

As I entered the school, I started crying hysterically. I could not control myself. I kept saying, "I want my mom, I want my mom." I went directly to the principal's office. When she saw how I was dressed and the disappointment on my face, she was stunned and immediately called my mom at the factory. The translator at Hart Shaffner Marx relayed to Mom that I didn't want to stay at school because I didn't feel well. The principal didn't want to insult or upset my mom by telling her the way I arrived at school that day. My mom left work, took the train, and transferred to the bus, finally arriving at school. When she walked into the principal's office, she saw me and stopped short. She was infuriated with my grandma. How dare she dress me in grandfather's clothes? Why didn't she get a dress from my aunt's closet and put it on me? My mom took me home, and I changed into my own clothes.

After she dropped me off at school, she marched to my grandmother's house to confront her. "How dare you hurt me and my daughter's feelings by putting her in her grandfather's clothing?" she said.

My grandmother responded that she was terrified of my aunts getting angry at her for using their clothes. This was a turning point for mom and her mother, and I believe they did not speak to each other for a couple of years. But I will never forget the way my mother protected and defended me. I discovered that love shows itself in all sorts of different ways.

I realized what responsibility and accountability was at a very young age. My parents endured much pain and made many sacrifices for us to achieve the American Dream of getting an education. Every lesson in my early life got me prepared for the future, eventually making me a stronger, more resilient woman.

My grandmother was an educated immigrant woman who withstood many difficulties in life. She traveled across the Atlantic in the early 1950s with a family of seven. She knew the consequences of hard labor and multiple jobs.

My mother was a young immigrant who didn't have money or an education. She didn't know much about life and knew even less about this new world. She had to overcome so many barriers in coming to a brand-new country with six people.

My grandmother, Eleni, and my beautiful mom, Bessie,—along with many other immigrant friends—never imagined what the other side of the Atlantic Ocean had in store for them. The language barrier was a huge obstacle to their arrival in a new country. They were deprived of sleep and food, and no one cared to translate English into Greek for them. They could not rely on any relatives. Everyone was a refugee or immigrant. They came to this country for prosperity and had to work to survive.

They didn't have degrees from Ivy League schools; in fact, they hardly had an educational background. Many of these immigrants were children under the age of fifteen who traveled alone and feared everyone around them. They were not from influential families. They were poor immigrants who set out with the goal of working hard, a dream to succeed, and a commitment to helping their families and countrymen back home. They were thirsty for education, survival, and the American promise of prosperity.

My strength came from witnessing firsthand their struggles, fears, pain, and joy. Strong faith, hard work ethic, loyalty, and empathy were instilled in me as they shared their inspiring stories and our family history. Through their examples, I learned nothing was impossible when you have the will to remain focused and humble. You were able to get closer to your dreams when you loved yourself first, worked hard, and had empathy for the less fortunate.

Dad always reminded us to never forget our humble roots. "Always remember where we came from and the sacrifices and pain we endured to make a home in this foreign country," he would say. "When you forget your past, you can never have a future." Dad would constantly remind us that he was an orphan and no one cared for him. "God has given you two hands, one to take and one to give," he would say. "I will curse you if you ever become the hand that takes and not the hand that gives. When you give to others, God will give you one hundred times more."

Life's unpredictable route took me through many ups and downs. There were hurdles, tears, sorrows, pain, laughter, joy, suffering, illness, poverty, happiness, and success. By accepting vulnerability and not being arrogant by thinking we are indispensable, or being insensitive to others' circumstances and situations, I was able to control many stressful situations.

No matter what obstacle came my way, I had learned from these strong immigrant women to see the glass as full. They taught me to be realistic in my goals and desires. Mom would say, "always see the bright light of hope at the end of the tunnel. God will shine a light of serenity and peace for your family. But never go beyond the length of your legs."

My parents, who didn't have an education, would teach us through parables, though sometimes the message wasn't totally clear to us. "What does that mean?" we asked. "Go slowly in achieving success," she said. "Don't try to achieve success by rushing to conquer the world or else your head will sink in the sand."

My parents were kind souls, selfless and giving. They never allowed us to judge or condemn anyone or anything. They were unable to help us with homework due to their illiteracy, but they would sit with us during dinner and tell us stories of their challenges. They were expert storytellers, sharing family history and global events. They taught us about the suffering and casualties of world wars. We learned real-life tragedies and historical facts from them better than we could have from any history book. We received education every day through the real-life events my parents and grandparents lived through.

They taught us gratitude by teaching us to pray before and after our meals. "Let's give thanks to God for the meal we have today, for there are many in the world who don't have anything but crumbs to eat." They had known this hunger all too well. Before getting tucked in bed, we had to kneel and pray and give thanks to our Lord for all the blessings he had bestowed upon us on that day.

Bold Resilient Women

Mom would say, "I don't have a school education, but I have street smarts, which no one will ever understand. People can't understand the stories of my life unless they survived in an impoverished environment. But I have kindness, love, and faith to know what is right and wrong—and that has taken me beyond where I thought possible." She reminded us of everyday struggles and her determination to give us what she and my dad were deprived of. Mom would tell us stories of people mistreating her by making fun of her while she sold hot dogs and snow cones on the streets of Chicago. During the day, Mom would push a cart to sell her products. And after putting the cart away, she fixed the soles and heels of women's shoes and found time to do alterations. This was her daily routine at my parents' store, a cleaner, tailor, and shoe repair that my parents struggled to buy and own.

When we asked Dad why he went into business so fast without knowing a word of English, he would look down at the table and pause before looking up at us, "My children, the first week I arrived here, I was washing dishes and a man said to me, 'Angelo, you said you will never work for anyone, that you are going to be independent.' I told him that when I crossed the Atlantic Ocean, I lost my rings, but my fingers are still here. Therefore, as long as I have my health, I will achieve success." He told us he took off the apron, threw it in the man's face, and walked from downtown to Gunnison and Marine Drive in Uptown, where we lived. All the way home, with tears in his eyes, he kept questioning God again. Why was he born to be tormented?

Dad and Mom were treated as second-class citizens. Many individuals in church didn't want to associate with immigrants. They saw them as inferior. They had assimilated into their new roles as Americans, and many of them changed their names, forgot their language, and severed their ties to their homeland, Greece. They would sit with other immigrant families in a separate section. Some individuals respected and treated my family with love and compassion; however, due to my grandmother's participation and position in the church.

Grandma was an active board member for St. Andrews, St. George, and the Hollywood House, which sheltered low-income elderly people on Sheridan Road in Chicago. She was an advocate for the poor and needy. She would bake the Holy Bread for every Sunday mass and every holiday. If they would ask her to bake the five loaves—*artoklasia*—for the well-being ceremony of a certain family or her family, she would gladly support the families.

Despite all the hardship they faced as immigrants, my parents and grandmother showed up for everyone: their family, their friends, their customers, their church, the Greek community, and even their relatives back home. As I watched them, I was always observing and taking mental notes on how to succeed. I felt like I would never have to have their level of courage, because I was establishing myself as an American. Little did I know I had other challenges ahead that would require my own resilience. I was lucky to learn it from them.

Inspirational Mentors

During grammar school, my favorite teachers were Mrs. Kathy and Sister Rita. These two women came from different religious and cultural backgrounds, one a laity and the other a devout Catholic nun. Although they demonstrated two different religious perspectives, both taught me respect, love for God, empathy, and equality. They were caring and loving women who had an enormous love and dedication for their students and the church.

Mrs. Kathy was a striking, soft-spoken woman with beautiful light skin, brown hair with red highlights, sparkling eyes, and a smile that took your breath away. She would discipline us with her sturdy and tenacious look, after which she would take us by the hand, lead us to the classroom, and teach us through empathy and kindness. She taught us to think about our actions and mistakes, making us aware that we needed to be responsible citizens and take control of our decisions. Sometimes, she left us wondering whether we were right or wrong with our conduct and actions.

Some of our male teachers were more vocal in their responses and teachings. They spoke with fierce, piercing voices, which were so terrifying we felt

Bold Resilient Women

like we would pee ourselves. They insulted us in front of our classmates, demanded apologies, or put us in the corner of the room to teach us discipline and obedience.

St. Thomas of Canterbury was a combination of a Catholic church and a school, and Sister Rita was a kind, sturdy nun who taught us to be focused and disciplined. Every morning, she would line us up before mass to make sure our skirts were below the knee. As girls walking to school, we wanted to be modern. We brought a string with us, and would tie our skirts up to have a mini look. But sometimes we would forget to drop the skirt below the knee, and we would get caught. Sister Rita was nice but firm. "Okay, young ladies," she would say. "I know you want to look good and be with the trends, but you need to respect yourselves and the house of God."

Sister Rita taught all of this without raising her voice—except for in one instance. She would raise her voice sternly if one of the girls didn't respect the rules of the school. She was fair and gave three warnings. But the fourth time you broke the rule, she would take the ruler and hit you on the rear. "If you do it again, we will call your parents to come and take you from school," she would say. We didn't dare have our parents leave work to come to school because of our behavior. This was the most important lesson of my life. You couldn't insult your parents, who were working three jobs to pay for a private school, and you couldn't take advantage of the love and opportunity the nuns offered.

Then, there was Father. When the priest walked into church and looked at us sharply, we would shake in our seats. His look penetrated your body.

He was a disciplined man who didn't hear excuses. He didn't have an issue with insulting or demeaning students in front of everyone. He would take a deep breath and then ask the kind of questions that hit you at your core. "Do you know what kind of sacrifices your parents are making to pay for your education? Would you like me to call them in and have a talk?" He only spoke once—there was never a second chance. He was petrifying, and I knew from my grammar school years that you must be obedient to a man.

This different treatment was confusing, even at a young age. I kept asking myself, *Why were men controlling women? Why was there a lack of respect? Why*

Bold Resilient Women

did men doubt women's emotions or discount their opinions? We were treated very differently from the boys in our class. Boys could not do anything wrong, and they received a different treatment when their homework was late. Teachers always had an excuse for them.

While Father treated us differently, his expectations were the opposite of other male teachers. Because most families in our school were immigrants, he wanted us to see the sacrifices of our parents. He had so much compassion for them. He wanted us to be grateful, and constantly reminded us about the responsibility to honor their sacrifices.

One day, when I was in eighth grade, a boy student turned in his homework late, and the male teacher didn't even bat an eye. One of my friends raised her hand and asked, "Why are boys treated differently than girls?"

"Excuse me?" asked the teacher, who was a man.

"Well, why does he get to hand in his assignment after it's due?"

The male teacher scoffed at the question. "The boys work after school.

So they get more time."

What? What did he know of our financial needs? Most of the girls in the classroom worked after school, too. Most of us were in the same financial situation.

It was as though lightning struck the classroom. I instantly understood, in my core, that a woman's role was going to be completely different than a man's. It was a lesson in the complexity women face by simply existing. It was so clear how men and women saw the world differently. Men focus on things being sustained and structured the way they want them, while women analyze things in a more holistic way.

The boys in school would make fun of our long skirts and our school uniforms. They bullied us for not wearing makeup and having our hair in a ponytail or an updo, as was the school rule. It wasn't uncommon to go into the bathroom and hear other girls crying because a boy had put them down.

Growing older, I've continued to see young men behave this way, and it's clear this pattern has to be from their family environment. From a young age, boys witnessed the mistreatment of women, and they became accustomed to degrading them and not having respect for equality, inclusiveness, and fair treatment. Men controlled the world, and it wasn't going to change in the near future.

They acted this way, but what I saw was that it was the women who held things together. The elderly ladies of the church—mostly my grandma and mom's friends—cooked and baked for the church bazaars and coffee times. They surrounded us girls with love and patience, teaching us the truth about life.

"Pretty girls," they would say, stacking sweets on a tray or slicing a loaf of bread, "it's irrelevant how hard we fight or how loud we speak. Men will continue to underestimate us. They will wear the pants of the family, and we will always wear the dresses. We will never be treated equally or be respected by men."

Strict Greek culture dictated that women had limited resources in achieving their dreams, ambitions, and goals. Women had to work, handle the

Bold Resilient Women

chores, and take care of the kids. Very few pursued an education. Many had to think outside of the box to find ways to get an education or to stand up for their beliefs without family knowing.

Women formed coalitions, creating sustainable organizations to feed the hungry, educate young people, care for the elderly, and help drug abusers, the mentally ill, and people who suffered illnesses across the world.

One example of a women-formed coalition is the Red Cross. This independent organization focuses on humanitarian needs, helping and evacuating victims of war and violent conflicts and bringing aid to injured war soldiers from across the world.

Another is Ahepa, the Daughters of Penelope. This group of women are faithful in promoting their Hellenic roots, as well as supporting arts, education, and philanthropy. And the Greek Orthodox Ladies Philoptochos Society, created by members of the church. *Philoptochos* translates to, "friend to the poor, needy, homeless, and ill."

These women became beacons of hope, as well as community pillars, as they supported people globally. They worked for different countries and our motherland. They built churches, schools, hospitals, and other institutions. They supported veterans, created homes for the poor, protected and cared for the vulnerable in different communities, built up neighborhoods, restored burned-down villages, established scholarships for children to excel in education, and so much more. They made a difference in the lives of people in the United States, Europe, and other parts of the world.

These inspirational women united in embarking and forming powerful organizations which were productive. They led by example. With these women leading the way, young women began believing in themselves and their purpose in this world. They became hope for generations to come. They believed in the power of working together.

"Work doesn't destroy you. It gives you reason to get up and conquer the world." My mom and grandma used to say this often.

What destroys you mentally and physically is psychological war caused by your family, workforce, or environment. Difficult circumstances are what devastate your peaceful life by damaging your health. By living an intense and stressful life, your body becomes fragile and exposed to many undesirable health risks. Persistent fighting, nagging, and anger will eventually destroy anyone's calm and inner peace, and ultimately break you down.

As a young girl, small and seemingly irrelevant things would torment me for days. I would get upset, becoming discouraged about my life and existence. Learning how to make different recipes for dinner, for example. I couldn't figure out the measurements correctly. Sometimes the dough would be stiff, likeit could hit the wall like a brick. Sometimes the food looked perfect, but I could not figure out how long to cook it, or what portion of water to add, so it was often overcooked or undercooked.

I would cry, blaming myself for not following the recipe correctly. I was a perfectionist who could not accept failure. If we didn't live on a budget, it wouldn't matter if I threw the food away and started over. But knowing we were poor, and food could not be wasted, impacted me severely. My parents never punished me or discouraged me from trying over and over, but I felt guilty. They would throw the dough or food in the garbage, clean my mess, and praise me. They would comfort me by telling me how proud they were that I wanted to learn to cook to help them out, and encourage me to start over. There was no punishment for trying and, knowing how sensitive I was, they didn't believe in discouraging me.

"You will never learn anything in life unless you fall a few times," my dad would say. "*Agapimou*, it's good to make mistakes."

This has stuck with me my whole life. The only way to learn is by making many small mistakes, and you'll see the impact on your personal life, career, and business ventures. By correcting your mistakes, you will think twice about repeating the same ones.

Bold Resilient Women

It's a good way to learn about the ups and downs of life. They just didn't want us to make the kind of mistakes that could ruin your life.

"Eleni, look in the mirror and love what you see," he would say. "Don't hate yourself for foolish things. Respect yourself for the person you are. What doesn't kill you will make you a stronger, more courageous individual in society."

 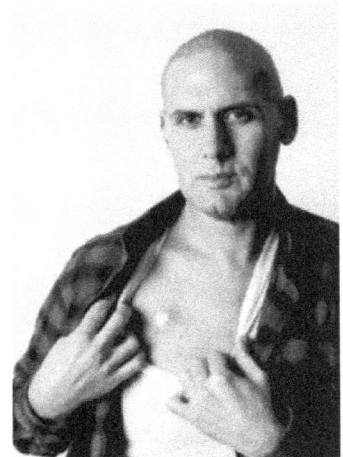

Chicago, a Big City

Growing up in Chicago in the 1960s was an adventure. The city had an interesting, energetic vibe. Hippie culture was everywhere, as people expressed their love for music, freedom, love, and drugs. There were also the riots. It was the era of the Civil Rights Movement, the Vietnam War, assassinations of both President John F. Kennedy and his brother, Robert Kennedy, and the assassination of Martin Luther King, Jr. All of this turmoil created divisions throughout the city.

We lived and had our business in the Uptown neighborhood. It was also the area where all of the big shots would show off their power and money. It was a social center of the city, with performing theaters, movie theaters, dance clubs, power, and glory.

It was easy to be dazzled by the area's bright lights, but you couldn't forget that riots, killing, violence, division, and racial segregation existed in our city—and the entire country. It felt uncomfortable to walk the streets of Chicago and be among big crowds. People were judging everyone by their skin color and economic status.

My dad would say, "We cannot accelerate the spread of hate and violence and the deterioration of our country.

We cannot destroy what people have built."

Bold Resilient Women

As a young and innocent child, I learned about violence and oppression by listening to stories from our beloved employees, Mr. Bogio and Mrs. Mae. Both Mr. Bogio and Mrs. Mae were born in Alabama, and told us horrific stories about the Deep South and how their family, friends, and Black people were treated. My siblings and I would help out in the store, and when we asked Mr. Bogio about his life, he would tell us heartbreaking stories of pain and suffering. Mr. Bogio was a renowned hat maker, and was known in Uptown, the city, and the suburbs as The Hat Man. One day, I gained the courage to ask about the marks on his arms.

"Missy, those are my marks of being a Black Southern man," he would say, his face filled with sadness and fear as if he was reliving those terrible days. With watery eyes, he would share stories of his parents, their tormented lives, and back-breaking work in the cotton fields.

"Missy, the weather was burning hot. My mother would wear a turban over her head and my papa would put on his hat. The heat was unbearable, but we just kept going on day in and day out."

As a child, I was traumatized by his stories, unable to understand how cruel people could be, how some people could treat other humans worse than animals. My brothers and I would talk at home, sharing our sorrow for him and his family. We wondered together, if we were old enough, could we have made a difference? If we were adults back then, could we have set people free of torture and suffering?

We ached for Mr. Bogio and Mrs. Mae. We cared and respected them both; they were part of our family.

"How did you survive?" I asked one day.

"Missy, we survived by our faith and trust in the Lord," Mr. Bogio said. "We had hope. We knew He wasn't going to betray us, and He was going to hear our prayers."

Whenever we asked questions, they shared truthfully.

"My father worked in the cotton fields, and my mama worked in the cotton fields and then cooked for the master and his family," Mr. Bogio told us one day. "She was the head of the household and in charge of all the other servants. As a young boy, I didn't know what it was to go out and play. My father would put me on the wagon and bring me out to help. If I didn't go to the cotton fields, I would shine my master's shoes and attend to his needs."

Mr. Bogio said he and his family were protected and sheltered by their master until one nightmare day.

"One Sunday morning, our master gave us the wagon to go to church and to visit our family on the other side of town," he told us. "Suddenly, out of nowhere, a group of white men jumped in front of the wagon and grabbed my father, throwing him on the ground. Missy, I witnessed my father's death at a very young age. Since that day, I can still hear the echo of his cries, my mother's screaming, and all of us begging these monsters to spare his life. They proceeded to torment him. After they had beaten him to the point where he was likely paralyzed, they hung him in front of our eyes without any remorse."

I was scared and terrified, yet I knew I needed to listen. My brothers and I wondered how we would feel if they hung our father in front of us. Would we ever forget it? Would it haunt us the rest of our lives?

Across the world, we knew that our Greek history contained stories not unlike Mr. Bogio's, as Greeks were tormented during the Ottoman Empire. Mr. Bogio would say, "I love Greek people. They know suffering. We share the same history, just in different locations and countries."

Whether it's war, depression, suffering, and both visible and invisible scars, these true stories of pain and agony can never truly be relayed in a textbook. When you are young, you have a difficult time understanding how people can possibly be ridiculed, killed, and discriminated against due to how they look or what faith they practice. It was painful learning firsthand the suffering of Blacks, Greeks, Spaniards, Italians, and many other ethnicities who have darker skin. Throughout history, racist individuals would seek them out; they were forced to flee or face death.

"One winter night," Mr. Bogio told us one day. "I'd had enough. I could not continue seeing my people being tormented and betrayed. I had seen too much blood being shed for freedom. My wife had lost several children due to overwork and beatings from her previous master. She was left infertile. We loved children but were left childless without a choice."

After his wife lost the last child and gained back her strength, they decided to flee. "I took my wife and escaped during the night and headed north to Chicago. I had heard remarkable stories of this big city. There were rumors that people of color were treated fairly here, and I even heard that there was the opportunity to work as a hat man." Mr. Bogio was obsessed with hats. As a young boy, he would go into town and secretly watch a tailor who made hats. He took it all in, and without anyone being aware, he taught himself to be one of the best hat men in the South.

Bold Resilient Women

Eventually, after many terrifying and exhausting days of travel, they ended up in Uptown. He knew it was the center of the theater community, where people came with their classy cars, chauffeurs, lavish mink coats, cigars, and stylish hats.

Mr. Bogio searched for a job as a hat and shoeshine man. He knew he had talents no other person had. He walked into Bennett Cleaners, removed his hat, and asked for a job. Mr. John, the owner of the cleaners at that time, asked what kind of work he could do. Mr. Bogio told us he smiled and said, "I was the best hat man in the South. If you give me an opportunity to work for you, your business will triple." Mr. John saw the potential and kindness in his eyes and hired him immediately.

Uptown was—and still is—filled with incredible landmark theaters: the Aragon, the Riviera, and the Uptown theater all tower over North Broadway Street, their bright, colorful lights promising something big. They were places to see and be seen. On the corner of our store's block was Broadway Bank, and opposite that was Senator Percy's office. All the corners were occupied with government buildings, and our customers were people like Mayor J. Daley, Senator Percy, Sheriff Elrod, Mr. Brown— the President of Uptown Bank—and other elite citizens. Word spread that the best hat man in town worked for Bennett Cleaners.

Everyone from all over the state came to Mr. Bogio to make their unique and rare hats. As a young girl, I witnessed long Cadillacs pull up on our street, and people walking out with big hat boxes.

Mr. John was a round, sweet old man who left Greece when he was thirteen years old. He didn't have a family or any relatives. He was surrounded by dear friends, but as he got older, he didn't have anyone to take over his business.

He met my dad when he was eating in a coffee shop. He saw my dad hustling, quickly cleaning tables, and carrying plates to the back to wash them. He saw that he was fast and fierce. He stopped him while my dad was clearing plates, stacking them onto his arms to work faster.

"Greek D Pee," Mr. John said, and motioned for him to come over. During those years, if you were a Greek immigrant and met another like you, you called them "Greek D Pee," not by their name. You didn't dare announce you were an immigrant. "When did you come over from the old country?"

"I have been here for six months. I brought over my wife, four kids, two suitcases, and one hundred dollars," he said.

"Why are you here?" Mr. John asked.

"I am an orphan who was deprived of a good life and education," he told him. "I want my children to be educated so that they can achieve the American Dream. I want them to have what I couldn't."

Hearing my dad's struggle, and seeing his work ethic and sincere heart, Mr. John asked him a question that would change our lives.

"I own the cleaners across the street," he said. "I would love for you to become my business partner."

"What?" my dad asked, still balancing the plates. Around them, the diner still buzzed, but my dad was frozen in place. He could not believe his ears. Why would this foreign stranger want to help them? "But I don't have any money."

"Don't worry, you will give it to me little by little. What do you say?" The answer was obvious. After talking to my mother, he accepted the offer and went into business with Mr. John.

Eventually, Mr. John became our grandfather. He was invited by Mom for Sunday dinner every week, and we loved him like he was our own. He had finally found a family to love and be loved by.

Mr. John and his assistant taught my parents the business. They learned how to do cleaning. They learned how to make shoes, heels, and soles. They already knew how to sew, but they perfected their tailoring skills. My father paid Mr. John a monthly payment, and they worked side by side, Mr. John translating Greek to English for my father until the day he died. Bennett Cleaners eventually became my dad's cleaning, shoe repair, hat, and tailoring business. With his hard work and commitment—which Mr. John saw that day in the diner—it flourished into a lucrative and successful business. With my father's expert tailoring and Mr. Bogio's gift for making hats, Bennett Cleaners became the go-to destination for Chicago's elite citizens.

Two years after my father bought the business, on April 4, 1968, Dr. Martin Luther King, Jr. was assassinated. People were furious. Some started destroying, burning, and breaking into businesses and homes across our country. I was working in the store that day when Mr. Bogio approached my dad in a panic.

"We must go right away," he said. He told him he would go buy plywood to secure our windows. "I've lived through chaos and destruction before. We have to go." I ran with him to the hardware store, where we saw other neighborhood business owners frantically grabbing plywood to protect their stores. Mr. Bogio and Mrs. Mae were terrified; they didn't want anything to happen to us or the business. They knew every day was a struggle for my parents and saw that they worked endless hours and days to support their four children. We saw and felt their pain so clearly. They were broken as they relived their past. When the riots ended days later, only one window was broken, and nothing was taken from our business. My parents were crying and thanking God over and over. I had never seen them so emotional, but it was just the start of many challenges to come. Mr. Bogio and Mrs. Mae had tears running down their faces, too. They didn't have kids of their own, and they had become our extended family. They cared for and protected us as their own, and we were just as protective of them.

My heart would race when they shared their stories of pain and suffering. I felt rage as I processed these stories of violence, segregation, and the mistreatment of innocent lives and people. I had heard similar stories before from my own family, and I prayed at night, "God, how can all of this pain and suffering happen?" It was difficult to understand how people were allowing this kind of intolerance.

That's when I first realized: We need to understand history. We must never forget or we risk repeating the same mistakes and suffering. Without looking back, we can never learn enough to truly look forward.

Laughter

My mom and dad loved *Zorba the Greek*. When the movie came out in 1964, I could not believe how excited they were to see it. Dad and Mom could relate to the way the characters would drink a glass of wine, then start dancing and partying. They were both great dancers, and when my father danced in front, Mom would be so proud of the different dance techniques he used. When Dad watched the movie, he would say, "Look at the zeal and passion he has for the music and dance! Bravo, *palikari*." That meant "bravo, young man."

It was difficult convincing Dad of Anthony Quinn's cultural background. Although we explained many times that Anthony Quinn wasn't Greek, Dad always insisted he was. He claimed that if he wasn't born in Greece, he was converted into being Greek the way many of our friends had.

Zorba the Greek started out as a novel, and my mom was infatuated with the author, Nikos Kazantzakis. He was one of the most important and talented Greek writers and philosophers of the twentieth century, but he gained worldwide recognition when *Zorba the Greek* won three Academy Awards. It also seemed to put us Greeks in the spotlight in a new way. My brother, Louis, would imitate Zorba, saying in a pitch-perfect accent, "Life is all about trouble. The only time, my friend, you don't have problems is when you're dead. When you are young and alive, you undo your belt and look for problems."

As children, we would laugh, and my dad would add his commentary. "Louis, you imitate him well because you are the same—always looking for problems to solve." We would call my dad the walking encyclopedia; he knew it all and wanted to prove to everyone the truth.

Bold Resilient Women

No matter how tired my parents were, there was always entertainment, laughter, dancing, and parties in our home. Dad and Mom would always invite Greek immigrants, who didn't have their families in the States, over for a warm meal.

Many times, I would point out, "Mom, we don't have enough food for u,s and you are inviting everyone!"

She would say, "Honey, you will see. God will bless u,s and we will have leftovers." She would put a big pot of water on the stove, add a sprinkle of salt, and ask me to grab the spaghetti. "You will see, we will have enough to feed the neighborhood."

Lo and behold, we always had leftovers.

Satisfaction

My mother believed you could know everything about a person through their eyes. She used to say, "If someone cannot look you in the eyes, they're hiding something. They're lying." But she also used to say, "Through a person's eyes, you can see if they have a clean and sincere soul.

Through their smiling faces, you can see if they have an honest and caring heart."

I have found this to be true, and I've learned it throughout my life, but especially in my work helping so many different people from so many different walks of life. The virtue of supporting and helping a stranger—even by simply respecting their worth in society—has given me the opportunity to view people as unique individuals. I've respected and admired so many people through my participation in the fights for human rights, religious freedom, the elderly, handicapped children, and discrimination against gender and color. This work has fulfilled me through fighting for those who may not be able to fight for themselves.

Growing up with three brothers and a strict, disciplined father gave me the courage and strength to be opinionated. I wasn't afraid to participate in different conversations and share my thoughts with confidence and resilience.

Throughout my youth, Dad would gather us together at the round table, and we would talk about the news and politics, and touch on how these issues impacted us at school and in our daily lives. He would encourage us to defend what is right and speak up against what is wrong. It was through him that I learned to be a passionate advocate for social justice.

Bold Resilient Women

"When you fall, get up, gain confidence, rise with positivity, and demand change," he would tell us. "Learn to voice your opinion to support those who are kept silent. Start making a difference in the world. Don't sit back, taking up space in society."

My parents—especially my mother—instilled in me confidence, patience, and love from a young age, laying the foundation for the woman I would become. While Dad taught us through words, Mom taught us how to live through her actions. We saw her work ethic and how she never commented on other people's lives or ordered us around. She encouraged me to never be drawn in by the outside influences intent on shaping young women. I learned by observing her charm, empathy, and love for others, and the way she avoided being pulled into toxic environments.

As a young girl, I wanted to know what events were happening across the world. I watched the news with my parents and explained to them what happened that day. Every morning before going to school, I would read the *Chicago Sun-Times* newspaper to my dad while he was making shoes.

But I wasn't only about the serious news. Many evenings after finishing my homework, I would read romance novels, which were hidden beneath my bed. I was fascinated by the twists and turns of a love story. When I received my weekly allowance, I would run to the train station to purchase a new novel. In school, my favorite subject was history. I wanted my mind to travel to different parts of the world, creating my own impression in my head of how I wanted the world to be. I wanted to broaden my mind with the different historical events and know every country's challenges and sufferings to gain their freedom and protect their flag. Dad would say to never disrespect any country's flag. Every country has shed blood in honor of its stripes. I loved reading about different cultures, traditions, and faiths.

Perhaps blending my love of news and history, and my fascination with the twists and turns of love stories, I was infatuated with kings, queens, and any country that had a monarchy. My dad had influenced me on this as well. He loved the King of Greece, Konstantinos; his desk and walls of our home were covered in pictures, letters, plaques, plates, cards, and other items that displayed the king and queen of Greece. He respected him as much as anyone. "When you are a king, you give up everything to serve your people with integrity," he would say. "The king is our country's identity. It is a continuation of the throne."

Until the end of his life, we never removed anything which symbolized the love and respect he had for the Greek monarchy.

This fascination with the social elite translated into my daily life as well. During my spare time, I would watch talk shows, eager to see the behavior of

Bold Resilient Women

this fascinating group of people. I wondered how they saw us. Were we equals or inferior to them?

As a vibrant and ambitious young girl, I loved to see how reporters announced the news. I loved the way newsmen, like John Davis and Walter Jacobson, of Channel 2 news analyzed the day's events with respect and integrity. There was no conflict or misinterpretation, just a strong voice and fair and unbiased commentaries. They reported without condemning or judging any side.

I started observing their comments, their movements, body language, and behavior to see if there was more behind what they reported.

Although Dad didn't understand what they were saying, only what I was translating, he would comment on it all. That's when I learned the meaning of respectful dialogue. Whether you agree or disagree, you must respect everyone's views and opinions, good or bad, and at the end of the day, you have to make your own decision to examine further or accept what is told.

It was through all of these assessments and observations that I gained a passion for psychology. I gravitated toward other people's eyes, trying to see their heart and soul, as Mom said. I wanted to analyze their body language and see if I could figure out what they were thinking.

Growing older and learning from so many people from different backgrounds, I began to be confident in recognizing the souls and hearts of many individuals. I gained assurance and faith that someday, I was going to love the profession of psychology. I would understand people's lives, fears, and outcomes, no matter what they actually verbalized.

Committed Parents

My mom worked endless hours without having a say in the decisions my dad made. She was a woman, after all. He would say, "I know what is good for our family." Dad—and all the men I knew—was the decision maker for everything from the house, to education, to work. Women had no choice but to follow their direction. Everyone had their role and responsibilities; the women worked and took care of the children while the men worked and were in control.

Dad never allowed us to disrespect Mom. When we misbehaved or fought with each other, all Mom would say is, "Wait until your dad walks in the house." We were horrified. We stopped immediately.

As a young woman, my mom was always encouraging me to voice my opinion, give my input, and stand up for things I value. Mom would always say, "Give your opinion with respect and don't impose your opinions and views with demands." Then she would smile. "My love, you milk from both sides of the lamb's udder, not just from one." She explained that when you are kind, people can see your intentions. Therefore, listen to both sides of the story before you make a decision. She never wanted me to be silenced by anyone, and not to fear someone if they disagreed with me. Every person is entitled to their opinion.

My parents were simple, hard-working immigrants. They believed that through hard work and sweat, anyone could succeed, as long as they had common sense, honesty, dedication, and drive. They firmly believed that education can liberate people by offering freedom to succeed and earn respect. When you speak, people will listen.

Mom and Dad merely shared their experiences, but they didn't realize that they were teaching us more things than any textbook possibly could. I would listen to how my friends' parents spoke to them. They were educated, but all they worried about was coming home and relaxing after a hard day. Their parents weren't teaching them about life, morals, values, faith, and hope—all of the things we talked about as a family every single night.

When I would share with my friends, the tales of our family's nightly conversations, or my parents' many stories and parables, they were enchanted. They wanted to hear it all, too. My parents knew a life they could never imagine. They knew what it was to fight, to starve, and to suffer. They knew war, torture, pain, and hiding in the mountains for safety. My friends, on the other hand, knew nothing about true suffering. I realized they wanted to hear these stories, too, and soon they started asking me what our family had talked about the night before.

Learning from my parents was easy. I saw their daily challenges and their ups and downs. They were the perfect role models, living out the life that they preached to us.

One late afternoon, I was sitting behind the counter of my parents' shop doing my homework when a tall, elegant cowboy walked through the door. He asked if someone could fix his boots. He wanted a pair of new soles and heels. But Dad was out selling hot dogs, and the store employee had already left for the evening.

My mom set down the pants she was mending. "Sit down, I do it for you."

"You can replace the heels and soles on my boots?" he repeated.

"Me, yes, I fix," she said without hesitation.

We stared, wide-eyed, but didn't say a word. What was she saying? She didn't know how to fix boots!

"Please sit," she told him, motioning to a chair. He sat tentatively. "Okay, but please do a good job," he said.

My mom suppressed a smile. She was excited she would make $15—$10 for the soles and $5 for the heels—and she wanted to surprise dad when he returned with the hot dog cart. It was half a week's salary.

But my beautiful sweet mom had never fixed boots. She only knew how to replace women's heels, and had not a clue about cowboy boots.

She placed the boot on the metal bar and began to work, grabbing the knife to cut the sole. Suddenly, the sharp knife slipped out of her hand and slashed open her whole arm. Blood streamed down her hand and dripped onto the floor.

Bold Resilient Women

Immediately, she grabbed my little brother and rushed him to the back of the store, where I watched her employ all of the old techniques. She had my brother pee on it, and then she smashed an onion and spread it on her wound. She grabbed a piece of material and wrapped her arm up in it, the whole time trying to laugh and make jokes, so we didn't see the extent of the cut.

"Don't say a word," she shushed us.

Although we could see Mom was in horrific pain, she continued, finishing the work she had started. I stood behind the counter with my brothers, holding back tears as I watched her suffering. I couldn't believe she would torment herself to support our family. I realized I was watching her sacrifice for us. She was bleeding, but was able to finish the boots. Mom covered her arm with a sweater so the man didn't notice the wrapping as she rang him up.

The man looked at his boots. "These are like brand new!" he said, clearly impressed. He told her she did a great job and gave her a $10 tip.

When he left, we thought Mom was going to pass out. When Dad returned and saw her, he closed the store and called the doctor next door.

We all went with her to the doctor's office, where he stitched up her severe cut. When he found out what happened, he stared at her in disbelief.

"Bessie, what were you thinking?" he asked. It was clear he saw her as a woman without limits. "I had to finish the boots!" she said. "I couldn't lose the customer!"

Mom's story spread around the neighborhood, and I believe the courageous act earned her the respect of the entire Broadway community. All of the Uptown bank employees became her best clients. Word spread like wildfire: "If you want a great job on heels, boots, cleaning, and alterations, go to Bennett Cleaners."

The police department, politicians, and Uptown residents knew us as a dedicated immigrant family who worked endlessly to accomplish the American Dream.

Their day would go like this: My dad would open the tailor/cleaning/ shoe repair store at 6 a.m., while Mom would get us off to school. Next, Mom would get the hot dog wagon ready for Dad, then go work at the cleaners while Dad pushed this enormous wagon across the streets of Chicago, selling hot dogs, tamales, and Polish sausage. He would return at 6 p.m., his feet and arms

Bold Resilient Women

aching from the miles he had pushed the wagon. I would run and grab the alcohol and start to rub his hands, arms, and feet, and he would always say, "My darling daughter, may God bless you. You have relieved my pain."

After dinner, he would go to the restaurant to wash dishes and return home at 11 p.m. Then he would work on tailoring with Mom's help. Mom, on the other hand, had additional jobs at Hart Schaffner Marx making suits while also working as a hot dog lady, a shoe maker, and being a devoted mother and wife. She was a multitasker without shame or glory. She wanted everything for her family.

I have many fond memories of our shop. Dad was the personal tailor for Senator Percy, and Mr. Bogio fixed Mayor Richard J. Daley's hats, which arrived in big boxes through a driver in a black car. I remember clearly when Senator Percy's driver brought my dad the politician's black suit to alter for his daughter's funeral. It was all over the newspaper, how she was killed in her home. This tragedy instilled in me a fear of leaving doors or windows open at our house.

As kids, we worked every summer selling snow cones in the city's parks and beaches. Because we had one hot dog stand and five ice cream cone carts, we all worked, but because my little brother was only seven and too young to sell, my parents made him the runner. His job was to take a taxi to the ice company to get bags of ice. My parents would have the taxi driver write his name, and we would get the license plate number—and with that information, they would send him to pick up ice while we were getting the carts ready. We were all accustomed to work. Reflecting back, we must have had a lot of faith in God's protection.

One day, a police officer walked up to our cart and kicked the wheel, telling us to never sell snow cones or hot dogs again. We didn't have a vendor's license to sell street food. Dad was furious. We took the carts back to the garage, where we had to throw everything away. My parents were devastated at being treated like criminals. This kept Mom and Dad up at night. They could not understand what they did wrong. As immigrants from a small village, they weren't aware of all the red tape involved in the U.S.

The next morning, I woke up with a steely resolve in my chest. School was off that day, and while I was in the cleaners, I looked up the name of the Cook County Sheriff and found out it was someone named Richard J. Elrod. I found his office address, and I told my parents I was going home to study. I couldn't bear to see them suffering, with a source of their income eliminated. I got on the El train at Lawrence and went into the city. I knew my way around Chicago well. We would ride the train to my uncle's restaurant, Taste A Treat, for lunch and bring it back home or to the store for our parents.

Bold Resilient Women

When I reached the office on State Street there were two officers standing at the door, one on each side.

I didn't even think, I just talked. "Hello, I am here to see the sheriff," I said.

They looked at each other and chuckled. "How old are you, kid?" They looked at me, a child in a summer dress with sandals, and no purse or bag on me.

"I'm eleven," I said. I stared them right in their eyes. "What's this about?" "I can only speak to Sheriff Elrod," I responded.

They called upstairs to his secretary and told them there was a young girl who was asking to speak with him. They escorted me upstairs, and as I was waiting to see this powerful man, I became frightened. But I had a goal, an important reason for being there. I summoned my courage.

After a few minutes—which seemed like hours—a man with a huge smile rolled over in a wheelchair. He instructed his secretary to pull up a chair next to him, and he asked me to sit down. Although he had been suffering and was in a wheelchair, his fortitude was humbling.

"Well, young lady? Why did you ask to see me?" he said.

I told him my parents' story, how they came to this great country to educate us, and about the many jobs they were doing to support four kids. I told him what the officer did to our cart, and he was distraught. He could not believe we were little kids working selling ice cones and hot dogs to survive. "Do you remember the officer's name?" he asked. I told him. He yelled for his receptionist to call the officer. When the call was patched through, he put the officer on speaker.

"Do you remember this family?" He described us to the officer.

"Yes, I do," the voice came through the phone's speaker, gruff and unkind. "They were violating city codes by selling food and ice cream products with carts in the streets."

"Okay, I see. Listen, I don't ever want you to bother this family again. I want you to protect them and take care of them. I don't want anything bad to happen to these children and their parents, and if anything does, I will hold you responsible."

I was in shock. Who was this man? Why did he have so much power, and more importantly, were we going to be safe?

Bold Resilient Women

After the phone call, Sheriff Elrod pulled my head down, and as I bent down, he kissed my forehead. "Little girl, you can go home. Nothing will happen to you and your family." He pulled out a business card and handed it to me. "If anyone ever bothers you again, you call me immediately."

I held the card in my hands as though it were gold. "Thank you, sir. And please bring your hats and shoes to my parents' cleaners if they need to be fixed for free. It's my gratitude for you seeing me today."

He promised he would, then offered to have someone drive me to the store. I said no, thank you. I was certain my dad would kill me if he knew what I had done.

I took the El back home, nearly jumping with joy.

"Eleni, why are you so happy?" Mom and Dad asked when I walked in the door. "Where have you been? What's going on?"

I took a breath to steady my voice, which was bubbling with joy, and I told them what I had done. They were shocked and angry that I got on the train alone, but when I got to the end of my story, they started to cry. They couldn't believe my courage.

My dad hugged me. "Elenitsa will be an interesting and capable individual," he said to my mom, laughing. "She will not fear doing great things. She will be a leader, and no one will be able to stand in her way." My dad continued with the reality of the world. "Your brother, Louis, should have been a girl and you a boy. You could conquer the world."

From that day forward, all the officers had great respect for my family. I guess they heard our story from the sheriff and wanted to make sure we were safe. Eventually, the police department and many politicians across the city became our best supporters and clients. We were protected throughout the city, and no one ever disrespected or mistreated us again.

Mr. Elrod kept all his promises. He even gained immense respect for my father's tailoring talents. He eventually became one of our best customers.

An Explosion

One Saturday, on a hot summer afternoon, Dad parked the hot dog wagon in front of Jupiter, a neighborhood store that sold many low-priced products. He then had to return to the cleaners to finish the suits and shoes for the weekend customers.

"Dad, can I work the stand?" my twelve-year-old brother, Peter, asked eagerly. "Sure," my dad said. "Eleni can go with you."

"No, Dad. I want to do it by myself," he said. Often Peter and I worked it together, or he worked it with my mom and dad. But he had never worked by himself. Not that it was a big deal. My parents never feared anyone harming us. Everyone in the neighborhood knew us; we were treated like celebrities.

"I can go with you, Peter," my mom said.

"No, Mom," Peter said, with an urgency in his voice now. "I can handle it myself." He was a salesman from a young age—he could convince you to buy anything he was selling.

My mom paused for a moment to consider this. "Fine," she said. "Eleni and I will go grocery shopping while you take care of the sales." My brother smiled. He was so happy and proud of himself. That whole day, he sold so much. It was going so well.

As we returned from the store carrying our shopping bags, Mom and I stopped by the cart. "Peter, can we help you?" I asked him.

He smiled so big. "No, you and Mom can leave," he said, practically bouncing. "I am having the best day of my life!" He told us he was on track for record sales. There's no way we could have taken away his glory.

Bold Resilient Women

We laughed, then took the groceries home, put everything away, and raced to the store to relieve Dad so he could leave and go pick up the wagon. It was too heavy for us kids to do on our own. My parents had made a space in the back of the store to store the wagon, as it was the only way Mom could prepare the ingredients for the hot dogs, Polish sausage, and tamales. As soon as she finished getting everything ready, she would start her daily jobs.

Dad still had a few jobs to finish, so Mom and I were running around, trying to help him, when my sandal broke. My dad bent down to fix it in a rush, when suddenly he peed on himself. We looked at each other. I was confused.

"Vaso," he called. He stood up and showed her the wet stain on his pants. They locked eyes. "This is a bad sign," he said. "It's not good when you pee without warning."

Dad had hardly finished the phrase when the manager of the shoe store next to Jupiter flung the door open and came running in.

"Fire, fire!" he screamed, out of breath. I started running after him barefoot, my sandals gone now, my family following behind. When I arrived at where the hot dog cart was positioned, I saw many people standing around, others crying, and others looking on in shock. There were policemen, fire engines, and park employees yelling and crying, everyone running around. The store manager was holding my hand tightly and pulling me through the crowd. I still couldn't tell what happened. I just saw pure chaos.

When I got to the front of the crowd, I stopped in my tracks. Peter was standing there, burned. He looked like a charcoal statue. I grabbed him, and he fell into my arms as paramedics stood around him, trying to stabilize him. The medics told me to back away but no one could make me.

"Sister mou, please help me," he said over and over again, his eyes looking up at me with fear.

"Peter, it's going to be okay. I will save you, just hold on, I will help you." I was shattered, crying hysterically, thinking, *My God, I am losing my brother*. We were so close. We never did anything alone; we were always together. We could not exist without each other. Wherever one went, the other was there for support.

As children, my parents paid us three dollars each week for working. They wanted to instill confidence in us and teach us that hard work pays off. When we got paid, Peter and I loved to go to the neighborhood stores. Sometimes,

Bold Resilient Women

Peter would give me his allowance to buy a new dress for church. He loved me so much. He would say, "Sis, you need to look beautiful since you are the only girl in the house."

One day, we were at Goldblatt's, and they were getting ready to throw a big box away. Peter asked if he could take the box, and the salesperson agreed. So we left Goldblatt's with the box and started the walk back to the store. We didn't see the two people following us. When we got to the cleaners, Dad asked us what we got.

"Nothing," we said. "They were giving away boxes, and Peter got one." Dad opened the box, and, stunned, he took out several sunglasses. As my dad closed the box, he threw his apron on the counter and told Mr. Bogio to look after the store until he returned. He grabbed me by the hand, and I grabbed Peter, and he told us we were going back to the store to return the sunglasses because they didn't belong to us.

We were in shock, too! We didn't know there was anything in the box. As we were walking out with Dad, two people stepped in front of us. They showed us their badges and told us they were security guards from Goldblatt's. They had followed us the whole way, and we had seen them peering in the store as though they were wondering how Dad was going to handle this.

"We'll take the box back," they told us. One of them held out his hands for us to turn it over. "It wasn't the kids' fault; it was the salesperson's mistake."

Dad wanted to punish me for not looking inside the box, since I was older. But I blamed it on Peter. "It was his fault," I said, pointing at him. "He shouldn't have said we would take it!"

Thinking back now, I believe the salesperson was put up to this. Maybe they were envious of our family because we stuck together and were beloved in the neighborhood. We were like speedy little mice, working at all the jobs. We were children, but did the work of adults. We didn't fear work; we enjoyed helping our parents persevere.

The following Monday, the store manager came to pick up his cleaning and apologized to my father. "The kids didn't do anything wrong," he said. "They didn't steal. The salesperson had no business giving a child customer a box." He explained that he believed someone had put her up to it, and she was fired instantly. Instead of being happy, my dad was sad that she lost her job. He hated people being out of work. Every little thing reminded him of his childhood and his difficult challenges.

∼

Bold Resilient Women

All around the hot dog stand, people were screaming. I was crying hysterically. I believed it was my fault. "Please forgive me, Peter, please forgive me!" I wept as I held him. The policemen were trying to clear the crowds while the fire department was working on making sure the flames were out.

Some of the onlookers had seen what happened while they were waiting to buy a hot dog. The firefighters and the detectives were asking for an explanation.

While the ambulance was trying to stabilize my brother, with me inside holding his hand, the policemen were trying to clear the crowds, and the fire department was working on making sure the fire was extinguished. Detectives were on the scene, asking people questions and taking reports. They were told a young boy was seen throwing a match in the gas tank. People didn't realize what he threw or what was going on—it happened so quickly, and suddenly they heard the explosion. Everyone was rushing desperately to overthrow the cart and to get my little brother free from the flames.

The manager ripped his shirt off, put water over his arms, and tried to push the wagon away with his legs and all his strength. Everyone was trying to help him, but the explosion was so fierce. He finally managed to get my brother free, but not before he had first and second-degree burns. If it wasn't for the shoe store manager, my brother would have been burned alive.

At that moment, all I could do was scream and cry. I was losing my little brother. My parents were running and yelling, and watching them approach the ambulance was a new level of grief. My dad was hitting himself and yelling, while my mom was pulling her long, beautiful hair and screaming. This was the most unforgettable and horrifying scene of my life.

They hooked my brother to different IVs in the ambulance, while my parents screamed like their insides were being torn out. The policemen and firemen were in tears, trying to be supportive. They all knew our family. They were our support system, protectors, and customers. No one was allowed to go with Peter in the ambulance, so I went with my parents. I translated for them: Peter was in critical condition, and they were doing their best to save him.

The policemen grabbed us and put us in their squad car. We followed the ambulance to the nearest hospital, Weiss Memorial on Marine Drive.

Mr. Bogio closed the store when the police informed him what had happened to my brother. He broke down crying; he had a special bond with my brother. Peter loved history, and would always ask Mr. Bogio questions about the South, slavery, and everything he had lived through. Mr. Bogio picked up his wife, Mrs. Bee, and they came to the hospital with my little brother, George, crying and praying.

Bold Resilient Women

By the time we pulled up at the hospital, the outside of the building and the halls inside were filled with policemen, family, friends, politicians, and firemen. It felt as if the entire city was supporting and mourning for my family. My brother was critical; they didn't know if he was going to survive. He had suffered first and second-degree burns all over his body, especially on his arms and face.

My dad cleaned and tailored clothes for many policemen, and they loved and respected my parents as one of their family members. They all stayed at the hospital to see what the outcome would be. Investigators escorted Sheriff Elrod, wheeling him into the waiting area to comfort and console my parents. He hugged us and told us everything was going to be fine; he was going to make sure of that. He said, "Mr. Palivos, look at me. I made it. I am alive, and your son is young and strong."

The police and fire department took care of us; they made sure we were safe working in the streets of Chicago. They were our gatekeepers, yet today, it felt like we were alone and betrayed, and Peter was victimized. We were lost. For hours, every policeman in Chicago took turns visiting. Mayor Richard J. Daley arrived with his security. He was in shock that this little boy was fighting for his life at Weiss Memorial Hospital.

The doctors had a conference where they updated everyone on my brother's health status. They said he had suffered trauma and severe burns. They could not open his eyes to see if they were affected. He needed extensive care if he was going to survive, and they didn't have the necessary burn unit for critical cases. My brother needed to be treated at Loyola Medical Center Burn Unit, where Dr. Howe, a renowned burn specialist, could try to save his life.

Immediately, Mayor Daley authorized the hospital to airlift my brother to Loyola. While he was in the air, we were taken to Melrose Park, where the hospital was located, with police escorts. We met with Dr. Howe. As he read the reports, he confirmed: He wasn't sure if Peter's eyes were burned, as they couldn't open them. It would take time for them to tell.

"Your brother," he said to me, "is up for the fight of his life."

Since my older brother was studying abroad, I became the personal decision maker and translator for my family. Because I wanted to save my parents from more grief, I tried to translate as little as I could, communicating only the essentials. I loved Peter so much. I hardly left his side. Every day after school, I would go relieve my mom at the hospital so she could go work. One of us had to be with him at all times. He had horrible nightmares, so I would sit next to him and study.

Peter fought for his life for almost a year. He had numerous skin grafts and surgeries, and all we could do was pray. There were times I thought we would lose him. Every so often, they would take him downstairs to the basement, where they had a huge tub. They would transfer my brother to a bed and dip him in these solutions, which stripped the burned skin, exposing the new skin to air.

It was an unfathomably painful process. You could see the skin and the bone exposed. They would apply a nonsteroidal, anti-inflammatory medicine, and then the skin was covered with dry dressing to let the skin breathe. This was the beginning of the process to heal to prepare him for a new skin graft. They would shave healthy skin from different parts of his body. We would see the skin grafts, which had small perforations so that the skin could breathe in order to adhere. My little brother would be in excruciating pain, yelling and cursing all of us. We could not bear the horrible things he was saying. He was suffering, fighting for his life. We felt for him. The nurses tried to comfort him, but everything was out of our control.

Every day after the doctors came to visit him, I would leave the room and fall into Dr. Howe's arms, sobbing and begging him to save my brother. I would wipe my tears with my long hair. The doctor was a heavy, sweet, gentle man who could see our family's desperation. Although his team came for a daily patient visit, Dr. Howe would come to see him two or three times every day.

My Mom would leave my brother's bedside in the evening and then work all night. She would come back in the morning, bringing with her a bag full of alterations so customer orders weren't delayed. She stayed all day until I arrived after school. We didn't have a car. We took public transportation and walked everywhere, so we had to take the train and transfer to the bus to go from Broadway and Lawrence in Uptown to Loyola Hospital in Melrose Park, which was about thirty minutes outside the city.

Mom was resilient. She never complained. She would take naps on the chair next to Peter's bed, crying and praying. Dad had to go from one job to the next, he had to finish the tailoring and shoes, he was the provider of our family. Dad was worried, he didn't know how he was going to pay the hospital bills. Sometimes, his bosses from his restaurant job would see his pain and let him leave early to visit his son. They kept reassuring him he didn't have to worry about losing his job.

My older brother, Louis, had no clue how extensive Peter's burns were. He could not understand our agony. My parents wanted to spare him from grief and distraction—they wanted him to pass his medical school exams so he could someday become a doctor and help the family.

When we were kids, we would make fun of Peter's plunky big cheeks. We called him "*mougasi*," which loosely translates to "stop moaning to get attention." Now, we regretted every moment we didn't show him all the love in the world. We wished we had never upset him or teased him about his weight. It felt like I prayed all day, begging for him to live. I didn't care about his weight or his plunky big cheeks, we wanted him alive, healthy, and back home.

One day, I asked the doctor why they were chopping my brother up. He was in such pain, and they kept sedating him with morphine shots. He took me to the lab and showed me the skin which was removed from him and how they were growing it in huge jars to help replace the parts that were burned. You could witness the stages of the healing: The skin would look blood red, then turn to purple bruising, and as it healed, become wrinkled, then take the look of a normal skin as time passed.

"Our priority is saving your brother from infections due to exposed bone," the doctor told me.

Peter had to have many skin grafts. The skin from different parts of his body wasn't growing healthily, so they had to start the process again.

Several weeks went by, and finally, they could open his eyes. His face was deformed: it was as huge as a watermelon, and his eyes were sunk deep inside. But when they checked his eyesight, they all started clapping. He could see! His eyes were not affected. You could see tears of joy rolling down our cheeks and even on the faces of some of the medical team. But they were especially noticeable on Peter's face, as he could finally see all of us.

"This is a great miracle," Dr. Howe said.

After a year of ups and downs and challenges, my little brother was able to come home with us. He was finally free of pain and suffering. We prepared the house with balloons and welcome home banners. Mom and I made all of his favorite foods and sweets, and spent all night baking. We didn't need sleep; we were all on adrenaline.

My mother's younger brother had purchased a new Cadillac, and he offered to pick up Peter with us. We pulled up to the hospital. I went in with my mom to sign all the release forms.

We had made Greek cookies for the doctors, nurses, and staff, thanking them for the support and love they had shown my brother and the family.

As the nurse rolled Peter over to us in a wheelchair, he was followed by all the nurses who had taken care of him, along with Dr. Howe. Everyone was crying and clapping. We were taking him home. Finally, we pulled away, leaving behind what was once our living headquarters, and my brother's suffering and healing place.

On the way home, my uncle had the music blasting. We were all excited, and we wanted to sing with joy and happiness. My uncle's excitement was overwhelming. He stopped in the middle of Lake Shore Drive, put on his flashers, and started to dance like Zorba the Greek. Everyone was stopping to clap and see what this so-called crazy man was doing. He was yelling, "My nephew made it! He is alive and going home!"

We had planned a huge reunion gathering. Everyone was anxious to see Peter, since visitors were not allowed at the hospital due to contamination of open wounds. Peter's fat cheeks had vanished; all you could see was a tall skeleton, and his bones were visible through his new skin.

He had lost an extreme amount of weight. It was alarming, but Mom would say, "At least he is alive. He is going to recover and get strong again. And if he survived this nightmare, he will be able to withstand everything in his life."

I wonder how my parents managed to keep it together. They never once complained about being sleep-deprived or tired. They never lost faith and hope. I have always wondered if Peter ever actually overcame this accident. Did he mentally, physically, and psychologically come to terms with his burns? Did the nightmare of almost losing his life affect him? And has he forgiven the young man who threw a match in the gas tank?

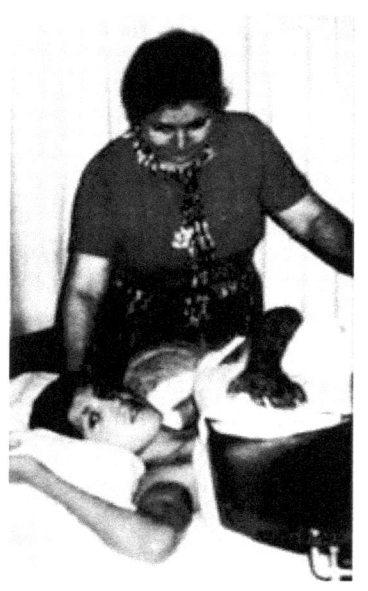

Sometimes, these questions keep me up at night, especially on his birthday. I don't know how life would have been for my parents and us, as siblings, if we had lost him. But how would it have been different if this had never happened?

My mom would change his bandages, go to work, come home, cook, visit Peter, do her tailoring, and do it all with a smile and a compliment for people around her. Dad was a Trojan warrior. He never slept, just kept working day and night. He would come home for dinner every evening between 7 and 8 just to see how our day was, and then go to work again.

After this tragedy, it seemed like life started again from the beginning. But now, my dad seemed to see his commitment to education even more clearly. Dad would constantly reiterate that he brought us to America for an education and prosperity. "I will give you the wings to fly," he would say, "and if someone cuts them off, Mom and I will catch you. But we won't do it if you don't have discipline in your life to listen and learn."

Bold Resilient Women

These were some of the darkest days of my parents' lives. They couldn't express their feelings for their struggling son and they were not able to communicate with the doctors. They didn't have a say in his treatments—they just left everything in the doctors' care and the protection of God. They felt useless as parents, expressing their feelings through body language and tears. But at the same time, while there was a language barrier, it was different. While my parents spoke Greek and the doctors spoke English, they all spoke the language of grief. They all saw and experienced suffering. "Please, *doutor*, son okay," my parents would say, holding Dr. Howe's hands. They didn't know how to pronounce *doctor*, so they said *doutor*

We could hear my parents talking at night, even after Peter came home. They would whisper about the cost of the hospital bills, which were going to arrive at the store any day. "It's okay, Vaso," I heard my dad say more than once. "We will make payment plans. They know we are poor." They waited for months to receive a bill. Dad finally told me to call the hospital and find out when they were going to send the invoice and set up a monthly payment plan, so I did.

The billing office told us to speak to the doctor, so I left a message for Dr. Howe and his assistant. Dad was an honorable man. He would say, "I don't owe a penny to anyone. People owe me." Once, he pulled out his book from his desk. He said, "You see this, my daughter? It's a book with names and the amounts people owe me from my little business. Many of them told me they were going to pay me back when I came to America. But up to today, no one has given me a penny. I am still waiting."

Dr. Howe returned our call at the end of the day. He asked how my brother was doing, and suggested that now that Peter had recovered, maybe we should send him away for a change of scenery and environment. He said it would be good for his healing not to think of the terrible accident.

When I explained what he said, Dad told me to thank him and tell him he would discuss it with Mom. Then he urged me to ask for the bill. When I translated, the doctor stopped me.

"Young lady, you need to call Mayor Daley and thank him," he said.

"Why?" I said, completely confused.

"He paid the entire bill for the hospital and the doctors," he explained gently. When I relayed this to my parents, we all sat in a silent shock. Why did he do this? How would we ever pay him back?

A short time later, Mayor Daley's driver brought his hats to be cleaned.

Dad had asked me to write a letter to the mayor expressing our gratitude and appreciation for his generosity. We passed it to his driver and asked him to pass it directly to him. The following day, we received a call from his secretary telling us it was his pleasure to help our family and to see my brother alive and healthy. He wished him continued healing.

"If you ever need anything, the mayor is at your family's disposal," she said. In the end, my parents listened to the doctor's advice. My brother was sent to Greece to be with my older brother and relatives the following summe,r and to attend high school. They wanted him to start fresh and leave behind so much grief and pain.

A Holy Woman

In third grade, my friends started calling me "Young Mother Teresa." I thought they were bullying me! I thought I was being teased. But my friends would say, "Eleni, our parents say you are like Mother Teresa. You never eat your lunch or chocolate bar and you always share with everyone." I didn't have a clue who this person was. I thought she was just another saint, a figure of the church. It was in my nature to give to others and help everyone in the classroom and on the playground, but I felt like my friends were mocking me.

As I got older, I became obsessed with reading about Mother Theresa. I was captivated by her global work with the poor, destitute, and vulnerable of the world, and how she showed mercy in sharing so much kindness and love with those who surrounded her. She cared only for others; she had selfless love for herself, but also committed acts of love for others.

I couldn't stop learning as much as possible about this inspirational figure, her life, and the amazing work she was doing in many poor countries—especially in Calcutta, India, where there was a tremendous need. Because of a decimated health care system, some third-world countries had an enormous spread of illness, and a lack of food left children dying from malnutrition. They lived in the dirtiest of places without clean water or anyone to care for them.

This incredible humanitarian gained international recognition and accolades and won the Nobel Prize for her mission of charity. She was of Albanian descent and was called to proclaim the Lord's name and follow His word. As a young girl, she went to live in a convent until she was ready to pursue her calling to serve others. She knew what hunger was—she had lived in poverty, and she wanted to spread the word of Jesus by taking care of the poorest of the poor. She founded the Missionaries of Charity, which served more than 133 countries. Her congregation managed homes in different parts of the world. Her focus was on fragile, persecuted individuals; the poor, innocent, and suffering; and people who were dying in their homes or on the streets from diseases like HIV/AIDS, leprosy, and tuberculosis.

Mother Theresa's congregation ran soup kitchens to feed the poor and needy, and many of the visitors were children who had never seen a decent meal before arriving. She had taken the vows of chastity, poverty, and obedience and was committed to giving wholehearted free services to the poorest of the poor. She was admired for her charitable contributions and her dedication and devotion to God.

Reading about this amazing model of kindness and clemency gave me the strength to persevere in my calling. This was a humbling testament. I realized that my friends in elementary school weren't bullying me. They admired me for my benevolent love for others. I don't ever remember eating my food alone; it gave me contentment and happiness to share with my friends.

As life has continued, I've been more involved with non-profit organizations, and in a lovely twist, the philanthropic community gave me the name, "The Modern Mother Teresa." I was featured on the cover of *Mia* magazine, along with an article written by the publisher explaining why I was given this title. She included many articles written about me throughout my life since I was a young girl. Many other global magazines started addressing me as "The Modern Mother Teresa." This global attention humbled me, as I knew I was walking in the footsteps of a great woman.

It's fascinating to see how, decades apart, I have been compared to this humble woman who is still admired by everyone. Her legacy has taught me that nothing in life is circumstantial or coincidental. Different paths and curves have surprised me, as I have almost unconsciously followed the same road of compassion and empathy.

Having learned from Mother Theresa, I want to inspire other women to believe in themselves so that they are strong and kind to others, and so that they can take control of their lives in order to extend a helping hand to others. Women are positive creatures who can take control of every challenge and obstacle standing in their way, if only they believe in themselves. The stories of this dynamic woman have spoken to my heart and given me the strength, inventiveness, and resilience to embrace the callings in my life's journey.

Stages of Life

*"Love and kindness are never wasted. They always make
a difference. They bless the one who receives them,
and they bless you, the giver."*
— Barbara De Angelis

I have always been an observer, and watching carefully every move people made around me, from all of these diverse cultural backgrounds, made me comprehend the different stages people go through in life. It's intriguing and fascinating to see my friends' lives integrate and intertwine through many unpredictable phases.

As I've grown into my adulthood, I've embraced every day as a learning experience. I became wiser witnessing dear friends and young women drop out of school. Some of them became overwhelmed and unable to balance their daily lives. Many friends ended up in disastrous divorces, with families torn to pieces financially, mentally, and psychologically.

In the 1960s, '70s, '80s and even into the '90s, immigrants who came to the States opposed a child or family member filing for a divorce. They believed that a divorce meant your family would be in the streets without a solid so-called family foundation. They worried about being stigmatized by family, friends, and society. Contrary to their thoughts or feelings, their children were forced to make certain choices, and didn't have any say in their decisions.

I was outraged watching these situations, where young women were inspired to have a successful life, but their aspirations were not supported by their family, partners, or peers. They were left speechless and hopeless, having their self-assurance and self-esteem crushed and demeaned.

In my opinion, these unpredictable situations, which I witnessed at a very young age, gave me the confidence and strength to go back to school and get my psychology degree. I wanted to understand the internal world of a human being and where the core problems begin. By understanding and accepting oneself, you can understand yourself and others. You will be capable of handling daily issues.

Understanding human psychology allowed me to gain the confidence to achieve my goals. I transformed into an optimistic individual with tolerance for co-workers, constituents, children, my husband, and friends. During my challenging trials, I gained immense admiration for people who became my mentors and advisors. These individuals inspired and encouraged me to proceed with my ambitions and dreams. They were intelligent, wise, creative, compassionate, loving, and caring. They had unwavering courage and strength to persevere and overcome all obstacles that stood in their way. These women had the ability and patience to connect with the old and young, eventually, many times, putting themselves in unforeseeable and unpredictable situations in a man's world of disapproval.

When I was a young girl, my grandmother and her friend, Maria Gouletas, two women devoted to God and the church, were challenged by the leader of our Orthodox faith in America, the late Archbishop Lakovos, on their faith. Their dream was to bring the icons of two Saints to the Greek Orthodox Church of America: St. Nektarios and St. Irene Chrysovalandou.

St. Nektarios was born to humble, poor parents in Istanbul, Turkey in the 1800s. His parents were good, abiding Christians who wanted their son to pursue a degree. He was educated in top Universities, and focused on writing books on religion and preaching about the Bible. He realized he had a calling and relocated to Aegina, a beautiful island in Greece. He built the Monastery of St. Nektarios, carrying every stone by hand. Many nuns were drawn to his teachings and love for God and people. He died in his 70s from cancer, and is today considered the healing doctor of those suffering from cancer and other diseases. His body lies in the monastery. My experience believing in St. Nektarios' miracles began in my twenties.

After I was healed from my illness as a young adult, my grandmother, Eleni, took my mom, my two children, and me to the monastery. She knew every monk and nun because she was so close to the religion her whole life.

Bold Resilient Women

When we arrived, the head nun had set up a huge bedroom for us. We were exhausted and had to get up at 5 a.m. to open the church and do a private service as a token of gratitude for healing me.

We put the kids to sleep and went to rest. As I fell asleep, I felt someone above my head, blessing me with essence. I could feel it on my head. My eyes would pop open, but I would see no one. This went on all night. I could hear footsteps walking, sense someone above my head, and feel the soft touch of a blessing. I started to panic. I woke up my mom and grandma and told them what happened. Mom was fearful, while Grandma thought it was just the mountains and the movement of forest trees due to the high winds.

I lay down again, but was anxious. They didn't understand what was happening. At 4:30 a.m., we got dressed and headed to the head nun's room. Grandma took her aside and told her what had happened. The head nun came toward me.

"My child, you are blessed. Before we go to church for the service, I want you to pray at St. Nektarios' tomb and place your head above it. Please come and tell me if you hear anything," she said.

I obeyed, and my family followed. I placed my head above the tomb, the cold stone touching my forehead. I jumped, startled.

"What's wrong, Eleni?" my mom asked, concerned.

"Mommy, it's what I was hearing all night, the steps and the blessing!" My mom and grandmother placed their heads in the same place, but could not hear anything. I put my head back in the same place multiple times and heard the same steps and a blessing. I smelled the essence of incense.

We went back to church, and I told the head nun what I heard.

"My darling child, you heard St. Nektarios blessing you while he was walking to his bedroom," she said gently, placing her hand on my shoulder. She explained that he used to sleep in a little cave right above where I was sleeping. I believe in my heart this was his assurance that I would be fine. If I could be patient, he would show me why I should continue having faith. I didn't understand what he was going to reveal to me in the future.

That's when I understood what the Lord says, in James 1:3-4. "For you know that when your faith is tested, your endurance has a chance to grow. So let it grow, for when your endurance is fully developed, you will be perfect and complete, needing nothing."

Or what the Lord says in Romans 8:25. "But if we hope for what we do not see, we wait for it with patience."

I have learned to wait with faith and patience for what God has in store for me, my family, and all those I pray for.

St. Irene Chrysovalantou was a princess who was betrothed to marry

Bold Resilient Women

Prince Michael, but she ran away because she wanted to dedicate herself to prayer and faith. She kept praying to God for the gift to foresee events and the godly strength for exorcism. She prayed day and night for people to heal, so intensely that she levitated, and the Cypress trees started to bend down, honoring and worshiping her. She died at over the age of one hundred. She is believed and trusted as the saint of healing, helping those who suffer from the fear of eternal death, preparing them for peace of soul, and helping women with childbearing.

It is said that St. John the Theologian gave her three apples as a token to heal. Even today, you can go to the monastery at the outskirts of Athens and get a piece of apple. These apples are blessed for many days at the altar. You can ask for a piece and give it to someone suffering.

In honor of my miracle, I have dedicated the icon on the left side of the altar at the monastery to my darling daughter, Victoria's, life and healing.

My grandmother and Mrs. Maria used to say that every time we are faced with many difficulties, we should pray to these two saints to help us receive their grace. They wanted everyone to get to know these two miracle saints. We've witnessed many miracles in our families. My grandmother and Mrs. Maria were both humble and unique women who wanted to share with others the glory of God. Everyone was inspired by their courage and perseverance to make a change. They maintained their beliefs and faith without fearing the position and the status of this great church leader.

These two faithful and courageous women made me understand how important education was in a hostile, controlling environment where your talents and intelligence were challenged every day. My grandmother was the epitome of a boundary pusher. She would constantly remind me of the amazing Bouboulina, the heroic woman who fought alongside thirty-nine men for freedom and independence in the war of 1821. She was one of the revolutionary warriors who wanted to liberate Greece from the Ottoman Empire. Grandmother would never forget Greece's suffering and endurance for freedom. "Look at what these women and so many other heroes went through for freedom, family, faith, and country," she would say, shaking her head in awe. She was a strong and influential force.

She believed so fully in the importance of education. "A person without education is like a piece of wood that's useless," she would say. When we looked at her, confused, she would explain. "When you have a degree under your belt, you have a secure future. You don't have to depend on anyone to support or feed you. You will succeed."

These inspiring words sparked a deep flame in my heart. I learned early in life that you had to take risks if you wanted results.

Bold Resilient Women

"You can accomplish and do anything in life if the stars are aligned, and the skies are open," my beloved mother would say. She wanted to make sure that I knew no one could stand in my way.

She showed me that you could quietly condemn your enemies with kindness and love, that you could learn to be silent so people would never know your thoughts. She would say not to express your feelings and ideas unless you have a clear view of your surroundings.

She believed in the saying to "kill them with kindness." "Never become confrontational when making your voice heard, Eleni. Have sweetness on your lips. Let those seeking confrontation be consumed with the venom of the snake."

"What does that mean?" I was young enough that I didn't understand quite yet that some people argue just to argue and be heard, and that some people just won't listen, no matter what you say.

"When you remain focused and still, you get a clear understanding of who is confrontational and overdramatic, and who is kind and generous. There is more substance in silent individuals. You will enhance your knowledge and understanding of life when you realize how hate becomes evil and how love becomes God."

The women in my life were successful and effective in their leadership roles. They had the authority to make changes by having the ability to connect and articulate with their colleagues without confrontation, but with responsive behavior. They were women giving out love.

Finding My Passion

I was asked by my dear friend, Neo, what inspires me to be a philanthropist. "Why do you care about making a difference?" He asked me. "Were you always like this? Do you really believe you can save people?" He told me, he and his wife had noticed me and started reading about my magnificent work with philanthropy. He said, "you have so much pathos to help everyone who comes in your path."

"It's easy," I told him. "I was always focused on helping others, even when I was a young girl. I cannot imagine not being involved in the church, organizations, or different institutions. It's engraved in my DNA and goes deep down to my bones. To be honest with you, I cannot verbalize or express the self-gratification and satisfaction I feel."

Faith is something deeply rooted in your heart and soul. I have shared my deep connection with God with very few people. It's a story of the visions I had when I was three years old.

I remember being a young girl and sleeping in a monastery at the foot of the altar for a couple of days. It started when I felt so vividly that I was being taken from my parents' arms in the middle of the night by young girls and taken on different journeys. These girls were beautiful. They glowed like the sun. They would show me different places and tell me things that would occur.

Bold Resilient Women

My parents sought help from monks and priests. They could not understand what was happening to their little girl. They would ask me questions about my whereabouts, and I would tell them where I had traveled and what I had seen. My parents realized they could not control the situation or keep me from being removed from their arms.

One evening, they brought a priest to the house to pray over me, but nothing changed. My parents were left hopeless. Mom decided to write a letter to her mother in Chicago, telling her what was happening to her granddaughter. My grandmother was terrified. She responded that she would take care of some matters and quickly come to Greece. She could not believe what she was reading, and wanted to witness this phenomenon firsthand.

Grandmother arrived at the village shortly after she received the letter. She decided to take me to her home to sleep in order to change my environment. Grandmother's house was filled with icons, holy books, and many other religious items. She believed I would be safe at her home, that I would sleep quietly without any distractions. Grandma and I prayed together, and when we finished, she lay me down to sleep next to her.

In the evening, the young girls, who looked like angels, called my name. My grandmother was startled. She tried to hold me in her arms, but it was impossible. She could not hold me down, and they took me from her arms. Grandmother was terrified. She thought she was going to lose me. What was she going to tell my parents?

In the morning, they brought me back to the house. My parents arrived at my grandmother's house and started to ask me questions. They wanted me to tell them what I saw and where I had traveled. My grandmother told my parents they had to take me to Panagia Ampelaki, a sacred monastery my grandmother was affiliated with, where children and people would go to be cleansed from different spiritual callings.

Looking back, I remember clearly that the nuns laid me at the foot of the altar while they and my family prayed.

After I came home, I recovered from the nightmares. I had lost my gift to see the future and predict events—but it wasn't forever. When I was nine years old, I started seeing different visions of things happening to my family or friends. I wanted to help everyone. I could feel, sense, or see if something out of the ordinary was going to happen. As years went by, my visions and dreams became more real. I became closer and closer to God. I felt I could tell him anything and he would listen. I don't fully understand the power of God, but I learned very young to trust and love Him.

I could not allow myself to see a vision of something bad or awkward happening and not try to help. I became compassionate towards my class-

Bold Resilient Women

mates. I would share my food and chocolate bars with them. If my teachers wanted a helper, as they called us in the Catholic school that I attended, I would volunteer. If someone was upset or insulted by a classmate, I would go sit with them to cheer them up.

Grandmother had many elderly friends, and after church, they would sit in the auditorium and have coffee and coffee cake. I loved to serve them. I cared for them as though they were related to me. Every week, Grandma would take me to the Hollywood House, a facility across from the church where the elderly resided, and we would bring them cookies and spiritual books, or giant potluck dinners that my grandma and her friends made. I would go and feed them and speak with them. I realized early in my life that elderly people just want someone to listen to their stories.

An elderly woman named Mrs. Ourania looked forward to my visits. One day, she brought me a beautiful doll that wore a huge green gown with lots of different fake jewelry. I fell in love with this doll. She told me it belonged to her daughter and she wanted to give it to me. I cherished this doll until I was in my late twenties. I had two children, and I was still playing with the doll with the large green dress.

This was the beginning of my journey and connection with the needy and the elderly.

When I was hospitalized at thirteen from a sinus infection, which eventually required surgery, I met a young handicapped girl who would change my life. My father's friends and employees were visiting me on a daily basis, bringing me many gifts and flowers. I had so many that I realized I could provide everyone on this floor with flowers for their rooms. As I walked through the corridors, I saw a young, crippled girl trying to get out of bed. I decided to help her. That was the beginning of a beautiful connection. I visited her every day during my stay at the hospital. I got to know this blonde, green-eyed, handicapped child very well. I wanted to provide her with all the gifts they would bring me as a way of showing her my love and compassion. She was grateful and happy. She shared the gifts and treats with the nurses and anyone else who stopped in her room. She felt important, not like a victim.

Zella became my best friend, inspiring me to support and care for handicapped children. Decades later, we are still close and still find time to connect. She gave me the confidence to listen to, defend, and become an advocate for children who are abused, and children who don't have a choice in life.

Bold Resilient Women

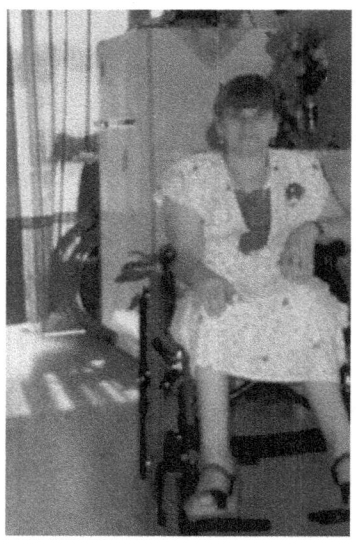

Zella was from Turkey. Her mother had died young, when she was in her twenties; Zella was only seven years old at the time. Her mother had been diagnosed with a disease where she had a traumatic large ball in her chest and she died. While the official cause of death was likely cancer, the true reason was neglect and poverty. She was poor and did not have access to medical treatments. Zella always had her mother's picture beneath her pillow. She said, "I carry my mom with me. When I am lonely, depressed, in pain and suffering, or I need something, I pray for her guidance and strength."

After a couple of years, Zella's father married a woman from his hometown. It shook Zella up—he was making a new life with another woman in what was once her mother's home. The stepmother didn't care about Zella, she just wanted security, and a man to work ,day and night, to take care of her. The stepmother never made an effort to become close to her, as she viewed Zella as an obstacle who stood in her way. The stepmother mistreated Zella and manipulated her husband, telling him that Zella always disobeyed her. She told him the only way she would stay with him was if he straightened Zella out. She told him his daughter should be helping him on the farm with animals instead of going to school.

One day, after a difficult day of work, her father went home searching for his daughter. Her stepmother informed him his daughter had disobeyed him and gone to school. The father, infuriated, waited for her by the door, an ax laying on the ground next to him. He asked where she had been and why she disobeyed him.

Zella never anticipated that her father would injure her. But he picked up the ax and hit her on the back, breaking her spine. She was rushed to the hospital by both of them.

"I don't remember what story they made up for the doctors," she said. "All I remember is being rolled into surgery. I came out of it with strangers taking care of me." No one would ever know the truth; in the northern villages back then, there weren't any kind of investigations.

"My father fled with his wife," she continued. "There wasn't a trace of them. I guess they knew I would end up in some kind of institution. I had no one to take care of me. Eleni mou, let's be realistic. Who wants to take care of a crippled child? They know there isn't hope or a bright future for me. I am confined to a wheelchair for the rest of my life, and my stepmother convinced my father that I would be better off in a handicapped institution."

Zella resided for many years in the Liosia Foundation. I would occasionally visit her when I came to Greece, and when I would leave, my parents would go see her once a week. One day, I walked in and found her in tears.

"Zella, what happened?" I asked, concern in my voice. "My father died!" she said tearfully.

I was mortified and angry for her. "So what? Why should you care about that man? You haven't seen him in years."

"I know," she said. "But I knew that somewhere in this world I had a family member. That was a comfort."

I was in a state of shock. I could not believe Zella's amazing heart and soul. She has been in a wheelchair since she was eleven, and yet she found it in her heart to forgive the man who took her fruitful future, life, dignity, and integrity away. Zella taught me to forgive cruelty—but not forget it. To this day, Zella has never criticized or condemned anyone for her reality of being isolated and confined in a wheelchair.

What inspires me most is the patience, love, and kindness Zella has for everyone around her. Sometimes I wonder if she doesn't despise or hate people for being free to come and go as they please in life. Does she wonder how her life could have been different? Often when I speak to her and find myself complaining about my children, or work, or life, before I can finish the sentence, she says, "Everything will be fine, just pray for peace and love, Eleni mou. Remember that God listens to our prayers. He will respond to our needs when He feels it is the right time. He wants to teach us patience, faith, and tolerance."

Many times, I want to ask how she can possibly have faith and pray day and night? How can she speak about challenges and trust God will answer? How does she find peace and serenity in her heart? She very well knows she has been praying to get out of the wheelchair all these years, but is still confined to it. Her patience, hope, and faith inspired me, and sparked my passion for children with disabilities.

My journey to philanthropy has taken many twists and turns, allowing me to hear stories and see firsthand the struggles and pain of others. Through

Bold Resilient Women

this, I have always been able to envision a world free of suffering. While it's an overwhelming task at times, giving to others is the only way we'll even come close to the world that I know is possible.

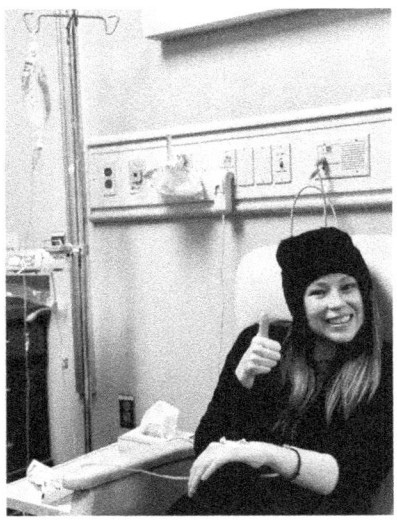

Young Innocent Love

Sometimes, love starts with a powerful, undeniable moment. Your heart flutters the first moment you lay eyes on a person. You find your heart beating so fast you think you will have a cardiac collapse. You feel immediately ready to give your heart and soul to that person. It's *agape*; you're ready to care for someone more than you care for yourself. You don't realize the butterflies you feel are love and pathos for that person.

My sophomore year in high school, I was walking up the stairs to go to class. I was a tall, slim, young girl with long, straight, dark hair and a summer tan. At the bottom of the stairs, I noticed a tall, handsome, young man standing with a group of boys, including my dear friends, Mike and Timothy. He didn't take his eyes off me. My heart fluttered.

Because I was a good student, a counselor recommended that I work in the principal's office during my elective classes. That day, as I'd just started with my responsibilities, I glanced up from the desk and standing across from me was the young man who had been staring at me from the stairs. He had just moved here from Greece, and I was instructed to work with him and to have his Greek degree translated to English.

Bold Resilient Women

I tried desperately to help, but my Greek was very poor. It took all morning to try and understand what courses he had taken back home. Afterwards, the principal asked me to give this new student a tour and show him the classrooms and the library, then take him to lunch.

We went to the counter to order food. I was starving, since I didn't have time to eat breakfast before I left the house. "I'll take a salad and fruit," I said to the lunch lady. I didn't want to fill up before gym class. "Do you want anything?" I asked Jimmy in Greek.

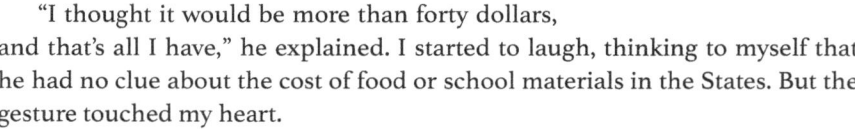

He shook his head, but as I pulled my money out, he shook his head harder and pulled out his money. We argued that I could pay for my own lunch. But he insisted and bought my lunch for me. When he saw my lunch cost twenty-five cents, he went back and got a hamburger.

"Why didn't you just get that in the first place?" I asked.

"I thought it would be more than forty dollars, and that's all I have," he explained. I started to laugh, thinking to myself that he had no clue about the cost of food or school materials in the States. But the gesture touched my heart.

Days and weeks went by, and Jimmy would follow me everywhere. One day during gym, I overheard the boys gossiping.

"That boy from the village has caught Eleni's eye," I heard one of them say. I marched over to them. "That's not true! He is from the old country and doesn't know anyone or understand English!" I said sternly. But the gossip didn't stop. I told Jimmy never to speak to me again or sit at the lunch table with my friends and me. I was panicked; if my father heard these lies, he would take me out of the public school, which I loved, and make me go back to Immaculata High School. I had cried for weeks to persuade my parents to let me go to the public high school—I was not about to go back.

I learned from Mike that Jimmy told him he felt something when he saw me. Mike told me that he said, "Someday I am going to marry her." Mike laughed, but he liked how bold Jimmy was. He recruited him to be a part of the high school boxing team, since he was tall and buff, and shortly after that, Mike introduced him to my siblings, thinking this would be a great way for Jimmy to see me and get to know me better. Jimmy eventually got to be good friends with my older brothers, Peter and Louis.

During the summer, I worked selling snow cones with my little brother,

Bold Resilient Women

George, at Foster Park. My parents liked it because it was close to our house; there were constantly people around, so nothing could happen to us; and we were stationed there all day until we sold out. At that point, one of our parents would come and push the cart back to the garages.

One afternoon, I was working at the park when Jimmy and his uncle walked up to buy a snow cone. Because Jimmy was now my brothers' friend and played soccer with them, I told them both that snow cones were on the house.

His uncle nudged him as I drizzled syrup on the snow cone. "She must be a good person," he said. Jimmy blushed. Later, I found out that when they walked away, his uncle told him I was beautiful with a great body and a generous heart.

Jimmy and I continued to be part of the same social circles, and he grew on me. I thought he was incredibly nice, and I loved how he had taken time to get to know my brothers and friends.

A couple of years later, life changed drastically for my family. One night, over dinner, my dad announced he was moving our family back to Greece. He had the opportunity to start a construction company, and he seized it. I was surprised, but not completely. I knew he was tired of rolling heavy carts loaded with food and drinks across Chicago neighborhoods. He complained often about being treated like an animal. Since arriving in America, he had gotten very ill and he almost lost his life, his wife had gone through cancer, and his son had been burned and fought for his life for a whole year. Plus, there were all of the other daily challenges that come with immigrating to a new country. All of this had destroyed him, mentally and psychologically. I knew he longed to be back where he knew the language and the culture and had close friends and family.

I spent the next few weeks enjoying as much time as possible with friends as I dreaded our departure. Three days before we left, we all went to a movie. Unexpectedly, Jimmy was standing by the entrance with his cousins.

"Hi and goodbye, Jimmy," I said to him. "I hope I will see you again someday."

"Why? What do you mean?" he asked. He looked at me, concerned. His English had gotten better, but he still spoke with a thick Greek accent.

"I am leaving tomorrow for Greece. Our family is moving back." My tears caught in my throat, but I avoided crying.

"I'm going to Greece too," he said. "I leave next week for a trip with my family." He smiled, and my heart fluttered.

The next day, I left for Greece with my family and all our belongings. We were starting a new life, and while my parents knew this place well, it was an unknown world for us children. While we had family there, we were separated from those closest to us—my grandmother, and my aunts, and cousins—as well as Peter and Louis, who stayed in the U.S. for college. My little brother, George, and I cried all the way to Greece.

My mom tried to make our life in Athens happy and fulfilling. She wanted us to be joyful in our new home and environment. She tried to make it fun to decorate our new house and make our bedrooms our own, but I was still lonely and missed home.

A few weeks later, Jimmy arrived in Greece with his family. When he arrived at his aunt and uncle's house, and after quick kisses on the cheek, he asked them one question: "How far is Nestani?"

His uncle chuckled. "Why are you interested in Nestani?"

"I am infatuated with a girl from Chicago, and her family is from that village. Where can I rent a car to travel there and find her?"

His uncle sensed there was no deterring Jimmy, so he rented a car for him to drive. In the end, though, given that he had never been there before, he decided to take a cab instead.

This turned out to be a fortunate decision. Greece is a small country, and coincidentally, the cab driver was from my village. Jimmy asked him if he knew anyone from my family, and the driver took him right to my maternal grandfather's sister's house.

"Do you know where Eleni and her family are living in Athens?" he asked her.

"I am too old to remember where they are," she told him. "But I remember it's near a church, St. Marina."

"Is there anyone else in her family who lives here and would know where I can find her?" he pleaded. My grandfather's sister directed the cab driver to my grandmother's cousin's house, who we were not close with, so they didn't know where we were. Jimmy was upset and frustrated and felt panicked—he had ten days to find me before his family returned to the States.

He returned to Athens disappointed, telling his uncle he had to find me before he left for Chicago. He told his uncle he heard I resided near a church of St. Marina. His aunt overheard the conversation and told him there were four churches in Athens with that name, and he could start with the one closest to their home. Jimmy took his first cousin with him, and they went out every day searching.

The day before Jimmy was supposed to leave for the States, he was looking near the final Church of St. Marina—his first three stops having come up empty—and asked someone if they knew where a Palivos family lived.

Bold Resilient Women

"The building at the corner belongs to them; they live on the second floor." Jimmy barely heard the last word as he sprinted down the street.

At our apartment building, George and I were running up and down the stairs, carrying the final things from our move into our apartment. The downstairs door was open, and as I ran downstairs the second time, I glanced across the street and to my surprise, I saw a young man who looked like my friend, Jimmy. I froze. *It couldn't be him*, I thought. *How could he possibly be here, right across the street from me?*

I walked across the street. "Jimmy? It's me, Eleni!" I said. I was so excited to see him, but also so confused. "What are you doing here in my neighborhood?"

"I was just walking from my aunt's house to the store and noticed you. I wasn't sure it could be you, so I wanted to stick around and see, and maybe say hi." He said this all so coolly, like it was the most possible thing in the world. I believed him. He didn't say that he had been searching for days to find me. He had walked up the stairs of the building, heard my voice, ran downstairs, and asked his cousin to leave. He was going to wait until I came down again.

It was late, and he was supposed to go to his family's house and pack, as he was leaving early in the morning for the States.

"Eleni, what are you doing the rest of the evening?" he asked insistently. In Greece, people rest in the afternoon and go clubbing or for dinner late in the evening.

"We are helping my mom unpack, and then she is taking us to hear Voskopoulos, my favorite singer." I had hardly finished the sentence when Jimmy responded, "Funny, I'm going to be there, too. He's my favorite."

I smiled, surprised. "Wow, I guess we have something in common." I felt tiny butterflies. When I went upstairs, my mom asked where I had been. Without thinking, I told her I ran into someone from the States who was friends with my brother and me.

"Sweetheart, a friend from the States and a friend of your brothers'? Why didn't you invite him up for a sweet?" she asked.

"He was in a hurry," I told her. "He had to get ready for the concert. He is going too! You will get to meet him." I tried to hide the excitement in my voice.

"Eleni, I am tired. I changed my mind. We aren't going tonight, we will go on Saturday, after I have had a chance to rest."

I was disappointed, and I wanted to go to the concert. I was also worried that Jimmy would think I was a liar. We were supposed to go, we had even purchased the tickets! But my mother was already on her way to lie down. Jimmy, meanwhile, went to the concert and waited outside till 4 o'clock in the morning. He saw that I didn't attend the Voskopoulos concert and, defeated, he left for his aunt's house to head to the airport.

There was no way for him to stay. In the 1970s, if you were a male Greek citizen attending college, you could visit Greece once a year and only stay less than a month. If you stayed longer without government consent, you had to serve in the Greek army. Jimmy was an immigrant, but also a United States citizen and a student, so he was given an exemption for not serving his country. But once he finished his studies, he either had to serve the Greek army or pay off his military obligation to the government. (Years later, my dad would pay the military dues for Jimmy, as well as all of my brothers. None of them had to serve in the army, and they were able to come and go as they pleased in Greece without being considered a deserter or traitor to their country.)

While Jimmy was away, his presence still loomed in my life. Not only did he cross my mind here and there, but Jimmy's aunt and uncle had a tenant with a beautiful daughter. When Jimmy and his cousins would visit Greece, they would hang around with her and her family, and this vibrant young girl had fallen in love with him. One day, she found my phone number written on the cover of a telephone book which Jimmy had accidentally left behind. She was enraged. She began to harass my mom and little brother with hourly phone calls, telling them she was engaged to Jimmy and I was standing in the way. She said I was not allowing him to marry her.

My brother told her she was a liar. He said, "My sister is not seeing anyone. Call back when she is home from work, and she will tell you it's not true!"

The next time she called, I was there.

"What is going on with you and Jimmy? Tell me!" she said.

"Jimmy is my friend from the States, but I didn't have an affair with him and I am not interested in him," I told her. "Nothing is going on between us."

"Please, can we meet tomorrow?" she asked. I obliged; I wanted to tell her to her face this was a lie, and she had nothing to fear. We set a time to meet in the park the next day.

"How will I be able to identify you?" she asked.

"It's simple," I told her. "I have a large beauty mole at the center of my chin, which I was born with."

I was waiting in the park when she arrived. She charged up to me and stood with her hands on her hips. She tossed her hair over her shoulder. "You are beautiful, no wonder he wants you and not me," she said.

"Jimmy is my friend, and that's all," I said angrily. "I would be more than happy to stand up at your wedding, if you wish. There are no romantic feelings between us, just a wonderful friendship." She seemed satisfied with my answer.

Bold Resilient Women

Meanwhile, I was miserable living in Greece. I cried day and night. I missed my older brothers, and all of my friends, and my familiar surroundings. But I started to establish a life. My dad had political connections, and got me a job as an airline ground hostess. While I got used to—and sometimes even liked—living in Greece, something was still missing from my life. My family tried desperately to make George and me love our new lives, but I was so homesick.

The following summer, in July of 1973, Jimmy returned to Greece. When he arrived at his aunt's house, he was greeted at the door by the young girl. She told him she had reached out to me, and we had met. Jimmy was angry and humiliated; he could not believe this young girl was stalking him without him having shown any interest in her. He told her to stay away from him and from me as well. He made clear he had no feelings for her and had no desire to be with her. The discussion ended as did their relationship.

On this trip to Greece, Jimmy had bought a bright red convertible so he and his cousins could drive around and attract beautiful girls. They kept riding around my neighborhood, which everyone noticed, as the red car was impossible to miss. Mrs. Stathoula, one of my parents' tenants, stopped Jimmy on one of his rides. "Are you trying to find Eleni?" she asked. Jimmy quickly shook his head, embarrassed, and left in a hurry.

Mrs. Stathoula told my mom, "I would bet my life he is looking for your daughter, Elenitsa."

"Don't you dare disgrace my daughter, and if you mention this to anyone, I will never speak to you again!" My mom was furious. Of course, Mrs. Stathoula was like family, and loved me, but my mom was terrified that people would start to gossip about me, especially since my dad was away in the States for a month. She knew what she felt, that she was watching a young man looking for his love. Later, she would tell me she was frightened because she saw the look in Jimmy's eyes and the expression on his face and knew he was in love.

One evening, the doorbell rang. It was Jimmy. He had called my mom and told her he wanted to bring greetings from my brothers, and of course, she invited him over, eager to hear any news about her sons.

That evening, when Jimmy rang the doorbell, I ran downstairs and flung the door open. He was dressed in jeans, with an open-zipped tee shirt, which emphasized his muscular body. His long, curly hair grazed his shoulders. We kissed on one cheek, and he waited anxiously for me to kiss the other cheek, as is customary in Greece.

"Can I have another kiss on the other cheek?" he asked with a smile. "Absolutely not," I said. "One is enough." I brought him upstairs and he satin the living room across from my mother. He looked nervous, and when my mom offered him a spoon of cherry sweet, he dropped it. He told her so many stories about my older brothers. I thought most of them were untrue, and he just wanted to be here, and would say anything to keep the discussion going. My mom saw the way he was looking at me and didn't like it.

"Jimmy, it's getting late and it's time to leave," she told him.

"Could I please take Eleni and George to get ice cream?" he asked politely. "Eleni's dad is in the States for the next month. She cannot go unless he is here."

I started to cry. I felt she didn't trust me and my brother to go with my friend, and I wasn't ready for him to leave. I felt something inside me. My mom looked at me and saw my tears.

"You can go for an hour," she relented. "Have them back by 10:30."

Jimmy had a bounce in his step as he led George and me out of our apartment. He wasn't familiar with our neighborhood, but remembered that there was a wine festival every year nearby in Haidari. As we walked there, when my back was turned, George whispered to Jimmy, "You and my sister make such a great couple." Jimmy kissed him on the head and bought George many little gifts; he knew how to get to a nine-year-old boy's heart.

All the way home, Jimmy kept trying to hold my hand, but I kept saying stop. When we arrived outside at home, George thanked him for all the gifts and dashed upstairs. I found out later that Jimmy didn't go back to his aunt and uncle's house. He was so excited by our night out that he slept in his car, next to the park by our apartment. The next morning, I was walking to pick up my paycheck when Jimmy pulled up in his convertible. He got out, lifted me up, and put me in the seat! As I was in his arms, I looked around and saw people peering over at us from the rooftops and balconies of our building. I tried to hide, but it was impossible. "I will take you to pick up your paycheck, and then I will kidnap you," he said. His voice was full of joy and determination. I thought he was kidding. "Jimmy, you are crazy! No way. My parents will be furious." I let him put me in the front seat and take me to get my check. I begged him to bring me home so I could face my parents.

When he dropped me off, my mom was standing by the front door, waiting for me. "Where have you been? Where did he take you?" Her hands were on her hips, and her eyes were focused on me. "How dare you disgrace us when your father is not here! People are going to say that the cat went away and the mouse started running around!"

"He took me to get my paycheck and brought me home!" I said, crying.

"You don't have any business with him," she said. "Stay away from him before your dad finds out and kills both of us."

I ran to my room, where I cried tears of sadness and anger.

Bold Resilient Women

The following day, I approached my mom while she was getting ready to leave.

"So, what do you think of Jimmy?" I asked.

"He is a handsome young man," she said, buttoning her coat. "His mother is lucky to have him."

I was feeling bold. "I think I'm going to marry him." I was only half-joking.

My mom bent down quickly and grabbed the first thing she could find—a shoe—and threw it at me. The heel of this shoe was broken, and it slid across my upper arm and scratched me. My mom saw the scratch and looked surprised, but she warned me: "Never say that again." I was furious.

Jimmy came to the house the next day, and my mom told him to leave. He looked at me for guidance.

"Jimmy, you have to leave me alone. My dad will kill me if you continue!" I walked him down the stairs.

"I have chased you for so long, Eleni." He said. He was standing in front of me, looking at me with pleading eyes. "If I leave now, I will never come back." Something happened to me when I heard this threat. I didn't want to lose my friend. We were so close. He knew everything about me, and I knew everything about him. He loved my brothers; he loved me. I had no secrets to keep. "Stay, Jimmy!" I pleaded. "Please don't go! I will talk to my mom. We will figure things out."

"I can't disrespect your mother, Eleni. We just have to do it on our own. I will wait for you tomorrow in the early morning, and we will elope."

The next morning, while the sun was just starting to rise, Jimmy pulled up. I was watching out the window, as I had barely slept all night. I was scared and excited, and most of all, I was overwhelmed with the feeling of falling in love. I ran down the stairs and jumped in the car, certain that once we were married, our problems would be figured out and we could start our lives together. We drove far away from Athens, and when we reached a small city at nightfall, we took care of tasks. Jimmy bought two wedding bands with our names and our elopement date engraved inside. I searched for a nightgown and, although it was summer, all I could find was a long, wintery gown that buttoned all the way up to the chin. It was one hundred degrees outside with no air conditioning, but I had no other choice.

We drove to Jimmy's village so we could meet his grandmother. When she saw me, she shook her head and, in Greek, told him to take me home, go back to his mother, and forget about me. Jimmy translated for me, and we were both angry. How dare she make a comment like that?

She didn't even know me! I respected her as his grandmother, but I absolutely did not want to see her again. We left for the city, hoping to find a hotel with two rooms, as we were not yet married.

It was so hot that day, and because it was the high travel season, hotels were limited. We searched for a hotel with two rooms, but we couldn't find anything. We finally parked the car at the square and started to look for a hotel on foot. After hours of searching, we found a hotel that had one room with two beds. I must have looked alarmed because the receptionist asked if I was okay. "We are newlyweds," Jimmy told her. "My wife is shy."

The room was small and plain. I was exhausted. I wanted to sleep. I changed into my winter nightgown in the bathroom, then tucked myself into bed, deep under the covers. I started to sweat. I was dying, beads of sweat were running down my face. I thought I was going to pass out from fear, and heat, and all of the adrenaline of the day. Jimmy walked over to the bed and asked if he could kiss me goodnight and I said no, I am too tired and upset. We fell asleep.

Meanwhile, my father had called home and when he asked to speak to me, my mother started crying and told him what happened. He started to yell, instructing her to take my uncle and my brother and search for me.

My mom remembered the name of Jimmy's village, so even though it was the middle of the night, she grabbed George and my uncle and found a driver to take them there. They sat together in the back seat, shoulder to shoulder.

"What are you doing going to an Albanian village in the middle of the night?" he asked them. "Make sure you keep your eyes open." My mother was mortified, but my uncle told her not to listen to village gossip. In the village square, a large group of young men were partying and dancing. It was their last night in town; they were departing for the army the next day. My uncle asked them if they knew Jimmy Bousis. One of the young men said, "Yes, he was with a beautiful young lady." They started to laugh, which made my mom start to panic. She told my uncle, "We need to find my daughter. What did he do to my daughter?" She didn't like his smirk or comment.

Though she was near hysterics, she was still thinking clearly. She remembered the name of the village mayor, who was also Jimmy's uncle. It was late, but they found his house and knocked on the door. The mayor answered, clearly having been woken up. He agreed that the marriage should not take place, which just alarmed my mother even more. Why would he say that? But he didn't have any information about where we were or what we were doing. Defeated, my family headed back to Athens—but they called in some help. My father knew the Minister of Defense, Papailliou Hlias, who had notified the Greek secret service and they were to arrest Jimmy when they found him. He told him Jimmy had kidnapped me against my will. My mom's uncle was the police commander in Argos, and my mom, uncle, and little brother went to see him. She wanted to find me quickly, not knowing what was happening to me and who this young man was who had whisked me off my feet. Her uncle told her his men were on it.

They searched and searched and finally spotted the car parked in the square. My mom had given them a perfect description, from the color to the engine. A red convertible is hard to miss. Several officers went to look at every hotel around the square to find us, while an officer stayed to keep an eye on the car. They knew that no matter what, we were coming back to pick up the car and go on our way.

Jimmy and I awoke to pounding on the door. "We are the *asfalia*," they said, which means secret service, but it also translates to "a defective light fuse." "If the light fuse is defective, get an electrician. Why are you waking us up?" Jimmy said through the door. We continued sleeping.

I woke up to the sun streaming through the window. It was clear Jimmy had been up for a while. He told me he would get the car while I got ready. We would drive to the monastery of Panagia, located on the top of a mountain, to get married on our own. Jimmy didn't believe in church ceremonies or priests to conduct a marriage ceremony. "We will go in front of God and exchange our wedding vows."

I got dressed and sat on the bed. I watched the clock tick as I waited and waited for him, fear growing inside of me. What if he had listened to his grandmother and left me? What if he walked out? I could never face my mother and brother again. I had disgraced my family by running away, and the only way out would be to kill myself. The clock kept ticking; I saw no other option.

A knock on the door interrupted my panicked thoughts. I flung the door open, thinking it was Jimmy. But it was the police.

"Follow us, Eleni." They led me down the hallway.

"Where are you taking me?" I wanted to yell, but I felt too nervous. "The station. Your mother, uncle, and brother are waiting for you."

I wanted to die. How could I have disgraced my poor mom like this? How could I have disgraced my family?

"Where is Jimmy?"

"He's been arrested for kidnapping."

"Why is he arrested? He didn't kidnap me! I left of my own free will!" "Tell that to the commander, we're taking you to him."

When Jimmy was heading to the car, the police had approached him and arrested him. My mom was nearby. She ran up to him and asked in a ball of fury, "Where have you sold my daughter? Tell me!"

"I didn't sell your daughter. I love her, and I will marry her, whether you or your family approves or not." My uncle gently put his hand on my mom's shoulder and told her to relax. "I like him," my uncle said. "He smiles. Let's give him a chance to explain."

The officers led me into the police station, where I immediately saw my mom, my uncle, and my brother sitting side by side. I wanted to die from embarrassment. I couldn't face them, even though George ran into my arms.

"Are you hurt?" my mom asked.

"No, he would never hurt me. He loves me!" I told her. I didn't understand why she couldn't see that.

Meanwhile, Jimmy was inside my mother's uncle's office, being harassed and interrogated as he tried to understand why he was being charged with kidnapping, as I had made the choice to come. My uncle realized he didn't kidnap me; he truly loved me.

My uncle emerged from his office, pulling Jimmy behind him. "Vasso, let the kids get married," he said to her. "This young man is a good boy. He loves your daughter. Go back to Athens and let them come back home." After a long conversation behind closed doors with her brother and uncle, they went back to Athens.

My uncle, the commander, pulled me aside. "If I were you, I would go to the archbishop and tell him your love story. He will help you."

We went to Nafplion, where the metropolis is, and asked to see the archbishop. He was waiting for us, as my uncle had called him. We explained our dilemma.

"I will tell you what to do," he said. "Go to the bakery and buy wedding almonds. Wear your wedding bands and say the Archbishop of Nafplion married you. We will be charged $5,000 if we marry you without the signed consent of your father. If you don't bring the consent by the end of the summer, that total will be doubled by the church. This will force your father to sign the wedding consent."

We listened carefully to his advice, then thanked him and did exactly what he told us.

We drove back to Athens to tell my mom, uncle, and little brother that the archbishop had married us. My mother started to fix up our wedding bed for us to sleep in, as newlyweds, as is our tradition and custom. Tears ran down her cheeks as she adjusted the sheets and blankets. I felt her tears in my heart. I could not fathom sleeping in her bed and disgracing her under God's eyes. I needed to tell her the truth. I went to the living room and told her what the archbishop had advised us to say.

"Please help me," I pleaded. "I will never sleep at your home without being married, but I love him, and I want to marry him." My uncle loved Jimmy from the start. Although mom was startled, she agreed to help us. I believe she didn't want to disappoint my dad's cousin. He was so pro-Jimmy. We were on a roller coaster trying to find a priest to marry us in August, which is a holiday fasting season with many evening sacraments taking place. Religious ceremonies didn't often take place during Panagia, except if a child was dying and needed to be baptized.

Meanwhile, back in Chicago, my father and my two brothers went to meet Jimmy's family. The meeting went quickly, and soon after, my father called me to tell me he did not approve and he would kill me. Louis sent me a telegraph saying, "Now that you broke up our family, I hope you will be happy." But my brother Peter said, "If you are happy, go for it, sister." That bit of love and encouragement from a family member kept me going.

We were celebrating the holiday of the Death of our Virgin Mary. We were supposed to be fasting, praying, and confessing our sins and problems, which were a burden to our soul for fifteen days, from August 1 to August 15. And here we were, trying to find a priest to marry us.

Finally, my uncle found a priest, who told us of another priest who could officiate—but we had to pay for both of their services. My uncle agreed to pay them after the wedding had taken place and he had seen the burned candles. They told my mom to pay half up front as a down payment, and the rest at the conclusion of the ceremony. If she didn't pay the priest the money, he would not start the wedding ceremony. My mom, a religious and honorable person, was paying a crooked priest to marry her daughter? She told my uncle this was a disgrace, but had no choice.

The next evening, we went to the far north of Athens in sight of the Hassia mountain range, where the priest resided. He was supposed to be waiting for us and ready to perform a ceremony, but instead, we found him sitting at table, drunk, finishing his meat feast—not fasting—and unable to hold a conversation. My uncle asked him what kind of priest he was, but my mom was in a state of shock. She had never seen this kind of behavior from a priest, especially during a sacred holiday.

We left immediately. It was as if God didn't want to bless this marriage. When we went to the priest who had made the introduction, he could not believe our story. He unwrapped the candles to make sure they were not lit. My uncle was so angry, and asked him how he could sell his body and soul to the devil during such a sacred holiday.

We were exhausted. We didn't know what to do. My father was returning to Greece soon, and he would be sure to separate us. My uncle, who was an incredible man, finally found a priest and explained our situation. This was a spiritual man who didn't judge or condemn anyone. He listened to my uncle's plea and agreed to conduct the ceremony. "God will see why I must conduct the wedding ceremony," he said. "I will marry these two in the Lord's church the way God wants." At last, it seemed like things were finally going our way. I didn't know how wrong I was.

Jimmy and I waited in the church while my uncle went to get my mother and George. We were not dressed for a wedding. I was wearing a mini white dress with a purple top and white sandals. Jimmy was wearing blue jean pants with a burgundy T-shirt and suede brown summer shoes. When my uncle told my mom they were going to a church, she asked him why.

"We are going to a wedding," he said. My uncle served as our best man.

He was an incredible person, vice president of the Piraeus Bank.

It was a simple ceremony. We didn't have flowers, a gown, tuxedos, bridesmaids, or anything else. Just Jimmy and me, plus my mom, and George, and my uncle's family. We had ten guests.

After the wedding, we loaded into the car with all ten guests and headed to the tavern for a party. The mood had completely flipped from uncertainty to joy. We were spilling out of the top of the convertible as we all piled on each other's laps. As we drove, people honked, waved, and laughed at us. It was the most hilarious day of my life. We were finally married under God's eyes.

A few days later, my dad returned to Greece. Jimmy was prepared. He had bought me a yellow mini pleated skirt with a white top and roses across the short sleeves, and kept it in the bag. My dad walked into the house wordlessly, kissed my mom and George, and asked to speak to me in his room, since his siblings, family members, and contractors were around. When I walked in, he closed the door and slapped me twice on both cheeks. I held my face in shock.

"This bum does not belong in my house!" he yelled. "He only wants my money. He only married you because they are village people and have nothing. You are to leave him now!" He didn't stop for a second, giving me reasons to walk out of Jimmy's life. My cheeks still stung. I couldn't believe he hit me so hard. He loved me more than his life.

Jimmy heard the yelling and walked right into the room, and when he saw my face, he was outraged. He couldn't believe my dad would slap me so hard as to mark my cheeks. I saw him take a breath, and then he spoke right to my father's face.

"Mr. Palivos, I am poor, but I don't want your money, or anything from you at all. All I want is your daughter, Eleni. I might have paid only twenty-five dollars for a ring and twenty-five dollars for a wedding band, but someday I promise you, she will wear the biggest diamond on her finger." (I guess the skies were open at that moment).

Bold Resilient Women

My father was silent, and Jimmy continued in a firm, loud voice. "Until today, she was your daughter. But from now on, she is my wife, and I won't allow you, or anyone, to ever lay a hand on her. Since you believe I want your money, she will change out of the clothes you bought and wear what I have bought her." He handed me the bag with the clothes in it, and instructed me to go to the bathroom and change clothes, placing the old ones back in the bag. I was stuck between two men that I loved. One who had always loved me unconditionally, and one who had walked into my life and upended it. My past and my future.

I had to listen to Jimmy. I changed into my new clothes, and Jimmy handed my dad the bag with my old ones. This was the start of a separation between my father and me. It destroyed me not being able to talk to him. "If you go with him, I will disown you. I never want to see you again," my father said. It almost killed me.

Two days later, Jimmy and I left for the States. I cried the whole way. I was departing from the first man I had fallen in love with, my dad. I felt sick the whole way home, though I didn't know if it was from sadness or something else was happening. I vomited the whole way home, feeling pain and weakness. When we arrived at the airport, Jimmy's family was waiting. From the looks on their faces, I knew this wasn't going to go well. My new father-in-law looked me up and down, and the first thing he said was, "Wipe the black ink from your chin." Jimmy told him it was a birthmark, but he didn't believe him because it was in the center of my chin.

Jimmy had to finish school, and had no money to support our new life together, so we had to live with his parents and sister. We continued to be challenged. I kept throwing up, and I couldn't get out of bed. I told my grandmother and aunt about my terrible symptoms. My Aunt Georgia took me to her doctor. She was worried about me. She and my Uncle Peter loved me as one of their own daughters. They knew what painful situations had transpired between my parents and me, and they wanted to make sure I was going to be okay. She brought me to see Dr. Bubala, a well-known and respected Bulgarian OB/GYN at Lutheran General Hospital, where I learned I was pregnant. I froze. It was impossible. I still felt like a child.

While I got dressed, the doctor took my aunt into his office. "Eleni should not have this child," he told her. "Her uterus is tipped, and she will have problems delivering this child—that is, if she doesn't have a miscarriage first." He advised us against the pregnancy.

Aunt Georgia brought me home because I didn't know how to drive. (She would drive from Glenview to Hoffman Estates with my five little girl cousins to take me to the doctor for my appointments.) Jimmy came home between school and work to find out what was wrong with me, and I broke down crying. I told him I was pregnant and was going to have a baby. He didn't understand why I was sad; he was so excited. "Great, now no one will take you from me!" he said, pulling me into a hug and laughing. I explained the doctor's warning, and he took a breath. "Let's take it day by day," he said.

My aunt was worried about my health and condition. She was older and experienced, and she knew this was not a good sign. She called Jimmy to explain everything the doctor said in detail. He said, "She will be fine. We will take it day by day. Let's see how things evolve." Jimmy told me we would stay with his family to get help until we had the baby. "We will decide what to do when I graduate and we have financial stability."

This was a huge mistake. We were newlyweds and had run away to get married. Everyone was angry, and no one approved. Additionally, Jimmy's sister was older and single, and in Greek culture, you marry off the daughter before the son starts looking for a wife—just another tradition we had trampled in our passionate quest to get married. Now I understand why my dad disapproved. This matter was brought up to him and my brothers, but he never said it until years later. Everyone knew that we were penniless runaways; we had no choice.

Challenges at Childbirth

From the moment we conceived Michael, my doctors were very clear that if I was considering having children, each one was going to challenge me during pregnancy and birth. But I was too young and naive to understand it. I thought he didn't know anything. All I knew was that I was a young, strong, healthy woman. I had no past health issues that could lead him to make assumptions about my pregnancies, so I was defensive. What did he know about me? And what was it I didn't know about my body?

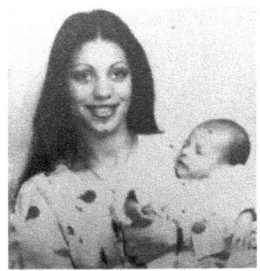

One night at the beginning of my third trimester, I woke up to excruciating pain. I had never had contractions before, and it felt like my insides were being ripped out. I doubled over and tried to go back to sleep, believing there was no way the baby was coming because it was too early. I didn't say anything to Jimmy. I knew he was stressed about his finals, but all day, I could not sit

or walk. The pain persisted, and eventually, it was clear that the baby was coming.

Jimmy was at school, so I told his mother and sister, between painful contractions, that I was having the baby tonight. It was too early, and they didn't believe me. Finally, I persuaded them to drive me to the hospital. They drove me to the door of the hospital and dropped me off.

I was a child having a child. I walked into Lutheran General Hospital alone, wearing a short summer dress and sandals, crying uncontrollably, and shaking from the fear and pain. I stumbled to the nurse's station, and as soon as I got there, a nurse grabbed me in her arms.

"What's wrong? What happened?" asked the nurse. She was wearing a white uniform and held a clipboard, which she had set down quickly when she saw me approaching. She thought I was a rape or abuse victim.

"I think my baby is coming." She looked at me with alarm.

"What's your doctor's name?" she asked. "Dr. Bubala," I said. She reached for the phone and immediately called him. He instructed her to take me to the maternity floor. She grabbed me by the hand and led me carefully to the delivery room. She asked me so many questions. "Do you have a husband?"

"Yes," I said between deep, painful breaths. "He's at school, taking his finals." During those challenging minutes, I felt like a lamb being taken to be slaughtered.

When we arrived in the stark white hospital room, my doctor's personal nurse met us. I put on a gown and lay down on the bed. I was shaking. I was terrified and felt so, so alone. Jimmy would know where I was when he got home, but I had no idea when that would be. While we knew a premature baby was a possibility, we thought we had much more time. "Honey, don't worry," she said, holding my hand. "I will stay with you until your husband comes. I will not leave you alone."

As I lay on the bed, I looked at the ceiling and felt as though I was out of my own body, yet the pain kept bringing me back. Why was I here? What was I thinking? I should have been out having fun. Why did I run away and marry my high school friend? Why didn't we wait? I had never imagined having a premature baby without anyone near me to hold my hand and to comfort me. I started yearning for the comforting hands of my mother. This was enough to destroy me mentally and psychologically, and when I think back on my first child's delivery, I sometimes have nightmares. I didn't realize what was happening. I didn't know the unknown. I also couldn't know that this trauma would remain with me for the rest of my life.

After many painful hours of yelling, screaming, and crying in the hospital room, Jimmy ran in. He was red-faced from the run. He came over and fell asleep next to me. I felt safe and secure, though I had no idea what was in store for my baby and me. At 3:30 a.m., the pain reached a new level, this time with more pressure than I had thought possible. I thought I had to use the bathroom, and as Jimmy carried me to the toilet, the midwife's nurse walked into the room.

She took one look and told me the baby's head was crowning. We rushed to the delivery room, and thirty minutes later, a three-and-a-half-pound baby was born.

I laid on the table, panting, sweating, and feeling so, so weak. But I just focused on the sound of the nurses rushing my baby to the incubator. "It's a beautiful, tiny, premature, little boy," the doctor said, sounding very far away though he was next to my bed. "He is strong but very small. Now we must focus on you." Turns out I was hemorrhaging and fighting for my life. It was the first battle Michael and I would face together. I was placed on close watch by doctors and nurses, while on the other side of the maternity ward, the doctors were trying to save Michael.

He was losing weight and becoming more fragile by the moment. He had jaundice and premature lungs that were not fully developed. When I was stable enough, they wheeled me to the newborn ICU to see him. One look at him, and I felt the physical and emotional sensation of falling in love for the first time. He was mine, and no one could take him away from me. Once I saw his face, I knew he was going to be fine. He was born to a strong mother, who was also born to a strong mother. Strength and perseverance were in his DNA.

After many weeks, I was finally able to bring my newborn baby home, where he was greeted with immeasurable amounts of love and at the same time with a lot of fear. I didn't know how to handle a five-pound baby. I was restless, anxious and frustrated. I had no idea what I was doing. I was exhausted. I slept holding the baby upright so he would not choke and I never actually went to sleep, as I was too afraid. All I could focus on was taking care of the baby, not myself. I was afraid of changing his diaper and his clothes, feeling as if I would break a bone. I would seize in terror when it was time to feed him; my absolute worst fear was that he would choke.

Back then, postpartum depression wasn't something we discussed. But every day, I was getting thinner and thinner. I truly could not stop crying. I desperately needed a shoulder to cry on. I had no one to lean on and no one's shoulders to cry on. I had no one to comfort me. I believe if I didn't love my son so much, I would not have survived this painful ordeal.

One day, I called my Aunt Georgia and described my feelings—the way I knew I should feel joyful, but I only felt sadness and fear. She understood; she had given birth to six girls. She advised me not to worry; she would come to help me. This went on for almost two months.

With her help and guidance, I became comfortable taking care of my newborn. My parents sent me an airline ticket, three gold coins and $1,000 to leave and go back to Greeece.

This was the first time I was going to see my parents since I disgraced them when I eloped with my husband. I sat on the airplane, racked with anxiety, sorrow, and fear. I didn't know how the encounter with my father would go. Was he going to forgive me? Was he going to love my child? Would he forget the past and start a new beginning? All of these questions tormented me throughout the fifteen-hour trip. Finally, I arrived home.

I exited the plane holding my tiny son, and immediately I saw my parents. They were standing by the door, the eagerness to see us almost radiating off of them. I burst into tears. I could feel my mom's joy as I fell in her arms like a little lost child, desperate to be loved and comforted by the woman who brought me into this world. Dad held and kissed the baby, but hardly looked at me. I was in tears as I took in my dad's firm and sturdy look. This was the man who worshiped me. I walked toward him and kissed his cheek, but I could feel a wall standing between us, and I didn't know how to tear it down.

That visit, I received all of the compassion, and support, and love I had needed from my beloved mom. I slept at night and rested during the day. I had time for myself while mom took care of the baby. I finally had a moment to take in my new son, and I was deeply in love. Michael was a little baby without much hair, lashes, or nails. He just wanted to be held and fed, and he loved to lie on the floor to play. Mom would sing to him, and he would laugh as if he understood the song. He was always awake. "He's not going to be an idiot," my dad would laugh, telling my mom. "He will be alert and a hard worker."

It's as though Dad predicted his future. Michael was always alert. He was observant of all his surroundings. Even as a young boy, he wanted to lead. When he was thirteen years old, he went looking for a job. Everyone who interviewed him thought he was much older, due to his height and language skills. When I asked him why he wanted to start work at a young age, he responded, "Mom, I know you and Dad give me allowance, but I like to make my own money."

The days and weeks of that first trip with Michael went quickly, and before we knew it, three months had passed. We were both leaving stronger than we were when we arrived. I was sad leaving my parents, and although there was friction with my dad, I felt safety and unconditional love from both of them.

When we returned home, I hired a babysitter to be able to work and support my husband while he finished his engineering degree. He graduated from the University of Illinois School of Engineering, after which he got a lucrative job working as an industrial engineer for Stewart-Warner, while

Bold Resilient Women

keeping his maître d' position at an upscale French restaurant in Chicago. For a moment, it felt like things were truly looking bright. Though we never stopped moving, we could finally see progress for the first time.

More Challenges

My life has taken me on a strange and unexpected voyage filled with many unseen curves. During my journey, I have had to deal with unforeseen obstacles and bumps, which made my stomach weak and anxious. Most of my choices were not made instantly or under pressure. They were thoughtful, made with caution and foresight.

Many nights, when I laid in bed, the house asleep around me, I stared at the ceiling feeling lost and betrayed. For a long time, my marriage was anything but romantic. I was a vulnerable, sensitive, young woman who was hurt with every comment my husband or his family would make. The only thing that brought me comfort was the tears, laughter, and unexpected adventures I had with my babies.

I lay there and wondered: *What is marriage? What is love?* My husband was going to school and to work, and I was constantly working to care for the kids and keep the house going. We were tired, exhausted, constantly working to accomplish our goals. We would meet like two strangers for a moment or two during the day.

One time, after we had paid school tuition, rent, and bills, I realized we only had enough money left for gas. I opened the refrigerator and empty shelves stared back at me. I started to cry in despair, wondering how I would possibly feed Michael. The only food available was *drahana*, which my mom had made in the village. *Drahana*, also known as barley, is a dried, cut-up pasta made from flour, milk, eggs, and sometimes yogurt.

I stood in the kitchen around midnight, trying to recall how my mom used to cook *drahana*. I put a pot of water on the stove, added a spoonful of olive oil and a pinch of salt. I fed my son *drahana* and gave him chamomile hand-picked from the village back in Greece, since there was no milk. The door opened, and Jimmy returned from work. Instead of coming in the door, he was ringing the doorbell repeatedly, and when I opened it, annoyed, I saw he was ecstatic. In his arms, he held numerous bags of groceries. He told me Lou Rawls had performed at the restaurant, and it was packed. Everyone was having such a great time that they were throwing extra tips at the staff. I couldn't believe it.

Our apartment was sparse. We were sleeping on the floor, having spent what we could on a crib for Michael, but the following day, we went and purchased a bedroom set as well as a living room and dining room set. These were the necessities in our home.

A wise, elderly woman, Mrs. Dee, would say, "Honey, if you have gone into your marriage to live a fairy tale life, you will fail. If you are realistic and know that six days you may cry and one day you may laugh, then you won't have false expectations." Mrs. Dee was strong and empathetic, and had lived a life of happiness and sorrow. She gave me the strength to not wish for unrealistic happiness. "Marriage is difficult," she continued. "You have to accept someone else in your life who was raised with a different background. It's like buying a dress when suddenly you realize it doesn't look that good. But while you can change the dress, you can't change your husband. So, you need to work to make it succeed."

I have always loved receiving advice on marriage and motherhood from women older than me. They have lived it, and they are not trying to sugarcoat the experience. They typically want younger women to know exactly how to navigate what they have experienced before.

My mother and grandmother used to say, "A man should only know his wife from the middle down, not from the waist up."

"What does that mean?" I asked.

"Never give your whole heart to anyone," they both explained. "Those closest to you will be the ones to betray and hurt you. Always hold your ace close to you as a last resort."

Grandma would often remind me that love is only a word, and while it's powerful, it could be used to justify bad behavior. Love can be used to engage in an affair, lead you into unknown situations, manipulate you to believing you only exist for him and he for you. Love can be possessive, a way of controlling an individual. A person who uses the word love to destroy a relationship is nothing but a user and abuser.

Agape, on the other hand, means you love someone as you love yourself.

Bold Resilient Women

You are not controlling anyone, but loving someone and working to meet their needs. *Agape* means two people becoming one. It's not the church or the wedding band that holds a person true to their promise, but the *eros*, *agape*, and *pathos*—the three types of love —that exist in a relationship.

"*Agape* is a powerful word that is misused by many individuals," my grandmother would tell me. She saw the world so clearly and delivered these messages to me at a young age. "Power, money, and greed have become the center of love. People nowadays connect to build a dynasty, not to build love and family. When you start thinking of what you gain in marrying someone, you have lost the essence of love. Think about how to build your home, then you will achieve true love and a successful life."

Second Pregnancy

A year later, I got pregnant with my second child, Vassiliki. From the moment my doctor told me she thought it was a little girl, I was in love. I was ecstatic. I was on cloud nine. I was going to have a little sister, a daughter, and someone to play with and dress up. I was thinking more like a child than a mother, yearning to buy a doll for my little girl. After being confined to my bed for months, facing many struggles and painful days, I went into early labor. I gave birth to a three-pound, premature baby, born at just seven months. It was a repeat of my first pregnancy.

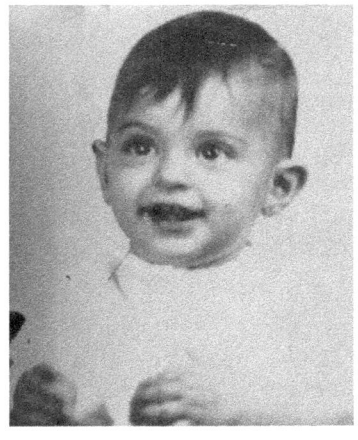

My daughter, Vassiliki's—Victoria's—birth had many complications. During delivery, her heart stopped, and my pulse and heart rate dropped drastically. All I remember are the voices of doctors and nurses speaking loudly and rushing around, and then suddenly, I heard the cry of a baby. I remember seeing her for only a second, as the intensive care maternity nurse rushed her out of the room, my baby hooked up to many wires from different machines.

I was too weak and ill to understand what was going on. I wanted my baby, and I didn't know where she was. The doctors were busy dealing with my hemorrhaging after birth. The next day, I was desperate to see my baby. I was terrified, consumed by a strange and curious feeling that I would never see her again. I remember screaming, and my mom holding me in her arms.

Mom kept reminding me that my little girl was a fighter. She came from strong women who fought for life. They were survivors; therefore, she, too, was a survivor. The nurses rolled me with a wheelchair to the ICU. I saw my little girl lying helpless, connected to numerous breathing tubes marked with an X, meaning critical.

I could not stop crying. How was this possible? After being confined to bed for seven months, with countless visits to the hospital, why was God challenging me this way? Why didn't he take her before I had laid eyes on her? I was terrified to hold her hand through the small, round window of the incubator tube. She was small and fragile. Her three-pound body was bare, without hair, and she didn't have eyelids, eyebrows, or nails, and hardly any skin covered her fragile body. She looked like a little mouse with large eyes and big, plump lips.

The doctors convinced my husband she had no chance, and he tried his best to prepare me for the worst. But there was no way. I was not going to accept this. I knew God wasn't going to take her from me. She was going to do incredible things for the world. My beloved Grandma, a dynamic and spiritual woman, brought the family priest to the hospital, where he baptized her. When the priest asked what her name would be, my grandmother said, "Vassiliki Irene Chrysovalantou."

During the christening, something magical happened: her little hands started to move and she was opening and closing her eyes.

"Didn't I tell you she was going to make it?" Father Vagia looked at me with a smile. "Someday, she will become a great woman and create many inspirational things." From that day forward, she started getting healthier and stronger.

After being in and out of the hospital for months, my little girl finally came home. It was such an emotional and incredible day. I couldn't sleep, I just kept looking at her and making sure she was breathing. I was trying to hold on to my job at the Millionaires' Club, trying to take care of my two babies, trying to balance a husband, trying to manage the house chores, and our home. I felt overwhelmed, but at the same time, I felt peaceful and content. Having overcome such significant challenges in my teenage years, I could handle anything that came my way. In my heart, I knew I had both of my grandmothers' and my mom's blessings. I had the protection from the Lord's angels and the grace and protection from our Lord and God.

Bold Resilient Women

As much as I tried, it was impossible to care for a sick child and a toddler while working, handling all household matters and taking care of my husband. I was becoming exhausted and weak. My parents wanted to help me. They suggested I send the kids to Greece. I had to make a very difficult decision. After weighing the pros and cons over and over, we decided to send my son Michael to Greece. My parents would care for him better than anyone; they loved him. My little brother was joyful; he would have company.

When it came time to send Michael to Greece, I felt like my heart was leaving my body. It was excruciating to part from my second love. But I had no choice. I wanted to give my children and family a better life, without poverty or suffering. As time went by, the distance from Michael took its toll. I didn't think I could handle this separation. Mom kept assuring me that he was happy, he never cried, and we were never missed. He was becoming familiar with his surroundings, and he had made friends with the children in the family who rented from my parents. My father's brothers and their spouses were entertaining my son every day. My mom told me of only one situation, where he got into a fight with another young boy when the boy grabbed his bike. My father was so infuriated, he threw Michael into his Mercedes and went to buy him a new BMW bike. Mom kept telling me, "Eleni, not even you could give him this much attention." I tried to breathe deeply. Michael was taken care of, and I could focus on my little baby girl.

I was determined to get Vassiliki healthy. My aunt helped me, holding my daughter while I did the cleaning, washing, ironing, cooking, and taking care of my husband and home. But while Vassiliki was getting stronger, she was still petite and fragile and didn't have an appetite. The doctors recommended we send her to Greece as well. They thought a better climate would help her weak lungs, and in Greece, she would be looked after twenty-four hours a day, seven days a week.

This suggestion was unfathomable. I couldn't believe I had to face the same devastating decision again. I discussed with my husband and parents the doctor's recommendation. My parents thought it was a great idea, but I just couldn't do it. I couldn't be separated from my daughter. But Vassiliki continued to be sick. She didn't eat or sleep. I didn't want her to leave my sight. I needed to be there to watch every bit of progress, but no matter what I did, she wouldn't gain weight. When she was a year and a half, she was only 17 pounds. Meanwhile, I had been to Greece three times to visit my son. Whenever I got there, he showed minimal interest in me, and every time I left, he was completely unbothered. This was beginning to impact me both physically and mentally. My son didn't see me as his mother. I knew that he didn't have the capacity to understand why he was there, and the difficult choice we had to make for our family's future. But it was absolute torture.

When Vassiliki was two years old, we decided to send her to Greece and bring Michael home. My parents didn't think this was a good idea. They wanted to hold both children. I expressed my gratitude for their immense support, but I could not bear to live without at least one of my children. I sobbed, unable to control my tears. I couldn't handle having to hand over both of the loves of my life. After my parents saw how distraught I was, they agreed. The following month, a relative of my mom's brought Michael home.

The adjustment was horrible. For starters, he didn't even want me to unpack his luggage, and he kept calling me ma'am, which was like a knife to the heart every time he said it.

"Ma'am," he would say in his high, bubbly voice. "I want to go home to my grandparents." I was trying to make him feel at home by explaining who I was and what his grandparents' role was in his life. After a couple of days, he began to feel comfortable, mostly because he loved playing with his little sister. He was not aware that this was temporary.

A few months later, I sent my beautiful baby girl to Greece with my husband's cousin. My parents waited at the airport to receive their little granddaughter. When they saw how tiny she was, they were heartbroken. It was very difficult for my parents to take care of the baby. She was a special little baby with many medical challenges and special needs, and she required a lot of attention and care.

Victoria received a lot of love from everyone. She was being chased around the *platea* by my younger brother, George, so they could feed her.

Michael had finally started adjusting to the States. Things were finally falling into place.

Kids are resilient, but I was still suffering from the choices we were forced to make. I was unable to leave Michael with anyone else —I didn't trust a soul. I would take him to work with me. The sergeant of the Glenview Fire Department and his wife were good customers at the Millionaires' Club and came in every day for lunch. Mary noticed I was always there, often with my son sleeping in the office or in the booth. She would bring him toys, candy, coloring books, and other gifts.

Thea Mary—which I called her out of respect—was an Irish woman with blue eyes and short hair, and Uncle Bob was a handsome, kind man who was respected by everyone. They always engaged with me, were never too busy to check in and ask me how I was doing. Thea Mary knew my struggles and commitment to my family.

"Eleni," she asked me one day. "Can I hold Michael for you while you are working?" I was in shock. It was the first time someone who wasn't related to me had offered to give me a helping hand.

Bob and Mary were compassionate people. As a fire sergeant, Bob had lost a young firefighter in a ferocious fire, and he was distraught every time he talked about the firefighter's young family. All he talked about for days was this horrible incident, and he and Mary visited the family daily, taking food and help with their needs.

Their kind and generous actions made me feel as though I had found a safe, special place for my son to spend time. Michael was already comfortable with them, and he would run, hug, and kiss them when he saw them. Thea Mary and Uncle Bob lived just a few blocks away from the restaurant where I was working as a membership director, so during my break between lunch and dinner, I would go to their house to visit him. He wasn't deprived of my presence. My son loved them, and they cared and attended to all his needs as though he were their own grandson. They didn't want Michael to feel lonely, so they purchased a little dog named Maki to be his companion and best friend. He was so happy. Thea Mary was a retired educator, so she was always buying him educational materials to help prepare Michael for kindergarten. He was very smart and advanced, identifying colors, letters, and knowing his name, address, and phone number. When he returned from Greece, he spoke very little English; within weeks, all he spoke was English.

"Children are like sponges. They absorb everything they hear and are taught," Thea Mary would say. "Teach them everything at a young age; they will never forget what they learn."

Uncle Bob and Thea Mary watched Michael until he started kindergarten. Once he was in school, I had to leave work to pick him up and then drive him back to work with me. This went on until I brought my little girl back. It was clear that we had to move to the city. It was impossible to continue working so many hours and running in between breaks to pick up the children.

One evening, Tom Jones was performing at the Millionaires' Club, and I was working the show and dinner. The room was completely sold out, and I was exhausted from talking and trying to sell as many memberships as I could. When I finally finished work at 1 a.m., I walked out into a dark, snowy blizzard. I picked Michael up from Bob and Thea Mary's, wrapped him cozily in the backseat, and headed home. As we were driving along Central, I noticed smoke curling up from underneath the hood, starting slowly and then gaining steam. I pulled over. It was pitch-black outside. Snow was falling, and the temperature was below zero. I was so afraid. The streets were empty and no one was driving by, so I pulled Michael out of the car, wrapped him in my winter coat, and started to walk for help.

Bold Resilient Women

There wasn't a person in sight. My hands and feet were getting frostbite, and all I could do was cry, and pray, and just keep walking until we found help. Tears ran down my face, and Michael would look at me and wipe them away, his small, soft hands cold on my face. "*Latria mou* Mommy. Don't cry. I love you," he would say, his words jumbled with a kid's pronunciation. I just kept putting one foot in front of the other, drawing strength from my child. Suddenly, a car pulled up next to us. An older man rolled down the window. "What in the world are you doing in the middle of nowhere in a snowstorm? Get in the car, and I can take you somewhere, please."

"No thank you, I'll walk," I said. My body felt stiff from the cold, but I wasn't going to get in a car with a strange man, especially with my child.

"Well, give me your phone number and I will call your husband," he said.

"No thank you," I said, focusing on holding Michael securely and stepping through the snow.

Suddenly, out of nowhere, I saw flashing lights. I thought I was delusional from the cold. I was ready to collapse when a policeman gently grabbed my arm and helped me into the car to take me to the station. When we got there, they covered me with blankets and gave me hot chocolate to warm up. They wanted to take me to the hospital, but I didn't want to worry Jimmy, so I asked them to take me home.

When Jimmy opened the door, he looked as though he had seen a ghost. The police explained what had happened, and Jimmy thanked them and ran a warm bath for me. With Michael now in bed, I finally took a breath and saw that my toes, feet, and fingers were blue.

Since that night, I often drive through that same area and remember how long I walked in the snowy, freezing night. I know deep in my heart God was with me. I should have died that night, and I consider this one of the many miracles I have seen in my life, which brought me closer to my faith and God.

Thea Mary, and Uncle Bob remained Michael's adopted grandparents, and we spent so much time together until they needed to attend to their daughters' needs. I am forever grateful for their endless love and support toward me and my son.

My father's sister-in-law came from Greece to visit my uncle and her sons, and at that very time, there was, coincidentally, an apartment for rent right above us. They moved in upstairs, which ended up being one of the biggest blessings in our lives. Thea was able to babysit and help pick up the kids from the school, which was down the street. It was a gift. "Someone above must be looking out for me," I would say to people with a laugh. "I think He is feeling sorry for me."

One summer on a visit to Greece, I was unpacking our suitcases and I begged Jimmy to go and glorify St. Irene while we were here. We needed to show our gratitude for saving our daughter.

"Absolutely not," he said. "I have been working so much and so hard. I am here to relax." But the next day, my mom asked him to change a lightbulb in the chandelier, so he grabbed a chair to reach the extra-tall ceilings. As he stood on the chair, he wobbled slightly, lost his balance, fell, and broke his wrist. He held his arm with a pained look on his face. "I think I need to go to the hospital," he said between clenched teeth.

We were on our way there when we bumped into my uncle. He told us about a holistic doctor who could fix Jimmy's arm, and so we went there instead. The doctor wrapped up Jimmy's wrist in a sling, and told us he would be fine—Jimmy just had to keep his wrist elevated and not use his hand for a week. "After that it will be brand new," the doctor told us.

As we drove home, I realized we were not far from the monastery of St. Irene. I had donated an icon to the monastery, and I thought it was magnificent. I wanted him to see it. The icon was marked in honor of the saint who saved my daughter, Vassiliki. But Jimmy wasn't into it.

"I just want to get home, Eleni. I'm in terrible pain," he said.

"Let's just stop and light a candle," I begged him. "Please, let's just stop for two minutes."

"I just want to go home," he said. "I need to rest." I relented, and my shoulders sagged in defeat. We drove north to the highway but encountered a detour, so we ended up on side roads. I looked out the window, watching the countryside go by.

After thirty minutes of a mostly quiet ride, we arrived at a dead end. In front of us was a large rock, and as we turned the car around, we saw what it said so clearly it could have been yelled to us: *"Welcome to the Monastery of St. Irene Chrysovalantou."*

I wanted to scream, and cry, and celebrate, and pray. What a miracle! St.

Bold Resilient Women

Irene brought my husband here whether he wanted to or not. She wanted him to pay his respects and honor her for saving our child's life.

This time was another sign that God exists. All we have to do is call His name, and He will be there to take care of us.

Adolescence

During my teenage years, my friends were grappling with the typical future decisions. Many were focused and working hard to be admitted into a top Ivy League school. Others were torn between their love lives and school, desperate to make the right choice between marrying the young man of their dreams or pursuing their education. Other friends were doing their best to find decent and secure jobs, while several of them were busy raising children and working hard to maintain a quality life for their family.

I, on the other hand, was consumed by proving to everyone I could handle being a wife and a mother of two young children. I was keeping a home going while working hard, which left me little or no time to think about myself in any way.

One day, my beloved friend, Debbie, stopped by our house. She sat at the table sipping coffee while I folded laundry. My children were napping, and I couldn't let this brief window of free time pass me by, even though my friend was here. It was too valuable.

"Eleni," she asked. She was kind and sweet and inquisitive. "What made you decide to get married at such a young age? Did you ever guess it would be so complicated?" Debbie's family owned the Greek theaters. She was always inviting me to see a newly released movie, since she knew I was on a tight budget. She never had to worry about money.

I was startled. I had never thought for one moment about my choices. Here I was, a wife and mother of two children at nineteen. I was such a capable individual, and I would let nothing and no one stop me from conquering the world. I was energized by doing everything. I may have been standing in a small kitchen folding laundry, but I wanted to make changes in other women's lives, leading by example. I may have been a child raising children, but I was learning from them every second.

I had never experienced—and I still haven't experienced—anything like being a mother. When my children cried, I wept in despair. When I punished them and they were breaking my heart, I would run to them and grab them in my arms and apologize. When they were joyful and succeeding, I would cheer and praise them. During the winter months, I looked forward most to rolling in the snow with them, making different snowmen using vegetables to emphasize their nose, mouth, eyes, and belly.

My kids loved to play baseball in the park near our house, so I would grab a bat and a ball, and we would play, and I would scream to them to run faster to the next base. On Saturday evenings, we went to the Glenview roller skating rink, and at the end of our time, they would fall on me, laughing as they declared me defeated. We started to go to Wisconsin to teach the kids to ski, and there was such excitement about who was the best.

As I played with them, though I felt joyful, there was a nagging loss inside of me. I felt deprived of my childhood. I never had the opportunity to do funny, joyful things when I was a young girl. I was too busy cooking, cleaning, babysitting my younger brothers, helping at my father's store, and studying. During the summer months, we didn't know what vacation meant—we were selling snow cones and hot dogs in the Chicago streets. Now, I was living a new role as a wife and mother. When I played games or did projects with my kids, while it gave me great satisfaction, I felt like a child who had missed out on doing crazy things.

On one trip to Wisconsin, we were going up the hill on the tow rope, and I lost sight of my little George. I turned around as best I could while trying to hang on to the rope, my head swiveling frantically, my stomach turning as I panicked. I released the rope, but I couldn't turn around. I was skiing down the hill backward! Suddenly, I heard a familiar sound. "You can do it, Mom!" My children were at the bottom of the hill, cheering me on. "Come this way! Land by us and not in the pond!" I made it to them and saw that there was fear in their eyes, but they greeted me with hugs and excited yells. "You did it!"

Playing with the kids daily gave me the opportunity to enjoy the simple things, which I had been deprived of in my life. Friday evening was pizza night after a basketball game or other sports event that they were involved in during that season. Afterward, we would go to Bakers Square in Niles or Skokie for pie à la mode with all their friends and parents.

Sundays were dedicated to God. I never missed one Sunday with the kids at church. Although you would think they would want to sleep in on a Sunday morning, they would all be ready and willing to go to church.

Of course, the fighting would begin when Michael wasn't attending to the altar and didn't go to Sunday school. He would fight with Victoria and pull her hair.

Meanwhile, Evangelo would pinch Georgie, who was the baby, as he thought I had stopped loving him and gave all of my attention to the baby. By the time I would separate everyone, there were friends and fellow parents coming to my rescue. I must admit, I had admirers at all the churches we attended. When the ushers saw us, they would say, "Here comes Eleni with her entourage!" I still don't know to this day if that was an insult, a compliment, or if they felt sorry for me.

Jimmy and I were poor and struggling, but we did what we could to create memories for our children. One year, we decided to take the kids to the West Coast. We could not afford the airplane, so we decided to take a road trip. The expensive hotels were outrageously priced, so we stayed at low-cost motels—Motel 6 was our favorite. It was clean, kid-friendly, and had free food for kids throughout the day. But most importantly, it was affordable.

All of the joys and challenges with my children made me realize I had a lot of growing up to do, since I had made the choice to be a wife and mother so young. I wanted to create a life for myself and my kids that allowed us to experience everything life had to offer.

Losing Control of My Life

Finally, we had stability. My two children, Michael and Victoria, were healthy. We were, after so many challenges, finally a happy family. I continued to balance children, marriage, work, and philanthropy. Despite all of the challenges of childbirth, not once did I regret having my children. I loved them more than my life. We played, laughed, and cried together. Every time I punished them, my heart shattered. We purchased my in-laws' little house because they wanted to live in Greece. We were finally becoming financially secure, but everything was closely budgeted.

The kids helped me paint the house, put in floor tiles, add wallpaper, and put mirror tiles around for the house to look bigger. After we had a hard-working day, we played baseball and basketball together to alleviate my stress and to let the kids enjoy the outdoors. Life was peaceful and smooth—finally.

One morning, I woke up extremely early to say goodbye to my husband before he went to work. It was something I always did, but this morning, when I tried to get out of bed, I felt dizzy and disoriented. I stood up and noticed I could not balance my body. I couldn't see in front either—everything was a blur. I felt the world close around me, and the next thing I remember, I was lying on the bed with my husband standing over me.

"Eleni, what happened? What did you feel? What's wrong?" he asked. His voice was panicked and alarmed. He was kneeling down to look at my face.

"I don't know," I said, holding my forehead. "I just wanted to say goodbye and to wish you a blessed day."

Jimmy didn't want to leave me alone, but I assured him I was already feeling better. I knew he couldn't miss the day at work, so I summoned all of my strength to walk with him to the door, holding onto his arm. I closed the door behind him, waved goodbye from the window, and sat down on the couch immediately.

I lied. I wasn't okay. Something strange was happening to me. I could feel my feet shaking and my body having spasms.

Both kids were still asleep, and I was desperate to wake them up and hold them tight. I was terrified. Different scenarios crossed my mind—if something happened to me, what would happen to my children? I felt grief and loneliness. I went to get up and fell again, convincing myself there was nothing wrong with me. *It's just stress,* I thought to myself. *I'm just exhausted.*

My mind was playing tricks on me. I thought I had tripped over a pair of shoes my husband had discarded on the floor, but nothing was there. Feeling disoriented and short of breath, I yelled for Michael to run to the phone and call my husband's aunt, Katina, to come take care of me. She came over immediately and stayed until Jimmy returned.

When he came home, I told him I was still not feeling well, but that I was sure it was because I wasn't getting enough sleep. "I'll be okay, I'm just tired," I assured him.

Meanwhile, we sold the house to go and live in Chicago near my aunt, her family, and my grandmother to take care of me. We rented in the same building where my dad's family lived. We didn't have much furniture; my brothers, cousins, and aunts furnished the apartment without my assistance. That first night, I couldn't sleep. I tossed and turned, and I was restless.

Something wasn't right. When I woke up early in the morning after finally dozing, I felt like my life was slipping away. I could not control my body. I called my mom in Greece and explained what was going on.

Without hesitation, she called her mom, my beloved grandmother Eleni, and told her to stay with me until she could get there. A few days later, my mom arrived from Greece.

My mom couldn't hide her worry. She was traumatized, and didn't know what was happening to her little girl. I kept going into shock, having seizures, then going into a deep, coma-like sleep for hours. I was hospitalized for many days at a time. Doctors were speculating that it was a rare illness that could not be detected. My husband and siblings were devastated. They could not bear seeing me in this condition. My husband didn't have an interest in being left a widower with two children at twenty-five years old.

During one stay at Grant Hospital, I slipped into a coma, and the doctors made a terrifying announcement to my family that I was going to die. They could not stop the bleeding. My body wasn't reacting to any treatments.

Instead of becoming better, I was rejecting all medication. My family was angry and in denial of my condition. They could not fathom that I could possibly be confined to a wheelchair, unable to come home healthy and take care of my small family.

While they sat for hours in the hospital waiting area, Jimmy told my family of the hopes he had for our future together as a family. Days seemed like years, and his aspirations of building a beautiful and fulfilling life together were diminished. "I feel betrayed by God," he told them.

He was consumed with anger and pain. He had dreamed of giving us a fairy tale life. Now, he felt like his dreams were collapsing. He would never experience life with me by his side. After many weeks of staying in the hospital, my mom proposed taking me to Greece. She argued it was the only way my husband could concentrate on his work. He wanted to work day and night endlessly. It was the only way he could cope.

We fought about the trip. He didn't want to let us go without having a prognosis from the doctors. Regretfully, the doctors had reached a roadblock. They could not figure out what was happening to my body. My mom was telling everyone, "I will heal my daughter from this cruel condition. I will travel to the ends of the world until I heal her. These two kids and I need her. She is a fighter, and she isn't going to give up until her last breath."

The longer I lay in the hospital, the longer I was deprived of my family and friends. I expressed a million times how disappointed and angry I was while watching my siblings, family, and friends laughing and sharing quality time with others, while I lay there, sick and alone. My parents felt guilty. I could hear them whisper to each other, "It should be us, not our beautiful and young daughter. She should be enjoying life and her babies." They felt helpless watching me alone in bed and not knowing the outcome.

While I was in the hospital, Jimmy had many lonely nights to think of our life together. He wondered how life would have been if we didn't focus so hard on work, and instead we did take those long trips with our kids to laugh, play, and cry together. He was so busy trying to achieve success, he never thought once about what could happen if one of us passed away.

Lightning struck, and he finally comprehended what was happening in front of his eyes. He couldn't lose me after we had overcome all the obstacles that stood in our way. Our life was based on hard work in order to achieve success. We did not depend on anyone.

After months in and out of hospitals, we decided the kids and I should leave with Mom for Greece. My father, meanwhile, had returned to Greece. He had a demanding construction company that needed him. He told Mom to stay next to me as long as she had to. To help me overcome the disease that was consuming my body. The doctors thought it would be a good idea to change the environment and scenery. I wondered if maybe the turmoil and the distance between my dad and me were contributing to my illness.

The day we departed for Greece was one of the most painful days of my life. I was torn to pieces. My husband, family, and friends had a difficult time saying goodbye. Jimmy couldn't speak, as he held back his tears. My childhood friend, Pam, gave the kids candy and bunnies for the trip. She thought she wasn't going to see us again. She was heartbroken, not understanding why I had lost so much weight and why the doctors could not identify my illness. I felt in my heart that I was never going to see any of them again. There were so many tears. Laughter and happiness were at a standstill. Sadness, grief, and anger had consumed the world around me.

The entire trip to Greece seemed like a lifetime journey across the Atlantic, although it was a one-day trip. My life was like a frightening dream. I was born, went to school, had wonderful friends, got married, had kids, and now the end was nearing. My life was winding down so quickly in front of my eyes, everything suddenly vanishing without a warning.

We stayed for seven extremely challenging months. It was painful for everyone: my parents, my little children, my family, and friends. No one could understand what was happening. I was losing weight, and I could not walk, eat, or function. My life was consumed by daily doctor's visits, experimental medications, a lot of holistic medicines, and priests praying over me. My dad was a contractor who had built many churches, and he was loved by the community and the clergy. Many spiritual fathers prayed across the country and the world for my health. I felt the power and love of God and the spiritual prayers of thousands across the world. I was learning the meaning of real love and how to live every moment without worrying about what the future holds.

My parents and my spiritual fathers were the pillars of my recovery. I felt their support guiding me toward a new life. Through the power of prayer and the glory of God, slowly I started to regain my strength. My doctors could not understand what was happening, but I knew that my deep faith in God had saved me.

Mr. Livaditis was the chief of the special intelligence of Greece, and also a dear friend of my parents. He and his wife, Areti, didn't have children of their own; therefore, they considered me their child. When they heard my parents had brought me to Greece very ill, they came to visit and were stunned to see a skeleton lying in bed. They could not believe what they were witnessing, that a young, vibrant woman who used to be so full of life was now lying hopeless. My dad explained everything to Mr. Livaditis, and he could not believe what he was hearing.

Bold Resilient Women

That evening, he called my dad to tell him about a spiritual man who performed many miracles. He wanted to take me the following day to see him and to pray for me. My mom and dad agreed, though they had planned to take me first to Northern Greece on the Bulgarian border to visit another spiritual man.

My mom and dad had learned that a monk at the border of Albania was healing many sick people. They carried me down the stairs with help from my dad's employees, and we drove many hours to reach his monastery. He prayed for me, and we headed back home the following day. I didn't want to be away from the kids for even one minute. I didn't know how long I had to enjoy them.

My parents did everything in their power to heal and make me well. They had physicians watching over me around the clock. They had spiritual fathers praying day and night. They had monks and nuns praying at the same time.

Every day was a struggle. The stabbing, sharp pains in my body were getting worse, but the most devastating part was that I was not able to get down from the bed and hug my children. My dad called Mr. Livaditis and agreed to take me to the spiritual man who was living in the old city of Athens, below the Acropolis. His name was Mr. Lamar, the police chief, and he said they used him to solve many unsolved cases.

Here we go again, I thought. Yet another person praying for me. But I could not disappoint my parents. They were up day and night attending to all my needs. They did everything, following every direction from the doctors and physical therapists. My parents didn't see anything or anyone besides their dying child.

My parents and Mr. Livaditis carried me down the stairs and into his car. "Where are we going?" I asked weakly, as they lifted me into the car.

"A spiritual man who will heal you," Mom said affectionately. I wanted to tell her that I was done, that I didn't want to keep doing this anymore, no one would be able to heal me. But I didn't want to hurt her.

Finally, we pulled up and a handsome, elderly man and a tall, blonde, gorgeous woman came out to greet us. They carried me out of the elevator and before I walked into his home, he stopped. He told me to take a breath. I was terrified. Who was this man? What did he know about my condition? Who told him what was happening? Was he aware how long I had been sick?

When we entered the house, he looked at me. "Why are you afraid of me?" he asked.

"I believe in God, not witches!" I said.

"Who told you I was a witch man?"

"My sixth sense. I am very scared."

A radiant smile spread across his face. "I would be afraid, too, if I were you."

My parents laid me on the sofa. Mrs. Livaditis held my hand, while Mr. Livaditis stood by anxiously, waiting to see what was next. My exhausted parents kept crying and praying.

"Eleni, are you close to a dead person?" Mr. Lamar asked.

I was horrified, but answered immediately. "My paternal grandmother, who I remember very vividly."

"Well, let's invite her to tell us what's wrong with you and what's going to happen."

I began to shake, wondering what was going on. I kept wondering if I was dreaming. *Do dead people speak? Was this man playing a joke on me and mocking my parents' pain?*

Mr. Lamar prayed for fifteen minutes. "She's here," he said. The Bible, which was on the cocktail table in front of me, was moving left and right. He closed his eyes and went into a deep sleep. All we could hear was him asking her questions, and when she responded, we could hear him say, "Yes, thank you." For a couple of hours, we witnessed something that will remain with me until my last breath.

When he woke up, he opened his eyes slowly. He told me my entire life, what would happen to me, what my future held, how many kids I would have, and what amazing things I would do for the world.

With every prediction he made, I was getting more and more agitated. I wanted to scream, "Can't you see, I am dying! You are giving me false hope!" I asked my parents and Mr. and Mrs. Livaditis to help me leave. I could not hear any more lies.

As we were departing, my dad asked to pay him for his prayers and mental support. "I don't want your money, Mr. Palivos," he said. "All I want is for your daughter to live. She will do great things for the world. You cannot imagine what I saw. She is an angel in this world." Though I was still frustrated, his words gave me comfort. All this time, I thought he was playing with my suffering and my parents' pain. "I will call Taki tomorrow, and you are to follow my instructions if you want your child to live."

That night, my parents didn't sleep at all. They were restless and kept asking each other, "Who was this man?" and "Why was he so confident I would be healed?"

The next morning, Mr. Livaditis came to the house. He had received a call from this man with many instructions. My parents were ready for the fight of their lives.

Mr. Lamar instructed them to open three churches at five in the morning, all at the same time. My parents sent three uncles to three different churches to open them and do a special prayer at the same time. He instructed them to buy twelve new handkerchiefs, tie them into a knot, and throw them into twelve crossroads on twelve different days at midnight. He told them they had to make sure they said the following: "I tie my daughter Eleni's illness, and those who pick up and untie the handkerchief will untie my daughter's illness to heal her." This went on for twelve evenings without my wonderful parents ever complaining.

Finally, he instructed my mom to go to an isolated mountain and start burning my clothes for three days, starting with my underclothes and then my outerwear. While this was all taking place, Mr. Lamar continued praying all night.

After almost two years of being severely ill, a miracle was about to take place. Unbeknownst to me, my parents, and my relatives, and friends, some power was healing me. Was it the numerous global prayers of many servants of God? Was it God's hand showing me His power as our savior, so I would never lose faith and hope? I will never know.

All I know is that I started getting better and feeling stronger day by day until finally, I was not having seizures or going into a coma. The doctors kept visiting and could not understand what had happened. Out of respect, my parents' friends who were involved didn't share with anyone what had transpired.

A few weeks later, I could get out of bed by myself and, most importantly, I could hug and kiss my children. My dad invited Mr. Lamar and his wife over for dinner so they could witness firsthand the miracle they had helped perform. When they walked in the house, they saw me standing behind the door. He did the sign of the cross and said, "God bless, for truly this is a remarkable miracle He performed."

I saw Mr. Lamar one more time before he passed away, just two months later. His assistant called my dad to inform us of the funeral arrangements.

Again, my mind kept wandering, asking myself who was this holy man? Why did he pass away after he healed me? What did he mean when he said that after I am healed, I will accomplish great things for the world?

I can only guess what he saw and knew about me. I had to be patient. I was eventually going to find out what the future had in store for me. But I'll never forget the miracle that I didn't only see, but I felt completely from my inside out. I also wonder if the distance from my dad and other family issues contributed to my illness. It definitely didn't help.

Reunited as a Changed Woman

In September 1980, I experienced one of the happiest days of my life. I got on the airplane in Greece to head back home to the States to pursue my family life. After a difficult year, we would finally be reunited with Jimmy. I was leaving behind my endless tears, poor health, and sorrow. I was on the way to finish what I had started, and nothing and no one would stand in my way.

When I got off the plane with the kids, Jimmy's eyes nearly fell out of his head. He could not believe what his eyes were seeing. I was alive and walking. I stared at him in shock, too. The person who was once a dark-haired, handsome wrestler and weightlifter now looked like a fragile man, complete with an all white head of hair. He had aged so much in a year.

Jimmy could not comprehend what happened. He thought everyone was lying about my recovery. Even if he didn't have faith or didn't believe in God or something bigger than us, he knew he was witnessing a miracle.

My entire family was grateful for what God had bestowed upon me. But I knew that I had no choice. I had to fight to live for my children, my family, my friends, and my beloved philanthropic projects. I learned a lesson: Never give up without a fight. When you believe you can do anything, you must give the fight of your life and win.

Although I had enormous faith, from that moment especially, I never stopped praying. I made a pact of faith and commitment to stand by every individual who needed my help and assistance. I knew I was empowered by a higher being as well as the woman who loved me unconditionally, my beautiful mom. She had embraced, loved, and taken care of me, nurturing me like a baby. From that day forward, I learned to cherish every moment without hesitation or regret. Life was not about making choices, but about navigating unpredictable, unbearable situations that come your way without any warning. I changed the way I lived my life after this. My illness set my life on a new course. When I returned to Chicago, I had transformed into a new woman. I had a strong desire to evolve as a mother and wife. I didn't want to be a yes woman or a follower. I started to believe in myself and my inner strength. Facing death in my early twenties was a nightmare, and it humbled me into understanding whether or not I was prepared to face future obstacles. I was confronted in very harsh and hard ways. I had overcome bed confinement. I had to suffer through not being able to hug or kiss my children. I had conquered grief and suffering.

With a new vision for my life, I started to focus on making a difference for abuse victims; for individuals who had no identity or voice; and for the old, ill, vulnerable, and destitute in society.

Day by day, I was becoming stronger and more confident in my ability to persevere in all my goals. I felt deeply that I could—and would—change the world. The love and empathy I felt from my family, friends, and everyone around me gave me the confidence to be sensitive to people's needs.

I knew I was challenged for a reason, and that reason was crystal clear to me: I needed to know my own pain and suffering so I could understand others' pain and suffering. I had overcome this terrible ordeal to help and support others in our society. I wanted to foster equality and peace among everyone. Before my illness, I tormented myself through sleepless nights, struggling to change my beliefs and attitude. But after it, I felt different. I learned to never contradict or question my abilities, gifts, and perseverance.

Alexander the Great said, "I owe my life to my mother but my knowledge to my teacher, Aristotle."

To me, this saying means that you can see how knowledge and power work hand in hand. The love, affection, shelter, and protection you have from your mother are the foundation that builds your character and self-esteem, while your knowledge comes from everyone and everything around you.

Bold Resilient Women

As it often happens, as time passed, Jimmy and I gained more distance from our challenges and suffering, and slowly forgot them. We became immune to barriers. We fell into the entrapment again of wanting to achieve the unachievable. We wanted everything, and slowly, we became desensitized to time and days.

My Third Child, a New Beginning

Coming home after my illness and my extended time in Greece was very difficult and strange. My family and friends, especially my childhood friends, Pam and Maria, could not believe what they were witnessing. I was alive.

Although Pam is a strong-headed individual, she has a caring and affectionate heart. She was thrilled I had recovered. When I was leaving for Greece, she had fallen into my arms weeping, not knowing if she would see me again.

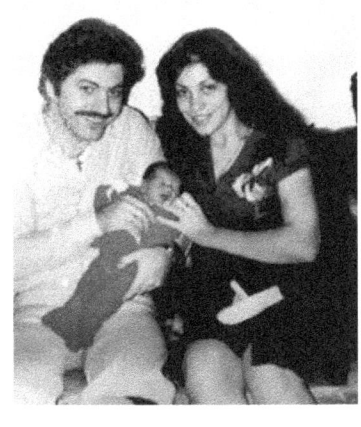

A few months after I returned, I had an amazing dream. In it, St. Nektarios, the doctor and healer, was walking on an unknown street with two women standing on each side of him, holding a beautiful baby with curly hair and big green eyes. In the dream, I asked if I could see this beautiful baby boy.

"Take Evangelo," he said. "He is yours to keep." When I woke up, I felt a powerful feeling inside me, and I knew I was pregnant.

I knew I was going to be challenged again, no matter how many pregnancies I had. I knew it was going to be difficult. I had been a rare and unique child, and now, as a woman, I was still rare—born with a tipped uterus, which is very uncommon. I was high-risk, but I had made a few promises to God, asking Him to heal me. I was determined to carry this child to honor Him, no matter how difficult it would be.

The challenges and struggles were the same. I was constantly in and out of the hospital. I was injected with 165 shots throughout the pregnancy to be able to carry the baby. But I was not angry or disappointed. I was happy and filled with so much love and confidence.

Every morning and night, I would say to God, "Give me my health, Lord, by allowing me to be pregnant, though I realize I will go through the same struggles and pains."

I could feel His power. He had listened to my cries.

After eight agonizing months, a premature baby boy came into this world. He was captivating; he looked like an angel. But then I noticed his head was slightly deformed—it was too long, and bright red. My husband and brothers were shocked, wondering why his head was so strangely shaped. The doctor reassured them that the baby would be fine in a couple of days. He explained that my body was pressuring my uterus to abort the baby, while on the other side, the doctors were trying to stop the contractions with medication. This is why he had a long, red head, due to the pressure of the uterus.

When Evangelo was born, everyone cried tears of happiness. By this time, my siblings and cousins had all learned the back doors and hallways to enter the hospital to visit me. Fear and anguish had consumed them as they prayed that I would be okay. But when they came in, they saw a baby with big blue eyes, and I was sitting up in bed, feeling good, and they were thrilled.

They only made comments about the size of the baby's head. It was the turning point of my life.

I had fully recovered from my illness. I was finally happy after many years of an unknown journey.

My grandmother and parents visited us at the hospital. Grandmother, being the midwife in the village when she was young, told us, "When babies

Bold Resilient Women

were born with heads like his, we would wrap their heads for a couple of days to form the right shape." She suggested telling the doctors to do the same. We thought she was joking, but she kept insisting.

My mother was furious. "Mom, here we were praying the baby and my daughter survive, and you're saying selfish village things." While Grandma was making her statements, all the men in my house were cracking up. They were laughing hysterically while Grandma was getting upset. She assumed we thought she wanted to hurt the baby. Looking back, Grandma would never make a statement to upset or hurt me. She just knew how they used to do things.

As promised, the baby's head became round and beautiful and the redness decreased as the days went by. Evangelo had the most beautiful features. Everyone would just stop and stare at him. I would too. I couldn't believe he was here, he was mine, and I was healthy enough to care for him.

An Exceptional, Beautiful Child

Evangelo was almost too angelic to be a little boy. There was something different and unique about him. As he started getting older, I could see how obsessed he was with dolls, fashion, makeup, and clothing. Deep down in my heart, I felt something was different. He was so loving, affectionate, and sensitive. He was a very special little boy who wouldn't leave my side for even one minute.

Evangelo loved acting, and when he was only three years old, his Greek school gave him a large part to play in *The Dowry of a Marriage*. It was a funny comedy: Evangelo played the groom, and asked the father, whose daughter was a little overweight, to give him more property. But the only thing he had to give to the groom was more animals, so the father offered him a pig, which was pregnant. Evangelo fully embodied the part, but he couldn't pronounce "pregnant pig" in Greek. Instead of *gourouna gastromeni*, he kept saying, "I give you *goulouna gatomeni!*" People were cracking up. The entire theater was packed. From there, he landed major roles in all the plays.

Evangelo spiced up our lives every day with his acting, modeling, and charismatic charm. He was born to be on stage and in Hollywood. Agencies started recruiting him for campaigns and projects, but I was too scared and frightened to let him participate. I was afraid he was too beautiful and sweet. I saw the way people were stunned by his vibrant looks. I decided I wasn't going to let him participate in television commercials. I didn't want an acting career for him at this young age—I wanted it to be his choice when he was older.

As he was growing up, I used to walk away from after-school activities or programs and hear people gossiping about his gender. I never paid attention. I hated gossip, and I didn't have time to sit and listen. I used to say to my friends, "When a woman doesn't work or doesn't have ambition, then she has time to spare for gossip."

People always talked about who was sleeping with whom, who was getting a divorce, who had a child addicted to different substances, and who had a gay child. They didn't care to focus on their own family issues. Instead, they wondered if my beautiful boy was gay.

As his mother, in my gut, I knew that my little angel was gay. As I looked deep into his huge blue-green eyes, I could see his innocence. I cried myself to sleep many nights thinking about how he would be treated by a rude and polarized society. It tore me to pieces. I kept thinking about his teenage and adult life. Were people going to be cruel or accepting? Were his siblings going to see him as one of them, or mark him as an outsider? Was his father, a man rough around the edges, going to accept and love him? Was he going to tolerate a gay child, or would he be worried about what his family and society would say? These and many other questions kept me up many nights, wondering about his future. But I knew God had chosen me because I was going to love and protect him. No one was ever going to harm him.

Evangelo never once complained about kids bullying him and calling him names. He was confident in his skin. He didn't care what people thought of him. He was more interested in his career in acting and modeling. He wanted to attend school in Paris, where he had many offers to model, and I knew that deep down, he wanted a new start. I believe it was very difficult for him to admit that he was gay. I didn't want my son getting hurt by anyone's cruel comments. At the same time, I couldn't share my fears with anyone—especially my husband and parents, who were old-school in their beliefs. I felt for him. It must have been awkward for him to identify what he felt and be open about his sexuality.

After he had been in Paris for several months, I went to Greece to visit family. I could not explain to anyone the pain I carried in my heart. One evening, there was an odd conversation about sexuality and gays. Hearing so much negativity from my own personal family members broke me to pieces. That evening, I could not sleep. I got up and went to the deck of our home to have a talk with God. I didn't know how to handle this challenge in my life and my son's life. I was seeking knowledge and strength. I knew I would have to be up for a fight.

As I stood on the deck, looking up at the sky, I heard someone come up behind me.

"Eleni mou, are you OK?" It was my father. Their bedroom faced the deck, and when Mom saw me weeping and wiping my tears, she woke my dad up and told him, "*Vagelaki mou*, go to our daughter, she needs you."

I fell into his arms, and he held me like I was a little girl who needed to be comforted. "My love, I want you to love your *Vagelaki* more than your other children," he said. "He will need you to support and protect him."

"How did you know?" I said through tears. I was stunned. How long had he suspected it? Why didn't he ever say anything?

"Let everyone talk," he said. "They should look at their despicable home lives rather than judge others." Just then, I remembered one of his favorite sayings. "It's easier for those watching the steps of a performer to judge, but those who dance, act, and perform know the difficulties they face in memorizing everything."

That evening was a turning point in my life. If I had gotten my dad's approval to defend and protect my son, I should not fear anything or anyone.

I was never a judgmental individual. I loved people for who they were and the good deeds they performed for others—not their sexual preference. It was always clear to me that individual views and opinions about people's sexuality weren't anyone else's business. Although society was becoming more inclusive and accepting, some people still stigmatized those they viewed as "different."

I could not (and still cannot) understand why people spoke with so much hate. Why they proclaimed gay people as evil and abnormal. They thought they lived in sin and had to be ostracized from society. This infuriated me. After all, what was "ethical and normal"? Many individuals making these statements would abuse their wives and children. They were individuals who didn't care about anyone's feelings. They could abuse, insult, antagonize, and humiliate others without feeling any kind of remorse.

How dare they judge and condemn gay people to isolation?

I started to research and work with many young people who were gay. I wanted to know how they felt and what kind of challenges they were facing daily. I learned so many lessons from so many kind and loving kids. I heard countless horror stories of young kids being physically and mentally abused by their friends, parents, and family members.

But the trauma went even deeper. Many of those children were traumatized by their parents, who told them they were a disgrace and disappointment to the family. Parents were more focused on the criticism they thought they would hear from their friends and society. They could not fathom how their children's homosexuality would affect them and their lives, and they didn't have a clue about the suffering and torment their children faced in an unjust world of judgment and oppression. They never stopped to think about how their child was being treated in school, in sports, in activities, at work, or in any other setting.

When you love your child, you want to know and accept everything about them. But rather than live in a loving and safe environment, some children are forced to change their sexual preference or end up taking their own lives.

As protective mothers and parents, it's our job to keep a close eye on our children and their peers. We must make sure they have an interesting and diverse group of friends who are open-minded and not judgmental. Children should be free to express themselves without fear of getting bullied or hurt.

As loving parents, we must ask questions of our children. We must realize the signs of a child who is being harassed, threatened, or teased at school, work, or in their social circle. If a child is acting out of character, a parent should intervene by asking as many questions as needed to find out what's going on. It's essential to help stop your child from doing something harmful. The greatest gift we can give to our children is reassurance. It's our job to reassure them that their sexuality is accepted. That's when we see excitement and relief in a child's face as they feel acceptance. Many young men feel that they are gay—or at least that they are different from other boys—before entering kindergarten. They don't understand how to express their feelings. I believe they are overwhelmed with the sensations they feel. Looking back, I realize that there was agony on my son's face. I just didn't know what his feelings meant.

The gay children I met and worked with told me they felt anxious and scared in relating their feelings. They were nervous, not knowing whether they would be accepted or neglected. They worried they would be kicked out and have to live on the streets and fight for survival. This is inhumane to me. We must accept our children with love—it's the only way for them to overcome fear and suicidal thoughts or avoid harmful drugs.

Bold Resilient Women

As parents, we need to protect and defend our children by exposing them to safe environments, including secure and accepting schools that teach love and acceptance rather than condemnation. We must find support groups, organizations, friends, and family members who will accept them without passing judgment.

Hearing the stories of so many young gay people has made me aware of how dangerous it can be to come out. One of the most painful stories I heard was from a fourteen-year-old young man whose parents found out he was interested in boys and had no intentions of kissing a girl.

This young man was verbally and physically abused by his parents and siblings. When he had endured more than he could handle, he decided to quit school and leave home. He was forcefully thrown out of the house without any clothes on his back. He went to a shelter where adult men made passes at him, so he ran away and slept under the highway. This young man ended up prostituting for survival.

When I heard this heartbreaking story, I asked to help him get off the streets. I believe he was deeply in pain. He left our group, and I never saw him again. I kept driving by the places I knew he could be, but I didn't have any luck.

Bold Resilient Women

I have heard so many traumatic stories during my feedings of the homeless, poor, and neglected. In any situation, I go around asking people to tell me their stories.

"Why, Mrs. Leni? Why do you want to hear about our messed-up lives?" they ask.

"We all have a unique story," I responded. "There isn't anyone without a story to tell, or else we have never existed in this world."

But hearing these sorts of painful life stories from young teenagers hit my heart differently. It made me want to become a guardian angel to these abandoned children.

Hearing these heartbreaking stories made me even more protective of Evangelo. Several years ago, I made a vow that I would never allow anyone to hurt or antagonize my son. I wasn't interested in listening to anyone's opinion about someone's choice in a partner or the sexuality they were born with. Everyone is entitled to live with and love anyone their heart desires. Life can be hard, but when we can be ourselves—and when we are with someone who loves us unconditionally—it's more joyful, easier, and more bearable. Why would we ever deny another human this experience?

Another Change

When Evangelo was a baby, my husband got an offer to work overseas as an industrial engineer. We discussed it, and when he said he wanted to accept the challenge, we didn't think twice. We packed our three children and started a new life in Greece. I was delighted to again be near my parents and receive their unconditional love and support.

In Greece, my parents had built me a beautiful home for investment with a gorgeous penthouse apartment for our residence. It was well constructed, and above all, it was made with love and hard work. My parents and I furnished everything and set up the new place while Jimmy went back and forth for interview after interview.

Everything was looking good for us. After all the challenges we had faced, moving to a different country—one we were familiar with—seemed like the easiest thing in the world. But things didn't turn out as promised. The company that had recruited Jimmy kept dangling the job in front of us, making him endure interview after interview. Because the political arena was very different in Greece, they didn't care that Jimmy spoke four languages, nor that he had an engineering degree and an impressive resume. All they were asking him was, "What is your registered political party?" Anyone who knew my husband—or knows him now—would know he didn't participate in any political party. He believed in the power of individuals and their integrity, strength, abilities, and passions to make a difference for the citizens of the country.

This ordeal went on for eleven months. His former boss from the U.S.

Bold Resilient Women

visited us in Greece and asked Jimmy if he had accepted the job proposal from the Greek company. Jimmy told him how things had transpired since we arrived. He advised him to take his family and come back to the land of opportunity. He informed him not to worry about his job—his position was still open. He just wanted Jimmy to return to Chicago. The following evening, my husband was interviewing yet again with a high-ranking supervisor for the job at his potential company. A wise old man asked him what he thought the chances were that he would get the job that he was promised. He kept asking questions about his family, about the move, about life in the States, about the position he held in the U.S.

"What are you doing here?" he finally asked. "You are dragged every day for interview after interview. Aren't you tired of being misled? You will not get the job. There is another individual who has political connections, so he will get the offer. He's not qualified or experienced. He hasn't even finished college. But due to connections, he is on the list for recruitment." Jimmy came home furious. And so, eleven months after our transatlantic move, we returned to our beloved country, America. We started again from scratch. We knew about challenges, hard work, and perseverance. We were going to succeed because we believed everything was possible. We had learned the hard way, through the many challenges we had faced, that when you want something in life, you can achieve it through believing in God, yourself, and your work ethic.

Bold Resilient Women

When we returned, we stayed with my brothers, Peter and George, for a few weeks until we rented a home near a school, so our kids could walk back and forth and be near family and friends. Jimmy and I discussed the possibility of visiting the West Coast before we both started work full-time. We had never traveled beyond Chicago and didn't know how the rest of America looked. We decided overnight we were going to hit the road with our family and see the beauty and the culture of our amazing country. After the disappointment of Greece, I wonder if we still had a bit of adventure in us.

Traveling across the country was the journey we had yearned for. One night while the kids were asleep, we made a promise not to miss the simple, meaningful things in life that brought us together. We were inspired to explore the beauty and the change of seasons as we traveled from state to state. We traveled across the country for three weeks. We were a young family, singing, laughing, and joking during the days and at night, sleeping at Motel 6. We saw many fancy cars and hotels as we traveled through many towns and cities. But it didn't matter to us that we didn't have an expensive car or that we stayed in cheap motels. All that mattered was that we were together. What was important was that we were setting new dreams to always be exploring together as a family.

At night, when we slept at these small motels, all five of us crammed into two beds, Jimmy and I could feel in our guts that the stars were lining up for us. We felt that one day, we were going to gain success and stay at those beautiful places and buy those hot cars. We had faith in ourselves, and we didn't fear work. We loved life and lived as if it were our last day.

Strong Women Never Give Up

We bought a house with very limited funds. We had to mortgage the house to receive a secure loan. To make our monthly installments, we worked endless hours. I had three young children who needed structure in their daily lives. I wanted them to succeed in school and improve their academic skills. My children were independent readers, but like all children, they had a difficult time managing their time wisely. I was an advocate for education and a hands-on parent, actively involved in their schooling and homework, which they often needed help with.

I was working from home, helping my husband with all our finances, but I also became a full-time chauffeur, driving the kids to school, acting class, art programs, football, karate, Greek school, and other activities. But I never stopped dreaming of finishing what I had started.

Whenever I had a spare minute, I would bury my nose in a book. I was obsessed with education, especially trying to understand and indulge in psychology. I wanted to assess and observe people's behavior and actions by gaining knowledge and understanding of human behavior.

I was committed to my Orthodox Church. I attended and participated in many not-for-profit foundation boards. I became the woman and mother who was known for multitasking. My life wasn't about making choices. It was about perseverance and success. I had to advance during the course of my journey. I was never thinking about the following day or the challenges that might come my way. All I knew was that a fresh day was rising, and all I knew was that I had to wake up every day with a positive outlook if I was going to get through. "Every morning, stand and look at the sky," my mom would say. "Thank the Lord for waking you up and being able to witness and preserve His creation.

Be grateful for another day. As long as your head is above ground, you can achieve anything your heart desires."

She would continue. "Eleni, life is a journey with many obstacles, curves and different paths. The only thing which is irreparable is death. When you're six feet under, it's difficult to rekindle your wishes."

Different obstacles that crossed my path sometimes felt unbearable. I didn't want to endure them. I wanted things to change overnight. Sometimes, it felt like life was a bad nightmare, but realistically, I was on the same course every morning when I woke up. Only I could change my path. I had to be proactive in making wise decisions and changes.

Everyone wants an easy fix in life. No one wants to face misery and mistreatment. You want to close your eyes and pretend things are terrific, but suddenly you wake up and can't bear it. You are at a loss for how to go on. You either want to end your life or run away, but you can't. You just have to find your inner strength and put one foot in front of the other until eventually, you're moving again.

Everyone shuffles their feet when they lose all hope. It's difficult to keep your feet on the ground and maintain faith during the dark moments in your life. When anxiety and misfortune overcome our faith, many of us who have faced the darkest moments of our lives are lost.

Many times, I would be disappointed, wondering why things I had anticipated going a certain way shattered my heart and soul.

It was difficult to accept disappointment. Unexpected feelings were arousing me. It was as though someone powerful shoved me against a wall, knocking the wind out of me. All I could do was try to hold onto my faith and secure my inner world by praying for peace and serenity. As a strong, bold woman, I had to learn how to continue controlling and handling my life. As much as I loved controlling situations, I had to come to terms. I was only able to control how I would react to different and difficult situations.

As a capable and determined woman, I had to believe through my strong faith, after the dark times in my life, that I could find light. Strong individuals actively keep faith in their daily lives. And this is how I, and many of my friends, were able to survive. We learned not to give up, crumble, or let our pain and suffering challenge our spirit. Powerful women have to stand up to difficult challenges. It's the only way of becoming wiser, better, and stronger in your life. When you have faith in God—and your ability to persevere—your

Bold Resilient Women

life will flow more easily by ensuring toughness and success even in the toughest and most unpleasant circumstances. You will continue conquering despite obstacles and barriers. Just persevere and persist in your endeavors.

Fourth Pregnancy

After three miscarriages, Dr. Levine—a high-risk OB/GYN—warned me not to attempt another pregnancy. I took his words to heart, but with so many miscarriages, I never anticipated I was going to get pregnant. One evening, I was feeling under the weather. I fell asleep and had a dream filled with beautiful scenery, but alarming scenes. I saw a young soldier fighting in a war. He told me, "If you don't leave, you will get killed."

Terrified, I started to run, but I asked him who he was. He said, "My name is George." He warned me to leave this place immediately, as the war was spreading. He said, "I want to save you." I asked him again who he was, and the response was the same. "George." As I turned around to ask him more questions and to thank him, he vanished.

When I woke up, I couldn't shake the disturbing dream. Why was he warning me? Why was he insisting I leave this place of war? In the morning, I told my husband the dream. He guessed I was thinking too much about the miscarriages and all the changes my body was going through at the time. An overwhelming, strange feeling consumed me:

I knew I was pregnant, and in my heart, I believed I was going to give birth to my husband's twin brother, George.

Bold Resilient Women

When my husband and his twin were born, Dimitri (known by the nickname Jimmy) came first, and George was born just minutes later. Soon after, Dimitri fell ill with a severe cold and high fever that lasted for about a week. The family's attention shifted toward George, and Dimitri's condition worsened. Despite the doctor and village priest urging immediate baptism, the infection persisted. Dimitri eventually suffered a seizure, and tragically, he passed away.

What we later discovered was the family's hidden secret: they told relatives and friends that George had died, not Dimitri. To preserve the tradition of carrying the father's name, they switched the birth certificates, a grave sin in the Greek church. From that moment forward, George lived under the name Dimitri, or Jimmy.

I always felt that the true Dimitri longed to return, that he belonged in our family. This is why I dreamt of George so often. I believed that Dimitri's spirit needed to be born into our home. I knew it would come with sacrifice, pain, and suffering, but I also felt the protection of St. George the warrior. And as with all three of my previous pregnancies, the moment I knew, I immediately fell in love.

My pregnancy was going to be extremely difficult, and when I told him, Dr. Levine said he didn't want to be part of it. He knew I was going to face a difficult pregnancy, labor, and delivery. I started having a panic attack for fear of not having a high-risk doctor to care for me and my baby. I paid Dr. Levine a visit, and after I finished crying, I explained my dream. He was a religious Jewish doctor who said, "I believe in King David's dreams and therefore I believe in your dream." He agreed to take me again as his patient. He warned me that if this pregnancy came to full term, I had to agree not to attempt another pregnancy.

A couple of months into the pregnancy, I was having the same pregnancy issues. Severe pain, nausea, and bleeding had consumed my fragile body. In my third month, I called the doctor. I could not bear the severity of the cramps. He advised me to go to the hospital immediately. He said I was likely having a miscarriage or might have to abort the baby.

As I was sitting on my bed in excruciating pain, waiting for Jimmy to take me to the hospital, I saw a vision of the young soldier from my dream who warned me to leave the war and be saved. He walked into my room and stood behind my body, kissed me on the cheek, and held me tight in his arms. I felt the pain departing my weak body. I was becoming stronger, and my bleeding stopped.

Now that this vision came to me clearly, I saw he was not a young soldier but a handsome commander with many medals of honor on his shoulders and sleeves. As Jimmy went to help me up, I kept insisting a commander was in the room. He thought I was delusional from all the medication I was taking, or that the pain was making me speak nonsense.

Jimmy searched the entire house and there wasn't anyone there. He reached down to gently help me up.

"We aren't going anywhere," I said firmly. "I will get through this pregnancy no matter what."

I had so much faith in God. He gave me this child. There was a reason for this baby to be born in our home and life.

Calling the doctor was difficult, as he also believed I was hallucinating. But he agreed to wait and see the outcome of the bleeding.

Throughout the pregnancy, I was admitted to the hospital on a weekly basis. The pain, cramps, and bleeding were persistent. Finally, on April 19, 1987, as I checked into the hospital again, there was a new document in front of me. It was a waiver, saying that if something happened during birth, they would not be responsible. They waived liability. I had no choice but to sign it.

After three days of excruciating pain, my cervix was not expanding beyond six centimeters, so the doctor ordered my labor to be induced. My blood pressure was dropping. I was hallucinating, becoming very scared and sick. All I could do was pray. I could hear my beautiful mom praying and crying, begging St. George the warrior to save the lives of my baby and me. Suddenly, I felt like I was dying. I remember begging for someone to save my life. I remember my mom screaming. Everyone was rushing around as my baby boy was getting ready to come into this world.

Another miracle: my baby was born on the eve of his name day, April 22nd. He had arrived two months premature, weighing almost five pounds. He was hospitalized for two weeks. Finally, he came home, where he was showered with love by his three siblings, my parents, my grandmother, and my siblings.

Life in the Bousis home was chaotic. It was a small home with a newborn and three kids who were envious of the newborn. They thought I favored the new baby. Instead of calling him George, they called him Mom's Golden Child.

Of course, I never favored him, but he needed more attention, and it was impossible to spend a lot of time with each one of them separately. My husband was too busy focusing on his new business to see the needs of our big family. He was about to embark on a new business adventure, one that he was unfamiliar with. We didn't have a choice. We had to make things work.

We started to outgrow our house. We didn't have enough space or bedrooms to accommodate our growing family. We decided to purchase a property and to slowly build our new residence.

Bold Resilient Women

What's Missing

When we returned home from our trip out West, we broke our newly established rules about simplicity and savoring the moment. We were energized to work hard, create a unique family life, give our children an exceptional education, and achieve everything our hearts desired.

Occasionally, in the back of my mind, I could hear my dad's voice. "When someone tastes the sweetness in honey, they want more and more," he would say. "It's never going to be enough." We had not yet learned that everything is better in moderation, even though we had faced so many challenges.

Slowly, we fell into the trap of power, success, and money. We were following the routine of wanting the next big thing. From our small two-room apartment, we went to a ranch home with two small bedrooms. Two years later, we set our sights on a four-bedroom home with a basement where the kids could play and do their school projects. We were very social and hosted a lot of dinners and parties. We believed in teaching our children to connect and respect others.

Having kids, we had to factor in the education. Our oldest, Michael, was an exceptional football player and wanted to play for the Glenbrook North Spartans. I didn't want him to go to a public school since all my life I had attended Catholic school, so I signed him up at Notre Dame. But he wasn't happy. When I asked him what he wanted, he said, "I want to play for the Spartans."

So, we purchased an empty lot in the Spartan's school district, which was attached to the back of my beautiful friend, Yiota's house. "Nothing can obstruct the views from my house to yours," she said. "All we need to do is walk across the yard, and we can connect." She knew how much Jimmy worked, and since she hadn't had anyone to help with her three boys, she wanted to be there to help me with my kids. We finalized the property purchase and began building our lovely home. Our funds were limited, so we could not add the finer finishes, but we didn't care. We knew there would be a time when we would be able to afford to make the changes we wanted. What mattered most was that Michael was happy at his new school. He could reach the stars and pursue his dreams.

Our next step was to purchase a nice car. We didn't want to be driving used cars in the affluent neighborhood where we lived. We also wanted to keep supporting numerous foundations, establishing organizations, supporting churches, and feeding and taking care of the poor.

Although we were on a budget, we still found the means to give as much as possible to all things that mattered to us.

One day, I was caught in traffic coming home from Michael's game, so I called Yiota and asked her to go pick up George when the bus dropped him off. "Of course," she said.

She went to our house, but he was nowhere to be found. She walked around our two yards, went back to our house, and when I arrived, she was frantic.

"Hi, Yiota. Where is Georgie?" I asked. Her demeanor was freaking me out a bit, and I had a pit in my stomach.

"I cannot find him," she said. In the rear of the house was a private lake available to people in our area, and we ran down there, praying he hadn't drowned. We searched and yelled and cried, screaming his name so it echoed around the neighborhood. I was losing my mind. I was panicking. I was hyperventilating with fear as the world moved too quickly. Suddenly, I heard a familiar cry and looked up the street. There was George, crying, his small legs running toward me. I wanted to spank him, but I scooped him into my arms. All I could do was hug and cry with him.

"Mommy, I just wanted the bus driver to take me to Thea Yiota's for a cookie and Greek coffee with milk!" We all started to cry and laugh at the same time. Turns out, when she was at our house, Georgie had gotten dropped off. When he didn't find her, he walked back into the yard and then started to walk around the neighborhood.

I had nightmares for weeks.

My dad used to say, "Always be aware of fire, women, and water." When I asked my dad what this meant, he said, "Fire can spread faster than the blink of an eye and will destroy everything in its way. If a woman is not a good partner, her husband will never succeed, and her children will never learn responsibility and accountability. And water can pull you so fast that you can drown without realizing the depth and strength of the waves."

I have felt all of this throughout my life. We found George that day, and of course, it was all an accident. While we remained focused on success at that point, we also received constant reminders about what's important and how quickly life can change, even when you're paying attention.

Staying With My Baby

Three out of my four children had left the nest, but as George was the youngest, he was stuck at home with us. He kept asking me if I would have another baby to keep him company. I would tell him that I could not have another child. It would make me very ill, and I wanted to be with him and not in a hospital.

"I understand, Mommy," he said. "I just want it to be you and me."

I had to entertain him constantly. He was lonely without his siblings. Being the youngest of four, there was always a lot of activity, lots of yelling, doors banging, things being tossed, football and basketball players constantly coming in and out. Our home was alive. Then suddenly, everything was quiet.

George was very mature from a young age. He grew up fast by trying to mimic his siblings, pretending he was wiser and smarter. He never acted like a little boy. He acted more like a perfect gentleman. When other kids argued, he would be the mediator. We called him The Wise Old Man.

In one way, George felt abandoned by his older siblings. But on the other hand, he would say, "Mommy, we don't need anyone else. It's just you and me. We are buddies." He wanted to be around me every moment.

He had many interests. He loved buying and collecting Beanie Babies, collecting G.I. Joe soldiers, collecting baseball cards, breaking and rebuilding computers, and competing in video games. With his adult-like demeanor, I sometimes wondered if he was too intelligent and smart for his own good.

As a freshman in high school, George competed in video games and won constantly. I don't believe they knew his age; his fellow competitors thought he was a senior or a college student. One day, I received a phone call informing me that George was invited to Las Vegas to participate in a gaming competition. They were surprised by my silence as they kept informing me of the logistics and the competition rules. I was in a state of shock when they told me he qualified because he was sixteen. He was actually fourteen.

When I confronted him about the unexpected call, he said, "Mommy, you were too sick. I didn't want to bother you. I didn't think I was going to make it to the final competition. I hope you will allow me to participate. I really want to compete." I had a bone marrow procedure scheduled and could not sit on a flight, and I wasn't okay with sending him alone. But no matter how hard I tried to have him reconsider, he was insistent on participating.

Seeing his passion, and how much he wanted to attend, I called my godchild and asked if she was available to accompany him to the tournament. She responded, "Absolutely." I called the director of the tournament and explained the situation. She reassured me the kids would not leave the convention center unattended, that they would always be in the presence of adult coordinators. They assured me he would be safe and accompanied by chaperones. Hearing this, I felt confident to let him attend.

The day arrived, and George was so excited that he hardly got any sleep. Later that day, he called to tell me he had won second place! He came home with two suitcases' worth of computers and all sorts of gifts.

George was a competitor, but now he was focusing on everything but school. He went from being an excellent student to failing many of his subjects. I asked him how we were going to correct this problem, explaining that school should be his number one priority.

"Go to the library, think about our conversation, and give me a resolution," I told him. "How do you want to handle your falling grades?"

Later, as I was stirring a sauce on the stove, George came over to me. "Mommy, I know I need to focus on studying. And the only way to stop being distracted by video games is to go to a boarding school."

I was devastated, I knew this was it, he was leaving. Once he went to boarding school, he would go on to college and never return home again. I cried all night but didn't want him to see me sad. I didn't want him to change his mind on my account. I wanted him to pursue what was right for his future.

The following week, we began visiting different boarding schools. We had made an agreement that he wouldn't go any further than a few hours away from Chicago by car.

We had an appointment with St. John's Northwestern Military Academy in Delafield, Wisconsin. When we arrived, he immediately fell in love with the campus and the headmaster, a compassionate and caring man. After the headmaster outlined the rules and regulations of the school, I saw Georgie becoming agitated. He asked to speak to the headmaster in private. I wasn't aware of what he wanted to say.

George was distraught when he learned he could not speak to me during the first month of school. It was a rule for everyone, as students needed to affiliate themselves with the school, students, and the different codes of conduct. The headmaster told him the adjustment would be hard. Students had to wake up at 6 a.m., fix their beds, take a shower, shine their shoes, buckle their belts, and get ready for school.

Georgie told him, "I want to attend this school, but I don't think I can follow directions." When the headmaster asked him to explain why, he said, "My mommy is very sick; I have to check up on her every day. I am the only one she has to take care of her." Being a compassionate individual, he made a deal with George: He could go to the headmaster's office every day to call me. He reassured him that he wasn't going to be denied the daily phone call as long as no one found out.

Later that day, I received a call from the headmaster. He shared how emotionally affected he was after Georgie told him the reason he was debating coming to the school. I could not believe what I was hearing. *My God, I thought. My son thought that because everyone else had left, he was solely responsible for me.* After dinner, we sat on the couch, and I asked him what he thought of the school.

"I'm excited!" He said, his face lit up. "I want to go there." I reassured him we were both going to be fine. He would focus on school, and I would start school again and finally finish my degree. We laughed and made a promise to take care of each other by being positive and supportive as we pursued our education.

The day came when my buddy had to leave for boarding school. This time, I was more than devastated. I was empty, lonely, and hopeless. I felt useless. I had been mothering kids every single day for so long that it felt like I had nothing to live for. My friends were having kids, and all of mine were gone. Fear and pain consumed my body again.

Georgie was hurting in his own way, too. He would always say that the buddies are separated. He sensed I was depressed and tried to motivate me to restart school again. "We will do it together, Mommy," he said. "I'll study hard, play sports, help other students, and take on extra work.

This way, I won't feel lonely. You have to do the same so you don't miss me as much."

I enrolled in school. We had taken an oath to help each other finish what we had started.

Bold Resilient Women

Remarkably, Georgie never took advantage of the headmaster's extended invitation to go to his office to call me. The headmaster told me that all my son needed was reassurance that he could contact me any time he felt I was not well.

After several years, graduation day was near. We both finished school approximately the same time. He was graduating from high school at St. John's Northwestern Military Academy, and I was graduating from North Park University with a psychology degree. I finally finished what I had started so many times in the past. My dream became a reality. I wasn't depressed or lonely as an empty nester. I had found a purpose to continue living. I saw what was possible in my life at this point.

As for my son, George, his passion for computers and gaming helped him achieve his dream of creating a tech company in his early twenties. When we talk about his experience in a military school, he says, "Mom, I became a man. I realized respect and discipline were the key to success." I like to think I could have taught him that, but I'm grateful that he had the experience and became the person that he is.

Being Open-Minded

On my bedroom wall hangs a poem in a bronze frame. It reads, "Love doesn't exist only for today, a moment or tomorrow. True love lasts and exists forever." Jimmy gave me this when we eloped, and it's been hanging in my bedroom ever since. Every morning, I look at it and I am reminded to fight for love and happiness. It has given me the courage and strength not to give up on my marriage.

When Jimmy and I eloped, my heart, mind, and soul were ready to jump into everlasting happiness without questioning my logic; I was ready to be submissive. I was in love, and nothing or anyone could stop me. Now, I realize that I had no idea what to expect from marriage. I was a child who had fallen for a handsome hippie. I didn't know what to expect from marriage, and I couldn't possibly envision the struggles that I was about to endure in raising a good and solid family. The simplicity of our romance was based on love and obsession.

Normally, this doesn't last; we were too young and naive to realize the commitment of marriage.

Many times throughout our marriage, I have felt lonely, lost, and discouraged, and I felt the void and emptiness of not having my parents or siblings as my safeguard. I had no one to turn to for advice and comfort. I found it difficult to laugh and be happy while I was struggling to live and survive. Every month, we struggled to pay rent and bills, and the stress was overwhelming. I would start my day by praying and reading little poems. Every little thing I read gave me comfort, especially during the many difficult days when things felt so dark, I couldn't see any light at the end.

Love and happiness are like looking for the flower that has the most spectacular aroma and fragrance. Flowers represent the innocence of beauty, as they are simple and beautiful to touch, see, and smell. But when you hold a rose the wrong way, the thorns can pierce your fingers. That's what happens when you don't cherish, nurture, and love the person who is holding you—they become thorns that will pierce your heart.

Grandma would say, "You see a bunch of flowers at a florist shop, so you reach to find the ones you love to place on your nightstand to smell and see when you wake up. As you move the flowers with your fingers, one rose can be filled with thorns that pierce your fingers. Although they have a beautiful aroma, they have made your fingers bleed. My sweet granddaughter, you can see a handsome young man with great manners and charm, but when your door closes, he could abuse you physically and mentally, making your heart bleed with pain and sorrow."

When a man loves a woman, he sees in her eyes the simple things he fell in love with. When he can bring you to smile and have joy in your heart, you will reciprocate with a singing heart. Your daily life will be full of laughter, singing, and dancing. Happiness is not regretting the person you sleep with and wake up to. Satisfaction is learning together to embrace the stars in the sky, the golden sunrise, the stunning sunset, the raindrops on your bedroom window, the flurries of snow, and the summer breezes, which bring the smell of fragrance of blossomed flowers.

Love and *pathos* are the glue that binds two people selflessly together without boundaries, monetary interests, power, status, or material things to fulfill their needs or void in their relationship.

When I was in my thirties, I realized that meaningless and materialistic things gradually die. They don't last, and they fade in front of your eyes. When you allow someone to transform the sparkle and gleam in your eyes, they have taken away your power, strength, and courage. I learned that, as difficult and challenging as it is, you can't let anyone drain you and leave you useless.

Stories of roses and wine are not realistic. My mentor, Carole, would say, "Life has many spills, and they come together like a wine spill destroying a beautiful tablecloth." What she meant is that when two people exchange hurtful comments, it destroys a delightful evening. Believing you will live a life without trials and tribulations will give you a false direction when it comes to hope. You will find yourself captive in a phony world of deception. You will always be chasing an unrealistic dream if you plan your future without living in the moment. Ongoing stress and worries for tomorrow will hold you in a detrimental cycle, where you worry about controlling your future instead of dealing with this moment's happenings. Life taught me to put the brakes on worrying about tomorrow. This gave me the freedom to enjoy my dreams for the future by looking forward to the opportunity for serenity and happiness.

Life is filled with struggles and sudden, unexpected ordeals. Every time I challenged myself to be perfect, I was destroyed mentally and psychologically. It was difficult to teach myself patience. Everything that was thrown in my path had its reason for a brighter outcome, and I gradually learned to become an optimistic and positive individual after many tears.

Learning not to expect things on my terms and time schedule, or to live by someone else's time and demands, was hard to accomplish. I was an individual who could not say no. But I kept reminding myself that God tells us things happen for a reason. We have to be patient to see the reason behind our struggles and challenges.

Neglect

As I grew into adulthood, my passion for giving back grew more intense. I felt I had been so fortunate, and I wanted to reciprocate by supporting the organizations and foundations that had supported me. I wanted to raise money for the hospitals and different foundations and institutions that had helped me through my struggles financially and psychologically, after my difficult pregnancies and childbirths. I was pulled to advocate for abused and neglected children, the silent members of society who are voiceless. I felt a calling to care for elderly, sick, and disadvantaged people, who are forgotten not only by society, but by their families and loved ones.

At the same time, I was a perfectionist. I demanded perfection from myself, and I fought to gain respect and loyalty from everyone who crossed my path. I was determined to stay feminine and fit despite my growing pains, financial issues, and lack of rest and sleep.

"Eleni, you cannot hold two watermelons in one hand," my parents would always say. It's a Greek saying that means that you cannot try to do a million things at one time. You will pay the price by exhausting yourself. Turns out my future was predicted by my parents.

When I was in my early thirties, I became very ill. It came on slowly, but I got weaker and weaker, and my mobility became so limited that I was hardly able to stand on my feet. The doctors didn't understand what was going on inside my body. They could not detect the root of my medical issue.

Finally, after numerous tests and procedures and an agonizing wait, I was diagnosed with a rare illness. It shook me and my family and turned my world upside down. Here I was, a dynamic and aggressive young woman with four young children, and no one to take care of me or them. During my diagnosis, Jimmy and I were going through a financial crisis that had consumed our marriage and home environment. This was the worst possible timing. I felt so hopeless, unsure of what I was dealing with and how fast it would progress. We didn't know where to start, how to even find the proper doctors who specialized in my rare illness.

During this difficult and unexpected time in my life, my children were my number one priority. I didn't think about anything else but them. I thought constantly about how I would protect them if I died. I didn't have time to focus on my illness—my immediate concern was the future of my children and their financial stability and safety.

I realized that when you are faced with the unknown, you must make arrangements for the security of your children. My children were the innocent victims caught in the challenge.

Going through this ordeal brought me closer to other friends who had suffered from different diseases, illnesses, and not knowing what may lie ahead for not only them, but for their families.

One of my dear friends, Tina, was a doctor who was diagnosed at a young and vulnerable age with cancer. As we discussed her illness over lunch, I was stunned by her first comment, "Eleni mou," she told me, as we discussed her young daughter, also named Eleni. "I have asked God to let me live long enough to see my Eleni admitted to high school. She is too young to be left without my guidance."

Listening to her gave me both nightmares and unwavering respect and inspiration. It brought back my fight with sarcoidosis and the will to live for my children and family. I learned from the greatest mentors in my life to never give up until my last breath. Just keep praying and fighting for victory. What a courageous woman. All she thought about was her three children and her beautiful mom, who was widowed in the prime of her life.

Tina's strength and will to fight for her children gave me the courage to be optimistic in every predicament in my life. Tina was a fighter, not a loser. She loved her family, faith, friends, and life more than anyone I have ever met. She mesmerized you with her laughter and jokes. Going through Tina's journey with her, I saw the power of faith and perseverance. Her wish was to travel to the Holy City of Jerusalem. She wanted to put closure on her life's circle. She knew her time was near, and she wanted to go pray and thank God for all his blessings. She was grateful to God for hearing her prayers to keep her alive to see her children become teenagers.

Seeing this beautiful, talented, kind doctor fighting and losing the battle to

Bold Resilient Women

cancer inspired me to raise—along with many dedicated volunteers and a supportive team—millions of dollars to support scientists, biologists, and oncologists at the Robert H. Lurie Comprehensive Cancer Center at Northwestern Hospital. At this unique institution, they do translational, outside-the-box cancer research. We established the Hippocratic Cancer Research Foundation to fund research with the hope of one day eradicating cancer.

In addition to my mom's miracle, throughout my life I have watched many young women who I love as my daughters or young siblings be diagnosed in their thirties with this treacherous disease. Two of those beautiful, remarkable, sweet, and intellectual women were Anna and Jill. Their diagnoses stunned all of us. We wanted to make a difference by ensuring they were able to see the top specialists. Today, they are well and healthy, both becoming amazing and caring wives and mothers of two beautiful children.

As a founding board member of the Hippocratic Cancer Research Foundation, I believe the organization honors Tina's legacy, as well as my mother, my friend Jay Michael, Vasuola, Pantelis and the others who were fighters. They taught us what faith and hope really are. Your will to fight is part of your healing process. Many cancer patients become advocates for others, as they understand life's battles in a new way.

Today, doctors, scientists, biologists, and cancer specialists are making tremendous efforts in healing many cancer patients thanks to clinical trials for chemo drugs. While I can't bring back Tina, my mother, Jay, Vasuola, Pantelis, and my other dear friends who have passed, who fought for victory but were not survivors, I can do everything in my power to help end cancer so others don't have to suffer. It feels like the least I can do.

Changing the World in His Eyes

Evangelo was my challenging, emotional, sweet child. He has always loved life and was never more comfortable than when he was in the limelight. He was infatuated with modeling and acting.

"Mom," he would constantly ask me. "When I graduate and I am asked to be a model in France, or to move to New York, will you let me go?"

"Of course. I will always let you pursue your dreams," I told him. I didn't want to disappoint him by explaining how hard it is to make it as a model or an actor since we were not involved in the movie industry. He desperately wanted to leave Chicago, go to Paris to model and then attend Parsons School of Design in New York. He had such a clear vision.

After graduating from Glenbrook North High School, Evangelo received a letter inviting him to Paris to model for a billboard campaign. He had been recruited by an agency.

When he read the letter, I was walking in with Georgie after his baseball game. He couldn't wait to announce the great news. His face was filled with joy, but I could also see he was nervous not to disappoint me. "Mom, I am leaving," he said, showing me the letter. I was shocked and stunned. He took me by the hand and walked me out to the patio. He saw I was holding back my tears. At that moment, I didn't want to keep my word. I wanted to break it, to shatter the promise I had once made without thinking of the consequences.

After we had a long talk in our blossomed backyard, filled with every flower that gave light to our intense conversation, I knew I had to let him go. "I will let you pursue your dream," I told him. "But don't you ever sell your body, soul, or spirit for glory and money." It was a very difficult and painful decision, but I knew I had to let him go if I loved him. He had told me explicitly that if I didn't allow him to go, he would leave and never come back. I knew that if I gave him my blessing, he would return. So, at seventeen years old, Evangelo boarded a one-way flight to Paris. All the way home from the airport, both Georgie and I were crying. He had lost his playing partner, and I felt I had lost another child.

A week later, after many sleepless nights, I decided we were going to Paris. I was falling apart. Jimmy didn't want to upset me anymore, but I knew he wanted to tell me I shouldn't have made such a nonsensical promise without discussing it with him; we never anticipated Evangelo would be chosen for the campaign ad. He was angry at me, but at the same time, compassionate when he saw how much I was hurting. My mom was also in disbelief that we would let him go to the other side of the world alone. I was packing for myself and George when my mother, my sister-in-law, and Victoria announced that they were coming too. Soon, we were all on a flight to see my sweet boy. We landed and headed straight to the modeling campus.

There were so many strange faces. I wasn't going to let my son share a bathroom with dozens of people, so I started looking for an apartment to rent for him. In his short time there, he had made three dear girlfriends. I insisted on meeting them. After we had chatted, I made a proposition.

"If I rented an apartment and paid the rent and all the expenses, will you guys take care of each other?" They were all from low and middle-income homes, different parts of the country, they too had wanted to pursue modeling to create a lucrative career and support their families. They were ambitious, motivated, and inspirational young adults with faith and perseverance. I had no doubt they would all protect and keep an eye on each other.

We spent ten unforgettable days with Evangelo and his friends. We rented a comfortable minibus for sightseeing. The driver was a French American who knew a lot of history and culture. I expressed my desire to learn about the Notre-Dame church, the Eiffel Tower, the Louvre Museum and the Champs Élysées. These were the important highlights of our trip to Paris. The adults focused on history and culture, while the young people were overimpressed by the unique food and pastries.

The young people in the group knew they would have many excursions of their own during their lengthy stay in Paris. Through our excursion, I learned everything about their lives, values, and morals. I was confident no harm would come to any of them.

As we were preparing to depart Paris and head home to the States, there

Bold Resilient Women

was a calming feeling. I hugged Evangelo goodbye. I knew in my heart he was going to flourish. He would stand tall by learning to cope with and handle different and difficult situations in his life. All he needed was the confidence, love, trust, and security that I had given him from the moment he was born. From there, he could create the life he wanted.

Conquering the World

As a young woman, I was aggressive and optimistic. I wanted to conquer the world. I listened carefully to elderly friends and family members for guidance, and I accepted their advice and criticism without pride or ego. Their wisdom rang in my ears. But the painful feedback was hard to accept; daggers were piercing my heart, and everything they told me felt like lightning striking out of nowhere.

As humans, we gravitate to people, and I felt comfortable reaching out to the family and friends who watched and guarded my back. These were the individuals who challenged me by telling me the truth about my actions, mistakes, strengths, weaknesses, pros, and cons. But I wasn't often ready to hear it. It angered me. I didn't want to accept my mistakes. Didn't they see how hard I worked? Didn't they care how far I had come? Behind closed doors, I felt like a loser who wanted to sink into a deep sleep and forget every conversation. I was desperate to overcome everything that stood in my way, and I didn't want to be called out on it. I was defensive, and because of this, many of my friends started becoming my enemies. Without realizing it, I was putting a divider between myself and those who truly loved me and wanted to protect me. I felt more comfortable walking away from my friendships and family relationships than facing the truth.

But after carefully viewing my internal thoughts, by reflecting on difficult conversations with loving individuals, a switch flipped. It was time to embrace true friendship and love.

When I was a child, my best friend was Debbie. But we had a contentious relationship. I would despise her for telling me to slow down and prioritize things. I was angry, and she didn't understand. She had money, power, and a wealthy family who provided her with everything her heart desired. She didn't understand budgets or having to be punctual for work. She didn't know the feeling of working endless hours to care for a young family.

As we grew up, we drifted apart. She loved and cared for me, and I for her, but she condemned my marriage and didn't understand the need for financial stability. Many years later, we reconnected, but we were circling in different worlds. She still didn't understand or have empathy for others. Though she had many misfortunes, she hadn't used them to motivate any change in her life. Debbie lived the same existence, and I was saddened to hear her lifestyle involved mostly parties, drinking, and drugs.

A few years later, when we were in our late forties, Debbie, my beautiful friend, lost her life. After abusing her body for so many years, her heart had betrayed her. She had a massive heart attack as she was sitting on her sofa.

I was shaken up by the loss of her, wishing I had not abandoned her. If I had stayed closer, could I have protected her?

This moment was an eye-opener for me. It was a lesson in understanding other people's pain and struggles. It was a moment to realize what it means to be someone's support system and not walk away. It was also a powerful lesson that money is not the answer; sometimes it brings destruction.

It's vital for young women today to take control of their lives. When you fall, you need to get up, stand on your own two feet, and regain your strength and motivation to change and succeed.

It was a lesson my mom preached often. "What doesn't kill you makes you stronger and will lead you to excel in all your endeavors," she would say. She believed that you couldn't rely on outside influence. You had to find the strength on your own. "If you are not confident in yourself and don't see why you are experiencing these challenges, you will not have faith in yourself. You should not marvel over someone else's beauty and talents. You must be satisfied with all the gifts God gave you, and that will make you a positive force in the world."

She believed fully that courage gave you the ability to succeed. She believed in tenacity, perseverance, and faith—but she also believed in kindness. She knew that you could be victorious silently without discrediting or destroying someone else.

Women have the power to withstand so much and rise to great heights. It just starts by taking control of your own life. It's your obligation to hold your empowerment tight in the palms of your hands with courage and endurance. We have the ability, fortitude, and strength to take charge if we can channel our confidence. Then it's our responsibility to show the next generation how to do it.

We have a moral obligation to build each other up. As women, we must support each other's goals, aspirations, and successes. Young, innocent women who are afraid to lead must be guided by mentors. We must inspire and empower them by validating their beliefs and opinions. Women must be supportive of intelligent and talented young women by giving them choices and opportunities.

My mother always said, "Give a young person the wings to fly. If you clip one, they will keep losing their balance, but let them fly and they will go to different destinations and lay their foundations."

When I asked her what all this meant, she explained it: "We want young people to succeed, but sometimes we hold them back for our own satisfaction. We clip one of their wings by never letting them make mistakes. But when you love an individual, you give them the strength to advance in their dreams by letting them fail; that way they know how to pick themselves back up."

Monumental Objects

Cleaning out my mother's home of seventy years was a challenging task. No one had an interest in any of her belongings, besides some old photos and pictures. For years, I would say to her, "Mom, you have accumulated so much garbage all these years, no one can even walk in your homes." I didn't feel connected to the many things my mom cherished, which had given her satisfaction and joy. I would go to her different homes and throw things out, or give them away with my dad's consent. I would hold something up or point to an item and say, "Mommy, you can give this away to the shelters and the poor. You don't need it."

Mom would take a long time to decide. Sometimes she would say yes, but other times, she would explain the story behind a certain item. She wanted to remember how hard she had worked to accumulate everything now that it was being given away.

When we went through the kitchen cabinets, she held up an iron kettle for almost half an hour.

"Mom," I finally asked her. "Are all these items really important? If you take an hour analyzing everything, we will be here for years!" We started to laugh. "Honey, my mother used to make hot meals with iron pots and kettles. She would leave them at the doorsteps of the neighbors during the Depression. As a child, I would help her deliver them, and the day after, they would appear in front of our yard outside the house. They would tie the pot in an apron so no one would see what we were doing. Many times, the neighbor would send firewood as a thank-you token for the stove and fireplace."

Bold Resilient Women

She had a distant look in her eyes, and I realized at that moment, Mom was reliving her past. Her attachment to material objects made sense to me. Every item symbolized an obstacle that they conquered, a challenge that they fought through. We haven't lived through the violence of war, communism, poverty, and suffering. We haven't lived long enough to have witnessed terror.

If you don't spend time relocating your parents to a facility or another home, you will not see and feel the pain in their eyes as their home is broken up. We don't realize that the time we spent picking cabinet colors, marble, tiles, or moldings won't matter in the later years of our life. Parts of our homes will be like a used dress, towel, or toothpaste you throw away. The only thing you will want is the photo memories.

I told my children that when I feel I am ready to go, I will decide what is saved and what is given away. Watching my mom's beautiful memories destroyed has made me feel remorse for not having appreciated all her little tokens while she was still here. My advice to my children and friends is to give Mom and Dad a chance to come to terms with the things they loved that were a part of their life.

What should be saved and thrown should be someone else's decision, not ours. We don't understand the psychological connection between a person and an item. We have to respect that it's often about more than just the item—it's difficult for someone to say goodbye to their past and present life and slowly prepare for their end.

We have to listen to our parents' and grandparents' stories as they go through the boxes of memories. It's difficult to get rid of precious memories that make up a life.

I got rid of many of my mother's things, but only later did I truly understand why Mom and Dad wanted to take their time. I wish I could turn back the clock and say to them, "Forgive me, I didn't understand every little thing has a place in one's heart."

Without Entitlement

When I was in my thirties, a young Black priest visited the Chicago area with his beautiful wife. There was something profound about this young woman's eyes. She was almost like a saint the way she spoke and prayed at the dinner table. We started to talk about God, His servants, His flock, and the Bible. I saw the sparkle in her eyes when she spoke about saving the lost, hungry, malnourished, and sick children in Kenya.

They told us how these Kenyan children have a zeal and passion to learn about God and His church. We asked them many questions about Africa. With tears rolling down his cheeks, the preacher responded. "What can I say?" he said. "Here, you waste food and throw away leftovers. But our children in the villages are dying from hunger. They don't have food to eat, clothes for their body, shoes on their feet, or a bed to comfortably sleep on. I see your homes filled with beautiful furniture, your children dressed in fine clothing and wearing different shoes daily. Yet, as I travel through this big country, I see so much hate, suffering, and anger. Your people don't greet anyone with a kind smile, gesture, or respect. They don't laugh or sing. My people are always laughing, singing, and dancing in the streets. They don't have anything, so therefore, they are not consumed by greed, power, money, or ego."

We were so inspired by his compassionate words and the passion in his voice and the intensity of his mission. We went home that night, and Jimmy and I discussed how we could possibly help these resilient children. After some discussion, my family and I decided to buy a plot of land in Kakamega, Kenya, and build the Mercy Orphanage.

Bold Resilient Women

After several months, the orphanage was finished. I was invited with my family to attend the ribbon-cutting and the opening of the orphanage. It was the happiest day of my life. I would travel to Nairobi, then four days later venture to Kakamega, Kenya. When my dear friends, Pat and Elena, heard that I was going to Africa, they came along to see what I had generously donated and to witness the poverty and suffering of the overpopulated communities.

As we landed and arrived at the Nairobi airport, we were welcomed by many little children singing and praising us alongside Reverend Charles, his wife, and some other community members. The ride to the village was filled with different emotions. I saw people barefoot and skinny, with their bones showing. Children ran and sang in the streets and fields, wearing hardly any clothes. Some people looked like the walking dead due to malnutrition. I could not bear to see so much suffering, poverty, and neglect.

Finally, after a few hours of a bumpy ride, we made our entrance through the gates of the orphanage. All of the children were waiting and singing joyfully, "Welcome Mama Eleni!" It was one of the most emotional moments of my life. Children were embracing, hugging, and grabbing us as if they wanted to hang on to a support system. Their love and excitement were overwhelming for all of us. They held tight to our hands. They wouldn't let go. We were all emotional, wrapped up in their love and welcoming songs.

After visiting for almost a day, in which they had arranged many activities, liturgies and local celebrations, we had the privilege of visiting the surrounding villages, different churches and gatherings. Everyone embraced us with comforting and grateful love. They didn't have much, but the little they had, they wanted to give it to us.

We saw firsthand the laughter, kindness, respect, and loyalty of these beautiful Kenyans. I found myself being called by our Lord to save these children. Although I had reservations about visiting, I glorified God for giving me the strength, courage, and health to see what I had passionately built. At the same time, we witnessed firsthand the pain, suffering, and malnutrition of children and adults. We saw peace and vitality in the simple things in their lives, which gave them hope. Everything we take for granted every single day is a treasure to the people in Africa. It was humbling to see the faith and love they have in their hearts. You could see in their faces the empathy they had for us and their surrounding fellow men. They didn't fear, envy, or hate us. They didn't care who we were, what we wore, or where we came from.

They saw us as their life savers, as fellow humans who were here to help support them and their children.

What I witnessed in Kenya reminded me of what my parents used to say. "Remain humble and be grateful for every little thing God has given you.

Bold Resilient Women

Glorify His name every day when you wake up. Be thankful for the food you will eat, the water you will drink, the clothes on your back, and the shoes on your feet to walk the rough roads. Remember, the garbage you toss away is a great treasure to a poor person."

The faces, smiles, laughter, and humility of these children and their parents, neighbors and clergy, will be engraved in my heart and mind forever.

A New Home

Finally, we were making our big move. After a year of construction, our dream house was ready.

We moved into our new home when our baby boy was 1½ years old. We were content and happy with our new residence. Everyone had their privacy and their own bedroom. The kids were happy that they didn't have to share their bedrooms, books, toys, or little gadgets.

Day by day, we were making little efforts to set up our home and make it ours. But something was missing. We didn't have the intimacy and the coziness of being together that we once did purely through the size of our spaces. I had to make more of a concerted effort to bring us together. Rather than let everyone drift into their own rooms, I would nudge everyone to gather in the family room, where we would lie on each other, read books, and watch movies. But the older the kids got, the harder it became, no matter how hard I tried. With so many activities and schedules, it became difficult having dinner together as a family every night. After dinner, I would have the children help me clean the plates, and pick up the kitchen, and then when the table was wiped, the children brought their school bags and spread their homework on the kitchen table to study together. I tried to get us all in the same place whenever and wherever I could.

Weekdays were filled with school, sports, and other activities. Every Sunday, the kids and I would attend church. The boys loved serving at the altar, and I enjoyed seeing them serving God with all their love. But something was missing: their father wasn't with us. He was always, always working. There were many times I left church and went to the bathroom to hide and cry. I was overwhelmed. Day and night with four kids and an unending cycle of washing, cooking, ironing, and all the other chores in between.

My children were growing too fast; the days and months and years passed too quickly. One by one, they were leaving the house, spreading their wings and creating their own dreams.

Michael moved into his own apartment. As an aggressive young man, he wanted to have his own space while he pursued his passion for football. He was going to go to college, play football, and work when he didn't have practice or school. He seemed to have it all lined up for his future. He was content with his lifestyle. He was ambitious in pursuing all his dreams and aspirations.

Victoria was a gifted child with many talents. Her heart drew her to the medical field—she was obsessed with science. She was a curious child who wanted to know how our bodies function. She won first place in her eighth-grade science competition by making the entire body of a person with electric wires. The judges found it very fascinating and interesting to see how she had made the body work by using electricity and light bulbs.

Because of her love for science, we got her a chemistry set. When she didn't have after-school activities, Greek school, or her Art Institute classes, she would lock herself downstairs in the family room basement and experiment with her chemistry set.

One day, I was in the kitchen cooking when we heard a loud noise. Michael ran downstairs to see what was going on. Victoria had mixed some chemical items, and they had exploded. There was smoke in the basement. Michael panicked and hit her in the stomach, anxiously thinking she was burning the house down. Victoria passed out from anxiety and fear, leaving Michael thinking he had hurt her badly. Screaming, I rushed downstairs, seeing everyone in a panicked fright. Everyone recovered, and we laugh about it now. Victoria made a decision not to go to medical school but to pursue law instead. We talked it through a lot. We would say, "It takes one minute and one incident for an individual to make a decision about their future."

During the time Victoria wanted to pursue medicine, the world was alarmed by the spread of the AIDS virus, which was taking the lives of so many innocent people. There was no way we could handle something happening to her. We advised her against going to medical school and to pursue another career. I think after her chemistry set blew up, her decision was made.

She decided to attend DePaul University in Chicago, and live at home while she commuted back and forth.

People in Your Path

God works in many miraculous ways.

Victoria would commute daily to the city to attend DePaul University. This skinny sixteen-year-old girl was on the toll road every morning at sunrise and every evening at sunset. One morning, a toll collector who had seen her regularly asked her where a young little girl goes every morning and every night? My daughter responded, "I go to the university. I don't want to live away from home so I commute back and forth."

"You are such a sweet young girl," he responded. "I will pay your tolls for you every day so you can focus on finishing school, since you are sacrificing sleep to commute back and forth. But when you graduate and get your degree, I want you to treat me to a cup of coffee."

My daughter, being a kind and giving individual, said, "Absolutely. I will treat you not only to coffee, but breakfast too." When she got home, she told me she had met a sweet, kind man at the toll booth named Mr. Jimmy, who had offered to pay for her toll. From then on, she would tell me how she and Mr. Jimmy would have lovely conversations almost every morning when they had time.

Two years later, we were at church when a beautiful baby came in with her mother for communion. The baby's face was disfigured due to a bilateral cleft lip and head, and as they walked up the aisle, the entire church started to whisper and stare. I was shocked. After mass, I ran back to find the mother, but she vanished. I told my husband and parents what happened, and vowed to speak to Dr. Mimis Cohen, a very dear friend who has traveled all over the world performing free surgeries on children who were born with a cleft palate. I wanted to ask him how we could help this baby.

The following week, I waited by the candle stand to find the mother. In our faith, after a baby is christened, the child has to take communion three times, so I knew she would be back. I planned to approach her after the communion and express my desire to help her child. My husband and kids thought I was out of place to say this to the poor parents, but I knew it was the right thing to do.

While I was standing by the candles, I saw her enter the church, and I was ecstatic. I told her about my friend and how he operated on so many children pro bono. I gave her my business card. "I can help your child," I told her.

I waited for days without a phone call. Weeks later, I was in the newspaper, as I had established the Frontida and Keso Centers for Abuse to help combat women and girls being sold for sex slavery.

This mother was working as a waitress when she saw my photo. She asked her customers if they knew me. "Who doesn't?" they responded. "She helps everyone who crosses her path." She told them about our encounter and how I had reached out during church to help her child. They advised her to call me immediately.

At 11 p.m., the phone rang. I sprang out of bed, tripping over my sheets. The only people who called the house late were my parents and children, and I began panicking, thinking something had happened to a family member. But on the other end of the phone, I heard a soft voice crying and apologizing for calling so late. I told her not to worry. I was ecstatic to hear her voice. I told her to hold on while on another phone, I called my friend, Mimis. After I explained the situation, he told me she should meet him at six the next morning.

I told her what Mimis had said. "I will accompany you to the hospital," I told her.

"No, no. We cannot impose to have you come so early with us." She promised to call after the appointment. In the end, Dr. Cohen helped this little girl. He fixed her entire face, nose, lips, and her head. After numerous surgeries, this little girl had a beautiful and normal head and face.

Weeks later, Mr. Jimmy, the toll collector, saw Victoria's license plate as she pulled in and noticed it said *"Bousis."*

"Is your mother's name Eleni Bousis?" he asked. "It is!" she said. "Did she go through your toll?"

He started to cry. "No, she didn't. Has your mom ever talked about a little girl whose name is Elizabeth?"

"Yes, my mom saved her life."

Bold Resilient Women

"Well, that's my daughter," he said through tears. Victoria teared up, then pulled off the expressway and called me, crying. I thought she had an accident. "Mom, remember Mr. Jimmy, the toll collector? The little girl who you and Dr. Cohen saved is his daughter!" The phone fell from my hand.

"What a miracle," I said. "God bless. How does He connect us with those who need help?"

With our support, Victoria attended an exchange program in France. During her stay, she worked on translating the work of St. Vincent De Paul into the English language. When she returned to Chicago, she was asked to paint a mural on the bridge which united the Wabash and State Street buildings of her school. She was very excited. The entire world would see the magical soulful work of this seventeen-year-old girl. I could often be spotted in front of the mural with my friends, showing them her beautiful work.

Bold Resilient Women

When Victoria graduated, she continued law school in San Diego. She was one of the youngest lawyers to graduate, and she chose to stay and study for the bar. When she passed, she worked pro bono, writing living wills for neglected people and AIDS victims who didn't have any protection or guidance from anyone. She told us, "Mom and Dad, I didn't go to medical school because I was worried about the prevalence of the AIDS virus. Now, I would like to give back to those who are neglected by their families, friends and society."

A couple of years later, she came and worked in Chicago for the State's Attorney. She wanted to make a difference in the world and be a voice for those who could not share their opinions or views. Although she worked for a few years as a lawyer, she witnessed so much injustice that she wanted to make others aware of what was happening in the world. So, she turned to filming, writing, and directing as a way to share these stories.

Victoria is the epitome of wanting to save the world by doing it all. Today, you will see her working endless hours and days, traveling the world to showcase her talent in the virtual, immersive experience space in storytelling. She was inspired by a book she picked up when she was traveling to Cambodia. She was touched by the unbreakable bond between parents and child. After she finished reading the book, she called me.

"Mom, if you had lost one of us, what would you do?"

I didn't have to think about it for one second. "I would never stop looking for you until my last breath in this world."

"Then I will help Mr. Pin Yathay find his missing son." Her voice was steadfast and committed. Her virtual immersive film, *Stay Alive, My Son,* showcases the complex feelings of guilt, love, and unwavering sadness of losing your child.

I am proud of my daughter's zeal in trying to unite families by collaborating with the United Nations High Commissioner for Refugees. She wants to support and highlight the dignity of refugees by educating people about the consequences of war, and the pain and brutality of abandoning or losing their children and family.

When it comes to my daughter, I see the stories of our ancestors in her face, the way she is drawn to experiences similar to theirs, but that are also uniquely modern. I also see the small interactions she had with people along the way—like Mr. Jimmy—and how they molded her into understanding how one person can truly make a difference to someone else.

Bold Resilient Women

Cancer Hits Home

When I was in my early forties, my world was turned upside down. My beloved mother was diagnosed with her third round of cancer. The doctors in Greece explained to my father and us siblings how severe it was: It was a rare form of cancer with a survival rate of zero. No one had ever lived more than two to five months.

During the night, as I tossed and turned in bed, my mind raced. I would get up and search the internet for ways to save her life. I looked for hospitals and doctors who specialized in this kind of cancer, known as AML. I googled all of the different medical options, treatments, and the survival rate. The doctors in Greece explained to my father and us siblings how severe Mom's cancer was and how long she would last. The doctors were afraid of what they saw, as the cancer was very aggressive and it was wiping out her blood. They said she would die.

She had no hope. Finally, after a week of sleepless nights and days spent on the phone, we found doctors who specialized in this type of cancer and a hospital with advanced research and treatments. The University of Chicago and Northwestern University were the top two hospitals that had oncologists who specialized in this kind of cancer. A decision was made, and we headed back to the States.

Upon arriving, we immediately went to the University of Chicago, where we had made an appointment before our departure from Greece. Mom and Dad still primarily spoke Greek, and asked us to discuss the different options for treatment. It was an extra layer of devastation: After listening to the recommendations and instructions of the doctors, we had the difficult job of explaining her options for survival. We needed to make her understand that if she didn't act fast, her life was at risk. She had to make a decision quickly, and the only chance she had involved getting her to a hospital where she could receive aggressive treatments. We admitted her to the hospital immediately, where she would have blood transfusions twice a week.

At our first appointment, we were hopeful. We sat in a room at the hospital with my mother, eager to hear something different from this new doctor. I held her hand.

The doctor looked over her labs, then sat down and looked my mom directly in the eyes. "Mrs. Palivos, you should go back home and enjoy your family without suffering," she said. "Live a quality life, although it's going to be for a very short time."

My mom was confused. She asked us in Greek to ask the doctor what she meant.

"This cancer is very aggressive," she said. "There is no chance for survival." Mom stood up defiantly, pushed the doctor to the side, and said in Greek, "I will live. I will not die."

She marched out of the doctor's office. "Let's go to the next hospital," she said. "I want to see what they say at Northwestern." At this point, we had to act quickly. Mom was having blood transfusions constantly.

We made an appointment and went to Northwestern Hospital. When we met with her medical team there, she felt confident. After listening to the two oncologists, Dr. Platanias and Dr. Talman, Mom seemed to breathe a little more deeply. She instantly trusted them. She felt comfortable because one of the doctors was Greek and the other Jewish. Somehow, she knew they would see her as a person and work vigorously to save her life.

"You will make me well and I will live," she said to them.

Dr. Talman looked at her and said, "We are not God. We are only the tools for God."

But Mom kept insisting. "I know with your support and your experience that God will give you the knowledge to heal me."

Yet another challenge and bump in the road for my beautiful mother. She was facing an uphill battle, a fight for her life. *Here we go again*, I thought to myself, almost bitterly. Hasn't mom gone through enough? It was her third cancer diagnosis, and it was so unfair that this horrible monster was attacking her again.

I started questioning God. "Again, why?" I asked Him. "Mom has been through enough. Why again?"

Bold Resilient Women

When she was in her thirties, Mom fell ill with colon cancer. We had only been in the U.S. for a couple of years, and the four of us were still young.

When she fell ill, she was taken to Dr. Voulgaris, a well-known Greek doctor at Chicago Grant Hospital. My mom was bleeding from the rectum. The doctor knew what she had from the start.

After arriving as immigrants, my parents worked day and night to build a life for us in a new country, and now this? Dr. Voulgaris didn't know how to prepare my dad for the news. He loved my dad; he had heard about him even before they met because their families came from the same town. He would see us in church every Sunday, and they would have coffee together and discuss the old country.

After the tests were completed, Dr. Voulgaris had to break the news to my mom and dad and provide a treatment plan, which involved Mom having colon surgery and an extended stay in the hospital. The cancer had to be isolated before it metastasized. My dad was devastated. He had to do what the doctor said if my mom was to live. She was too young to die.

∼

One morning, Mom and I were having breakfast on the deck of our home in Athens. The sky was a vibrant blue, and a soft breeze flowed over us. I took a sip of my coffee and asked her something that had been on my mind for years.

"Mom, why are you always in a good mood?" I said. "You're always smiling, you're never judgmental or harsh, you always..." I had hardly finished my comment when my mom jumped in.

"My darling daughter," she said. "When you are in your thirties with four little kids and hear the word 'cancer,' you are horrified," she explained. "Suddenly, you stop thinking about yourself and all you can think about is surviving for your children. The little things are insignificant, and every day is such a gift. It changes everything about how you view the world."

While she beat colon cancer, she was faced with a cancer battle again in her forties—this time in her thyroid. History was being repeated. While we thanked God that it wasn't as critical as her first round of cancer, we were, of course, afraid, and Mom was terrified. It was the first time I ever saw her losing faith and hope. She was wondering, *What's next?*

My grandmother came to visit from the States and told my mom about a famous monastery. "Many miracles take place there, my darling daughter. I want to take you there to pray." She handed her a book called *The Miracles*, which she had purchased at the monastery.

But though my mom was devout in her love of God, her response this time was unpredictable. She refused to go to the monastery and didn't want to hear anything about it. She looked at the book for a moment and then tossed it to her next-door neighbor. She wanted nothing to do with it. (Coincidentally, the neighbor's daughter, Vicky, would eventually become my mom's daughter-in-law and my sister.)

On that hot July visit, we traveled to our summer home at Oropos, at the outskirts of Athens, to spend the next two months on the beach with the children. It is a peaceful, safe suburb where everyone keeps an eye on the kids, and parents can relax without the fear of abduction or violence. One day, we were all taking our afternoon siesta, with the house doors and gates closed. As Mom was sleeping, she was awakened by someone smacking her legs. Startled, she rose out of bed and looked around to see who had hit her.

She was furious, thinking her mom, my dad, or one of us kids was playing tricks on her. But when she saw all of us were sleeping, she realized something strange had taken place. She lay back down uneasily but couldn't sleep. She stared at the ceiling, wondering if she had dreamed this mysterious encounter. She got up to explore, and as she was heading toward the gate, she suddenly saw the book thrown at the end of the pathway. She picked it up and started reading it. It only took a moment before she was asking God to forgive her weak spirit. When the siesta was over, she revealed to us what had happened, and immediately the next day, we were traveling to the Island of Lesvos, Mitilini, to visit the monastery.

Life had been calm and we had felt as though our dreams were fulfilled, when once again, Mom, who was in her sixties now, got her deadly diagnosis. We were all devastated. We could not imagine what Mom was feeling, what was going through her mind when she received another cancer diagnosis. However, this was not like the previous ones. It was vicious, and two to five months was the maximum life expectancy. We started seeking doctors globally who specialized in AML, and that's how we found Dr. Talman and Dr. Platanias at Northwestern's Robert H. Lurie Hospital.

Mom was a notorious fighter, and she proved it to us and the world every single day. She showed us that life was about being resilient. She believed the only way to survive was through prayer, faith, and hope. Immediately after the diagnosis, mom was admitted to the isolation ICU floor at Northwestern Hospital. The doctors were stabilizing her, and their plan was to treat her for a month, evaluate, and then try a different chemo drug. This pattern would go on for three months. She had already failed two chemotherapy treatments, and the doctors didn't know what to do. They were hitting a brick wall.

One morning, the doctors called our entire family in for a meeting in my mom's room. They explained to us that they had developed a new, advanced cancer trial drug treatment, and they asked permission from Mom to agree to take the chemo. Mom would receive this trial drug along with two other patients. All three would be guinea pigs in helping to save those affected by AML.

We were silent for a moment, the question lingering heavily over the room. Then, we started asking many questions. "What are the effects? How soon will we know the results? And how would they give it to her? And how would we know if the drug was a success?"

"This drug is very invasive," the doctors told us. "It's administered intravenously, and it could possibly kill her." We told the doctors we wouldn't tell my mom this part, so we didn't freak her out. Next to her bedside, we asked her if she would be willing to fight one more time for herself and all of us. Mom saw the anxiety and fear on our faces.

"I will do one more round of chemo," she said, her eyes watery. "But if it doesn't work, I want to be left alone to go to my creator."

We had no choice but to grant her wishes. We kissed Mom goodbye, told her we loved her, and went to the waiting room. While they injected my mother with the drug, we sat in the waiting room in uncomfortable chairs, sipping black coffee, and staying up all night, waiting and praying for the results. Dr. Platanias sat with us. During one of the many exhausted, terrified silences, we asked what the drug was called. He told us, "It's a trial drug, so it doesn't have a name. It only has a number."

"How will we know that it's working?" we asked him. "What will we see?" "If the trial drug works, we will see spots on her fingers and toes, probably between five and six in the morning."

We had no idea we were about to witness another miracle in our lives. Just as the doctors predicted, when it was 5:45 a.m., we looked at Mom's fingers and toes, and they were filled with hives! We all started crying, and yelling, and hugging each other. Mom was a living miracle; she was being cured from this monster due to a brand-new trial drug. She fought for her life. She battled to live a life free of cancer, and she won! What a great victory. She was free to live and enjoy the fruits of her labor and struggles.

While we were celebrating my mom's health win, her sister, my beloved aunt Katerina, wasn't feeling well. She had started working at Hart Schaffner Marx as a young seamstress and eventually became a manager. Sixty years later, after her retirement, she was honored as the most lucrative, hard-working employee of the company. She could not wait to travel and go see the world she had missed.

My cousin, her son, a doctor, arranged to have her do certain tests. We weren't sure what to expect, but we were shocked to find out it was lymphoma. Here we go again with this monster called cancer—one was being healed, and one was starting her journey. My mom kept telling Katerina not to give up hope and to believe in God and the doctors.

Through my mom's oncologist, Dr. Platanias, my Aunt Katerina was introduced to Dr. Winters. They hit it off well, and Thea Katerina started chemo. She fully recovered. It has been almost twenty-five years, and she is still cancer-free.

My mom lived for another seventeen and a half years after her lethal cancer diagnosis. Her fight and survival were the pivotal points for many changes in my life. I wanted to be a beacon of hope and make a difference to those who are fighting the battle of their lifetime. Mom was the prime example of a trial drug making a difference in people's lives. This drug—which was approved—is called GLEEVEC. With her bravery, Mom helped save hundreds of lives globally.

I knew there was a calling, a reason God had put me in this predicament, but I was not aware which path I should follow.

After my mom fully recovered, I made a promise to create a foundation that would fund "outside of the box" cancer research. I returned from Greece in 2013, and one day, I met Dr. Platanias for lunch. He explained to me the process for funding cancer research. I promised him I would see what we could do to help. We had to unite with scientists, doctors, researchers, biologists, and philanthropists—everyone making a difference in eradicating cancer.

I truly believed in the cause, and I cared deeply about helping. But I was distracted due to numerous other obligations and foundations. I was not yet committed to begin the process for another foundation. I was overwhelmed until four of my dear friends all lost young children to cancer. This left me angry and deeply sad. I could not believe that in the twenty-first century, we were still losing so many lives to this horrible illness.

One summer afternoon, I was having lunch with my friends, Anna Sophia Loumis, Jay Michael, and Danielle Samolovich at Carmine's in Chicago. We continued to discuss how we could impact the world by making a difference in the fight against cancer. I expressed my vision and my life's mission: to support Northwestern by funding experimental research. My friends thought it was a great idea, and we made a plan to start a foundation. During the course of our planning process, we were joined by Dr. Nicole Boufis, a cancer researcher; my sister-in-law, Dr. Lisa Palivos, who worked in the emergency room at Cook County Hospital; and attorney Peter Karahalios. Collectively, we all decided this was our mission, and we wanted to be a part of a challenge and change. The Hippocratic Cancer Research Foundation was established in September 2014 without knowing what the future held.

The excitement and planning didn't last long. Shortly after, we learned that our beloved friend, Jay Michael, was diagnosed with cancer. Jay was a tall, handsome, ambitious, and loving friend to all. He was a visionary who dreamed of saving the world. One day, he called to tell me he needed to see Dr. Platanias. He was not feeling well. After a series of tests, to our shock, he was diagnosed with a terminal cancer, stage 4 Hodgkin lymphoma, at the age of thirty-three.

We were left speechless. But we knew that Jay would fight until his last breath. Jay fought so hard to live. He wanted his story to be different. He was ambitious. He wanted to fulfill his wishes by enduring his own cancer challenge. He wanted it to give hope to other cancer patients. Jay cared selflessly for every fellow patient who crossed his path. Once, when I asked Dr. Platanias how he was doing, he told me, "Jay never asks about the latest cancer trial drugs for himself, but for the patients he has referred." He would constantly remind Dr. Platanias he wasn't worried about his cancer—he knew he was in good hands. He was more interested in others' prognoses than his own. Jay's heart was bigger than the world. He cared so deeply for everyone, and was always asking questions about their lives, children, and how he could help. His smile never left his beautiful face, and his engaging, vibrant, green eyes pierced your heart. The only complaint he would tell me is, "My tongue burns after the chemo, but it feels good when I eat ice cream or something cold."

Jay lost his battle with cancer in January 2016 at the age of thirty-four. This tragedy invigorated my passion—as well as many others—to establish the Hippocratic Cancer Research Foundation for the Robert H. Lurie Northwestern Comprehensive Cancer Center.

The Hippocratic Cancer Research Foundation's mission is to support the tireless efforts in eradicating all types of cancers through experimental research. We honor the memory of those who fought courageously against cancer and honor the resilience of all cancer survivors. We are committed to funding translational research by discovering, developing, and implementing effective new therapies for cancer patients. These treatments can be carried out through advanced, groundbreaking research.

The Hippocratic Cancer Research Foundation works diligently to support the heroes behind the scenes. Collectively, they are on the front lines against cancer. We applaud these resilient fighters, those who fiercely and bravely battle cancer and we honor the memory of the warriors who bravely showed strength and tolerance after their valiant journey.

We held our first fundraising event in November 2016, and since then, we've raised millions for the foundation. With every dollar raised, we honor the memory of Jay Michael, my mom, Bessie Palivos, and founding board member Dr. Tina Mantis.

May their zeal and passion in making a difference for the world be the force and inspiration for us to never give up the fight.

Unconditional Love

Loving my four children unconditionally has come with heartaches, pains, and sorrows, as much as I tried to prevent them. As a mother who loves and cares for her children, I refused to have them go through the growing pains I faced at a young age. I wanted to protect them from making bad decisions that could impact their future. There were times I wanted to shake them and say to them, "I am not your friend and I am not your enemy. I am the woman who sacrificed her life, dreams, and ambitions for you to be able to live and flourish in a fragmented world."

I raised my children by myself while Jimmy went to school and worked long hours.

How does someone know at seventeen years old to balance children, a demanding and hard-working husband, school, and organizations? Somehow, my life was always filled with challenges and difficult—sometimes excruciating—choices. I would sob exhaustedly, not knowing if the decisions I was making were sensible and vital for my children and our family's future.

I wanted so desperately to instill in my children the many words of wisdom my grandmother and mother passed down to me. I wanted to teach them everything about life. In my little free time, I devoured books about parenting and childbearing. I knew the only way to raise my children was to be a loving and patient mother with lots of tolerance. I had many bright ideas for their future. Failure wasn't in my vocabulary; I could not fathom being defeated in this role.

I knew by having faith in God and trusting my intuition that I would feel power and strength and be guided into making the best choices for my marriage and children. I never felt the pressure to choose between having my children, going to school, or having a career. God gave me strength, resilience, tolerance, and extreme patience. Even when I would go days without sleep due to the many illnesses my children had while they were young, I had the power to persevere. I didn't believe in limitations. I knew hard work could not kill me. In the back of my mind, I knew my biggest danger was daily stress, but there was little I could do to help it. This was my destiny in life. Eventually, this stress was going to turn into a big and unpredictable nightmare, but I couldn't know that now.

My spiritual father, Gerontas Fillipas, gave me some of my most treasured spiritual advice. "You can find God and witness his power in everything that's simple in the universe. It's those simple things that will give you comfort and happiness." He explained that musical hymns in our church connect you with your inner soul and mind and can set you free to think from a different perspective. When you are a positive thinker and hope for great things for your family, friends, and everyone around you, desirable things will come to you, for you are a part of God's creation. He told me to ask the Lord for what I yearned for with humility and *agape* in my heart, and I would receive His blessings.

"Set yourself free to thirst for the simple things in life," he said. "It is strange to accept the simple, meaningful things which surround us, since our concentration is consumed by possessing everything we see. When we believe in ourselves and the universe, we should continue to teach ourselves discipline and honesty; then great things will come unexpectedly in our life."

The Archbishop of Greece, His Beatitude Chrystodoulos, was my confessor. Every time I met with him for confession, I would tell him I needed to confess what made my heart heavy.

"We all face a heavy heart," he would tell me. He was a kind and gentle man of God with a round, white-mixed brown beard, red cheeks, and a bright smile. He was without judgment or condemnation. He was a spiritual leader who supported social services and saw (and spoke) the truth. He cared about mothers and children being raised in abusive homes. He provided assistance for young single women by educating them and setting up different opportunities to learn skills for those who could not attend school. He opposed children not being treated for drug addiction. He cared for the victims of sex trafficking. He insisted that people can make a difference in the lives of others.

When I spoke at the World Conference for the Family in the 21st Century, he was seated in the front row, clapping and giving me strength. He became known as the bishop who believed in equal rights, humanitarian intervention, and the rights of everyone to attend church, no matter what they wore. He was respected for his outpouring of compassion for youth and their issues. "Come, children, to the Lord's home any way you want," he would say. "I am not here to judge you. I am here to spread my open arms with love."

He was smart and passionate about the church and the country. I don't believe any politician will ever have over three million people attend a protest at the capital for the removal of religious identification. The government wanted to change our Greek IDs by removing "Greek Orthodox Christians" as a designation and removing the cross from our flags. The Greek population opposed this, and rallied to protest with the vote to remove the cross from our flags. The country opposed both changes and came out to voice their frustration, led by His Beatitude Chrystodoulos.

I have been blessed to have had amazing church leaders for guidance. I have been honored to serve on numerous boards with Cardinal Francis Eugene George of the Catholic Archdiocese of Chicago, a humble servant of God. Together, we have served in different roles at Maryville Academy for orphans, Little City Foundation, and Misericordia, which supports intellectually and developmentally disadvantaged children.

Cardinal George reminded me of Archbishop Chrystodoulos. He was a lovely, intellectual, and faithful man, who would raise his eyes above his glasses to analyze you. Cardinal George believed in walking side by side with all faiths and defending human life with respect and dignity. He worked to combat poverty and child pornography. He believed in leaving your worries in God's hands. "Leave your burdens and have faith and confidence in God," he would say often.

He was a man who didn't fear learning and growing, and after making comments that hurt the LGBTQ+ community, he made a formal apology, recognizing that he hurt and damaged many of his own family members and friends who were gay. He said his position stemmed from his fear for the church's liberty. This made me understand how difficult many individuals' positions are in speaking out the truth. His apology was well-received by LGBTQ+ advocates. It was genuine, and he took full responsibility for the comments he had made.

By witnessing his humility, I realized that we are all creatures who make

Bold Resilient Women

mistakes. It takes a humble and sincere individual to ask for forgiveness by admitting he made an inappropriate comment. It takes strength to use your missteps to learn, and grow, and become a better person. Yet again, it all comes back to simplicity. This brave yet quiet act can bring us closer to God and each other.

India, Kathmandu, Nepal, Fish Island

Traveling to India was one of the most exciting trips I have ever taken. I was traveling with my beautiful daughter, Victoria, and friends who were responsible for starting an eye clinic that was involved in saving children who were blind. They were doing eye surgeries pro bono, giving them back their eyesight to see, read, and view their loved ones and all great, good, or partially bad, things which were inconsequential.

We landed in Kathmandu, and I was shocked to see that you could not see three feet from where you stood. There was so much pollution. I wore a heavy mask on my face, and gloves that were essential to protect myself from different illnesses. I took the whole scene in: multiple people on bikes, overcrowded buses, monkeys running around, electric poles filled with hundreds more wires than I thought possible. And through all of it, it seemed everyone was smiling and happy. I was in a state of shock. How did Nepali people live happily while we were miserable? Why has our society not realized how spoiled we all are? And why can we all not see and be exposed to experiencing how the other side of the world lives? Maybe then we can all understand humility.

The following day, we were pulled by a rolling boat to Fish Island, where we stayed for two days. After dinner, my daughter and I would sit outside by the lake. I said, "Honey, look at the stars and watch the people across the river dancing and singing." The next evening, following dinner, we looked with curiosity at the photos of the hotel's elite guests on the walls. We went again to sit on the lawn chairs, and view the stars, and the calmness of the lake, and all its greenery surrounding this peaceful place. Again, we witnessed the people across the river dancing and singing.

"Victoria, my darling. What do you think is wrong with this picture and scenery here at this location? What is striking you about what we are witnessing?" I asked her. The stars glowed above us, and we could hear the gentle lapping of the lake. My daughter responded, "Mom, I see us and the other guests at this hotel rushing after dinner to work on our computers and then retreat for the night early. Yet, those people across the lake don't have food to eat, or nice beds to sleep in comfort. But they are alive. They have no computers to work on and no chairs to sit on, but they seem happier than most of the people here. There is laughter, singing, dancing, and parties all night. There is life. Here, everyone is muted, too busy worrying about their jobs, finances, and tomorrow's accomplishments." I knew she was right. I took it all in, the sights, sounds, and this treasured moment with my daughter.

When we traveled to Delphi, we were received by many at the Oberoi Hotel, which was located behind tall walls. I was shocked to see the extreme differences between the wealthy on one side of the wall, and the extremely poor on the other. All that separated them was a street and a tall wall. On one side, you saw extreme wealth and ease, with bellboys, servants, housekeepers, and other staff standing on the balls of their feet waiting to be called. On the other side, you saw hunger, poverty, and people who looked like the walking dead, their skeletons visible beneath hanging skin. It was clear they had not eaten for days.

The following day, we were to visit the Taj Mahal. The Taj Mahal was designed by an Islamic architect, who infused it with illuminating light, arches, and domes. It is one of the seven wonders of the world. It was a symbol of love, as a tomb dedicated by Emperor Shah Jahan for his wife, Mumtaz Mahal. Our tour guide told us to look at the temple across from it, which was partially built of black marble. He told us the emperor was so hurt by the loss of his beloved wife that he built his own tomb in black marble. But he died before it was finished. Today, it stands as a bombed temple depicting the suffering and true love of a man for his wife.

Traveling across India, we saw it all, so many extremes within a couple of blocks: wealth, suffering, death, burning dead bodies, people walking barefoot and half naked, women and men washing themselves and their clothing in dirty rivers. The most revealing thing we witnessed wherever we traveled was serenity, peace, and contentment. Their religion has influenced them to be good-natured people. They believe in reincarnation. If they are good in this world, they will be reincarnated again in a more peaceful life filled with their heart's desires and a better life.

Bold Resilient Women

It was refreshing to see people feel lucky and satisfied with simple, fundamental things that brought them alive, like enjoying time with their loved ones.

Afterwards, we traveled to Nepal for a wonderful birthday party for Dr. Tultul, a world-renowned OB/GYN. It was fascinating to see how joyful everyone was. People treated each other with respect and love, and every time people turned around, they were doing their best to accommodate others. What I saw and understood was that there was beauty in every country, culture, and ethnicity. If we stop judging others and refrain from wanting and expecting everyone to cater to us, we may finally be able to embrace the simple things in life.

Traveling back, I could not sleep on the airplane. I kept wondering all the way home, *What are happiness, satisfaction, and joy?* Reflecting on the three weeks we traveled in these amazing and unique places left me speechless and humble. I learned to respect and love those who were at peace with their surroundings. Their souls have a serenity that so many people will never reach.

Success

Today, looking at my four children—Michael, Victoria, Evangelo, and George—and recognizing the many sacrifices, transformations, and transitions I made from day one, makes me wonder how my life would have been if I had made different decisions.

I am proud of all the amazing things I have achieved, among them raising four successful children while helping my husband flourish and become a self-made entrepreneur.

I graduated with a degree in child psychology. At a young age, I was elected president of the board of directors of the non-profit Greek American Rehabilitation and Care Centre, and I currently serve as chairman. This home is dear to my heart due to the fact that it houses the immigrant heroes who sacrificed for all of us to enjoy the fruits of the American dream. It's a safe haven and home to many elderly, ill, vulnerable ,and destitute community members, regardless of their economic status.

I was one of the two founding members of Frondita Foundation for abused children, women, and families. This organization is an advocate for abused women and children from third-world countries. With my colleague, Bonnie Miller, we made the world aware of child sex trafficking through the Mediterranean at the global conference, The Family in the Twenty-First Century, in Athens, Greece.

I am proud to have made a difference for children with developmental and intellectual disabilities by serving on the board of directors for Little City Foundation. I was eager to educate people not to judge or condemn children born with disabilities. They had no choice at birth; we have a choice to support them.

As a society, we have an obligation to attend to their needs, reassure their care and security, and support the foundations that highlight their importance within the community. I serve on the President's Council for Maryville Academy for orphans and neglected children, which also has a support system for parents who lack help for their children while they work.

My Orthodox Christian life has ignited me to work with numerous religious organizations. I serve on the board of directors for The Leadership 100 Endowment Fund, which perpetuates Hellenism, faith, culture, and heritage within the Greek Orthodox Archdiocese of America. With extreme humility, I became the godmother to St. Haralambos Greek Orthodox Church in Niles, Illinois. I have built numerous churches globally and renovated many monasteries.

My husband, Jimmy, and I built and founded the Dimitri and Eleni Bousis Family Mercy Orphanage in Kakamega, Kenya, Africa. This is a home for orphans to be sheltered and protected from a corrupt society.

I established and founded the Hippocratic Cancer Research Foundation, raising funding to support the efforts of scientists, biologists, and oncologists to eradicate and cure all types of cancers at the Robert H. Lurie Comprehensive Cancer Center at Northwestern Hospital in Chicago.

I have served on the Human Rights Commission for the State of Illinois, which gave me an opportunity to be active in the fight against discrimination. As a commissioner, I was the voice opposing discrimination based on color, race, religion, or gender.

Bold Resilient Women

These and many other roles have given me gratifying and meaningful experiences and fulfillment which cannot be compensated with any monetary gifts.

Receiving many accolades globally has made me realize how my involvement has energized those who have crossed my path through my love for the world, children, family, and country. My dear and beloved friends, who were able to push and support me the extra mile, have made me view things from a different perspective.

Knowing the experiences of my mother and grandmother, being brought into their memories of challenges and hardship, has given me the motivation to keep going. With sorrowful eyes, they would tell me how they woke up at the crack of dawn to go work in the fields, fifteen-hour days, seven days a week.

These painful stories always left me speechless. I could not fathom how these women worked day and night, taking care of large families, yet they were always singing and dancing, smiles on their beautiful but tired faces. They were honorable women who never complained about their daily nightmares; their goal was to just keep going.

Part Three
Everyone Has a Story

A Mother Losing Hope

My friend Dina's mother was a beautiful woman with long, curly, brown hair and an amazing sense of humor. She was the youngest of eight siblings. She came from an influential family, and she was beyond spoiled by all of them. Everyone thought she would end up marrying one of the best available bachelors in our community.

"She is going to be so lucky," I would say to my mom, imagining myself married off to an affluent, eligible bachelor. My mom would stop me quickly. "My love, you don't know that. Sometimes, honey doesn't attract bees; it attracts bugs that can contaminate the honey." When I asked Mom to explain, she elaborated. "A nice, sweet, and kind individual can attract the opposite—a miserable and horrible person."

One day, we heard a young man was chasing her, pursuing her all over town. She was falling for him, but it was clear he was a narcissist. We could all tell that he was in love with himself—how could he love her? She became possessed by his handsome looks and false charm.

When I would lie in bed at night, I heard my parents talking in the other room about how worried they were for this gorgeous young girl. Finally, the marriage took place, and they moved into their new rented house. In the early days, it seemed lovey-dovey. They had three children back-to-back, and she cared for them while he worked as a maintenance engineer at a lucrative company.

We saw her less and less, but when we did, she was always bruised up. There was always an excuse. She was too embarrassed to share what was going on behind closed doors. One day, word got out that the husband had tried to drown her. Upon hearing this, her older brother, who was well off, picked up his sister and her children and brought them back to his home. They pressed charges, and fearing he would go to prison, the husband left the country.

Eventually, the wife started to live on her own and support her three beautiful children with help from her family.

She was the epitome of love and sacrifice, and raised her children with dignity. All three of them became educated, thanks to their mother and her family, and they never saw their father, nor did they have knowledge of the horrible things he did to their mother. She wanted to protect the children from this monster and the horror he put her through.

One day, my mom asked me about this woman and her children. As I was telling her what I had heard, my mom handed me a story in Greek. I translated it into my handbook. I was touched by the true statements a mother can make after she has sacrificed so much for her family.

The story goes like this: A mother was tossing and turning, unable to sleep. She was tired, exhausted, and anxious. She was angry and frustrated with life. She was tired of being mistreated by her husband and children. No one had any respect or empathy for her, although they knew she had given her life so they would not be deprived of anything.

One day, her husband came home and said, "I lost my job, but it's okay. I will rest until something else comes my way. But for now, I'm heading out with the boys, and I'll be back late."

After months of this, he announced he had a job interview. "It's okay. Do whatever you want," she said.

One day, her son came running inside the house, out of breath. "Mother, I did poorly on my finals, and the school will kick me out."

"It's okay. You will have to repeat the grade. How fast you forgot that I mopped and cleaned floors to educate you. Now it's your turn to pay for your tutors."

One day, her daughter came running into the house in a panic. "Mother, I took the neighbor's car for a ride and smashed it into a wall. How will I pay to get it fixed?"

"It's okay, my dear daughter. Take it to the body shop and get it fixed." "But I don't have money for insurance," she cried. "Where will I find money to pay for the damages?"

"I washed and mopped floors to raise you, so you can get a job as a waitress and make money to pay for the car."

One day, her sister-in-law came in crankily, bitching about her life. "I am exhausted from the baby crying day and night. I don't have time to see any of my friends. I need a break. Help me."

"My dear, I had many kids and I had to work, clean, cook, and wash. But I always had time for God and my friends."

The oldest son arranged to have a family meeting to discuss the sudden change in the mother's attitude. "I think our mother has gone insane, she is out of touch and out of control. What is wrong with her?"

As the mother walked in the house silently, she stood outside the room, undetected by anyone, listening to the children she had sacrificed her life to raise. When she couldn't handle any more, she opened the kitchen door and walked in. Her grown children stared in shock.

In a calm voice, she said, "All these years, I lay sleepless at night worrying about you and your lives. I prayed for your health. My stress in seeing you walk bad paths gave me anguish, anxiety, and nightmares. But I realized all my stress did not solve any of your problems. It only made me lose my own health and my own peace of mind."

She paused and stared at her children, looking each of them in their eyes before continuing. "I promise I will never again agonize over your actions, decisions, and happiness, or be responsible for your unworthy and ungrateful comments. I will become a spectator, watch you from afar, and let you solve your own problems." She noticed the way her daughter's brow furrowed and the way her son rubbed his hands together nervously.

"Don't worry," she said. "You will find the solutions. But I have come to realize that I can only be responsible for myself and my own problems, no matter how difficult that might be.

"From this day forward, I leave things up to you. You are responsible for the consequences you face, bad or good. The only thing I can do as the woman who brought you into this world is to pray for you to have wisdom, the grace of God, and an abundance of health." With that, she exited the room, leaving her children behind, speechless.

I read this story many times over. Greek culture is about unconditional love and feeling responsible for your family until your last breath. We like to take control and fix everything for those we love. We don't want our children to face the same difficulties we all had. We don't want them to struggle for food or be unable to pay the bills. We want to shoulder this burden for them, no matter how they treat us in return.

The hardest parenting lesson I had to learn was that it is an act of love to let go. I was not put on this earth to create a family and to carry everyone's burden to the end. Everyone has to make their own choices and mistakes. It's the only way to set yourself free. I have done my job now; it's their turn to continue their lives.

Eye Openers

As a little girl, I had taken care of all those who crossed my path, and now, as a woman, I had to fulfill my promise to take care of the poor, vulnerable, elderly, and sick of the world. God had opened the way to a new life. My role as a mother had changed. I had given my kids the wings to fulfill their dreams and desires. They knew that if their wings were clipped, I would be there to catch them. But it was time for me to spread my own wings in fulfilling my vision and dreams.

Being involved in numerous organizations and attending night school was an eye opener. I saw firsthand how women were disrespected by professors and classmates. They were treated as third-class citizens, dismissed from conversations and unable to speak their views and voice their opinions. They were looked down upon.

One spring afternoon, I went to the study hall to finish a project when I saw a young woman crying. She had a compact in her hand, and she was frantically trying to cover bruises on her face with makeup. I was so alarmed and upset at what I was witnessing. I approached her and asked if I could help, but she shook her head with so much fear. Her red eyes penetrated my heart. I could not walk away. I had witnessed firsthand similar excruciating scenes, and I insisted on helping her. I took her across the street to McDonald's for coffee. At that moment, she was all I could think about. I forgot about the work assignment that I had to finish. All I wanted was to help this young woman.

I was stunned to learn about her strict father, who was obsessed with educating his two sons while sending his three daughters to work in a factory to support their brothers' schooling. This young girl knew this treatment was unfair. She was extremely smart and articulate, and she wanted a bright future for herself.

One day, she decided she was going to sign up for classes without her parents' consent or knowledge. But they somehow found out, and when she got home, her father was waiting to greet her with a belt in his hand. He struck her, and after he fell asleep, she decided to leave the house and went out, roaming the streets.

She reached out to her close friend, and her parents were so upset with the family's behavior that they invited her to live with them. She felt awkward, though. They were poor immigrants, and she knew they could not afford to feed another person. After living with them for a few months, she accepted a wedding proposal from a friend who had a crush on her. It seemed the only way to move forward in her life.

While she thought her problems were solved, she never anticipated what this marriage had in store for her. When she expressed her dreams of going to school to her husband, he immediately cut her off from the world. He told her she was to work with him from morning until night. When she resisted, he took her head and smashed it against the wall, hammering and punching her until she passed out. She had nowhere and no one to turn to for help. She was alone, destroyed, and ashamed. She came to school to get away from this monster and figure out where to go and where to stay.

I felt distressed and angry, but at the same time, I was in disbelief. How can this happen in the U.S., a democratic country where everyone is supposedly free? We were not living in a third-world country where the man ruled the family and the wife had to be obedient and treated as a slave. I took her in my arms to comfort her. We were both crying and shaking. I told her not to worry, I was going to give her money to stay at a hotel. I took care of this young woman, and the only people who knew were my parents. They offered to help me financially so I could, in turn, help her out.

She was a smart and vibrant young woman who wanted to stand on her own two feet. She wanted to succeed and prove to everyone that she was not a battered woman and wife. A couple of weeks later, she got a full-time job while attending school part-time. We graduated together, and although no one was there to clap and congratulate her, she told me it was the happiest day of her life. It was an emotional day for both of us. I yearned to finish school, and she yearned for freedom and survival. As she walked near me, she kissed me.

"Thank you for saving me and making a difference in my life," she said. She had tears running down her cheeks, but she glowed with relief, peace, and happiness. "I will always be grateful to you." As I walked away, I felt an inner gratification. I realized how beautiful life could be if everyone was responsible for saving one other life. The world could be free of pain and suffering. She decided to move to a new state and start a new life, leaving behind her identity, family, and friends.

She was not going to be a slave to anyone again. She was going to be an independent woman who would help and support other women who were victims of domestic violence. She wanted to tell her story to other abused women, helping inspire them not to live in fear and to remove themselves from disheartening, obsessive relationships. Her desire for her own life was simple: She would never allow another man to dictate her life: where to go, what to wear, when to laugh, when to speak, and who to associate with.

Today, I believe going back to school, finishing my major, and receiving my degree gave me the courage and confidence to observe, analyze, and view people's lives through a more educated lens. But it was the stories I heard from fellow classmates that changed me forever. I could not fathom being isolated and tormented behind closed doors.

North Park University has a large number of foreign students, many of them married. I was shocked at how many spoke about their mates with so much anger and animosity. They confided in me about their family life. They had gained my trust and told me stories about how they were expected to treat their husbands, family, and friends. Whatever they felt for any family member, they were not allowed to be obnoxious, angry, or opinionated. They were only allowed to speak after receiving permission. They were never to disrespect, disagree, discredit, or express an opinion in front of others. One time, I asked a fellow student. "How do you treat your husband when he returns home from a long day at work? Do you speak to him with an angry tone if he is tired and speaking poorly to you?"

"No," she responded immediately. "I must rush to the door, welcome him home, take off his shoes, and set his meal on the table. We don't discuss anything. He is always too tired, and there is nothing to say—after all, nothing is my business."

"Maybe you need to give him time to eat, relax, and unwind," I suggested. "Then tell him about your day and what is going on with your boys."

"I can't," she said. "He must give me permission to speak." This reminded me of my own family members who had come from the old country, relationships where the men would make decisions on their own and never acknowledge the wife. When the wife asked a question, the husband would slap her across the face. I had witnessed this several times, and it left me angry and distressed at not being able to help them.

As a young girl, I thought it was just women from the old country who were programmed to obey men's commands. But as I grew up and got involved with organizations and went back to school, I realized abuse happens in every country, culture, ethnicity, faith, and income bracket. Day by day, I became more and more aware of what was happening in many homes behind closed doors. It wasn't about loving your husband and wanting to take care of him. It was about control: Do what you were told or you would be punished physically, mentally, or emotionally. Men had brainwashed women to contradict themselves, and convinced them they were not fit to be good wives if they were not obedient to their husbands' requests and commands.

I was raised similarly by my immigrant parents. A woman had to take care of her working husband. He was the provider, and the woman was the homemaker. My responsibility as a woman was to take care of the kids, cook, clean, iron, sew, run errands, take care of the bills, and also show up and be an elite young woman in the social circle. My mom would always say, "Never show the world outside of your home what is happening behind closed doors. No one needs to know whether you have food to eat or not, whether your clothes are new or from a department store, or whether you have money to pay your bills."

Coming from the old country, Mom knew life could be unfair for women. Often, her life advice contradicted what she knew I saw through family and friends. But she wanted better for me.

"Always walk with your head held high with grace and sturdiness," she would say. "Never be forced to participate in situations beyond your means. A wise woman should be able to voice her opinion without fear. Do the things that make you happy and give you satisfaction without feeling guilty. Just remember that intelligent women and men should never disgrace each other in the presence of family members and others by making unethical statements or unrealistic demands. Women and men should never condemn or bash each other by putting down every comment or kind gesture being made. We cannot blame others for our actions, as we have the mind and a heart to make decisions that can affect us and our family. We should not focus on changing others; we will spend a life of unhappiness. We must be responsible for our own words and actions.

"When an individual is raised in a loving and caring environment and given the opportunity to voice their opinion, they build strong character and a solid foundation," she would explain.

"If a young man hasn't had a good role model in his life to guide, teach, and explain to him how to conduct himself as a man, he will never be able to make solid decisions. When I hear young men speaking about their fathers, you can tell which father has had an open, loving relationship with his son, and which one has never shared a normal father-and-son conversation."

What I hear from numerous women in my life is how painful it is for their spouse to engage in a conversation with them or their children. They have difficulty expressing their feelings, and as a result, don't know how to speak to their kids about life. They can't discuss family issues with their wives, and it's all due to a childish relationship with their father. Men would rather walk away angry than sit and have a meaningful family discussion.

I witnessed the painful expression on the face of a young friend when he lost his father. But the first thing he said after we hugged and I offered my condolences was, "My father, the man I looked up to, never wanted to know how I felt."

I realized at that moment how vital it is for a father to praise his son and respect his opinion, whether or not he approves or disapproves of his decision. It's important for young men and young women to know that failure is a part of life and it creates a strong character. When you fail, it means you are learning. Failure leads you to succeed the next time.

When a young woman has witnessed her father physically, mentally, or psychologically abuse her mother, she lives with the perception that she, too, can be abused by her partner. It teaches her at a young age to be obedient to a man's wishes and commands—or else you will be punished. I believe a young woman can resent her mother for not having the courage to stand up and voice her opinion by putting a stop to abuse. If a young man has lived in an abusive environment, when he grows up, he too will be abusive to his mate. He feels that is how he proves he is a man.

Throughout my life, my friends have all had access to my phone number and knew they could call at any moment, day or night. I have heard so many stories throughout the years from my involvement with people. Every story was an eye-opener and a lesson.

A dear friend once shared with me the story of her parents. Her father was a dominant, self-made entrepreneur who demanded absolute obedience from his wife. Her mother, though intelligent, lived quietly in his shadow, rarely voicing her own opinions. When she discovered his affair, she finally confronted him and gave him an ultimatum: leave the other woman, or she would walk away.

His response was cruel. He told her she could either accept his betrayal or leave with nothing. Devastated and humiliated, she felt trapped. Coming from a humble family that could never support her lifestyle, she convinced herself she had no options. Overcome by pride and fear of society's judgment, she made the tragic decision to end her life.

Bold Resilient Women

The next morning, I got the call: my friend had driven her car into Lake Michigan. Hours later, they pulled her body from the water and pronounced her dead. I was shattered. We had shared coffee every morning after dropping off our children at the babysitter—how could she not have said something? How could she leave her two-year-old son in the care of such a man? These questions still haunt me, and I know I will never have the answers. Now, every time I pass Peterson Cemetery, I pray for her soul to rest in peace.

This tragedy taught me that you don't need anyone to tell you they love and care for you. You don't need anyone else's financial means to support and sustain you or your child. When you don't have the fear of God or work, you should not fear being alone. I wish I could tell her this. I wish her story could have ended differently.

Carole, a Dear Mentor

During my teenage years, when I was a young wife and mother, I didn't have anyone to advise or mentor me. Carole became my adopted mother, a woman who gave me strength, advice, and mentoring. She told me, "When you smile, your soul smiles, too." She explained that your soul radiates through your eyes. When a person has good intentions, their eyes and face glow like a lightbulb, revealing the joy that's in their heart and soul. At the same time, if an individual has jealousy and envy, they lose the sparkle in their eyes, and their face shows anger, revealing the dark side of their inner world.

What an understatement. As I got older, I experienced firsthand how souls and hearts speak through a smile or a deceiving face. Carole constantly said, "Sweetheart, your entire body smiles. You speak with your hands, your face, and your entire physique." My mom said something similar too. "Eleni, you have never stopped smiling since the day you were born," she said. "People with a dark heart can only bring you pain and disappointment in your life."

"Carole," I asked her many times throughout our relationship. "How can you really tell if people are honest or shady?"

"As you go through many confrontations and conversations with different people, you too will learn to identify the good from the bad," she would always remind me. "The reason I give you examples is to protect you from harm's way. You're too naive to think of bad intentions."

Being a teenager, I could not understand Carole's advice. I wanted her to be straightforward in her explanation of why you must be skeptical in trusting others. "When you are confident and secure in your morals, values, and inner world, you don't have hate or animosity for anyone," she shared. "You won't be able to hold grudges or seek revenge on those who have hurt you. Just leave it up to God. You can love and have compassion for everyone around you—but you have to learn to be cautious and apply limits and boundaries with everyone who comes into your life. When you learn to have tolerance and endurance, you will be able to face the world. Hopefully, you will become a true leader, one who has learned through enduring many challenges and obstacles. It's not difficult to embrace someone who crosses your path when you both share the same values and willingness to teach and encourage others by being an example."

What she said was life changing. I began to view the world with awareness, caution, and maturity. I tucked her words into my heart and tried to live them every day: Lead by example and people will believe in your vision and be willing to support every effort.

Carole reminded me that there are no limitations to success. You can achieve anything in this world.

"Dream of great things, set goals, and everything will work out your way," she would always say with confidence. "Remain focused and don't allow anything or anyone to distract you from your desires and ambitions. When you start something in life, make sure you finish. It's the only way you will feel confident with your decision."

Carole was a force of nature. She never stopped teaching me everything she knew. When I made a mistake, she would correct me gently with constructive criticism. Every time I achieved anything at all, she would crochet me a scarf. She believed in an individual's potential. With a bright, charming smile, she offered words of encouragement to keep going. But when she disapproved of an individual's behavior, her smile would turn to a stern look, and she was never shy about sharing her thoughts and feelings.

She was especially passionate about the role of women in society. "Young women need to be smart," she would say. "You cannot try to outdo a man, but you can put him in his place with your wit, charm, and elegance. Never be intimidated by a man's derogatory comments. Men fear women, and they know they cannot exist without a woman's opinion and foresight. They just want to believe everything is their idea.

"The best advice I can give you is to just say, 'Yes, honey,' and then turn around and do what you think is right. If your mate thinks you agree with everything he says, whether or not you follow through, you have the key to a man's happy life.

"In today's world, you have to be your own voice and have your own opinion. Unless you are a woman who sees only material gain and money from your partner, you can manipulate him by saying, 'Yes, honey,' to all his demands."

Carole mentored many young women, and she taught us all by example. When we visited her at her house every week, she would take us all by the hand and walk us through her home, showing us her closets, her bedrooms, her living spaces, and all of the beautiful blankets and scarves she had made. She would stretch out her arm in each room, inviting us to take it in.

Each space was neat, clean, comfortable, and well-decorated but not gaudy. "A man should never see you sloppy," she would tell us. "Even if you don't have time to take care of yourself, just put on lipstick, brush your hair, put it in a ponytail, and wear your studs. Now, you are ready to greet him and send him out the door for work in your clean PJs, and your illuminating smile."

Carole believed women needed to be smart and wise, and that we had to wear many different hats in order to have a happy marriage.

"Wear your apron in the kitchen, your gown to a formal event, and your nightgown in your bedroom," she would say. "Then you will understand how to make your partner happy. Most men are simple creatures. They want food on the table, a clean home, and children cared for. They want their partners to be engaged in their daily lives and know their friends and family. You must be able to entertain them with charm no matter what or how you are feeling at the time."

I loved Carole, but a lot of what she said didn't line up with what I saw. Though I was young, I saw a different story playing out in the world around me.

"But Carole, you see disrespectful girls get the best guy on the block!" I would protest. Every day, I saw girls who were unkind or malicious get their way, and those who were role models were disrespected and not appreciated. "Sweetheart, men and women eventually get sick of making the wrong decision in choosing a partner. Mistreatment of an individual doesn't last long. There will be a time when someone will cheat or walk out of an unstable relationship."

She explained a pattern that I have seen play out as my life has gone on. "In the beginning of a relationship, you are distracted and influenced by material things," she said. "As time goes by, all that becomes old. You mature. You start to see what's really important in your relationship. The focus will change, and eventually, people want someone who can be an example for their children."

∽

Reflecting on the many days, hours, and years I spent with Carole, I realize that Carole knew me, my life, my passions, and my inner world better than I will ever know myself.

One day, about thirty-five years ago, my four kids and I were traveling to the Leadership 100 conference. We learned of this organization from Carole and her husband, Jack. Jimmy and I were young, and we had three children at that time, so we didn't have the money to travel to the conferences, but Carole and Jack would always take the children and me with them. Jack was one of the founding fathers of many organizations and a huge supporter of different churches across the United States. Eventually, Jimmy and I became members of this esteemed group of people. They were immigrants or children of immigrant parents who had achieved success, but they had never forgotten their humble beginnings. We were happy to be a part of this wonderful organization.

"If we don't preserve our faith, culture, and language, we will be lost," Jack told me. "I believe in Leadership 100 because it perpetuates faith and Hellenism." Those words were engraved in my brain immediately. We joined the Leadership 100, in part, because we believed in this great slogan.

Bold Resilient Women

Traveling to the conference with Carole and Jack was always full of fun and excitement. When we arrived at the hotel, Carole would go straight to the slot machines, while Jack, the kids, and I would walk around, taking in the lights and sounds, and cheering Carole on. One year, as I was pushing the stroller and holding Evangelo, and Jack was holding Mike and Victoria and laughing, we saw lights flashing, heard a machine beeping, and above it all, Carole's shrieks of joy. "Jack, Jack! I just won $50,000!"

Jack had a great sense of humor and responded, "Oh, honey, you have lost $200,000 all these years!" I will never forget the laughs we all shared.

Twenty years ago, before we left for this particular conference, Carole and Jack wanted to have dinner with us. Carole, who was usually so vibrant, full of laughter and storytelling, barely spoke during dinner.

As we left the restaurant, she stopped me right outside the door. Jack and Jimmy were still discussing business, as usual. They were always happy in the presence of each other. Carole looked at me and hugged me for an extra-long time. "I love you very much, Eleni," she said. "You are the daughter I always wanted. Please take care of yourself and your mother." I walked her to her car and helped lower her into the front seat. My stomach churned. I knew something wasn't right.

The following day, we left for the conference in Florida. Carole and I had arranged to sit together at all the meetings and at the evening functions, while going shopping during the day. But when I showed up at the board meeting and didn't see Jack, I knew something was wrong. I found out from another conference leader that he had left almost immediately after he arrived. I sat outside the board meeting and kept calling and calling until Jack answered.

"Thanks for checking in, Eleni," he told me. "Carole doesn't feel well, so I had to leave right away. I will keep you posted."

I asked him, "Did you fly alone?"

"Yes," he said. "I came to attend the meetings and go back, but things changed quickly."

I couldn't find peace. I stumbled through the conference almost as though I was half there, as my mind was with Carole back home. I could not wait to fly back and see her. The moment I landed, I called to find out where she was so I could get to her. I found out she was very ill and was at the hospital. I rushed there.

I walked into her hospital room and my heart caught in my throat. Carole was lying in the hospital bed, looking small under the blue blanket, surrounded by machines. I immediately started crying, unable to control my tears. This was the woman who had taken me under her wing. She had protected me from the day I was married. She was my support system and my advisor through every stage of life, guiding me, advising me, helping me become a woman. I sat down next to her bedside, and she opened her eyes. We looked at each other, and it was true what she said. Even though she looked frail, I could see her soul smile.

Jack filled me in on what had happened. "I made coffee that Tuesday morning and put the newspaper on the table for her, the way I do every morning," he told me. "I left for the office. When I got there, I called her to check in, and she didn't pick up. When she called back, she told me she had tripped over the telephone cord and fallen. Eleni," he said, looking right at me. "We don't have a telephone cord. That's when I knew something was very wrong."

He told me he raced home. She had recovered and was sitting at her kitchen table, sipping her morning coffee. He told her he called the doctor to take her in for tests. She was infuriated. She wanted to attend the conference. She assured him that when she returned, she would go take the tests immediately. Jack flew to the conference, and as soon as he arrived, he got the call. Carole had passed out on the floor. Her son called the ambulance, and it took her to the hospital. After extensive tests, they diagnosed her with an advanced glioblastoma, an extremely rare, aggressive form of brain cancer. The oncologists had to perform emergency surgery to alleviate the pressure in the brain, and this would be followed by extensive chemotherapy.

I visited her every day, talking about our times together. I was leaving for Greece in July, and I had to make the trip. I told her I would be gone for a month, but I would be back by her side as soon as I could. She squeezed my hand. She understood the love I had for her. Every day I was gone, I called Jack for updates. He was frank with me: It was not good, and just a matter of time before she passed away. Now, it was all about making her comfortable. They transferred her to Warren Barr Rehabilitation and Care Center. I told Jack she wasn't going anywhere until I came back. The night we returned home, I went straight to Warren Barr Rehab Center to see her. I sat by her bedside, holding her hand. Jack stood near the door, a cup of black coffee in his hand.

"Jack, I had the most incredible dream," I told him, still holding Carole's hand. "In it, Carole told me to tell you she wanted her green-blue rhinestone dress with her."

His eyes got big. "I have been looking for that dress for the last few days," he said. "I haven't been able to find it, but as I was leaving the house, her mirror closet door opened and the reflection of the sun on the dress blinded me. There's no way you could have known."

It was suddenly so clear to me. She wanted to be buried in that dress. Jack took it to the funeral director.

The following morning, Jack called me at 6 a.m. Carole, my beautiful adopted mother, lost her battle with glioblastoma brain cancer, just six months after being diagnosed.

Carole's death was devastating. I had lost the woman who molded me into the woman I am today. She was my mentor, teacher, and confidante. But I carry her with me every day, in my heart, and in the way I move through the world, and the decisions I make. I put her advice into practice every day, and I like to think that when you look into my eyes, you see a little of Carole peeking through as well.

Zoe

Zoe was a 5'9" brunette, a young woman with long hair down to her waist and deep green eyes. She was a gifted individual with a high level of intelligence and a brilliant mind. When she was in her early twenties, she fell for a very talented and hard-working basketball player named John.

They were madly in love. She supported his passion for basketball by working day and night to make sure they were cared for financially. All she wanted was for him to succeed.

His family was angry. They didn't care for her. They didn't want anyone interfering with his career or distracting him from his basketball practice. They told him he was too young to think about marriage, that he needed to continue his studies and pursue his athletic career. Zoe didn't care about their feelings because she knew the love that they had for each other. They continued dating for almost a decade. She had promised him and his family they would not get serious until their dreams were fulfilled and they had secured their future.

John came from an influential family, and after his career ended in a car accident, he went to work at the family company. "Fate has something else in store," his father told him. "Don't worry, it's for the best."

John became infatuated with money, power, and prestige. He loved how all the employees praised him. Zoe supported him psychologically, and she was cleaning, washing, and maintaining life for him behind the scenes. Without any warning, John also became infatuated with one of the company secretaries.

Bold Resilient Women

This secretary was a poor girl who was desperately trying to seduce John, the owner's young son. She dressed provocatively with mini dresses and tight jeans—she wasn't going to lose this great catch. One day, John wanted to go out, but Zoe was exhausted from working all day, so she turned him down. His secretary heard the conversation and started making demeaning comments about her.

"Why would your fiancée not want to be with you?" she taunted. She knew he was angry that she had turned him down, so she offered to join him.

Days later, they were the talk of the company. Zoe heard from mutual friends what was going on behind her back. When he came home, she confronted him and he said yes, he was having an affair. She was devastated. She threw the engagement ring at him and walked out of the house. He immediately went into the arms of his lover. Zoe was out of the scene, leaving his secretary free to move into his bed.

A few months later, an announcement was made: She was pregnant and John was going to marry her. Many of the employees were angry. They knew he had been manipulated into this marriage, which left Zoe heartbroken. Soon after the marriage, the secretary miscarried. The marriage was stressful, and John started to believe what his best friends had been telling him, that he had been played by her and her family.

John decided to leave her and rekindle his relationship with his real love, Zoe. He invited her out to dinner to beg for forgiveness, but Zoe could not trust him. She was too hurt and embarrassed to forgive him. She left the restaurant without accepting his apology. He had no other choice but to go back to his wife. John and the secretary went on creating a family together, and Zoe married a young man who had been enchanted with her since he was young.

After being married for a few years, she realized she wasn't happy. She didn't want to admit it, but she didn't share the passionate love she had with John. She decided to leave him. Weeks later, she wasn't feeling well. She had horrible pains and swelling in her body. Her stress levels were creating severe complications, so she was treated and released from the hospital. After she fully recovered, she moved to another city to forget about John and her past life.

Years later, John and Zoe bumped into each other at an event. When they looked at each other, everyone saw the sparkle in their eyes. It was clear nothing had changed for either of them.

Time stood still, and the love was still there. When John's wife witnessed the look on both of their faces, she passed out. She was a victim who loved drama, and she wasn't about to let him go. Zoe left the event, her heart aching.

Bold Resilient Women

She wondered why she had let her guard down. She had been through so much pain and suffering.

Zoe and I caught up over lunch one day. Her face was pained, and she leaned close to me, desperate for answers to her many questions. "How can someone pretend they love a person, when they know their heart belongs to someone else?" she said. "When you love someone, you don't care where you live, what you wear, or what you drive. All you think about is being in his arms, feeling safe and loved."

I realized she had sacrificed so much by loving him more than her life, but he was too blind to realize true love. Years later, John's wife passed away from a rare disease. Shortly after, he went looking for Zoe. When he found her, he told her he was now alone and expressed his deep feelings for her. He asked her to give him another chance to spend the rest of their lives together. He told her he realized they had lost time together due to other people, and he yearned to start over. She told him she needed time to think about their future. She said, "So you want me to tell you how much I miss you and want to be with you? Don't you understand, we are old now. What is there for us? We lost our youthful years of love, and we lived nothing but pain and suffering. Is there anything for us left to cherish?"

Over another lunch, hearing about this encounter, I asked her what her decision was. "I don't know, Eleni," she said. "All I know is that age doesn't matter. I still love him the way I did when I was young."

"You just responded to your own predicament," I told her. "Love doesn't die, no matter how old you two are." She started seeing him again, and they were like two young teenagers in love. I bumped into them during my vacation, and I have never seen two people look at each other with so much passionate love.

Zoe's love story was one of the most real ones I have ever heard, full of tolerance and patience. I realized again that God is the only one who knows what the future holds for everyone. We just have to be patient. We need to have hope and faith that He is looking out for us.

Losing a Young Child

When your phone rings in the middle of the night, your heart nearly stops. And when it turns out to be an old friend, your mind starts to spin. It's either very good news or, more likely, very bad news.

One night, I was in bed when my phone rang. It was my dear friend, Chang. We have known each other for a long time and served on the Human Rights Commission together. I switched on the light and sat up to give him my full attention.

"I am so sorry, Eleni, for disturbing you this late," he said.

"Chang, there is no reason to ever apologize for calling," I said. I could hear a slight tremble in my voice. I knew something wasn't right.

"Did you hear about the tragedy tonight in the Greek community?" he asked. "No," I said, the word struggling to come out. "Please tell me."

"My dear friend is a landlord in Wilmette, and one of his tenants is a young Greek couple. He just called me to say that their seven-year-old daughter died in her sleep." Before he could finish, I started to cry. I had so many questions. *What is he talking about? How did this little girl die in her sleep?*

"Please, tell me more, Chang. What else do you know?"

"I don't know anything else, Eleni. I don't know their names; all I can give you is my friend's address, who lives a few doors away."

I thanked Chang for calling and told my husband that I had to leave.

I was already jumping up to change out of my pajamas.

"Jimmy, I have to go," I said. "Chang told me a Greek family lost their child, and they don't have anyone here."

Bold Resilient Women

"What are you going to do?" Jimmy asked.

"I need to find out who they are and how I can help." I hopped in the car and drove through Wilmette, searching for the landlord's house. Once I could identify the landlord, I could try to guess which was the house of the family.

It was late, and one house on the block had bright lights on in the living room window. Though my heart pounded, I knocked on the door.

A tall, thin man in his late forties opened it. He was holding a little girl with long, black, curly hair, who was crying.

"Hello, I am friends with your landlord," I told him. "Did your family recently have a tragic loss?" I didn't know what else to say.

"Yes," he said. "I lost my little girl, and my wife is in the ICU fighting for her life." I started to shake, and he invited me in to sit down. He told me his name was Peter, and he sat down across from me, still holding the little girl, who buried her head in his shoulder.

He told me their story. Peter and his wife, Tatiana, worked in finance. They asked to be transferred to Chicago for work and to seek help for their little girl, who had a difficult medical condition for which she would eventually need surgery. They knew no one in Chicago when they had arrived a few years before.

The whole family got the COVID-19 virus, despite the extreme precautions they were taking because of the little girl's medical condition. The daughter was asymptomatic, and while the wife was the last to get sick, she got it the most severely. Tatiana had to be transferred to the hospital. Initially, they told Peter she would be fine and would soon be released from the hospital.

After a week, his wife's condition got worse, and Peter learned that she would be intubated that day.

The next morning, he got the older daughter ready for school and took her outside for pickup. When he returned to the house, he went to wake up the younger daughter, and she was dead. Doctors said it was cardiac arrest, likely caused by COVID-19 and her underlying health condition. His wife, now fighting for her life in the ICU, was unaware of what was going on.

The following day, I returned to his house to help him understand what was going on with his family. We called the doctors, but they weren't giving him any hope. The child was in the morgue, and he was waiting for his wife to pass to send both bodies to Europe at once to be buried. Along with him and his little girl, I couldn't believe what was happening. I have many friends to engage in prayer.

My daughter and I decided to go to the Serbian Monastery on Good Thursday to pray. That evening, there were numerous priests and bishops there, and after mass, I approached the bishop and asked him for Holy Oil. He instructed us to go to the icon of the Holy Mother and get Holy Oil from her burning candle. My daughter and I took several pieces of cotton and dipped them in the oil, then on the way home, we stopped and gave them to Peter. I kept insisting he go to the hospital and to keep blessing his wife's entire body with oil.

After a month, Peter decided, with the help of many, to send his daughter's body to Europe to be buried. He only had his mother and brother to receive the body. My husband was abroad for business, and I told him to please be with the family to help bury the child. It was a blessing that he was unexpectedly there at the right time. The girl was laid to rest.

Peter could not lose hope and faith. We were all fighting for her. We knew God could not take Tatiana, as she had already given her daughter to God. Days, weeks, and months went by. The doctors had decided to disconnect the machines when the other daughter, who was nine years old, requested a meeting with the medical team. They were shocked to receive a meeting request from a child, but they granted it.

The daughter instructed her father not to be in the meeting, and she approached her mother's medical team like an adult.

"If you have done everything in your power and followed all protocol to save my mother's life, then we will discuss what is next," she said confidently. "But if you haven't done absolutely everything the medical protocol says, I need to know who is responsible. I will have to obtain a lawyer and file a lawsuit." The medical team was amazed at this little girl's courage and strength, and they assured her they had done everything to save her mother; there wasn't anything else to be done.

On Wednesday, Peter was to sign the forms to disconnect his wife from life support, but he wasn't ready. He asked to wait until Friday morning, and the doctors agreed.

But then: a miracle.

A doctor called Peter early Friday morning to tell him Tatiana had regained consciousness, opened her eyes, and requested her glasses.

Everyone came to visit her: doctors and nurses from every hospital, clergy, family, and friends. No one could believe what had happened. Peter told me his part of the story. "Eleni, when I went home to call our friends and family in Greece to let them know Tatiana was alive, I saw some papers on the kitchen table. One of them was from the hospital, and it had the date of the surgery for our little girl. It was exactly today, the day her mother came out of the coma." He was sobbing.

I was amazed. "Peter, maybe God wanted to save you, your wife, daughter, and family from a bigger permanent tragedy. Your little one might have died

Bold Resilient Women

on the operating table or been left handicapped." I don't know what God has in store for this family. All I know is that Tatiana has fully recovered after being in the ICU and enduring physical therapy. She lost a year of her life and her little girl. Today, she cannot face the loss of her little girl, but she says, "I cannot challenge or question God."

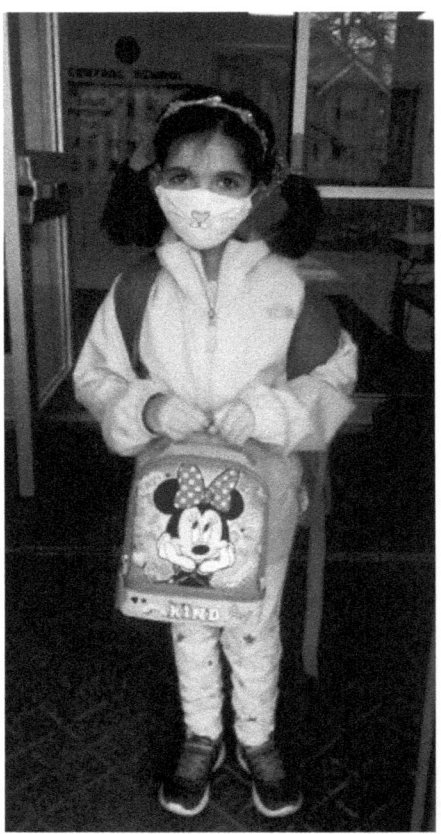

Connection of Pain

Once, while traveling on a flight to Florida, I was helped with my luggage by a kind couple. To my surprise, they were Greek, though they didn't look like it. Their English was superb. The gentleman kept reading a medical journal. His wife happened to be sitting next to me. I offered to change seats, but she said no, he had a lecture coming up and had to focus. Her name was Marina, and she asked me where my family came from, which was expected. This is the first question any Greek will ask another. We need to know your roots and homeland so we can know how to identify your beliefs, culture, and foundations. We shared our family histories. I fell asleep, but before we landed, she took my phone number.

By the time we arrived home, she had called to invite us for dinner.

We became very close. She said I reminded her of her daughter, who visited her rarely. We met up in various places: Chicago, Greece, and Florida. I had a strange feeling they were hiding great pain and burying it by traveling all over the world, taking numerous trips, healing their wounds. One day over lunch, she broke down crying. "What's wrong?" I asked.

"I want to tell you my life story. Mario is my second husband," she told me, sniffling. I said, "Well, that's not a big deal. Why is it painful? Are you not enjoying yourself?"

"It's not that, but we have a painful journey together. Pain connected us," she explained. Mario was a famous eye surgeon who specialized in corneal transplants. He was head of the department. He had a huge mansion in a suburb outside of Cleveland. Her first husband was a surgeon at the same hospital, and he and Mario were both very successful, esteemed doctors with beautiful wives and wonderful families. They were all family friends from the time their children were born.

The couples were chairing a gala for the hospital, and together, they had an appointment with the country club manager to decide on the menu. When they arrived, they realized Mario had forgotten the contract at his home office. They had left his sixteen-year-old daughter at home with the housekeeper, but when the housekeeper left for the evening, the daughter invited a young man over to watch a movie. As they sat on the family room sofa holding hands, her father pulled into the driveway and witnessed an unfamiliar car. He looked inside the family room window and saw the young man and his daughter, hands clasped together. He immediately marched inside the house and punched the young man in the face. He asked him to leave right away. The young girl was destroyed and insulted by her father's behavior. She ran upstairs, opened her father's safe, and pulled a gun out. Suddenly, the father heard a gunshot. He rushed up the stairs and opened the bedroom door. He saw blood splattered everywhere and his daughter's dead body lying lifeless on the floor.

His wife, friends, and the catering manager started to worry because he wasn't picking up the phone. They thought he was involved in a major car accident, so they all left to go to the house. As they were driving up, they saw many police cars, ambulances, and cars being diverted to other streets. They saw people coming out of their house. The group parked the car and started to run, yelling at the policemen to let them through. This was their home. The police escorted them inside, where her husband was sitting on the sofa, crying and pulling his hair.

As she approached him, he told her of the trauma that had transpired in their home. She was devastated. She was screaming and running up and down the stairs, trying to see if this was a reality. Her friends and everyone took control of the funeral arrangements.

After the burial of this young, beautiful sixteen-year-old, nothing was the same again in their marriage and household. His wife fell into a deep depression. She didn't want to live, and she was institutionalized for a few months. She started to feel better with the support of her dear friend, Marina, and Mario.

After a year, he wanted to take her on a trip to Greece. A few days after they had recovered from jet lag, he left her on the sidewalk while he went to get the car from the garage. He told her he was going to make a U-turn to pick her up in front of the house, so she wouldn't have to cross the street alone due to the extreme traffic. She didn't listen. She proceeded to walk across the street when a car came out of nowhere and struck her. She was rushed to the hospital where she remained for months. Eventually, she was airlifted on a private airplane and brought back to the States. She was left crippled for years.

Meanwhile, Marina's husband died from a heart attack. She was a widow in her thirties with two children. Months later, Dr. Mario's wife passed away. Now he was a widower in his fifties with a young girl and a broken heart after losing his daughter and wife. Mario and Marina kept in touch, and supported each other through their respective tragedies.

A few years later, over dinner, Mario made a proposal. He said, "Marina, we are two dear friends who have gone through so much pain and tragedy. Why don't we connect our sorrows and see joy in our lives?" She agreed. They married and lived a happy life. After twenty-five years, they were traveling back from Spain when Mario received a call from his other daughter. Marina's son was swimming in his pool with his children when he died of a massive heart attack.

Mario could not say a word until they arrived home. He did not want to alarm Marina. The driver picked them up at the airport and headed home. As they pulled up to the garage, he realized he had to tell her of this tragedy before her friends did. She thought something horrible was happening because she saw cars in the driveway, which she recognized belonged to her friends. She asked immediately, "What is the new tragedy in our lives?"

He told her their beloved son had a major heart attack as he was swimming with his four children. She was despondent. She could not stop screaming and yelling. She could not imagine why God was challenging her with so much grief and pain. She was so depressed that she isolated herself with heavy sedation. She felt she had nothing to live for. Her son was the love of her life. He had never disappointed her or displeased her in any way, and he was a perfect son, husband, and father. She didn't leave the house for months and could not attend the funeral, nor did she accept any visitors for condolences. She felt that God was punishing her. It took her years to adjust to the loss of her son, and it wasn't until ten years after he passed that she could even visit the cemetery.

In 2022, we received a call from her friends telling us that Dr. Mario had passed away. Every day at 6 a.m., he would go to the beach and swim for an hour. Marina waited for him to join her for breakfast, and when he didn't show up, she began to worry and started to walk toward the beach. As she approached the water, she saw many people standing around an individual as paramedics tried desperately to revive him. She noticed the color of his swimming trunks. She started crying and screaming his name. She started yelling, "This is my beloved husband!" The paramedics told her they could not do anything for him. He was pronounced dead. At the hospital, they told her he had a massive heart attack and that he was likely already dead when people saw him floating and swam to help and pull him out of the water.

I began crying; I felt her pain so acutely. She was a woman who had the world at her feet, but her life was filled with so much sorrow, grief, and pain.

"My God, how much have these two people suffered?" I said to Jimmy shortly after it happened. "Why was there so much pain and suffering in their beautiful life?"

"Only God knows," he said.

When we finally met up after Mario's passing, we hugged and held each other for what seemed like hours, crying in each other's arms. She told me she fell to the ground saying, "My life is over. Everything I loved God took away. Why should I live?"

Shortly after, she was rushed to the hospital. She had suffered a major stroke. She remained in the hospital for a couple of weeks. I flew to Florida to visit her, but she didn't recognize me.

After a few weeks, she was transferred to a rehabilitation center where she would have to start from scratch, learning again to walk, talk, and be independent. Again, I went to visit her. One moment she recognized me, the next she wondered who I was.

Her caregiver and her personal nurses told me they wished they had known this remarkable woman before she had gotten ill. They had heard her life story from multiple friends who visited her on a regular basis and shared the tragic tales of losing her children and husbands.

I visited her every time I traveled to Florida. My heart wept for her. I saw a remarkable, beautiful woman who was once vibrant, elegant, healthy, and full of life deteriorating in front of my eyes.

Her daughter admitted her to the rehab center and left the following day to go back to Europe. This woman, who had gone through so much agony, torment, pain, and suffering, now had no one around to rub her feet, to speak to her, to love her, or to hold her hands. It broke my heart.

To this day, I wonder how strong her will was to continue living in this world. I have never met someone with so much strength. Why didn't she get discouraged? How did she not give up?

How strong must one woman be to endure so much grief and continue smiling?

My mom used to tell me, "God will not give you a cross you cannot carry.

Bold Resilient Women

Eleni. He will only give you the weight you can carry." But it felt so unfair that some people were capable of carrying so much, while others seemed to glide through life.

I was so angry that she had mentally died, and even more furious when I thought about her life.

Marina was one of the strongest, toughest, and most meticulous individuals I have ever met. If you asked her to bring some food, or grab something from the grocery store, she would take the initiative and order everything for all the guests. She didn't want people or friends to pity her. She would say, "Your presence is more important to me than anything else. Taking time out of your busy life is enough to make my grieving process easier and more comforting."

She was fierce, facing head-on every challenge that came her way. Instead of wanting comfort, she would ask how you and your family were feeling. I could not understand why she never expected my support. She was so optimistic in facing her loss. She wanted her friends to listen to her, to be able to relive her life and the loss of her loved ones.

Thinking of her daily gave me the opportunity to understand and think about what her needs were. She was lonely in a big two-room condo, her only comfort coming from old photos of family, friends, and memories. She just needed people to talk to her and keep her company. She had faced death, happiness, marriage, and the pain and suffering of spending her last years cared for by strangers. She had her dignity taken away.

When I visited her the last time, I could not bear to go alone. I took one of her dear friends to accompany me. When she saw us enter the room, she kept telling us what a wonderful husband she had. She had recovered from the stroke, but was now faced with dementia. "Why did he leave me here alone?" She would say sadly. "Why hasn't he come to take me home?" She showed us photos from when she was a young bride and mother. I asked her who the person in the photo was. "A friend," she said. I was heartbroken. This woman was so active with hospitals and philanthropy. She was so motivated and strong. She was brilliant, and was now stuck in her own world without hope of ever coming back.

Her story reminded me of my involvement with the Greek American Rehabilitation and Care Centre, where the fourth floor houses many patients with Alzheimer's, and it's an extremely painful and challenging place. I have seen how this disease strips people of their integrity and dignity. It is cruel. It leaves families feeling hopeless as they watch their loved ones fade away without knowing who they are or recognizing their loved ones. The residents don't know where they are or who they are, and the family struggles to make them aware that they were once a part of their lives.

One day, you remember your past and present, and you are looking forward to a future filled with family, and friends, and goals. The next day, you don't know anything about your existence and your identity. It truly puts the fragility of life into perspective. Then again, some people don't need the reminder. They have learned it every step of the way.

Dorothy

One of the things my parents truly emphasized to me is that everyone has a story. This has been illustrated to me throughout my life, but never more clearly than at the Greek American Rehabilitation and Care Centre. Every person who came through our doors had their own vast, complex history. Sometimes we learned their stories, sometimes we didn't. But even if we never knew anything about their past, it was as though we saw the impact of every choice they ever made play out daily at the nursing home.

Dorothy was a beautiful, chubby woman with blue eyes so sad that they pierced your heart. She joined us at the nursing home from day one, and I was drawn to this kind, melancholy woman. She reminded me of my late grandmother, Eleni. Their skin texture and eyes were so similar that one could say they were related.

Every day, Dorothy would sit at the dining room table by herself. She didn't want anyone around her. She wanted to live the rest of her life alone. The staff and I were upset as we watched her. Usually, people come to the nursing home and find friends and communities. It is a beautifully social place. We all wondered why this woman kept her distance.

I started looking into her file, digging into her family history and her personal life. As Greeks, the first thing we ask one another is, "What part of Greece or Europe are you from?" This is how we identify the culture, values, and morals of an individual. I wanted to know her history, including where in Greece or Europe she was born and raised.

But after looking into her life, I realized this gorgeous woman was not an immigrant. She was born in the United States and had gotten married to a prosperous farmer in Northern Illinois. They had three children. At a young age, her husband suddenly passed away, and I never found out how. She became a young widow in her late twenties, with three young children to raise.

Dorothy would work all day at a doctor's home taking care of the house, then come home and work all night tending to the farm and animals.

She was an honorable woman and never cared about getting remarried. All she wanted was to raise and educate her children—and she accomplished dreams for her children through hard work and endless nights without sleep.

In all the years she resided with us, no one ever visited her. This was extremely puzzling to all of us. She would sit alone and cry, staring out the window with tears running down her face from morning to night. I wondered what could have happened to make her children dump her at the nursing home and never look back. Holidays came and went without anyone visiting.

One day, I decided to call one of her children and advise them to come and see their mom before the Thanksgiving holiday. I told him I was sorry to bother him, but his mother hasn't eaten and all she does is cry. I suggested he or one of his siblings visit her to cheer her up. To my extreme shock, he said, "Thank you for the call, but I am very busy."

I shared this story with my executive board during our next meeting. "Good for you, Mrs. Bousis," said our director of nursing. "But I doubt it got through to him. I have seen this play out so many times in my career. Children leave their parents and forget they ever existed." I was horrified. This could not be true. I could never renounce my parents, no matter what. On Thanksgiving, I was setting the long dining room table for my children and their families to arrive. I had a mental list of what I still needed to do for the holiday, but my mind kept drifting to the nursing home. I called over to the nursing home, asking if anyone had visited Dorothy. The nurse responded sadly that no one had come. I told my husband and our housekeeper to keep an eye on the food in the oven and I would return in an hour. I needed to have lunch with Dorothy.

I walked into the dining room at the nursing home and went straight to Dorothy's table, where she sat alone. She was crying and mixing the food with the fork she was holding. I told her that I was also alone this holiday and wanted to have Thanksgiving dinner with her. She looked at me with a fierce yet sad expression and said, "Thank you."

I could not make Dorothy eat anything, and while I tried to make conversation, it was clear she just wanted to be left alone to die with her pain and sorrow. Driving home, I broke down crying. I prayed aloud, asking God, "What kind of children are these? Didn't they see her sacrifices?

Bold Resilient Women

Didn't they know she could have given them up for adoption and lived her life? I was devastated for her, and didn't understand how a life could come to this point.

Dorothy died after the holidays. She is still a topic of conversation at the nursing home. Now, we know a little more. She was born to an Irish family. Her parents immigrated to America with their grandparents, and met at a church event in Wisconsin. They were farmers who grew crops and raised animals. They were hard-working people. They had four children, three boys and one daughter, Dorothy. I never found out what happened to her parents or brothers.

She married an Irish-Scottish young man after he returned home from the Navy. They met through mutual friends right before he departed for World War II. In those days, couples who were separated by war got married quickly. When her beloved husband returned, he was injured, but he continued to work on the farm with her in-laws. They were happy until he was struck ill as a result of his war injury. Dorothy was carrying her fourth child at the time. We were never able to fill in the blanks of her life after that.

Her story has stuck with me since. It's just one of the many lives that have come through the nursing home doors, each one filled with love and pain, joy and suffering. It's been an honor to witness and learn about it all.

Irene, a Dynamic Woman

During one of my visits to Washington, D.C., for a Greek holiday celebration, I met a very interesting woman named Irene. From the first moment I met her, I admired her zeal and passion for peace and her willingness to make a difference in all people's lives. She was an attorney, politician, and author. (I particularly love her book, *I, Iakovos*, which is the memoirs of Archbishop Iakovos of America.) She worked for the State Department and left to get involved with Greek politics. She was a candidate for the Democratic Party. She ran for Governor in Kalamata, Peloponnese. After she got tired of the political arena, she went to Albania to work with the Red Cross. Irene was sharp and intelligent. She was incredibly well-versed in Greek and American politics.

We had a delightful conversation about both of our countries. We exchanged stories about our immigrant families.

"Our people shed blood for both countries," she said. "They were not traitors." During WWI, many Greeks left the U.S. and went back to fight in Greece, leaving behind everything they had achieved. After the war, many came back to retrieve their properties, while many never returned to get back what they had earned with their blood, sweat, and tears.

When Irene and I met, it was like we had known each other in a previous life. We were both passionate about making a difference in the lives of abuse victims, and we wanted to be a voice for the innocent and vulnerable in our society.

She expressed her idea to build an abuse center for women, children, and families. During my visit to Greece, I decided to visit the different sites she had picked. We had a big networking Rolodex of connections; we knew we could make a difference for abuse victims. We reached out to several officials who oversaw neglected buildings. To help propel this change, they designated two buildings: one near the center of Athens and one on the outskirts of Pandeli, Athens.

When the process was finalized, we proceeded with help from my father's company to restore the buildings, turning them into secure shelters for those who were running away from abusive situations.

During the many years I served alongside Irene as chairman of the Frondida Foundation for Abused Children, I witnessed so much pain, suffering, abuse, and neglect. I never believed anyone could treat people worse than animals. Children were afraid when you reached out to hold their hands. They looked at you with red, watery, and terrified eyes, thinking you too were going to injure them.

To my surprise, when I visited the shelters during the night, I witnessed mothers sleeping with their children, comforting them, and holding their hands. They wanted to protect each other. It was very difficult to gain their trust. Irene and I were very committed to making a difference in these people's lives. We thought we could save every abused person who reached out to us.

A few years later, I was invited to Greece to speak at the EU Convention for the Family in the Twenty-first Century, which had attendees from seventy different countries. Walking to the podium, I stood in front of the Archbishop of Greece, His Beatitude Chrystodoulos, one of my dearest spiritual fathers. I received his blessing with teary eyes. I wanted to reassure him that I was committed to helping all those in need. Staring at representatives from different European countries, I realized we had the same goals and ambitions, and we had a lot of work ahead of us. We were going to make a difference in society.

Plans were underway to make a change. The American Ambassador to Greece was Ambassador Miller. His wife, Bonnie, and I worked diligently to make people and organizations aware of child sex trafficking throughout the Mediterranean Sea. By simply alerting people to the issue, we became a beacon of hope for many young and old people. Our voice was heard loud and clear. Our work continued for many years, until Bonnie left Greece to return to Washington, D.C.

Irene started feeling tired and sick. She had gone through so many struggles to save children from all parts of the world. She kept saying, "Why didn't we start earlier in life to save more people from abuse?" That's when I realized that you will never have enough time in this world to achieve everything you want. You would have to be born several times over again and live many lives in order to feel confident you have succeeded in everything the way you want to.

When I heard Irene's words echo through my mind, I immediately thought of my beloved mom. After her morning coffee, she would tell her caretaker, "Please get my clothes and purse ready. When are we leaving?"

"Mom, we have hardly finished our breakfast, and you're already on the go. Sit down for a moment," I would say.

Mom would respond. "Sit down, my love. I need to speak to you." Her voice was sweet but fiercely demanding. "I will tell you a story." Due to the immense love and respect I had for her I did what she asked.

"When you are in your thirties, and you are sitting in an observation room not knowing what your test results will be, your thoughts are consumed by your past, present, and future. I remember that the oncologist walked into the room and kept looking at me with teary eyes. He saw my age and the fear on my face. He could not fathom telling me I had cancer. I had four little children who needed my unending protection and love."

She continued. "At that moment, I realized how quickly your life can change. It just takes one minute for someone to tell you if you will live or die. I had to believe in the Almighty's power and my own will to gain the strength needed to fight for my family and my children. My love, if you want to do something, don't waste a moment. Get out and do it. You don't know what the next minute brings."

Years later, Archbishop Chrystodoulos fell ill with advanced liver cancer. This was the beginning of the end. No one was as passionate as he was in making a difference for the destitute, sick, elderly, and abused. He was a spiritual man ahead of his time. After he passed, the Greek government closed both shelters. No one had an interest in saving lives. People were too consumed with their personal lives and material things. Our dreams fell apart; they didn't exist anymore.

Through my various involvements with many global foundations and their activities, I have experienced what it means to be humble and genuine. Abstract lessons become a reality when you walk down different paths and streets and meet a variety of people with different morals, values, interests, environments, beliefs, faiths, and upbringings.

I learned the best way to relate to someone is to simply pause and listen to their story. Every human being in this world has a story about their own challenges and triumphs. When I feed homeless people in impoverished areas, I ask them to tell me their life stories, and I am always surprised at the touching, fascinating stories from these victims who roam the streets, alleys, and docks. I am always alarmed to learn what makes people turn to the streets and live in extreme temperatures without a roof over their heads or water to clean their dirty faces, hands, and bodies.

To my astonishment, I have met doctors, lawyers, businessmen, fathers, mothers, and children with fascinating stories that broke my heart.

After inhaling their backgrounds and observing their heartache, I left feeling unworthy. I began to wonder, *why would I think I am better than them? What made this person give up on their talents, aspirations and ambitions? Can people ever overcome hurdles like mental illness and addiction?* I learned never to judge or condemn anyone in life until you hear their painful past. We don't have the right to ever pass judgment on anyone.

Sometimes all it takes is the right person at the right time and place to bring someone to life again.

On Christmas Eve every year, we serve the poor and homeless at the Annunciation Cathedral of Chicago alongside His Eminence Iakovos, as well as family and friends. As we started singing Christmas carols one year, everyone stopped. From the rear of the church hall, we heard the most magnificent angelic voice. It shook the Cathedral with beautiful lyrics. I looked over at our metropolitan (a spiritual leader similar to a Catholic Cardinal), and tears were streaming down his cheeks. We walked over to thank the singer and to ask him who he was. He bowed to our Bishop and kissed his hand, saying, "I was an opera singer and now I sleep in the streets."

The metropolitan and I tried to ask him more questions about his previous career, but he remained silent until we finished dinner. When everything was done, we tried to look for him everywhere, but he had vanished. We were all sad. We were unable to help him. This man, who once had so much talent and passion to entertain many, was now living on the streets of Chicago. It shook us all.

Over coffee with the volunteers, we discussed this man, asking each other what caused an individual or someone like this talented person to end up homeless and living on the streets, alleys, or in shelters. Everyone seemed to have the same thought: If this happened to him, it could happen to any of us. I guess we will never know the answer. Only he knew the pain he was carrying. Suddenly, I remembered what my dad would say. "Pray for people not to lose a screw from their brain." When I asked him what this meant, he said, "A brain is like a car engine. When things slowly break down, you won't have a car. That's how a person is when he keeps falling and falling, he falls into a lost place in his life, and it's difficult for him to come back."

I have learned the meaning of life—or one of them, at least—is to be observant of peoples' reactions and feelings. No one is born knowing anything. It's life and circumstances that give you wisdom and knowledge. When you

Bold Resilient Women

approach an individual without judgment, you can better understand their actions.

A beautiful homeless young lady said to us once, "Life is simple when you are open-minded. When you live alone, you make your own decisions, and you are responsible for yourself and your actions. Once you invite or involve others in your life, everything becomes a big unsolved puzzle. You can never again get a grip on what makes you happy, content, and satisfied." She was once a wife, mother of one child, and a teacher. We never found out what circumstances made her homeless. Our church is full of stories like hers. As compassionate humans, it's our job to listen to them. It's the first step in helping to restore someone's dignity.

Andrea

Andrea was a tall, handsome, stern musician who could play the bouzouki better than a professional. When I met him in the nursing home, he was ninety, but he didn't look a day over seventy. He was self-sufficient and mobile, and made his way through life unassisted. He loved to play his instrument for fellow residents.

Every morning, we would gather together in a cluster of chairs right outside the gift shop, where residents would grab coffee. Often, Andrea and I were joined by eight or so other residents around the same age. I was almost like a talk show host or a young child; I asked so many questions. Each answer led me down another path and to more questions. I wanted to learn everything about these people, their childhoods, families and their immigration stories. I wanted to know where they came from.

Many of them hardly spoke about their past lives in Greece or the other European countries they had immigrated from. Many adapted so fully to this new country as a form of survival, changing their names and identities, and assimilating into the American way of life. Andrea was often quiet as other people shared their stories, but one day I turned to him.

"Mr. Andrea, where did you come from?" I asked him. "Northern Albania," he responded.

"When did you come to America? What do you remember about it?" I continued. The rest of the group was equally curious. Andrea was an incredible listener, but shared little about himself. Like so many other residents, it was clear he had a fascinating history. We just needed to give him the space to share it.

"I left my country and immigrated to Greece with my father. It was the best way to get a visa. They wanted workers to work for America. When I was eleven, we left Albania and took the ship from Piraeus to America. We left my mother and sister behind. I had a small suitcase with two shirts, two pants, one jacket, and two pairs of underwear, and in my arms, I carried my bouzouki. When I came to this great country, I wanted to study music. Bouzouki was part of my heart and soul. I went to school while my father peddled fruit on the South Side.

"I was clear with him that I would always help the family, but he better not ever tell me to drop out of school. My father saw my passion for music. He allowed me to attend school, and in the evenings and on weekends, I washed dishes to help the family back home and support our life. We lived in a small room with about twenty-five other immigrants. We all cared for each other. We were all in the same predicament, and no one was better than the other.

"When I got older, I got a job at Grecian Garden, a nightclub on Halsted Street. I was providing the entertainment there when I met Claire, a beautiful and attractive young girl. We fell in love and got married within six months. We wanted to rush the wedding because my father was very ill. He died shortly after from some kind of undetected illness. He never got a chance to go back home to see my mother or my sisters. Shortly after that, I received notice that my mother and sister had passed away. Back then, people would die, and the doctor would say that they ate something and got food poisoning and died. They never tried to find out more."

At this, the other residents nodded knowingly. I wondered how many people had friends and family lost in mysterious ways and doctors who wouldn't—or couldn't—help them.

"I never wanted to go back and see the mountains, or remember the sacrifices or the torture I went through."

"Now that you are ninety, what are you feeling? What is clear to you now that wasn't before?"

"Eleni mou, first and foremost, I hope no one ever lives through the hell we did in our youth. I loved my parents so much that I was obedient. I just left my mom, sister, and everything I knew to support my family. I loved my wife, my son, and my dear friends. But I never had time to assess and love myself. I know it's late in life, but finally I feel free in this place to care about *me*.

"I realize age is just a number; you are only as old as you feel. A little late, but I realized I wasn't born to carry the burdens of the world, and no one is relying on us to solve their problems.

Bold Resilient Women

Problems should be left up to God. We have to learn to lay our burden on His shoulders and hands.

"I stopped bargaining with friends and especially family members. I realized that there are people who love you and those who want your money, and those who want your money might never save you if you're tumbling down. I learned to be generous with the extra money I had, and the money I didn't need, I would loan to my friends and family. I learned that for some people, borrowing money is easier to accept and difficult to return."

Mr. Andrea paused to sip his coffee. The group of us was silent as we listened. I never discouraged him, or any other resident, from narrating their life story. The simple act of sharing allowed them to walk down memory lane and rekindle their past. Being at the nursing home reminded me that someday, we will all be sharing our stories with those willing to hear them. I want people to listen.

"Darling," he said. "I learned not to correct anyone but myself. No one is perfect in this world, not even me. At this age, all I want is peace of mind. It's more precious than perfection.

"I learned that every person needs a compliment, but sometimes it's difficult for people to give. There is too much ego. Always walk away from people who are negative and don't value you.

They might not recognize your worth, but I assure you, they will lose out in life someday.

"Never be ashamed of your feelings and emotions toward others; this is what makes you a human. And never let your ego get in the way. That's where you see relationships fall apart. It's like knowing your son has stolen everything from you and yet you keep forgiving him, not admitting to yourself that he was your destruction.

"Live every day of your life as if it's your last. Only you are responsible for your happiness, and you owe it to yourself. Don't allow toxic people to destroy your happiness. Remember, we only have one life to live."

Mr. Andrea stopped abruptly and stood up, asking to be excused to go for a walk. I stood up too, and touched his arm. I thanked him for sharing and told him I would be in the office, and we would talk later. It was clear he needed a moment. I saw him walk out the door onto the grounds of the nursing home.

An hour later, the police walked into the office, holding Mr. Andrea by the arm. When they asked to speak to me, I could feel something wasn't right. I walked outside my office.

"Please don't talk, Eleni mou," Mr. Andrea said. "I need to speak to you." I looked at his face and saw blood dripping from his forehead and bandages on his cheeks.

"Officer, can I talk to Mr. Andrea in the office?" I asked. I knew the officers—they were a part of our community at the nursing home, so they said yes.

As soon as Mr. Andrea sat down, and before I could say a word, he started to talk. "I did something stupid. I have my old Cadillac, and every afternoon I just take it for a little spin in the back of the park."

My jaw was on the ground. Residents weren't allowed to have cars at the nursing home, even if they were vintage Cadillacs. "What happened?" "The car was running out of gas, so I had to turn out on Milwaukee Avenue, and the car went crazy. It wasn't stopping, and it just hit one car after another."

I wanted to laugh, because it was clear what happened. He confused the gas pedal and the brake.

"Eleni, I am scared. What if everyone I hit comes after me? I won't have enough money to live here. Please, let's go to the bank and turn my account over to you."

"Andrea, I can't do that," I said gently. "I love you, but I can't be responsible for your bank account."

We wanted to figure something out, so the nursing home CFO went with him to the bank. We persuaded him to turn everything over to his son. He was resistant, but there wasn't any other family. After he signed the paperwork, he held his head in his hands. "He will take everything," he sobbed. "He has destroyed me before, and he will do it again. I won't have money to live here. I washed dishes, I played my bouzouki all night, I was deprived of my youth, deprived of my mother and sister, and now I will be left with nothing." His shoulders heaved as he cried.

We assured him this would not happen, but as I rubbed my hand on his back, I remembered what he told the residents and me in the chairs outside the gift shop. He knew better than all of us that your family can take your money and sink you to the bottom. He was a wise man.

I left a couple of weeks later for Europe. While I was gone, the accountant went to make a transfer for his monthly payment when the bank said there was an overdraft. To everyone's shock, his money had been removed; there wasn't a penny left.

When the team called me to tell me what happened, my stomach dropped. I felt guilty for persuading him to transfer everything to his son. I never imagined this could happen. I asked to speak with him and reassure him that he didn't have to worry—we would figure it all out when I returned. But two days later, I received another call from my office. Mr. Andrea had suffered a heart attack and died overnight.

To this day, my heart aches for allowing this to happen. I should have believed Mr. Andrea's stories and intuition. We talk of him often, remembering his humor, his love for music, love for the person next to him, and his passion to entertain everyone in the nursing home. He will always be remembered as the mysterious music man who lived and died with honor.

Friends Losing Faith

One of the most heartbreaking and profound sadnesses in growing old is watching friends lose sight of their worth due to their old age and the challenges of becoming frail and losing their strength. Many of these friends had parents who believed children should work and not attend school. They saw education as a form of abandonment, that by going to school, they were not supporting the family. Other friends had parents who forced their daughters to marry young and live at home. With no way out, many of them ran away and were never found.

These parents were not meant to be parents. Many of them were born during the war, when calm and security were just words and not something to be felt. Many grew up in poverty, sharing a loaf of bread between ten people. Many were abused, or victimized, or raised by parents who had also suffered. The damage of earlier generations continues to ripple into the present.

Other friends have lost their parents, or had their parents return to their home country once their children were grown. Many families have changed, with surviving parents moving on in a new marriage, while some parents have fallen off the radar and are lost to their children. Some parents were and will always remain a mystery to their children.

My friend, Evangelo, had one of these complicated fathers. His father was bright and intelligent and was recruited by Harvard out of high school. He didn't want to leave his wife and his country, Greece. He had married right out of school and was deeply in love with his wife. But Harvard reached out, and they saw a new path forward, one filled with opportunity. He would move to

Bold Resilient Women

Boston while she stayed back, continued her job teaching, and waited for her opportunity to join him. While he was away, she wrote to her husband to share that she was pregnant! They would both soon be with him. She was ecstatic.

But the young man was so consumed with his new life that he didn't respond. When it was time to give birth, his wife brought a baby boy into the world without her husband by her side. Her friends and family kept asking when she was leaving to be reunited with her husband, and she told whatever lie she could: It was difficult to get a green card, he had to finish a project first, she needed an attorney. Meanwhile, she went about her teaching and cared for her son with help from her mother. Her heart was big, and she was honored for her commitment to education by the Red Cross, the Greek Church, the Greek government, and many other foundations.

Time passed, and the son, Evangelo, fell in love with a beautiful woman named Matina, who helped care for his mother without question. One day, she asked his mother why she never went to the States, or why this man never came back for his wife and son.

"I was told he had started a new family," Matinaa told me. "He met a young American student, married her, and they had four children. He forgot them."

Matina, my friend, was devastated. How could this man forget everything about his former life? How could he just forget his wife and son and begin a life filled with lies? She found his address and wrote to him, introducing herself as his daughter-in-law. She invited him to come to Greece to meet his son and granddaughter. To her amazement, he said yes.

It was Easter. Matina was cleaning the house, preparing for her father-in-law. Her mother-in-law kept asking her why she was painting and cleaning the house in depth. She didn't want to hurt her, so she didn't tell her that her husband was returning after so many years. Finally, the day arrived. A driver pulled up outside their house, and a handsome, well-dressed man emerged, put on his stylish hat, draped his raincoat over his arm, and walked to the front door. Matina's mother-in-law stood up to get the door. Something in her gut told her that finally, after so many years, she was coming face to face with the man she once loved.

She opened the door. "Welcome to your home," she said. "You were late coming, but at last you arrived." She gestured for him to come in and sit down. She sat across from him and never asked him to explain why he never came back: why he abandoned them, why he started a new life, and how he could ever forget the love they had shared since they were young children. All Matina's mother-in-law could think was, "Finally, he is meeting his son."

Matina was kind to him. She was happy to see father and son reunited and starting their relationship from the beginning. During Holy Week, they would go to church together. On Holy Wednesday, just outside the church, when he was standing alone with Matina, he finally broke down.

"I am a ruthless man," he said, tears streaming down his face. "How could I have forgotten my love? How could I have abandoned my son? Why did I blindly marry a woman who just wanted the privilege of being married to a Harvard professor?" Matina let him cry, put her hand on his arm while she listened. "I am a nobody; a piece of rusted metal."

From that point on, this man returned to his home every year, though he never reconciled with his wife. Her son, her students, philanthropy, and her family filled her life, and she never wanted a man. She was satisfied serving others and her Lord. People from all over respected this amazing woman who stood firm, honoring her past but creating a beautiful life for herself and her son.

One day, I received a call from a Harvard administrator. They were inquiring about the Greek American Rehabilitation Care Centre, and wanted to bring a private paid resident there. I was surprised. Harvard clearly wanted to make sure this man was well cared for after a minor stroke. He must be someone very special.

Shortly after, the day came for the transfer. I was at the nursing home to greet him. They wheeled him in, in a transport bed, and I saw a tall, handsome man being rolled through the lobby, assisted by an elderly blonde woman and two men. He was taken to a private room, and I confirmed things were comfortable and taken care of. We left the man to rest, and I offered to give the family a tour and show them our home, our chapel, the amenities, and surroundings. But his family showed no interest. They were in a hurry to leave.

The following day, I was late leaving the nursing home, and while walking through the lobby, I was introduced to three people who had recently arrived from Greece. I invited them to come inside for coffee. I asked them who they were visiting. They told me the gentleman's name, and I stopped in my tracks. It was the professor.

Nothing made sense to me at that moment. One day I was meeting an American family who didn't speak a word of Greek and couldn't get out of the home fast enough, and the next day, I was meeting people who spoke no English and had traveled all the way from Greece. I sat with them as they shared their story—being left behind, abandoned, reconciling with this man years later.

I listened to the story and I felt like I had walked into a movie. *My God,* I said to myself. *How can this man cry for the father who had abandoned him? Why was he feeling so much pain?* I didn't think I would have been this forgiving if it were my father.

Bold Resilient Women

This Greek family stayed another day, not leaving the man's side, while his other family never visited. I began gravitating to this Greek family. I saw the meaning of love and forgiveness in front of me. Somehow the past did not matter; what mattered was today. I gained so much respect for them. They so fully put into practice the saying, "One cannot love unless they know how to forgive."

This man never stopped crying and holding his son's hand all day. You could see the regret in his eyes. His heart could not contain his suffering. His health started to worsen, and we believed he was overwhelmed with a heavy heart and a sorrowful conscience. After a few months, he passed away.

One day, I received a call from Matina. Her daughter had been accepted into Harvard with high honors. She was brilliant, like her grandfather. She was his pride and joy, and she was following in his footsteps.

"Eleni, my daughter cannot attend Harvard," she said. Her voice was thick, and it was clear she had been crying. I expected her to say something about expenses or missing a deadline. But what she told me next almost knocked me over. "Someone from the family reached out to the school and demanded that she never attend Harvard Medical School." Of course, Matina and her family were devastated. Why would someone stand in the way of their daughter's future? They knew who was behind it, but Matina and her family didn't have the inner strength to start a war. They decided it was wiser for her to continue her studies at Athens Medical School, where she graduated with high honors.

I am extremely proud of this young girl. She had the opportunity to leave and live abroad, but she stayed in Greece to care for our countrymen. I gained even more respect for her after she was hospitalized with a serious case of COVID-19, and after she had fully recovered, she continued sacrificing her life for others.

I still remain in contact with the family. Through their story, I witnessed what it means to forgive. The trauma of the man's abandonment began the moment he left for America. So many people whispered about the wife he left behind. Were they even married? Was this really his son? Was she an honorable woman?

I can say with confidence that people thrive in making up lies. Everyone questioned her, her son, and their story, but with patience, tolerance, and love, she proved to everyone what an outstanding and ethical Christian woman she was until she took her last breath. From Matina and Evangelo, I learned that she always loved her husband and could never accept his betrayal. He was her knight in shining armor. It was an eternal love filled with pain, sacrifice, commitment, and betrayal, and while she built a life that served others, she always held her love in her heart.

Innocent Girls Left Behind

Like the Harvard professor, many men in Greece immigrated to America and never looked back. They didn't care if they had left behind a wife and children. They wanted to create a brand-new life. It created an epidemic of innocent girls who were left behind to deal with the embarrassment and shame, and who had to create brand-new lives for themselves and their children.

My mother told me about a young woman who was so embarrassed when she heard her husband had another family that she poured petroleum on and burned all his traces and belongings. She didn't anticipate the strength of the petroleum, and the flames spread so fast that her dress caught on fire. When her fellow villagers finally saw the fire, they rushed to her rescue, but it was too late. They found her burned body.

"Her husband, his new wife, and his new family never visited the village," my mother told me. "He knew he would be ousted by everyone in the village. He might not have physically killed her, but mentally he condemned her to death."

It wasn't only the girls in Greece who were left behind. Even when they were able to immigrate, they were tossed aside. My grandmother told me about Elizabeth, one of her beloved friends who was like a younger sister. Elizabeth was brought to the States when she was fourteen to be educated. When she arrived, she was welcomed with an apron and a little bed to rest before they called her to take care of the children. Days and weeks went by, and she asked when she would start school. They told her they didn't have the money

Bold Resilient Women

to educate her or to pay for her expenses. She would take care of the children and handle the chores. She was treated as a slave.

One Sunday, she went to church to ask for help from the priest. In the 1950s, the church was a safe haven for many immigrants. My grandmother spotted this young girl walking in nervously, looking lost and malnourished. My grandmother immediately approached her and asked her name. The young girl broke down, begging someone to send her back to her village. My grandmother brought her back to her house; she wasn't going to let this young girl go back to poverty and suffering. My grandmother had five kids—one more wasn't going to hurt her.

Elizabeth became a family member. She left my grandmother's house when she was twenty, when a friend from church introduced her to a charming young man, and they married. At first, my grandma said she was happy. But as soon as the children arrived—three girls—he became a monster. He demanded the girls get jobs at a young age to support the family. The children were straight-A students, and their mother wanted them to finish their education. The father beat her for supporting them and going against him, and also beat the children. But the girls were intelligent and motivated, and all of them finished high school in three years instead of four.

One day, the oldest girl found out she was accepted into medical school. When her father heard the news, he flew into a rage and beat her badly, leaving her passed out on the floor. The mother had had enough. She summoned the strength and willpower, and that night, when he was sleeping, she grabbed her three daughters and fled the house. My grandma assisted her again in getting settled with her children.

The three young girls didn't have good luck. One died young from a rare illness. The other two were both married, but they were both abused by their spouses and ended up physically and mentally destroyed. Elizabeth told my grandmother many times it was her own fault; she should have left the marriage when the girls were little, so they would not be traumatized and almost accustomed to abuse. One time, over coffee with Elizabeth, I asked her.

"Why didn't you leave?" It's a delicate question, but she was a remarkable woman who was not afraid to be honest and vulnerable.

"I was afraid of not being able to survive with my girls," she said. "During those days, my dear, you were stuck with the person you married. It didn't matter if he was violent. People didn't get a divorce." She told me that she cried day and night, blaming herself for her daughter's outcomes. "When you live with abuse, you think that it is normal for a man to be the boss, and you to be a slave." This real-life story shattered me because she was so connected with my grandmother in so many ways.

Bold Resilient Women

These stories are all too common. Girls were isolated in abusive relationships with no one to turn to for help and support. Girls couldn't leave, because they believed their families—who struggled to support themselves—couldn't take them in. Young girls were faced with terminal illnesses. When I was a child, I attended a classmate's funeral, and to this day, I have never heard so many screams in my life. Her mother's world had collapsed. This traumatized me for many years. I could not attend funerals until my father finally said to me, "My love, the dead cannot hurt you. It's the living who can eat you alive. Don't fear the dead, only fear the living."

I grew up with strong female role models in my mother and grandmother. Through their stories and through my own experiences, I learned that complicated and unwavering situations can spin out of control within a second. A small circumstance can change your entire life. My grandmother would always say that the strongest creatures that roam this world are human beings. She truly believed in the power of people to change, that with faith, hope, confidence, and trust, one could rebuild their life and achieve whatever their heart desired.

Often, Grandma and Mom would say that your daily life goes on without your control. You find yourself making unexpected choices. Somehow, you find the inner strength not to be distracted by your goals and ambitions. Having confidence can give you the ability to find yourself and to move forward with optimism and courage. Once you realize nothing is impossible, you will be inspired to do things beyond what you believe you can.

Laura

Laura was a tall, busty, and beautiful woman, with blonde hair, green eyes, a great smile, and deep dimples. She was sweet and kind. She would walk in a room and all the men would turn their heads to look at her.

One day, as she walked into my father's office, a friend saw her innocent smile and kind manner. He said, "This is the kind of girl I would love to marry." My mother said it was as if the skies opened and God heard his words. He kept coming around her and her family, indulging her with precious gifts and showering her with compliments. He was a very wealthy man. She was raised in a middle-class family, lived in beautiful homes, and attended private schools. She became attracted to his compliments and his elegant nature.

He was patient and tried every way to win her heart. Two years after he first spotted her, he went to her father's home and asked for his daughter's hand in marriage.

"You have my blessing, but it's my daughter you need to convince to marry you," he said. That evening, he proposed to her and she said yes. Laura had fallen in love with her prince.

The wedding was magical. She wore a beautiful, flowy gown with a headpiece that looked like a crown. She was a princess. As she appeared at the doors of the church, walking arm in arm with her father, the whole room could not take its eyes off of this gorgeous, blonde, young woman who had stolen this young man's heart.

For their honeymoon, they traveled throughout Europe. All the stars in their life had lined up. Everyone said Laura's luck was beyond great. Although she was deprived of her own mother, who had passed away after birth, she was raised by her maternal grandparents, her beloved father, and older brother. But there was always a sad side to her, which could be seen deep in her eyes. She had missed the loving hands and the warm shelter of her mother. Throughout the years that I had known her, she never spoke much about her mother. She only said, before her wedding, that she wished her mother were there to dress her as a bride.

Laura began her life with this young man living in a dream world. He provided everything her heart desired. She gave birth to four beautiful children and raised them with a lavish, loving, and caring lifestyle. But she never forgot to be humble and kind.

She embraced her mother-in-law and father-in-law with love and respect, but her husband's two sisters were her rivals. They made her life miserable. Every time they would walk into her home, they would put her down. They would tell her she wasn't worth what their brother provided for her. She was an innocent individual who did not like controversy, and she never wanted to put any barriers between her husband and his family. It was becoming a nightmare. It felt like the beginning and the end of the destruction of her family.

She became exhausted and infuriated by their constant demeaning comments. Many times, she expressed to her husband how she felt, but he sought to protect his sisters instead of his wife.

He would tell her, "Let them say whatever they want, as long as they are fine." Nothing mattered. He could not understand that they were killing her with daggers the minute they walked into her home. She could not do anything right. They would flip stories around. Her only way out was to walk away and leave two of her daughters behind. She took one of her daughters and her son and fled to a new life.

I asked my mom years later if she was happy where she was with her children. My mother said, "She would either have gone mad or had to do what she did for survival."

"How did you come to this conclusion?" I asked.

"I know the family too well," she said. "And those sisters are very evil women. That is why the young man had never settled down. They never anticipated that he would fall head over heels for a beautiful woman. She became a threat, and they wanted the lavish lifestyle and the vacations for themselves. They did not want to share with any other woman." She paused for a moment. "Sometimes I wonder if they saw him as a brother or something else." Years later, Laura returned for her daughter's wedding. She stood far away, witnessing her beloved daughter getting married. Her daughter finally found out that her mother stood silently behind a tree, witnessing what was once her

Bold Resilient Women

little girl becoming a bride. She asked her friends to connect with her. She wanted to hear her side of the story. Laura's son and daughter—the ones she had taken with her—were in college, and she worked two jobs to support them. This beautiful woman, who once had it all, had become a slave, raising her two children alone while her other two children and her husband lived in a mansion in a wealthy suburb.

It was arranged for the two daughters to finally meet the woman who walked out of their life. Laura was never warned that she was going to meet the daughters she left, but as they walked into the restaurant, she saw two beautiful girls who looked exactly like her. She walked over shaking and crying. She realized she was in the presence of her daughters.

Her daughters wanted to ask one million questions, but somehow, nothing mattered at that moment. The only thing that mattered was getting to know the woman who had given birth to them. After a couple of hours, Laura finally said, "I had no choice but to leave you behind. You had already established the bond with me, and I knew I had taught you to be strong young women. It was my turn to teach the two younger children what foundations they needed to have in their lives." The girls understood their mother had no choice. She either would've ended her life from the cruelty of the aunts, or she had to choose to walk away.

They had always heard stories about how mean and evil their aunts were, so they empathized with their mother. They could only imagine how difficult they had made her life. They were happy that they got reacquainted.

When Laura passed away, she was only in her sixties. She had lived a life of pain, then a life of happiness, and then a life of misery and sacrifices. I remember when we heard that she had passed away, I wanted to scream and yell about the way her life had gone. I asked my mom, "Why does God not punish those who destroy people's lives?"

Mom was a very religious woman. "Honey, I don't know what kind of sins the aunts committed," she said. "None of us know. That's why spiritual fathers tell us to ask the Lord to forgive our ancestors for the known and unknown. You must always remember that you are born in this world alone and you die alone. You suffer by yourself, and you deal with your pain and suffering alone. Therefore, my beautiful daughter, let this be a lesson. Take care of yourself.

"As your grandmother always said, it's hard to take care of one parent, but a mother can take care of ten children." She explained that this parable illustrates the way a mother loves her children unconditionally. She doesn't care how many she has; she loves all of them equally. She lives and breathes her children day and night. Mothers can have a dozen children, but they will never complain or be discouraged.

Bold Resilient Women

Through their mother's painful life, the daughters understood and realized they had to protect themselves. The friends who stood by her side were crying, unable to believe such a kind and beautiful soul was destroyed through the evilness of envious people. They believed her looks, demeanor, kindness, and empathy were a threat. When I saw her being placed deep into the ground, I was shattered. I started to understand that you can never change anyone. You can only change yourself.

Marie

One day, I was invited to be interviewed about a fundraiser I was organizing and chairing. As I was making corrections to my comments before the journalist walked over to the table, I happened to glance over his shoulder. I saw a young, fragile woman crying hysterically. I immediately excused myself and walked over to comfort her. Her face was familiar. I had met her before, but I could not bring myself to remember where and when our paths had crossed.

Soon after, I realized this was the daughter of one of my dear friends. I was shocked to see this beautiful, gorgeous, blonde, blue-eyed, young woman slurring her words. I asked her if she was okay. Could I help her? Was there anything I could do for her? I was beyond horrified and saddened to hear she had suffered a major stroke at the age of forty. I wanted to pinch myself. I could not believe what I was hearing and witnessing. I thought my ears were deceiving me. Being naive, I didn't realize you could suffer a stroke at such a young age.

I was so shaken up that I canceled my interview. I could not bring myself to discuss my involvement with my organizations. It was my passion from a young age to care for others, and at this moment, all I could think about was how I could help this young woman recover and overcome her struggles. I was born to protect, defend, and support individuals, including those who suffered from different illnesses and substance abuse. I was honored to be interviewed for this publication, but I could hardly talk about why I devoted so much time to helping others while simultaneously feeling as if I was turning my back on this young woman if I did not volunteer to help with her health issues.

Bold Resilient Women

We stayed for hours talking. She opened up to me about her narcissist ex-husband and her cruel in-laws. He had problems with gambling and cheating and was mentally abusive. He would belittle and insult her, calling her fat and ugly, which only amped up after she gave birth to their children. Through her bright features, you could tell how strikingly beautiful she was before her illness. She told me, "I didn't have the strength to lose the weight. I was too depressed. Look who I have become. I don't even recognize myself when I look in the mirror."

I asked her when she had the stroke. She said, "I was upset, angry, and tired of being harassed. I wanted to get out of the house and go to my mother's arms to vent."

On the way to her mother's house, she suffered a major stroke, which left her entire right side paralyzed. She went to rehab for physical and speech therapy. I was heartbroken. Why didn't she see the writing on the wall from the first year of her marriage? Why did she stay with him to allow herself to get sick, to strip her of her youth and integrity?

She told me that one day, she finally had enough. "I knew he was seeing someone else because of my stroke. He was ready to leave me." According to Marie, her ex said he would grant her a divorce, but would fight for custody of their children since she could not even take care of herself. After dragging her to court daily, she decided to give him custody of the kids. He could provide for them with money, homes, and cars—everything their hearts desired. While every day she was faced with excruciating pain and struggles to care for herself, her children were living a lavish lifestyle with their father and his mistress.

I asked her why she didn't reach out for help from her siblings. She said that her ex was a great provider. "He was rich, and we had everything we wanted," she said. I wanted to shake her up and ask her if it was all worth it. She was in a wheelchair, while he was off celebrating a new wife and family. No one stepped in to help her overcome this situation. Her self-esteem was crushed, and she felt worthless.

"Marie, you are smart, intelligent, and strong," I told her multiple times. "You can overcome this bumpy road and gain back your health, strength, and confidence. You need to get better and stronger. Then you can fight to win your children back." I didn't believe her children would give up the love they had for her just for their dad's money.

"It's not possible that they don't want to see you again," I said.

"Eleni, you don't understand. I was admitted to the hospital in intensive care, and they never came to visit me once. They have denounced the woman who brought them into this world. They now have a new mother whom they admire, love, and respect."

I was crushed. I spoke with her sister, trying to make sense of all this suffering.

"She is telling you the truth," she told me. "We don't say anything to upset her anymore. We want her to recover fully, but he has turned the kids against their mother with his money. They haven't seen her in years." That's when I remembered that my mom would say, "For money, Christ was crucified. For money, we sell our souls to the devil. For money, we sell everything precious that is in our lives. Money becomes the evil strength in a family."

When I left her sister, I broke down crying in the car. I could not believe I was hearing this story. He already destroyed her physically and mentally—why couldn't he leave her alone? Why did he turn her children against her? I felt like picking up the phone and dialing the children to have a talk with them. But I realized it could backfire and make things worse.

I decided it was best to let some time pass and see if she regained any of her strength. I knew her siblings were doing everything in their power to help her out. Her brother-in-law told me, "I will not stop nagging her until she gets off the wheelchair and throws the crutches away."

I knew Marie was strong and ambitious, and she had so many people cheering her on. She was a dominant, strong, and resilient woman. Though I knew she would make it, it didn't make it any easier to see her struggle—or to know that cruel and vindictive people like her ex-husband exist in the world.

Susan and Charlene

My friend, Susan, can charm anyone. She has a vibrant smile, a petite figure, and a soft, kind voice that electrifies you with love. From the moment you meet her, she makes you feel loved and wanted. She is a classy woman who dresses with elegance and charm. Everything is coordinated—her dress, hat, shoes, and purse. She has an empathetic heart and is grateful to her friends. She is one of those people who tells you how much you mean to her.

My darling friend always told me that a dignified individual never has time to think of anything bad. When you embrace life with humility, good things will come your way. The key is to live a simple life of happiness and joy. Good deeds come back to you, and bad things will never go unpunished. Life is simple. It's made up of short memories you accumulate throughout your life from your family, relationships, friends, and your career.

She was an incredible resource for parenting advice. She would always remind me, "My dear, your children need to feel wanted and loved. You are the only person who loves them unconditionally. You are the person who has restless nights of sleep worrying about them. You are the woman who sacrificed her own body to bring them into the world."

As a parent, you're obligated and responsible to tell your children the truth, but also advise them on how you see things and what your opinions are about different matters. A loving parent engages in a conversation with a compassionate *agape*, tolerance, and patience. Susan would say, "Truth and honesty are the virtues of happiness."

Susan came from a wealthy family. Her father was a prominent judge, and she was well-mannered and articulate; she could socialize in affluent circles. Later, she married a lawyer who eventually became a very respected judge, so it seemed she was always surrounded by wise conversations. Her world was intense and interesting. Her family gave her the tools to be patient and tolerant. They provided her with a strong educational background. Living life to its fullest taught Susan how to inspire those around her, and she has inspired me with her comforting words as a wife, mother, sister, and friend.

Having coffee or dinner with Susan enlightens and broadens my horizons. It's almost like she brings me into a fantasy land. Her life stories are captivating. She could write volumes on life, challenges, pain, and struggles. When I mention someone influential, she always has a story to add about someone who crossed her path. Her life is like a scripted movie of power, success, and suspense. You are drawn to every story she and her husband, Roger, tell.

You don't need to see a movie when you have these amazing characters narrating their stories.

Susan lives by example. She knows how to get her point across without raising her voice. She is frank about the reality of marriage—that it's difficult and complicated.

"You need to work with your partner and try to see things eye to eye," she would say to me as we discussed life, families, husbands, and more. "Every marriage has challenges, Eleni. It's how you handle them that matters. I am married to a sweet and gentle man who loves, respects, and admires me. He would never raise his voice to make a statement. We share ideas and come to an agreement together."

I asked her once, "Does Roger ask you for advice and opinions before making a decision?"

"Absolutely, honey," she said. "We are one. We are not two people in a relationship. I would not have been married if we did not respect and support each other with family, personal, financial, and all-around life matters."

After my mother passed, Susan continually reminded me that she was my adopted mom. Throughout our friendship, she has listened to me with a loving heart, comforting my problems and worries, and sharing soothing motherly advice. Smiling, she would say, "Honey, everyone has problems. It depends on how full you see the glass."

Susan always tells me how important it is to listen and understand people. "You cannot change anyone," she says. "So don't expect them to alter and transform themselves if they don't want to change." As a loving and caring individual, you need to remain focused on your commitment to your word. You must be comfortable in what you are doing and committed to passing along positive energy and happiness to your family and friends. Be a force of good and love by giving and spreading happy vibes. Susan always reminds me that we are all responsible for ourselves, our actions, and deeds. People need to take responsibility for their actions and inner demons. All we can do is wish them well and let it go. When you are an individual who gives and cares for others, you don't have time to focus on those who cannot handle their own regrets.

∼

Charlene is a spicy, sweet, blonde, petite, Irish woman with bright, sparkling, blue eyes. Charlene's loving heart captivates you from the moment you meet her. She and her husband, Scott, have a beautiful, tenacious marriage filled with love, optimism, charisma, talent, and incredible stories. They can inspire you to become a better, more loving, and more caring individual in an oppressed, complicated, and unstable world. They inspire hope in a world filled with animosity, vengeance, and hateful comments. Some people are consumed and distracted from reality. They don't see the problems and suffering of others as they fight for their lives.

My dear friends would give you advice, sharing their experiences of pain, loneliness, family feuds, a daughter's hardship, cancer struggles, or heart disease. They are always willing to inspire others by sharing their experiences. They are the epitome of perseverance and determination.

Having seen firsthand their courage and compassion in supporting individuals who are homeless, individuals afflicted by cancer, or others who have undergone personal tragedies and heartaches has left an impression on my life.

Charlene and Scott are big supporters and advocates for fighting cancer. They have educated people by speaking out through their many social and media platforms. They support preventative medicine and the treatment and cure of all types of cancers. They are also actively involved in promoting a healthy diet and daily exercise, and helping to reduce the rate of obesity in school children, which in turn will decrease the rate of cancer and other diseases. Charlene is one of our nation's leaders in supporting the efforts of doctors and scientists in eradicating cancer. Throughout their journey, they have persistently tried encouraging and advocating for volunteering and community service in support of important diseases and medical issues affecting our country.

Together, Charlene and Scott wrote an amazing book, Conquering and Curing Cancer: The Cancer Survival Book. This book provides a vehicle for them to communicate with everyone affected by cancer by providing accurate transparent information. It also provides a place to share important insights and events with them since they have firsthand travelled down the path of conquering cancer. They keep telling me that their wish is for everyone to join their mission and see their vision for a cancer-free world.

This book highlights an inspiring story of a couple fighting cancer together. It provides a poignant look at cancer from the perspectives of patient and caregiver, covering the highs and lows from diagnosis, to surgery, to chemotherapy, to radiation, to follow-up visits, to gaining back strength. It also serves as an important survival resource for patients and families battling cancer. It's a compelling story of two people continually fighting for themselves and for the millions of Americans impacted by cancer.

Today, Charlene is still fighting to conquer cancer. She says, "I am a tough

Bold Resilient Women

cookie who will achieve the healing process." Many nights, I lie in bed thinking how this amazing woman gets out of bed to help herself and others fighting this terrible battle.

Charlene and Scott—both founding board members of the Hippocratic Cancer Research Foundation—have inspired the entire board to become proactive about our mission and work toward advancing our goal to fund "out of the box" research to eradicate all types of cancers.

Charlene and Scott emphasize the importance of uniting together. They continue to say, "If doctors, scientists, and philanthropic leaders join forces, we will save the world from tears, heartache, and grief." I can't help but think they are absolutely right.

Love Is Blind's **Shaina Hurley Was Diagnosed with Cancer While 3 Months Pregnant: 'Nothing Was Going to Stop Me'**
People

Claire's Nightmare

The persistence of trying to find out who you are and what you aspire to achieve should start with searching inside your soul. My friend Claire's needs and wants led her to the unknown world of abuse and suffering. At the age of sixteen, she was promised to a much older man.

Claire was a young, innocent child from a very poor family who hardly had food on their table. An elderly man wanted a slave as a wife to bear his children so they could contribute to his wealth—and he set his sights on Claire. Soon, she found herself in a marriage that was both physically and psychologically abusive.

She never learned the English language. She was not allowed to take classes on basic communication at the local church with other immigrants. As a child, she was deprived of formally learning the Greek language because she was working on her parents' farms. Now that she had the opportunity to gain knowledge in a free country, once again she was not entitled to learn anything that could provide her freedom.

Claire was held hostage by an oppressive, strange man, who treated her as a mistress and slave. Her daily responsibilities were to take care of him and the children, and clean, wash, cook, and cater to his entire family. She was never allowed an opinion or a say. For fifteen years, she endured pain and suffering until she finally gained the strength and courage to tell him she was leaving. She wasn't going to put up with his behavior anymore.

He gave her an ultimatum: Forget about leaving and crossing the line, or you will have to give up your children and never see them again. He knew the only reason she was willing to live with him was for her children. He threatened full custody, and said that she would never be able to come back. She could not believe what this horrible human being was doing to her, but it was clear she had to give up her three children in order for him to set her free. As Claire shared her gruesome story, I got chills down my spine. This man wanted to kill her existence as anything other than the mother of his three little babies. He didn't care if his children were raised in a dysfunctional family. All he cared about was winning his trophy and keeping it on a shelf. She thought things over for months and tried to stay for the sake of her children.

Although her heart was desperate to stay with her children, her brain was telling her to make a decision of freedom. She could not find the strength to leave the three babies she had suffered to bring into this world. One evening, he was angry. One of his friends told him he had bumped into Claire, and he expressed how beautiful, kind, and polite she was when he introduced himself. The husband was furious that she dared glance at him. When he came home, he was outraged and went on a rampage, screaming at her, trying to engage her in an escalated fight. Before she could defend herself, he grabbed her by the hair and started knocking her head against the wall.

When he fell asleep, she packed her clothes and walked away, never looking back. *What a devastating decision for a mother*, I thought when she told me, *to leave her only true loves: her children.* She basically had to choose to live or die. Her children were raised to despise and hate their mother. Claire was never allowed to ask family members about their health, education, or accomplishments.

Although she lived far away, she made it a point to stand outside the playground near their home or outside of their school when no one was looking, just to see them. She was not allowed to share in their graduations, marriages, baptisms, or any other happy occasions.

Days, weeks, months, and years passed by, and her anger and hate for him were almost tangible. "No one knows how many tears I have shed behind closed doors," she said. "If only the walls of my home could speak, they would reveal my pain and suffering. They would tell how this monster destroyed my life and family."

"I should have killed him," she told me as time passed. "But he was too powerful and always threatened to lock me up. The police were called many times, but they never did anything."

One day, Claire received a call from a distant relative who was a state trooper. He was someone who had loved and cared for her, and was one of the only people who was there for her throughout her life. In fact, he wanted to marry her, but she could not get over the fear of being with another man

Bold Resilient Women

When she picked up the phone, he informed her that her younger son was involved in a four-car collision. He was in the hospital in critical condition. Now, no one was going to stop Claire from seeing her son.

She had horrible images of what could happen as she walked through the door of the hospital. When her ex-husband saw her running to the reception area, he asked security to escort her out. Instantly, her cousin stepped in and took her defense, telling him furiously, "She has every right to be here. She is his mother. You deprived her of her son all these years; let her be with him now." Claire was lucky to say goodbye to her son before he took his last breath.

When she spoke of her painful life, all she would keep repeating was, "So what did I do? I left to save my life and killed my son." She fully believed she should have stayed and taken the punches, abuse, and insults. "If I had stayed, maybe this wouldn't have happened," she said. She was overcome with guilt. She couldn't see that her husband was the murderer. That he had stripped the children from their mother, and when he did that, he stripped them of happiness, safety, and security. No matter how hard I tried to convince her, my words fell on deaf ears.

She was too stuck in her pain and unwavering situation. She could not comprehend what was happening to her. This man was a selfish and self-centered individual who chose to destroy women and children, whether he was cutting them down in the home or taking revenge when they gained the strength to leave. People like this man are hypocrites and narcissists. They don't want women to have a voice or a say. They don't want them to stand up against violence.

"Having more children does not resolve a dysfunctional marriage," she said. "It only adds more layers of harassment, a bandage to hold the wound from getting wider. It's hard to find the strength and willpower to leave your abuser when you are alone and fighting a losing battle.

But when you have kids, you have to face the choice of removing yourself rather than letting someone else destroy you and those around you."

I realized, through my conversations with Claire, the different ways women have convinced themselves to stay with an abusive man, they feel they have an obligation to the family and society, and once I started working in the field of domestic violence, I realized how common it actually is.

My grandmother would say, "You are a steward to your children, and you have a responsibility to protect them." But Claire's story taught me that, while absolutely true, it's sometimes more complicated. You teach your children to become vulnerable to abuse.

Not Seen as Beautiful

My friend's daughter, Maria, was a tall, thin, beautiful brunette with green cat eyes and a white complexion like snow. Her dream was to become a famous model and travel the world while enjoying the good life. In the 1970s, women rarely became famous models, and usually didn't make much money doing it. As her dream failed to materialize, she became depressed. She felt unwanted. She felt ugly and saw herself as a failure. Her depression increased to the point that her parents committed her to a rehab center. This once young, vibrant, and beautiful woman was medicated, and people feared she would harm herself. After years of treatment, unconditional love, and a huge support system of family and friends, she overcame her skeletons. I spent nights and days with her to make sure she didn't harm herself. She shared her deepest nightmares with me. I helped to save her.

Beauty is in the eyes of the beholder. Maria was more solid and respected than many people who live in other individuals' shadows. She started believing in herself, her intelligent mind, and her kind heart. Years later, she found peace and love with a young man who also had many challenges in his teenage years. Without judging each other's pasts, they became model citizens, a great, loving couple, and outstanding parents.

Marilyn was a striking thirty-six-year-old young woman who had gone through college on a full ride scholarship. She was a successful pharmacist with a young son and a happy family. Every day, I would encounter her outside of the building we both lived in, and I could see fear and pain in her eyes. Yet when I asked how things were with the family, she would smile and say everything was amazing.

She had olive skin with long curly hair that reached down to her waist. Everyone was envious of her success and thought she had it all: a handsome husband, children, a lucrative job, a brand new house and a world of luxury around her. The entire neighborhood thought she had a fairytale marriage. One morning, a dear friend called us and told us Marilyn had walked away from her marriage. We were all stunned.

What had happened? Why didn't she share anything with any of us? What made her walk away from her luxurious life? These were all unanswered questions none of us could explain.

Years later, we found out her husband had a mental breakdown. She could not deal with it. She had fallen in love with someone else. After a huge ordeal full of courts, verbal hate, and abusive behavior, her husband passed away in his early fifties.

I think of Marilyn, her husband, and family often, especially when I drive by the cemetery. I question how we didn't see anything, and why she didn't share her painful life with anyone. Maybe she thought we could not understand her, or that we would judge and condemn her. We were all much younger and inexperienced in life and marriage. She must have thought we were the last people who would be able to advise her or understand her ordeals. But age doesn't matter—love and support can come from anywhere. I wish she had known we were there for her.

Anna

Anna was a sweet, innocent, young girl from Italy who had moved to Chicago at the age of fifteen. Her uncle and aunt had brought her to the United States to babysit their kids while attending school. To her surprise, she spent so much time taking care of the children that she hardly had time to study.

This went on for a couple of years. She was told that they needed to work, and she had to take care of the kids and the household. When she protested, she was punished by going to bed hungry. They would not provide any food for her. She was treated as a maid instead of a family member. The only way out was to find someone to marry.

During those years, you would meet your future spouse during coffee after church, or at church festivals or functions. Anna was introduced to a young man after church by one of her friends. When she went out with this man, he treated her with love and respect. It didn't take him long to propose to this gorgeous, brunette, tall, busty, and curvy young woman.

A few months later, they were married. But something changed. He isolated her from her family and friends. From the start, he started abusing her physically, mentally, and psychologically, even after she had given birth to three children. Things persisted as before. Constant feuds and put-downs. James was not a good father. There was something possessive and evil about him. When his niece came over to play, she would flinch when she saw him. She told her cousins she didn't want to go to their house to play, and instead asked them to come over to her house. When her parents asked her what the issue was, she told them the reason she was terrified to go to the house. They confronted James at his house in front of his wife and kids. Her father grabbed him by the neck, beat him up, and told him he better not ever go near his daughter again or he would kill him.

It turns out he had inappropriately touched her when she went to use the bathroom. At that very moment, Anna's younger daughter chimed in. "Mommy, Daddy touched me too when you were at work." She didn't know this wasn't supposed to happen. He was the father she respected and feared. Anna lost it. She started hitting him in front of the kids and his family. She grabbed his clothes and threw them outside the house.

Anna filed for divorce the next day to save her children and herself from sexual and physical abuse. This tormented the kids well into their teenage and adult years. They were traumatized by hearing what kind of monster their father was. They could not trust any man in their lives.

Their mother moved very far away and took custody of the children, but the kids never faced their wicked father. They hated and despised the fact that they shared his DNA.

Time heals everything. Through the unconditional love of their mother and family, the healing process began. All three children got married with a frightening shadow hanging over them. They became great parents due to their mother's love and support, but they were forever impacted.

Years later, Anna's children and I became adults. Anna had passed away. Her older daughter told me their mother never remarried. She dedicated her life to her children, grandchildren, and her church. I could not believe it. Her mother could have had any man. She was tall and beautiful with long brunette hair and gorgeous, silky skin. Yet she dedicated her life to her family. *The injustice*, I thought.

I asked her daughter how her husband and family were, and she said everyone is fine, but she is better than everyone. When I asked her what she meant, she said, "I finally forgave my father. I had to do it for myself and my family. I could not carry this burden any longer." I stood silent as she continued. "I learned forgiveness from my mother, who was tormented by him. She was a naive young girl who didn't have the support of anyone at the time. She could not trust anyone. She thought that if her immediate family had betrayed her, how could she trust anyone else?

This, my dearest Eleni, is the painful reality. She dedicated her life to raising us as a single mother, due to her fear of another monster in her children's lives."

I was stunned that this beautiful girl forgave this horrific man. How could she have found the strength to forgive? I looked into her light blue eyes and saw peace and love. She had come to terms with her past.

Bold Resilient Women

One thing I always say to my friends is, "Those who you love and those who love you unconditionally are individuals who will support and stand by you through thick and thin. It doesn't matter if they are related to you. Sometimes a stranger can take care of you better than a family member."

We will meet so many people in our daily lives. Many of them will continue a relationship with us, and many others we will leave behind. It's through difficult times that you need the support and love of your family and friends, not when things are pleasant.

Relationships are like being on a voyage and meeting different people from different paths of life. Some you will like and be fond of, and many are unnoticed by you. Through this journey, you will find many common interests with some individuals that will eventually become lifelong friends. Life is about accepting it all—sorrow, happiness, goodbyes, tears, death, good, and bad relationships—if you are going to be a survivor in this strange world. We live in times of uncertainty, and we never know what the next moment will bring our way. Mom would always say, "It takes one minute for a doctor to tell you bad news about your health. It takes a second for a tragedy. It takes a second for your life to come to a standstill. Everything in life is a split second. All we can do is take responsibility for ourselves. For us to understand our purpose in this world, we need to accept that nothing in life is certain. If you want to succeed, you must sweat and have painful backaches."

As my father would say, "You cannot enjoy good fish if you didn't get wet while catching it. You will see it is harder than you thought. It's like struggling to climb many flights of stairs to reach the top of the building," he continued. "You struggle, you sweat, you become weak, tired, and very thirsty, but when you finally reach the top, someone decides to throw you over. At that moment, you will see, you can get to the bottom very fast."

"Dad, what does this mean?" I asked one day.

"It's hard to have a stable and effective marriage, relationship, position, or career. If you cannot accept the skeletons in your closet or painful times in your life, if you can't admit your failures, you will continue putting on a bandage without healing your wound. You have to face the most hurtful incidents in life to achieve success. It's very easy to lose your soul, life, dignity, and everything you have achieved in a split second. Always walk without fear, my darling daughter, and have stability and courage. Don't ever be the flip-flopper in your life. What you say today should be your empowerment for tomorrow."

Dad and Mom would always say, "If you are not content with your decision, take two steps back, analyze the situation, and then move forward. Don't throw yourself in a situation where you're not one hundred percent sure it will be a good outcome for you."

Bold Resilient Women

I personally believe the secret to life is to live every day as if it's your last moment on this earth. We are all on a beautiful journey, a train ride, which will take us to many destinations and places. We never know when the trip will come to an end, and we will have to exit.

Often, I take a long car ride without knowing where I am going. I just want to release stress, or think about a situation, or solve something. I find myself looking outside at different cars passing me by. I look inside to see if people are alone or with company. I always wonder what people are discussing during their journey. Are people bewildered by their daily problems? Or do they take each day as it comes?

I love seeing the green grass and the beauty of all the things in my life. Often, I end up at the Serbian monastery to walk and pray. I like to find peace in the simple things in life. I find myself being distracted and needing time to pray for myself, my family, friends, and those who are sick, those living in war, poverty, and those that are in dire need of vigilant prayer.

Through the gift of prayer, I have found peace in my heart. I believe there is nothing more powerful than a connection with our creator. He is a loving God who has his arms open to accept all of us.

When I reach my office or home, I normally look up in the sky and say a prayer of gratitude that I have walked with the beautiful things that are left: my memories. What great discussions and interests I have built with those I have come into contact with on this journey.

At the monastery, I often have beautiful discussions about life. One of the priests said something touching: "God will bring you the people in your life he wants. These people will always bring you a calm and peaceful smile, while others who come your way will surpass your journey and travel ahead, watching your smile fade away."

Resentment

My dear friend, Julie, had a handsome son who resented seeing anyone. Tad had anger. He resented everyone around him. Hearing others express happiness or laughter would set him into a rage. He was formerly intelligent and kind, and no one could understand what was happening to him. Out of nowhere, he would make inappropriate comments about anyone and everyone. A friend of mine told me he had several issues with his marriage and had problems with his parents as well. He was unhappy in his marriage, which everyone thought was perfect. He had gone to his parents many times complaining and expressing his unhappiness, but his parents didn't want to hear about it. "You made your bed, now you lie in it. It's too late for you to think about mischief. You have four children to think about." That's all they would say. It seems this is a common sentiment in our culture.

His family opposed his filing for divorce. He told them he was exhausted with his wife's unpredictability and her outbursts, which always took place behind closed doors. He was tired of sacrificing himself and knew he wasn't giving his best to his boys. His wife was known to be a gossip, a thief, and a manipulator. Every day, he felt the stress and tension of going home after a long day at work. He didn't know who to turn to. His pride and ego were bigger than the love he had for himself and his kids.

One winter day, he took his gun and went for a drive. He found an isolated place and took his own life. When he didn't come home, his family started searching for him. When they could not find him, they notified the police. His body was found a few days later.

Bold Resilient Women

I understood at this point that it's the person who dies who loses out in life; those who remain behind figure things out. His family grieved, but as time passed, they all prospered and went on with their lives.

We witness the behavior of parents affecting the decisions children make. I can confidently say his parents and siblings never anticipated things would be so bad that he would take his own life.

Society's discriminatory and judgmental comments and gossip perpetuate oppression in a relationship.

Men and women must learn to fulfill their own needs first and take care of themselves and their happiness before they think of others. When you know your own worth and self-respect, you will lead a life of contentment and peace. As the most powerful animal who roams the earth, we can receive love and reciprocate it. We can learn to love and respect each other and live in a world of equality and loyalty. We can be collective in our efforts in achieving successful encounters.

There shouldn't be restrictions in pursuing anything that brings peace. Everyone is entitled to happiness, whether it's a wonderful marriage, an inspiring career, a productive existence, or whatever else brings them fulfillment.

Mary Kay

Mary Kay had the kind of life women dream about. She had a mansion by the lake, two beautiful children, exotic cars, and a handsome husband with a successful hedge fund company.

Our group of four friends would join Mary Kay to take the kids to the park after school. Occasionally, we could see a bruise or two on different parts of her body and asked how she got hurt. Before we could finish the sentence, she would say, "Look at these kids. They play so roughly, hitting each other. They do the same to me."

We believed what our friend told us at first, but then we noticed it happening more and more. Her excuses got old. One Saturday morning, as planned, we waited for her to bring the kids to the park. She never came. I went home and called her number, but the phone kept ringing and ringing. There was no answer. A chilling fear consumed my body, and in my gut, I could feel something terrible had happened. After a couple of days, rumors spread like wildfire. Mary Kay was hospitalized. Supposedly, she was hurt in an accident and had severe head trauma and broken ribs.

We wondered what had happened, but no one knew anything. We assumed there were hidden secrets in that house. Her husband did not allow visitors after her injury. He said that she was recuperating from a horrible fall and needed her rest while she was in the hospital. He put restrictions on who was allowed to visit her. Surprisingly, only her parents and family were on the list.

A month later, I received a phone call that left me speechless. This once-strong woman with a fierce voice wasn't making any sense. All she could say was, "No one will ever understand my story." I had to get a grip and focus on what she was saying. I took control of my fear and begged her to see me. She agreed after nearly an hour of convincing her.

We met the next day, and before she even sat down, she looked me straight in the eyes.

"I want to ask you a question," she said. "Can you believe a twisted story? I want to tell you, but I am afraid you will betray me and think I am crazy."

"Why wouldn't I believe you?" I asked. "What do you have to lose?" I had heard numerous love stories that had ended in destructive ways. I knew loving couples who seemed happy around their family and friends, but became violent behind closed doors.

Our conversation gradually became more personal, emotional, and intense. She shared the severe suffering she had covered up all these years. It turns out that rather than the perfect life, Mary Kay's days were filled with excruciating pain and anger.

"I am tired of telling my family and friends lies," she said. "I would cover up his abuse by telling them I was clumsy and self-destructive. I was prone to having accidents, I kept hurting myself playing with the kids. When I was stressed, my blood pressure would go below normal, I would get dizzy and pass out." Disbelief overwhelmed my chilled body.

She finally said, "I need to get far away from my abuser." I realized how much she had endured throughout her marriage. "Eleni, I don't ever want anyone to know where I will go with my two children. I need to savor their innocence." I understood completely. It was her job to protect them. I had to control my tears of disbelief as she continued sharing. "I am a victim of violence," she said. "I remained in a violent marriage of convenience for my entire family." She told me she had confided in her mother about the abuse and was alarmed by her response. "She said that he is a good man and father, and he works hard to provide for everyone. I told my mom that he was an angel to his friends, partners, and constituents. The minute he left the house, he was reborn with a great personality. However, as soon as he came home, he became an unknown creature. Eleni, he has a split personality. I am constantly walking on eggshells."

Mary Kay always thought her mother loved her unconditionally. But every time she complained, her mother would tell her to stop exaggerating and over-reacting. Her mother defended him, saying he had a lot of stress due to his demanding job. "He is a good husband and provider," she said. "You never have to worry about having a roof over your head, money, or cars. Your children are lucky to be raised in an influential community."

Bold Resilient Women

Her mother, who came from a poor village in Greece, suffered during the war. They didn't have food on the table or decent clothes or any kind of transportation. Her family fought every day for survival. She worked two jobs to educate her daughter so she could meet a wonderful and educated man to marry. When Mary Kay met this fine young man, her mom saw how he wined and dined her, the expensive gifts he bought her, and how she was cared for. She thought her daughter would live the sort of life she was deprived of. Her mother was happy for her.

"Eleni, my mother saw the material things in my life. She was witnessing a different lifestyle for me, her daughter." She told me that her mother repeatedly told her marriage was made in heaven. She said her home was cozy, without challenges or financial needs. "My mom saw many bruises on my body, and not once did she mention anything," she told me. "She never had the courage to ask me how I had gotten those marks on my arms. I don't know if she was in denial or she just didn't care." Mary Kay believed her grandfather and father were both physically abusive to her mother, and that she had erased her painful memories of the past.

Her parents never understood. Yes, he provided financial support for them, but she was sacrificing her life. She was monitored like a little child. Everything had to be neatly placed in the cabinets, closets, and in storage. She had to have the meal on the table and the kids fed, bathed, and in bed. He said he was mentally exhausted and didn't have the capacity to sit and talk or hear any noise.

One evening, he came home unexpectedly. His meal was not finished, and the kids were all over the house playing, laughing, and throwing their toys around. He started yelling in a rage for the kids to stop, demanding that she put them to sleep. She put the kids to sleep with tears running down her face; she was exhausted from being treated as a slave.

She stood at the top of the stairs and told him she wasn't going to put up with all his abuse anymore. She was finished. He sprinted up the stairs, grabbed her by the shoulders, and shook her. They got into a terrible fight, and suddenly, she found herself at the bottom of the stairs. She woke up in the hospital with a concussion. She had a bruised face and many broken ribs, and she could not believe she was alive. She could have died in that fall. That was the beginning of the end, the day she realized she had to take charge of her life. She owed it to her two children.

Listening to this tragedy made me furious. Why didn't she tell us what she was going through? We would have helped her even if no one else wanted to. I certainly would have gone out of my way to make sure she was safe. I told her that whatever decision she made, I would stand by her side to support and help her. She could not trust or tell anyone what she was going through. She was terrified of filing a police report. He always threatened to take the kids away.

A few years before, when she threatened to call the police, he told her this: "They will never believe you. I will take the children away and institutionalize you." This terrified her, and her fear became her captivity in an abusive marriage. That's how he got away with years of abuse. It would be his word against hers, and no one would believe that a wealthy, educated man could ever be an abusive husband.

Days and nights were difficult for me. I couldn't focus on anything else. I kept wondering what she was going to do. Where would she go? Who would take care of her? Had she saved any money?

Days later, she called to tell me about an affluent family who knew her and had always suspected something was not right in her marriage. They thought he was just a little too nice and perfect to others, and his behavior did not make sense to this intelligent elderly couple. The husband knew how to study people, and he and his wife believed her story. They recognized the excuses coming from a battered woman. They made arrangements with another couple who resided out of state for her to leave. They were very close friends who would never betray their trust and friendship. In the beginning, it made her sick that her escape was being plotted like something out of a movie. She was caught. Why should she leave the city she loved? How would her children feel about leaving Chicago and never being found by him or anyone? She didn't know if she was making a wise decision.

At that moment, I remembered my beloved mom always saying, "Look at the individual. Don't focus on a family, background, education, or wealth. Out of roses come thorns and out of thorns come roses."

When I asked my mom what this saying meant, she simply said, "You can never judge anyone by what they show."

I had never imagined this was just the first of hundreds of abuse stories I would hear. At the time, I didn't yet know, but I was embarking on a life of hearing and witnessing many terrible and difficult stories. Despite my work in this area, every time I hear about life-shattering experiences, I have empathy and sadness in my heart. No one deserves to live in a dysfunctional, abusive environment.

When Mary Kay came to bid me farewell, I was heartbroken. I knew we would never see or talk to each other again. She was going to be given a new identity and a new life in a new place.

Although it was painful saying goodbye to my dear friend, I felt peace inside. I was proud of her courage. She had placed her emotions aside and had decided to set herself and her children free.

Weeks, months, and years went by, and I never heard from her. We completely lost contact. Her mother passed away, and she didn't come to the funeral. Years later, her father passed away, and again, people expected her to show up. But she never came back home. She had erased the memories, friends, family—everything about her previous life.

This frightening story made me a stronger woman. I started seeing deeper into different situations because I wasn't naive in thinking abuse doesn't exist. While I never saw Mary Kay again, her impact on my life still lingers to this day. Wherever she is, I hope she knows this somehow.

Mr. Bouras, a Man of Steel

Mr. Bouras and my family met many years ago through Leadership 100. He was known in Chicago as a unique spiritual man who worked in the steel industry. His parents, Dimitri and Rina, had arrived in this country as children from Tripoli, Arcadia, and Leondari, Arcadia, the hometowns of my parents and grandparents. Many Arkadians fled to the United States as children during the late 1800s and early 1900s. All they thought about was coming to work and sending money back to the family. They were all very faithful to our churches, family, and country.

Mr. Bouras was an honorable man who enlisted in the army during WWII. Right before he left for the war, he married his sweetheart, Anna, whom he had met at a church function. He was awarded the Distinguished Flying Cross from the President of the United States for flying forty-four combat missions. He ended his military career as a major.

When he returned, he graduated from Northwestern University with Mrs. Amalea Alexander and her sister, Helen. This is how I met Mr. Bouras, from these amazing and inspirational sisters.

Anna was an ambitious woman with character and wisdom, and she persuaded him that they should start their own steel company. She said she saw that he was the best salesman, and because he knew his work so well, his potential was huge in the steel business. In 1960, he and Anna established Bouras Industries, eventually producing fabricated steel components for the real estate industry.

His steel company was evolving fast. He helped build the New York skyline, beginning with the World Trade Center Tower 4, followed by Bloomberg, Bear Stearns, Goldman Sachs, Time Warner Center, and many sports stadiums across the country, including those of the Yankees, Giants, Patriots, Ravens, Redskins, Celtics, 76ers, Wizards, and Devils.

Mr. Bouras gave credit to Anna for inspiring, motivating, and pushing him to start and grow his own company. He was nicknamed the "Man of Steel." In addition to his work, he and Anna were devoted to philanthropy and supported numerous organizations and not-for-profit institutions. When asked if he had regrets, he would say, "I did it the way I wanted to."

His biggest joy was sitting in his large office surrounded by photos of his skylines, stadiums, and the airplanes he had flown in WWII. He would have a large pillow behind his back. "It relieves the pain I got in the war," he explained.

I would sit hours with him at the office, hospital, and his home during his final year, asking him questions about life and success.

"Eleni mou, because you are young and naive, I will give you a piece of advice I want you to keep very close to your heart," he told me one day. "When people around you start kissing up to you, stay far away from them. They have bad motives. Always respect those who tell you what you don't want to hear. They are the ones who will watch out for you."

"Mr. Bouras, how do you know?"

"Honey, I know many people who surround me don't care about me," he said. "I know their intentions. I am old, I have no children, and I am wealthy. I will die and leave much behind. But you, who are young, beautiful, innocent and kind, and genuinely care and love others, will get hurt. I don't want people to use your kindness as a weakness. I want to protect you."

I thought I was listening to my dad. *It's got to be the same Arkadian water,* I thought to myself.

"Mr. Bouras, why didn't you ever go back to Greece?"

"There was no need. My family was here, and there was no one left behind to go visit." He would always stop there, as if he never wanted to discuss the old country. He always said, "My parents taught me at a very young age to love and worship God with all my heart and soul. You need to work hard if you want to enjoy the fruits of life."

I would often drive with him around the city so he could assess the construction of different buildings and identify whether the steel was bought from him or another company. I remember one time when we were driving, he was looking out the window and said, "These buildings aren't using my steel. I wonder why the salesman didn't get the job." I was stunned that even in his nineties, he was worried about why he lost the account.

Bold Resilient Women

I asked him how he noticed, and he told me his steel was in the form of a cross, like an X. He reminded me so much of my father. They knew their work, and they were filled with wisdom and empowerment.

We were invited to Mr. Bouras's eightieth birthday party at his favorite Italian restaurant near his office. They would always reserve a private room in the back where we would eat together and share stories, many times joined by his friend and executive, Bill Crane. I was unsure what to buy someone who owned the world, so I decided to buy him two Chanel ties. He opened the box.

"I love them, Eleni, but don't you like mine?" He held up the bottom of his tie and showed me. "Sir, it is beautiful," I said.

"Sit and I will tell you the story of the tie." He loved to have you sit with him for hours to share his unending life experiences and stories. "Well, I went to Walgreens to get my medicine and I saw a rack of ties at the great price of $9.99, so I asked the cashier to give them all to me." I could not stop laughing. "You don't like it, do you?" he asked. "No, sir, but the price just blew my mind."

"If you like something, don't look at the price. Just think about how good you look in it."

I gained so much respect for Mr. Bouras. He wore $9.99 ties, drove his old car, and still lived in his first residence. This unique and kind man taught me what a good and secure person is, and how I should feel safe in my own skin, my family, and who I am. He would tell me, "My family and the people around me know who I am and what I am worth."

"Never let money or power buy your integrity and honor," he told me. "Let your passions, love, and knowledge make your way for you."

One time at the house, we had a little debate about this conversation. "Sir, you said you knew many people around you were there for your money, not because they loved you sincerely."

"Yes, that's true. I said that to you because the world has changed. Or maybe it's always been this way. People have the tendency to associate you with your worth."

"Sir," I said. "There are many people who are loyal to opening the churches every Sunday for us. There are many caregivers who take care of the sick. There are many individuals who go out in the streets and feed the homeless. I am asking you, are all these people seen as good, honorable Christians? I think so."

He said, "Yes, they are the true, honest, and dignified individuals in our society. But when you have money, you are identified with your money. Doors will open more easily for you, people will call you often to see how you are, they will buy you accolades and awards, and they will wonder exactly what you are saying. But why aren't the people who usher and clean the church honored? Why haven't the people who clean the streets and take care of the sick and homeless been awarded? So you see, my dear, what the answer is to your question."

It wasn't long after this conversation that I walked into his office at the same time his assistant told him he had a call. I motioned that I would leave, but he waved for me to sit. He wrote on a piece of paper: *"Sit down."*

I sat across from him and found myself listening to the most profound conversation I had ever heard. After he hung up the phone, he said, "I had to tell Warren what I thought."

"Sir, I am glad you did, but who is Warren?" I asked.

"Don't you know Warren?" He said.

"Warren who?" I asked.

Warren Buffett." I spilled the water all over myself.

"Why didn't you tell me he was on the phone so I could talk to him too?" I joked. We could not stop laughing. "Sir, do you know many people who can just speak to Warren Buffett? I sure don't know anyone. See, money travels where money is."

He just shook his head and smirked with his loose saliva coming out of the side of his mouth.

Mr. Bouras taught me not to trust anyone but God and my instincts. "When a woman is wise and faithful, she will lead her husband to success. But if she is taking space in society and sits around without any purpose, she will eventually destroy him and his family—unless he is a very strong, stand-up man."

I told him it reminded me of something my mom used to say: "When a woman works, she doesn't have time to file her nails or stir up problems. She's too busy taking care of someone else." In Greek, there's a saying: *Xenis ta nehia sou na vriskis provlimata*, which roughly means, "If you have nothing meaningful to focus on, you'll start looking for problems."

Many times, I thought he, my mom, and my dad had lived and been raised in the same home. They all spoke with so much compassion and wisdom about life, work, and faith. Their whole lives were devoted to philanthropy and giving. Mr. Bouras and my parents were all from the same era and the same

Bold Resilient Women

country, and they had the same morals and values. They were born into different backgrounds and raised in very different family environments, but they were united by their hard work ethic and their sense of analyzing people. Their sixth sense could identify a person who was real and one who was along for the ride. Mr. Bouras and my parents would teach you through showing and sharing tales of their strength, struggles, and challenges. They were storytellers who had lived life to the fullest. They also both believed that though young people had more today, there was a distinct lack of happiness.

"The world is more complex. Technology rules them. People don't know how to change, it's as if their brains are fried." This always made me laugh. They all believed social media had advanced society, but at the same time destroyed relationships, friendships, and marriages. They saw how people had become too dependent on computers.

"People have forgotten the simple method of picking up a pen and writing," Mr. Bouras would say. He was a big reader and always had a huge basket with different books and newspapers. "You need to pick up a hardcover book and feel the flip of the pages, then you will understand the concept of the book."

The man who took personal calls from Warren Buffett believed intensely in the beauty of a handwritten letter. That's just one of the ways that Mr. Bouras consistently reminded me of what's important in life.

Lost Love

George and Ria were two young lovers in their teenage years. They attended high school in the city during the week and, over the weekend, they would go back to their village to help with the farm, animals, and family. They both came from humble and poor beginnings. They wanted to succeed and make their parents proud. They could not stand living in poverty, and they dreamed of making a better life for themselves and their future family.

There wasn't a day that went by that people didn't see them together. They had many dreams and ambitions to finish high school and pass their tests to be admitted to Athens University.

They were determined to get their college degrees, secure careers, and eventually get married and create a wonderful family together.

George passed and attended Athens Medical School while Ria passed her tests to attend the College of Education in a different city. This brought much pain and anger, as they desperately wanted to attend the same university to continue their love. George reassured her that no matter the distance between them, their love was everlasting and no one could ever destroy it.

They both started college in different cities. A lovely brunette student started pursuing George. Weeks and months went by, the letters began fading, and Ria could not understand what had happened to the man who promised to love her forever.

Christmas came, and they had plans to reconnect in their home village, where they had gone to high school and where their love began. Ria waited at the *platea* at their meeting place for hours, but George never showed up. The next day, she went to the village, thinking he had gone there to rest. She knew medical school was very difficult, and she thought maybe he had fallen asleep from studying for his finals before the Christmas holiday.

Ria knocked on the door. His mother answered it. "Is George here?" She asked hopefully.

"I'm sorry, Ria," his mother said. "George isn't coming home for the holidays." Ria broke down crying, unsure of what was happening. His mother had known Ria since she was a young girl and was very fond of her.

"I don't know why he made this choice, but maybe you should travel to Athens and surprise him?" Ria didn't know what else to do, so she took her advice. The next day, she went shopping for him with what little she had and then took the bus to Athens.

When Ria arrived at George's house, she rang the bell eagerly. A tall, brunette, young lady answered the door. Ria was horrified.

"Who are you?" she asked, confused.

"I am Tina, George's girlfriend," the girl responded. Ria handed her the packages and told her to tell George they were Christmas gifts from Ria, a friend from the village. She left quickly and went and sat in the park for hours. She could not believe how he could have so easily discarded their relationship, love, and all of the dreams they had made.

Ria went back to her city to go back to school. She wanted to finish what she had started so she could get as far away as possible. A year later, she heard George was getting married and his girlfriend was expecting. She was destroyed. She wanted to end her life. How could she get married when she had carried on a love affair for years with the man she had given her heart to? Ria left the country and never wanted to return.

She moved to New York and resided at her aunt's home. She registered at a local university, where she met a wonderful young professor who helped her with the English language and introduced her to a new country and big city. She had never seen so many people, such busy streets, such huge buildings, and such a range of different cultures, languages, and races. Even through adventures in her new home, she was a village girl who was devastated after losing the love of her life and leaving her beloved family behind.

Every year, she would learn of George's life. He and his wife had three children, and he had finished medical school and become a successful surgeon. He moved to Los Angeles to attend medical school in the United States to specialize in a particular field. Everyone assumed George was happy, but he wasn't smiling or making jokes the way he did when he was with Ria. It was as if he had checked out of the past. He was only living for today and focusing on the future.

Bold Resilient Women

Several years later, the professor asked Ria to marry him. He was madly in love with her, and she cared for him, but she didn't want a partner. Fifteen years had gone by since she lost her love, and she was lonely, working day and night as a social service coordinator for a hospital. The professor told her he had an offer for a transfer to Chicago. He was going to accept, but only if she accepted his marriage proposal. She agreed. After many years of pursuing her, she finally decided to marry him, move to a new city, and start a new life. Meanwhile, in a twist of fate, George was now head of surgery at a hospital in Chicago.

Twenty-five years after George broke Ria's heart, there was a Greek dance, and both couples were invited to attend. All of a sudden, they walked through the door and came to a stunned stop when they saw each other. They were in shock. They didn't believe it could be real. Was God playing a joke? Or was there a larger meaning that they had come back into each other's lives?

It turns out that the previous week, George's wife was diagnosed with Stage 4 cancer and was undergoing chemotherapy. His three children had all graduated from college and were set in their careers. George had too much to bear, and he couldn't think of Ria. At the same time, she tried desperately not to be in the same circle of friends.

A year went by, and Ria decided to leave her husband. She didn't think it was fair for her to love one man and live with another, as she knew she still had feelings for George. The professor was unsurprised because he had always known he had never really had her heart. A few months later, Ria was at the hospital for tests and bumped into George. He told her that his wife had passed away from cancer. She felt sad for him and his children.

A year later, George and Ria ran into each other on a flight to Greece. Stuck in the air with nowhere to go and no way out, George and Ria finally talked, and Ria was able to tell him how he had destroyed her life. She told him how he had deceived her and had disgraced her in front of her family, friends, and villagers. She told him she had to leave her beloved parents and country, and flee to an unknown world.

George was shocked to hear this. He told her on that fateful day, Tina, his then-girlfriend and future wife, closed the door after a visitor and told him it was Ria, who said she was with someone else and didn't want to see him. He was devastated that she had betrayed him and their love.

When Ria heard how this woman had lied and manipulated their love, she broke down crying. She explained to him what had happened, how she waited for him for hours at the *platea* and he never showed. She told him she had visited his mom, and she gave her the bus money to go see him in Athens, and to bring him his Christmas gifts. Tina answered the door and said she was George's girlfriend and they lived together.

At that moment, they both realized how they had been played by someone who wanted to break them up. She may have gotten her wish—but it didn't last. After the long plane ride, George and Ria realized their love was everlasting, one that had continued for a lifetime. They rekindled their love and restarted their life together. They didn't need to date; they were best friends who knew each other inside and out. There were no surprises between them.

George and Ria married and have been together for over twenty years.

Today, I see them together at different events, and I am always struck by how they look at each other. You can see the true affection. They act like teenagers falling in love.

My friend Stella always says, "Be patient and see what God has in store for all of us." When there is true love between two people, God will bring those souls together sooner or later. People can lie, plot, and manipulate others, but eventually, the truth comes out. One can never be happy or rest easily when they know in their heart they took their partner from someone else's arms. God eventually tests love. And when it's real, he brings those people together again.

Marianne, a Woman of Strength and Courage

It's nearly impossible to identify all of the amazing women who have influenced me throughout my life. Since I was young, I have been surrounded by so many mentors, who led me to follow in their footsteps. It would take volumes of books to write my connection and affiliation with each and every one of them.

They were precisely the role models that you want to have. They were all charismatic, charming, honest, and loyal. They stood tall with grace and empathy for others. They taught me by example what strength and persistence mean. They guided me in establishing a secure self-esteem with the ability to focus on positive thoughts and drive toward the things I wanted to achieve and accomplish in life.

One of those amazing women was my beautiful, charming friend, Marianne. Marianne was a tall, slim Italian woman with blonde hair and a statuesque body. As a young woman, she could charm anyone who crossed her path. She was vibrant and charismatic with a passion for living life to its fullest. While these qualities were always ingrained in her, they dramatically increased when she was diagnosed with cancer in her late twenties. The dramatic news was a terrifying curve, one that changed her life drastically.

Bold Resilient Women

Marianne had a difficult time accepting her diagnosis. She wanted to pretend nothing was wrong, that there was no way her life plans would be derailed. She wanted to live, travel, and see the world, and nothing was going to stand in her way. She was insistent that she would conquer cancer.

Marianne always told me, "Cancer isn't going to wipe me out, Eleni. I am going to fight and win. I have too many things to do and many people to support."

She was a resilient woman with faith and hope. Little did she anticipate that when this monster wakes up, it can spin out of control and take your life at any moment.

Marianne never considered herself a victim. She lived a full life until she was in her fifties. She had good and bad times, but she never once complained, no matter how much pain she was enduring. She was always smiling with joy and confidence, and fully believed she was going to beat all odds. Her biggest delight was passing $100 bills to busboys, bellboys, homeless people, or anyone who needed her help.

Although as a young girl I witnessed my mom's battle with colon cancer, I didn't understand the side effects, and the way it could be cured or be lethal. At the young age of eight, I was too young and naive to understand how this monster almost destroyed our family. All I knew was that everyone had a role in alleviating mom's stress level. She was terrified and angry. She was in her thirties and didn't think once about her own life, only the lives of her four children. Mom's smile drifted away from her frail face, taking away her ability to be resilient. She felt lost and lonely, not knowing how to communicate with her doctors. She was stripped of her integrity. At this vulnerable age, I was made aware that cancer has the capability of taking over a person's looks, body image, and life. Your self-confidence diminishes and leaves behind someone who is hopeless, lost, and has no idea what steps to take next.

Marianne was my first close friend diagnosed with cancer and fighting for survival. Marianne loved life, her family, and her friends more than anything. She wanted to live for her beloved mother, her brother, Michael, and her two beloved nieces, whom she treated as her own daughters. Marianne didn't accept Cancer, and unless she was visiting MD Anderson Cancer Center, where she had her procedure, treatments, and her yearly test, she rarely thought about it, only steeled herself to fight it.

"I will beat all odds," she would tell me. "Nothing can take away my fight." Marianne would always say, "I thank God for money, because I can buy my medicine, and see the finest doctors, and receive the best care and hospitals. But my darling friend, you can never buy time: The clock never stops." It was a shocking eye-opener in my twenties, watching a graceful woman close to my age fighting for her life. It was scary, the first time I witnessed someone so beautiful, talented, and charming face an uncertain future.

One late summer afternoon, we met for lunch. Marianne was such a supportive friend, and she had planned to purchase raffle tickets for an upcoming fashion show fundraiser for one of my foundations. We greeted each other in the doorway of the restaurant, and paused as we waited to be seated. Around us, the clink of silverware and plates rang through the restaurant, and busy waitstaff bustled around us, setting and clearing tables.

"Eleni, I wish I could be there," she told me. "But I am too weak and tired. I just can't."

Suddenly, my legs were shaking uncontrollably. I stood like a statue, unable to speak. I was standing in the presence of this elegant, fierce woman, and I couldn't say a word.

She grabbed me and hugged me as though I were a lost child, and I let her. I didn't want to tell her that I felt I was passing out when I approached her and saw her bald head without a wig. I was horrified, wanting to yell and scream from the pain my beloved friend was enduring.

"Don't be afraid," she said in a soft voice. "I am tired of wearing a wig. I want to be myself. I've lost my beautiful hair, and I'm pale as a ghost." I looked her in the eyes, and while she looked different physically, her eyes radiated her bold, brilliant heart. "Money can't buy you a better life," she said. "It only pays for doctors and treatments to prolong it. Honey, always remember: money talks, and bullshit walks." These realistic words of pain and suffering kept echoing in my ears.

I started feeling agony and anguish. How could I lose someone so dear to my heart, a mentor and a friend? Although she was facing her own struggles and demons, she had time to think of others, especially my loved ones. Marianne never forgot someone's birthday, anniversary, name day celebration, or any other monumental holidays. She also reinforced the importance of giving to the poor and homeless. When we would go out for dinner, she would be holding a pocketbook with at least $5,000 in $100 bills. She knew the doorman at the Four Seasons and the homeless people in the street by their first names. She would greet them, genuinely check in on their lives, then silently put a $100 bill in the palm of their hand.

Through Marianne, I learned the meaning of unconditional love and saw the different ways people with empathy and love reveal and express their emotions for others. When she returned from the MD Anderson Hospital after her treatment, she instructed her driver to come directly to my house to congratulate my daughter, Victoria, on her high school graduation. I opened the door and I was taken aback by her pale color, her weak and frail body. I was speechless. I told her she should have gone straight home to rest, but she said she wouldn't dream of it.

When she left, I could not control my tears. I kept asking myself, *Why would she exhaust herself after her treatment and long trip?* After she gave me a kiss and a card for Victoria, she left, looking exhausted and distraught. She started to deteriorate quickly after that.

Throughout her fight with cancer, Marianne never forgot to love and glorify God by saying, "Who is not to be tested? He was the son of God and only thirty-three years old. They tormented and tortured him as if he were a criminal, and at the end, they crucified him in front of his mother."

She would remind me that we were both good Christians, though one was a devoted Catholic and the other an Orthodox Christian. Though we could spout off all of the differences between our faiths, Marianne would say that we both had the same values and morals.

The following week, I was set to travel to Jerusalem, but my trip was postponed due to political issues in Israel. After several days, I was informed by the Patriarchate that it was safe to travel there again, and immediately, I arranged to go. That year, Marianne was too delicate and brittle to accompany me, but she wanted an icon of our Lord and Savior Jesus Christ from the Holy Land. I had the opportunity to visit the Patriarch of Jerusalem, and I explained to him Marianne's case. I asked him to bless the icon I was given by one of the nuns, which I would bring back for comfort. This Holy Icon of Our Lord was sacred, and just by looking at it, you felt at peace. I accepted it faithfully; this was a precious gift I was going to give to Marianne for peace and healing.

I returned home with hope and faith. The following day, I took it to her house. She prayed, crying for encouragement and peacefulness. She held the icon and embraced it before setting it beside her bed. A few days later, we went out to celebrate her new transformation. After a very long time, I saw her face beaming and glowing, her skin flawless.

A couple of weeks passed, and I didn't hear from her. I knew she needed downtime to rest and rejuvenate between treatments. She called me to set up dinner, and over the phone, she told me not to be alarmed when I saw her. She was a woman of acceptance.

As I pulled up, I saw a woman waiting outside of the revolving door of the Four Seasons. But there was no way it was Marianne. This woman was small, fragile, and bald, and leaning on a cane. The skin on her face was drawn, and her clothes hung off of her frail body. I was so startled when I realized it was her, but finally I gained the courage to hug her before opening the car door for her.

"I'm sick of wearing wigs, Eleni," she said again, as I extended my hand out to support her. I marveled at her remarkable strength and courage—even if it was an act. I was witnessing the new Marianne. Unfortunately, she never shared the burdens and pain with me. She would say, "Honey, you have too many children and responsibilities to carry my burden, too." I was witnessing the distress and anguish of someone I admired and cherished.

Sitting across from her in the club restaurant, I was numb, shaken up by the sight of her. I was furious that my dear friend had to endure this fight. "Why didn't you tell me you weren't wearing your wig again?" I asked her. "If you had warned me ahead of time, I would have considered shaving my head!" We both laughed, and finally, the ice was broken. Our dinner played out the way our time together always did, with twisting and turning conversations about current events and people we knew. We laughed our hearts out, which turned into tears. We were both overwhelmed with fear and terror; we knew the end was imminent.

Every evening, Marianne would call me at 11 o'clock. She was aware of my schedule. I had to feed the kids, help with homework, and the evening chores, and then we could talk for as long as she needed. We discussed death, everlasting life, and what happens to us after we die. She kept wondering: *When we die, do we cease to exist? Or do we go to an eternal life where someday we will be reunited with our loved ones?*

"Our spirit and soul will continue living," I told her. "The dead are around us. They guide and protect us. We don't have the godly power to see them, but they frequently communicate with us in our dreams and visions. I can assure you that I can feel the presence and protection of my grandparents and the loved ones I have lost every day."

Many times, we discussed euthanasia and what it meant to induce death. She thought many times of ending her own life. She wanted to visit Dr. Jack Kevorkian. Dr. Kevorkian was an American pathologist who was a euthanasia proponent. After a lengthy conversation about our Christian faith and God, we both agreed that no one had the right to take their life or someone else's life. God brought us into this world and He is the only one to take us back to His eternal home. She would start laughing loudly and say, "Okay, I guess that's not a good idea."

I had many restless nights of sleep thinking of the discomfort and distress my dear friend had endured through her cancer battle. I was witnessing her agony and fear without understanding what her vulnerable body was really going through.

Marianne wanted to remain positive in her dreams and endeavors. She continued calling me every night to tell me of her dreams for her nieces and everyone she loved. She had hopes for everyone to achieve and fulfill their dreams in this compelling world. She loved to close the phone or dinner conversation by laughing and saying, "Even those I don't like, I wish them luck." She constantly verbalized how lucky she felt to be alive and to have lived with her loved ones many years after being diagnosed with cancer. Marianne was grateful for her family, the friendship and love we had for each other, and the wonderful times we had together. She said, "I am appreciative of the beautiful icon I have beside my bed. Our Lord's image has become my comfort and peace during my ups and downs."

A couple of weeks later, her brother, Michael, called to inform me of her passing. I was devastated, wondering what her last minutes were like. Was she at peace? Did she have regrets? Was she ready to depart this world for everlasting life? I knew the only regret she had was breaking off her engagement after she was diagnosed with cancer. She would laugh, saying, "I didn't know I was going to last this many years. If I did, I would have gotten married."

At Marianne's wake, I walked slowly up to her casket. She looked as if she had fallen asleep, and her face radiated peace. She was beautiful and calm, and finally her suffering and pain were over. She slept serenely. The following day at Holy Name Cathedral, I sat next to her beloved mother, Margaret, and her family. I grieved with so much sorrow and heartache.

Although I knew she was in God's kingdom, I was distressed. I had lost my beloved friend, and even though I knew we would meet again, I was really going to miss her.

As a mother, I could feel her elderly mother's pain. There were no comforting words. What can you possibly say when someone is crying after losing their daughter?

I kept asking, "Why God, why?"

Marianne's passing left me angry and disturbed. I kept questioning why this vibrant woman, who had so much potential in life, didn't survive. Why didn't she conquer cancer?

Marianne's love for life, people, family, and friends taught me many lessons. She taught me how to fight battles with dignity, hope, and honor. She didn't want anyone to pity her. She would say, "It's better to have people envy you than pity you. Never give your enemies a reason to laugh at you; keep your dirty laundry in your house, don't spread it to your enemies."

If you didn't know Marianne's story, you could never imagine how painful her daily life was.

Marianne's experience showed me firsthand how to appreciate every moment in life. Wealth, power, and success are irrelevant when an individual is told their life and existence in this world are only for a short time. Plato said, "There is a distinct collaboration between the mind, the body, and one's

Bold Resilient Women

health. The cure of many diseases is unknown to physicians because they are ignorant of the whole. For the part can never be well unless the whole is well."

No one wants to leave. Everyone finds a way to transcend their problems and feelings when the end is near. At the end, we all pray to the higher being to have mercy on us and to forgive our sins and transgressions. It's a painful lesson to acknowledge that from dust we are made and to dust we will return.

It's hard accepting and understanding that we are not indispensable—we are here today, gone tomorrow.

As the Bible says in Mark 13:32-36, *"However, no one knows the day or hour when this happens, not even the angels in heaven or the Son himself, but only the Father."*

At that moment, I understood what my beloved friend, Yiota, would say. "Eleni mou, do you understand why a child cries when it's born? It cries because it's aware that with birth, death will come. No matter who you are and which family you are born to, ultimately, you will not remain in this world." From that day, I realized we are all here for a very short journey, a train ride that will take us to our final stop. Then, we will start our long walk to everlasting.

Riches to Rags

My beloved friend, Stephanie, came from a wealthy shipping family. She was the only daughter, and the whole family admired and doted on her. She was talented and extremely smart—she could tell you everything you needed to know about the shipping business.

Stephanie's mother was one of four girls, also raised with golden spoons in their mouths. Stephanie's grandfather had many manufacturing and shipping companies, and her mother was a great prize for any handsome man. She was beautiful, talented, artistic, and charismatic, with smooth olive skin and deep gray eyes. A young man working for her family had set his sights on her. In the beginning, the family opposed the unity of these two young people. But when the parents saw the way he pursued her with loving determination, and also treated them with honor and respect, they started liking him.

Because her father didn't have any boys, he treated this young man like his own and held him to the standards of a son. Very fast, this young man moved into the family. He became bossy and in control of the manufacturing business. Eventually, the wedding took place, and the family gave her a good dowry as a wedding gift. They purchased a lovely home near them and the other sisters.

The father and his son-in-law were together all the time, commuting back and forth to the office. The marriage seemed to have been made in heaven. Within three years they had created a lovely family with two young children, a boy, and a girl who was Stephanie. This young man, Stephanie's father, was

Bold Resilient Women

tall, handsome, and intelligent. Every woman wished he were with them, not with his wife.

Eventually, he fell into a trap. Two young women had set their sights on securing two healthy, wealthy, and powerful married men. Stephanie's father had taken the bait and fallen in love with another woman. Her mother was devastated. She didn't want to disappoint her parents, so she kept quiet about her heartbreak.

One day, the banker stopped by Stephanie's grandfather's office to ask how business was going. Her grandfather couldn't understand why the banker would ask such an out-of-character question, so he asked what he meant.

"Well, according to accounting, two of your factories are overdrawn. Money has been drawn out in large amounts by someone with authority." Stephanie's grandfather froze as he realized his son-in-law was scamming the company by spending money that wasn't his on the mistress and buying her luxurious cars, homes, and clothes. When the banker left, the grandfather fell onto his desk. They called the ambulance, and he was rushed to the private hospital near the office. Two hours later, he was pronounced dead. The family arrived quickly, not knowing what had transpired. A doctor greeted them at the door with his head down.

In one day, everything had changed. Instead of checking in on an ill or exhausted man, they had arrived at the hospital to say farewell to Stephanie's beloved grandfather. The entire family started falling apart. No one knew when and how this devastating destruction had started, but the enormous empire, built through her grandparents' sweat and hard work, was slowly crumbling. The family was losing everything. The house was going into foreclosure. Stephanie and her brother had to be pulled out of private schools and transferred to public schools. From that day forward, there wasn't anything the family could do to control the destruction.

Stephanie could not handle the disgrace and the anger she felt for her father. She never wanted to see him again. He had sold out his family and left them starving in the street. Before, they would drive to school with a chauffeur, and now they were hiding from their friends. Instead of getting the best quality organic meat from the butcher, now they had one small piece that they would split into thirds. Many nights, Stephanie's mother would go to sleep hungry. All she thought about was feeding her children and doing her best to protect them from the disgrace and gossip of their friends.

When she was old enough, Stephanie left to attend school in London. She had gotten a full-ride scholarship. She was working part time at Harrod's, which is where her former friends from her private schools would shop. They

Bold Resilient Women

would mock and degrade her, demanding she bring them different clothing items to try on, and when they didn't like it, they would throw it on the floor to have her pick them up like a slave.

She was humiliated by these spoiled and rotten young women. Back when they were younger, they were always jealous of Stephanie and her bright intelligent mind. This was their vengeance. Stephanie could never believe how cruel people could be when someone loses everything.

Eventually, things started to change. Both children finished their education in London and graduated at the top of their classes with high honors. They returned to Greece, where doors were open for them at many major companies. Stephanie and her brother were both brilliant, hardworking, and motivated to succeed. They had made a promise to their mother—and to each other—to rebuild their wealth from scratch. They knew how to work hard and remain focused, and nothing could stop them. They had lost everything overnight, so they knew it was going to be a hard uphill road. But they were going to work hard to regain admiration and respect. While Stephanie shared some details with me, overall, I knew very limited information about her painful youth. Every time we started to talk about it, she would break down crying. "I don't want to remember anything," she would say. "I have tried very hard to erase the disgraceful and painful years my father put us through." While Stephanie knew all of the details of the story, there was one detail she didn't know: the identity of the mistress. She was protected by her mother, grandparents, and aunts.

They didn't want her to find out who she was.

Stephanie put the dots together one day while working at a boutique, when the mistress and her friends approached her for help with their holiday shopping. The women knew who she was and they ridiculed her, making fun of her, and her mother, and what she was doing now instead of driving around with a driver. She realized, by what they said, that she was face-to-face with the woman who had unraveled her life through her interference.

One evening, Stephanie and I were invited to an event. While chatting and mingling with people, I saw Stephanie freeze. Then I noticed three women, glaring at each other with intense, angry stares. They looked outraged when they saw each other. I could not understand why everyone was standing like a statue.

I grabbed Stephanie and pulled her to the restroom.

"Stephanie, what in the world is going on with those women?" I asked her. I noticed her face was pale and she was shaking slightly.

"Those are the mistresses who destroyed two families—ours, and my mom's best friend's. They destroyed marriages, wealth, and families." She looked like she had seen a ghost. I could not believe what I was hearing. I felt so much pain for her. I never wanted her to be again faced with women who had brought so much destruction into her life.

When we came out of the restroom, Stephanie followed the lead of her mother and aunts, who acted as though they didn't care. They pretended the women didn't exist.

Her mom leaned over and whispered in my ear. "They should run away, since everyone in this room is aware of their past and present," she said. "I, on the other hand, don't have any guilt. Therefore, I don't care whether they exist or not." Though her words were strong and forceful, as a woman myself, I could feel and see deep down her annoyance and anger beneath her gray eyes and beautiful, rosy face.

I could not wait for the event to be over. I knew everyone was reliving their past, a past that caused heartache and death. The next day, Stephanie and I spoke about everything. She said she had to forget about all the suffering. It was the only way to look forward to a bright future.

She said her spiritual father had advised her that forgiveness would be the key to her success, but that she shouldn't forget what happened so she would never be hurt again.

"People learn from the many obstacles and hurdles in their life," he said. God had seen Stephanie's hard work, pain, and fear, and I believe he granted her everything her heart desired. She has achieved so much simply due to her work ethic, morals, and faith. She showed everyone who mocked her what intelligence and a great mind can do when they have fierce determination. She didn't have to sell herself or her youth to anyone for money. She had built her own success.

Today, Stephanie is considered one of the top women CEOs in the world. People come from all over to hear her presentations and opinions on the global environment and the shipping industry. I am so proud of her; she has come out strong and resilient.

Her mother is proud of Stephanie and her brother. When I had coffee with her, she said, "My kids suffered a lot. It was difficult to go from riches to rags, from drivers to walking, from being served to serving others with courtesy and respect. Neither I nor my children deserved so much pain and suffering." She reflected and paused for a minute. "Who knows? Maybe God wanted to humble us and teach us to remain balanced in life."

She continued. "All I can say is that I am grateful for the support and guidance God gave us, and the individuals who saw my daughter's brilliant mind and provided her with an opportunity to succeed. My children learned the hard way that the way to success was standing on their own merit."

Once again, after many painful years, Stephanie is chaperoned around with a driver and lives in beautiful homes, as she did once when she was an innocent young girl. Only this time, she did it on her own. She is in control, and she won't ever let anyone take that away from her.

Part Four
The World Today

My Calling

As a passionate and ambitious voice for faith and family, and against violence, trafficking, human rights, and gender discrimination, I feel I have been called to this place through my connection with God during the many difficult times in my life. But I've also been inspired by the numerous inspirational people in my life from diverse cultural backgrounds. A friend or a human being can inspire you through their challenges.

Bold Resilient Women

Friends and family members losing a young child to illness, parents losing their battle to cancer, or other unknown pandemics or illnesses. Family members losing their homes, villages, and families during the wars. Many individuals have touched my soul through witnessing their fight through a challenging life. I've been blessed to know a network of amazing individuals who fought to the end, becoming beacons of hope and perseverance for future generations.

Born to two humble and poor immigrant parents, I learned firsthand hardship, suffering and pain. From a young age, I witnessed their challenges and fears in an unknown world. I began to see life through a different lens. My parents made a perplexing decision to travel to an unfamiliar world with four little children, impoverished resources, two suitcases and $100.

Witnessing their distress empowered me to strive for success.

My immigrant parents' calling was to travel to a strange world, crossing many barriers, obstacles, and enormous hurdles to motivate us to acquire a passion for education and knowledge. They were hard-working people who depended on their hands and physical strength to succeed. Mom and Dad didn't have any educational background, and didn't know how to read or write. Sitting at the round table with their children, they were eager to learn even the most basic writing and reading skills. They constantly reminded us, "My beloved children, the war deprived us of education. We were two very smart and young people without guidance or an opportunity. We want better for you."

Strong Women Among Us

Throughout my life, I have had the honor and privilege to be affiliated and connected with many strong, inspiring, and motivated women, dynamic individuals who stood firm and strong in their morals and values. These women were forced to make difficult life decisions that affected them, their families, and their personal sustainability in a modern society. These exceptional and influential women became advocates for women who were too scared or incapable of voicing their need for equality.

These strong women had eagerly succeeded in many diverse fields. They were wives, mothers, doctors, lawyers, politicians, entrepreneurs, athletes, news reporters, scientists, teachers, and many other leaders. They have become role models for young girls and children, aunts who share their trust and confidence, sisters who share in their pain and laughter, mothers who cry and laugh with their successes and failures, teachers who guide and mentor us, and our future spiritual mothers who pray and keep us grounded in faith and family.

They walk among us, committed to loving and nurturing us, connecting us like dots and making the world a unique place to live.

Strong women are willing to fight for their beliefs. Unfortunately, many hardships overshadow the great things they have done or do for others. Sometimes, small things are hard due to their compassionate heart for success and love.

My mother would always say, "Laugh with your family and friends. Never forget laughter is the healer of pain. It helps you get through the bumpy daily routine."

When my mom and dad visited us, they would start imitating people, laughing hard without anyone else laughing. I would be caught up in my own issues. I felt like I had no time to play around, or stop to have a laugh. Dad was a comedian. He could imitate anyone you asked him to mimic.

Sometimes, I would be consumed by my thoughts. I would ask Dad, annoyed, "Don't you have something serious to say?"

"Eleni, if you keep taking life seriously, you will forget what happiness, laughter, and joy is in life. There is a time, *agapimou*, you would be surprised how it uplifts you."

Life is about learning. It's the only way you will be able to embrace life's complications and turmoil. Tolerance and patience can resolve the kind of controversies that can affect your future. If you remain ignorant and selfish, people will never trust and have confidence in your ability to make wise decisions.

Mom would say, "Life is about accepting the good and bad. If you don't, then you will never know what life is about, and you will never live a fulfilled life."

Always say something comforting to those who see you as a support system. See people for who they are and how they represent themselves. I have learned never to listen to statements and remarks but to be supportive and kind-hearted among others.

This is what women of character and wisdom teach those around them. Love is not judging or condemning. It's about looking deep into a person's inner world to see the good and bad in individuals. A strong woman disciplines herself to believe in herself and care for others selflessly. When life teaches you lessons of pain, you become optimistic and productive.

When you become strong, you become a visionary. You can see your mission in life. You want to achieve success for yourself and your family. You will witness serenity in your home life and see your household as smooth and happy, living in a calm and serene environment. Through many painful situations, I have done my best to live optimistically and not take life for granted. I have understood what it's like to be brave and resilient and be an example to those around me.

It's easy for a strong woman to deviate from painful situations and obstacles. It's difficult to be vulnerable. You can become fearful of being a voice for truth. By being honest and strong, you have the power to never give up, no matter how many mistakes you make. As people, we must realize we can fall hard when we face hurdles. What makes us strong is the willpower and tolerance to get up, stand on our own feet, and continue our path forward. A strong woman becomes her own worst enemy when she can't see her own resilience. She doesn't see things clearly and makes rational decisions that impact herself and all those around her. We must use reverse psychology. By providing confidence to our inner world, we can influence ourselves into believing in our ability to overcome anything. We must never forget that we are the strongest animal in this universe. We have the knowledge to decide our future and make wise decisions for our existence.

The most important thing I learned from all these inspiring women was to affiliate myself with other intelligent, intellectual, articulate, wise women. Through their tolerance and charisma, I learned how to empower and encourage myself and others to be honest and positive. Even if other women's poor behavior and bad judgment have impacted your friendship with others, infiltrating your relationship with hate, you should ride out the wave and continue doing the things that are meaningful to you and those beside you.

When your friends are strong, together you can achieve anything. No one can stop you. You become unstoppable in your mission. You don't have to take validation from anyone other than yourself first, then your family, friends, and those you love. No matter how hard and difficult your relationship is, you should not walk away without completely telling your mate how you feel and how their actions speak louder than words.

My father would say, "Words can cut you like a sword, but your actions can heal all wounds."

My mother would say, "Remain strong in your beliefs, ambitions, and goals. Never be distracted by any promises or misleading comments. Be strong and look ahead. Don't ever allow anyone to take away your courage, stamina, and zeal to achieve anything your heart desires. You are the leading force of your future desires and successes."

When you are a confident and strong woman, you should not be afraid to voice your opinion and concerns for your family, children, friends, and all those who surround your life. People will see your stability and you will achieve respect, faith, and loyalty—sometimes from those you least expected.

As a strong and sturdy woman, you can offer your family a good, solid life. All your children need to know and hear is the unconditional love you have for them. Through this love, you are providing a solid and stable environment. My mom would remind me, "It's not the quantity of time you devote to your children and those who impact your life, but the quality of time, where you listen and hear their concerns and fears. You can spend hours with those you love, but when your conversations are meaningless, it doesn't matter. You can have limited quality time and find out more things that affect your children and loved ones' behavior, daily problems, and issues that need to be addressed."

My mom once stated, "I was faced with making many decisions at a very young age. If I were not a strong and optimistic individual, I would have fallen apart through all the tribulations and unwavering curves that came my way. The only way I made it through was to see a positive light at the end of the tunnel."

She continued. "My love, when you are a solid and strong individual, you can achieve your goals and anything you set your mind to. Even if others think you have a fierce personality, they will admire you for your resilience. Always refuse to have negative thoughts or surround yourself with toxic people. Have a positive outlook on the world and remember the greatest gift given to a person is the free will to do whatever they want. People are pessimistic, but you should embrace everything with a ray of light and not perceive the world as dark and frightening."

Being strong means having confidence, faith, tolerance, openness, and the ambition to fight for what is ethical and moral. People might be envious of you, but those who are confident will respect, admire, and praise you for your honesty and diligence.

You will achieve the respect and the loyalty of those you least consider as friends.

Love Conquers

Life has taken me on many different paths and journeys. I felt like I rarely planned or made drastic choices, yet somehow doors and unexpected paths opened my way to success. I didn't get distracted by thinking or dreaming up ways to be effective. I have always known the plan was already set for me. Therefore, I knew to follow my instincts. If I failed the first time, I didn't give up. I would gain endurance to get up and start over. I was a fighter. I was a survivor.

Strength and courage are engraved in my DNA. I come from bold, strong, and powerful women who had overcome tremendous obstacles and pain through times of war, suffering, deaths, and unbearable heartache. They had seen much more than I could ever imagine or comprehend.

History books could never tell what the women of my family have endured.

Love and *pathos* are two words that echo in my mind and are engraved in my heart. When you love anything in life with passion and empathy, you will succeed. Many of my spiritual fathers reinforce what my ancestors would say: Never lose hope and faith, no matter how difficult things get. Through *agape* and patience, the inevitable is possible. Love does not make choices; it embraces humanity with humility and sincerity.

Thea Rina told me, "Eleni, *agape* comes as a fragrance. The wind blows, and either you sense the smell or it goes by as if it never existed."

"But Thea, what does this mean?" I asked. "When love knocks at your heart and you don't listen and grasp it, then it will find someone else to love."

Bold Resilient Women

I learned through her wise advice that you should use wisdom and never judge, never have pride, never condemn, and never criticize or manipulate situations, circumstances, or people. Everyone catches up to a scammer and a liar. Every individual has a story of happiness, pain, or suffering.

Thea Rina would say, "Eleni, two of the worst words in our Greek language are *ego* and *misos* [ego and hate]. *Ego* is being selfish, where you don't care for anyone but you, yourself, your body, and everything affecting you personally. *Misos* is hating someone with vengeance, taking an eye for an eye, wanting to take revenge and eventually destroying them."

I learned about judgment at a very early age. I would walk with my mom, my grandmother, and their friends to church early every Sunday morning. We could not afford to take the bus back and forth; $1.20 was a lot of money for us. As we were walking, playing hopscotch with our friends, we came to the red light and stopped. Suddenly, my mom's friend looked across the road and pointed at a young girl, probably sixteen years old, dressed very provocatively. It was obvious she was waiting in the street to be picked up by an escort.

Mom's friend ferociously said in Greek, "Look how she is dressed! She is selling her body for money." Without hesitation, my mom responded. "I am an uneducated woman, and will never make this kind of a statement." As we kept watching this young, innocent girl, my mom's friend did not stop criticizing. Mom was so upset, her voice raised with empathy. "You don't know what has made this young girl roam the streets for money," she said. "You don't know her story."

All the way to church, Mom was furious, and the argument escalated. My mom told her friend to wash her mouth with soap and to go to church and ask for forgiveness from God. But her friend kept going, railing against this young girl and calling her a tramp.

My mom could not resist. I am surprised she didn't hit her with her purse. "A tramp is someone who destroys families and people's lives," my mom said. "If you are a good Christian and human being, then reach out and help her. Give her hope, emphasize how precious and beautiful she is, and praise her to boost her confidence and self-esteem. As a mother and woman, you need to help young girls and young men get out of prostitution, not make fun or make obscene comments and pass judgment without having any remorse."

I was in awe of my mom, and I know now this is one of the best lessons I learned from an early age. I realized I wasn't worthy to condemn or judge anyone. Mom would tell us that it was important to listen to a person's story. You had to make that individual feel safe and comfortable to open up and proceed to a healing process. Mom taught me many lessons about condemning and judging. She told us that we should never ignore violence, discrimination, segregation, and oppression. We should see everyone as one. Under God, we are all created equal.

Mom and Dad would tell us that violence and discrimination are horrible things.

Dad would say, "I lived through the violence of World War II, which took many family members' lives. Villages were burned to the ground, and people were tortured and killed in the squares of our city. I saw the brutality of the Civil War, my cousins stripped of their youth, abducted from their families, and taken to the mountains to be trained as guerrillas. I witnessed the Communist Party take away our rights by starving us without having any food to eat. I have witnessed discrimination in the way others have belittled us since we were poor and uneducated. My darling daughter, I have lived through so much pain and suffering in my life that everything now is irrelevant; nothing can penetrate my thick skin. Young people today have everything their heart desires. Sadly, many young people feel entitled to wealth and power without sweating."

Mom would tell us, "God didn't mention color, race, faith, or culture. He said, You are all created in My image as one. Weak spirits label each other to separate and divide people by culture, heritage, faith, or gender.

"In order to succeed in your career or personal life, you must have patience, tolerance, and steadfastness. Never become arrogant and deceive people. Pride will end up hurting and destroying you and your future. You must see people as equals.

"I learn to love and appreciate people for what they are, not what they can do for me in return. Don't judge people by the clothes, shoes, or car they drive. Beneath all this, you never know an individual's lifestyle, education, and financial security. Your eyes can deceive you."

It's been repeatedly demonstrated throughout my life that patience is the virtue of excelling in what you do and making wise choices. Choosing what to wear, where to go, or what to eat are not priorities or critical decisions in one's life. Freedom of choice is unique. God knew us before we were in our mother's womb. He was aware of our sins. God gave Adam and Eve the freedom and the free will to make their own choice, although He knew they were going to sin. We have the freedom to make decisions based on our honesty and moral sense. We need to act with an empathetic conscience for others and our family.

People often use the word "freedom" to destroy or dishonor an individual, a country, an organization, or institution. But choice is the free will to do honorable things that affect someone's daily life. You cannot base your life on making choices without consequences. You should make a decision based on effectiveness and productivity.

As women, we have the honor, privilege, and endurance to bear children and bring future role models into this universe. To do this, we face and endure excruciating pain. God has chosen women to be mothers because we know from biblical passages, the serpent—or the devil—enticed Adam and Eve to eat from the forbidden Tree of Knowledge. The punishment from God was exile from paradise and the curse on both man and woman.

Additionally, the woman was to experience excruciating pain and suffering at childbirth, a pain that spreads to the entire body. We won't be able to tolerate pain and suffering until we endure the birth of a child. Although men tend to be strong, they are resistant and fragile to pain and suffering. As the biblical passage says, man will sweat to get food from the ground to support his family. Women have the courage to be resilient in painful circumstances. As women, we love with our whole heart and soul and have the power to calm situations and heal from unbearable emotional suffering.

We can conquer and achieve anything we set our minds to when our inner world is calm and harmonious. Our children will mimic the *pathos* and passion that they see. When a child lives in a calm environment, and sees love, and feels stability, they will learn how to be compassionate to others.

We must believe in our existence by validating the path we are traveling on in life. When we do this, we set the right example for the next generations.

The Elderly

In my early forties, I was elected by the Greek American community to be president of the Greek American Rehabilitation and Care Centre in Wheeling, Illinois.

Bold Resilient Women

The home was built by Greek immigrants, who knew firsthand not only the struggles that immigrants face in coming to an unknown world, but the challenges of growing old in an adopted country. These people should be considered heroes; they came to create a better life for their families and many of them never returned to their beloved homeland. They achieved the success we enjoy today through pain and suffering. They deserved a place for their final stage of life that was comfortable, loving, and supportive.

After several months in this role, I resolved to dedicate my life to this elderly home. I was so touched by the painful stories I heard on a daily basis from the residents. They were fathers, mothers, children, and siblings. While many residents were treated with love and respect by their families, many of them were placed here and forgotten.

I soon started a routine. Every morning, I would visit the nursing home. I would sit and have coffee with the residents and listen to remarkable life stories, the kinds that can't be found in textbooks. The stories were profound. Some were joyful, some were tragic, some were unbelievable. I am continually amazed by the way others can transform and change you through their life experiences.

One particularly lively morning, I was walking through the dining room, and I felt drawn to a particular woman. She was sitting alone, sipping a cup of coffee, and I joined her. Like I always do, I started asking questions. She revealed one of the most profound stories I had ever heard about a friend of hers who was sent to another home.

A mother and father had one son. He was their miracle child, as the couple couldn't have children for more than fifteen years of their marriage. Back in the 1940s, fertility medicine was limited, and women didn't have options. So, they left it up to God. The mother got pregnant in her forties and gave birth to a healthy baby boy. The parents worked day and night. They wanted to provide this boy, the only child God had given them, with whatever his heart desired.

When the son was grown and his parents were old, his father died. The son didn't care about taking care of his mother or overseeing her medical care, so he sought out a nursing home and placed her in permanent residence. His mother was content living at the home. She had made friends, and the staff cared for her well. The son seldom visited, only when it suited his busy work and travel schedule.

One day, he received a call that his mother was deteriorating and had very little time left. He came to visit and say goodbye. She hadn't seen him in a long time. "Mom, do you need anything? Is there anyone you want to see? Any restaurant you want me to take you to?"

Bold Resilient Women

She looked at him with tears in her eyes. "Son, I sacrificed so much for you because I loved you so much. But you don't know how to love. You have no love in your heart, not even for the woman who gave birth to you." He was shocked as he sat by her bedside, and she began listing her final wishes to him. Though her health was poor, her voice rang through clearly and certainly.

"When I die, I want you to make a donation to this place, which has been my home and shelter. Find someone to help with the things that need updating in this place. It's sweltering during heat waves, and the air conditioning hardly works. In the winter, the heat went out.

"Purchase personal room refrigerators so patients can have their own snacks. Find a way to help the kitchen staff. They serve over three hundred people three times a day, and because they have to buy so much food, and the refrigerators have limited space, the food can spoil. You won't believe how many nights I went to sleep without eating.

"Order cookies and chocolate to bring to the residents. You don't know how many times I wanted a cookie with coffee, but didn't have money to purchase one.

"Buy some diapers for those without family to support them. I expected you to change my diaper once in a while since I changed your diapers for so many years. When you were a baby, disposable diapers were for the wealthy, so I had cotton diapers that I washed in the bathtub every night. "Buy some body cream. My skin got dried out from the hard factory work I did. Now that I am older, I spend more time in bed, and my skin itches. How many days have I scratched my body and seen skin flakes falling from the dry skin? When you were a baby, creams were too expensive, so I used olive oil to moisturize your wrinkly skin."

"Why are you telling me this on your deathbed?" he said, crying. "Why didn't you tell me you wanted these things?"

"My son, I am used to hunger, as I grew up begging for food. I am used to sacrifice, as I lost my family to the war. I am used to medical treatment, as I battled so many diseases as a result of the war.

"I wanted so much for you, so I gave you the wings to accomplish all your heart's desires. You made wealth and you gained power, but you forgot about where you came from and who sacrificed herself to bring you into this world."

She held his hand. "My biggest fear is that your wife and children will throw you aside, send you to a home, and never visit you. That they will dump you, take your money, and pretend like you never existed."

The mother looked into her son's eyes. "Just remember, everything you did to me, you will receive it back. You had your chance to love the only mother you had. You forgot my love was an unconditional sacrifice."

Bold Resilient Women

With these last words, his mother passed into the Lord's everlasting life, leaving behind a lifetime of pain and sorrow. The son lay his head down on her chest and sobbed, pulling at his hair in pain.

I am captivated by every story I hear. Our residents have lived lives of love and pain, success and disappointment. It's devastating to see people cast aside as though their lives don't matter. With the nursing home, we hope to make every resident not only cared for, but feel as though they matter. It's the least we can do for people who have lived such remarkable lives.

Life and Learning

Throughout my life, I have had countless conversations with individuals from different parts of the world, which has reinforced one of my most foundational beliefs: Every human being has a story.

While, years before, I've listened as many women share their confusion and torment over what the future holds for their families, it seems that lately, people are stressed and confused about the state of their relationships. Many people struggle to keep up with our culture's fast pace, where technology moves faster than the speed of light and communication has so drastically changed.

I've learned that the best school in this world is not in a building—it's sitting at the feet of an elderly person. They will teach all of us that no matter how advanced the world becomes, your core values in life should never change. We must never forget our role in today's unpredictable and unprecedented times. While technology advances rapidly, we must continue to work toward uniting and teaching young people how to overcome challenges and think of positive outcomes.

People want to build their own paths and futures by writing their own stories. But this can be done only when an individual has love and kindness in their heart, and is not confused by unknown forces and events. When you have love in your heart, it shows in your eyes and your actions.

Young people must learn from our mistakes, and in order for them to do that, we have to be willing to admit them. It's better to admit them than to have an ego and live a superficial life. It eases someone's self-doubt and stress if you can pay them a compliment and say, "Thank you for calling me and making me laugh. You've made my day." I assure you, however you are feeling, it will make you feel better, too.

Life is about accepting the beautiful and sentimental moments that come your way. For example, when your baby falls asleep peacefully in your arms and your heart feels warm and serene. These emotional moments and feelings cannot be ignored. Life is about kindness. It's about listening to others and understanding what their fears and expectations are in this world. It's wiser to love and be kind than to be a manipulative and selfish individual. We must realize it's not social media that's hurting our children and our relationships: it's the demons inside us that manifest in dark places. It takes effort and patience to sit and play with a child, but they aren't the only ones who benefit. You will be shocked at how many stories and lessons you can learn from their innocent perspective on life.

No matter how serious your life is at any time, you should not discourage yourself from laughter and joy. There is no such thing as perfection and peace. Life requires us to be hopeful, confident, and willing to accept what comes our way. We might as well accept that perfection is a word that we have to accept, but we cannot let it overpower our lives. Today's complicated environments can evoke anxiety. You may not know where to turn. We must remember that at the end of the day, what a person needs most is a hand to hold and a heart to understand them without passing judgment.

Let's look back to our childhoods, where simple walks with our parents and the conversations we had around the block or at the park were the real lessons of life. My parents taught me not to be manipulated into becoming too accessible to others. They taught me never to discourage someone or belittle their intentions or intelligence. The precious moments a child spends next to an elderly person will do wonders in their adult years.

My father used to say, "You fill a cup of coffee and you start sipping it until it's all gone. That's how life is. You start, stop, start, and stop again. Life is about starting something, and when an obstacle comes, you stop. Then you fix the problem and start again until something else comes your way. Then you start again until all is fine again."

Many of my dear friends have hidden behind their husband's money and power without realizing that money doesn't buy happiness or class. Those small daily fights and arguments bring confusion and stress to our lives. It diverts our focus from the simple things that can truly make our lives spectacular. Despite power, wealth, and position, everyone wants to be appreciated and loved by their family and friends.

Bold Resilient Women

"Even in hell it gets hot, and you don't want to be left alone," my mom would say.

I've learned to ignore situations that I cannot change. All I can do is try to mollify them to the best of my ability without defeating and insulting others.

"Don't try to get even with someone," my mom would always remind me. "Let God, who is a loving but vengeful God, take matters into His hands. Don't try to rationalize with someone's toxic heart. You are only allowing that person to continue to hurt you. Walk away and cleanse your hands, you have enough of your own worries on your own."

She showed me how to surround myself with positive, energetic, and thoughtful individuals who will make me a stronger and better human being.

Through my sufferings, I've learned that no one is perfect. Life throws you tough curves, and it's at these moments that we have the choice and opportunity to make life better. We cannot harbor bitterness. Happiness comes from the most surprising places—often where you least expect.

"People are like your fingers," Mom would say. "They are not the same size." I loved this one because you see it every day. People are far from the same. You see someone, but you don't know or realize what painful burdens they are carrying. Everyone's cross to bear is a different size and shape.

Life is a difficult journey, and everyone wants to get to the top of the mountain and be king. But remember that you climb, you fall, slip, and laugh all the way up. As soon as you achieve your goal, you are left thinking of your next project, agonizing so much that you barely enjoy this moment.

The women I have connected with have shared that they feel as though their lives and families were being controlled by an unknown force. They were losing connection with their husbands and children. There was no longer a family dinner, where everyone sat together and discussed daily happenings. Their lives and everything around them had become superficial. They were more used to seeing their relatives hunched and buried over a small screen than looking them in the eye. They didn't understand the importance of daily habits, and that their own tendencies to stay online were part of the problem. Hearing these concerns has made me want to connect with other women and share my struggles. I want women to consider the larger question of our existence. Being confused many times as a young woman, I tried hard to control things that were affecting me emotionally and psychologically, or creating anxiety and stress. But learning to embrace and accept things out of my control taught me to see things in a positive light.

I am speaking with empathy in my heart to young women who are confused and disoriented, believing the pictures they see on social media reflect perfect families, perfect homes, and perfect lives. We are taught from a young age that no one is perfect, but we seem to have forgotten. Perfection is impossible. My mom used to say, "You want to become a saint, but the devil tempts you." She would explain that you don't want to be involved in drama, but as a human being, you get tangled up in things.

Let's not forget that we all have our own crosses to bear. Everyone has problems that can or cannot be rectified. We all face challenges in different ways. Illness, poverty, money, divorce, disabilities, unemployment, and death are among the many challenges that will arise in people's lives. These situations can become a burden and a source of stress and anxiety. But they are part of our stories. Perfection is a losing game.

Learning the Facts of Life

As I have journeyed down the path of life, I have had to venture down many different roads that led me to such different places. Happiness, sorrow, pain, joy, marriage, parenting, grief, frustration—every emotion and feeling has been part of my adventure. It was difficult learning and understanding what my existence was about and how fast I was evolving into the individual I would become.

As a woman, I had to understand that I had come into this world through two loving and caring parents, people who nurtured and nourished me in becoming myself. But eventually, I had to venture out to find my identity and my existence. One by one, I met my siblings, and later, I met aunts, uncles, cousins, and more extended family that I had never known. The puzzle of my life became bigger, and my journey became more complex and longer, with many curves and stops. I did my best to make the right choices for my family, career, future, and friendships.

As a human being, I have learned that the biggest animal to freely roam the earth is a human. We are not chained or caged; we are free to make choices, and no one can ever force us to make an unwanted decision. When a friend of mine asked me if I think our destiny is written when we are born, my response was, I don't think so. I have asked many of my spiritual fathers the same question, and their response was the same. If there is a lot of traffic coming, would you freely cross the street and get killed? God gives us the free will and knowledge to make choices.

Today, I believe in my heart that while we are capable, we lack the desire to be compassionate, empathetic, tolerant, and ethical individuals. We stay in our safe bubbles and worry only about ourselves. We just want things that make us happy and satisfied. Little do we understand that it offers us just minutes of satisfaction before our joy fades away. Our ego is bigger than our love for our neighbors or friends. We don't have the capacity to put someone else ahead of ourselves. We feel superior to others. Kindness is often seen as weakness; we cannot see it as a gesture of love and compassion.

A wise friend asked me, "Eleni, when you give a gift or go out of your way to help someone, do you expect something in return?"

"Not often," I responded. "I forget what I have done for someone. I don't tend to share my good deeds with anyone but those I help and God."

"I figured that out when you approached me to help this person," my friend said. "And you were going to make his payments to save his life."

"Why would I see someone suffering and not reach out to help them?" was my instinctive reply. I hold this true, but I also have a deeper belief about life. What I plant in my time on earth is only temporarily mine. When I depart from this world, it will all be left behind. I won't be able to take anything with me, so why not help someone in need? Why not plant the mustard seed and let it spread?

I thought the conversation began and ended with this one question, but to my surprise, he continued.

"If someone gives you a glass of water, will you forget it?"

"No," I said. "I would be obligated to this individual for helping me."

His response was profound and truthful. "Can I ask you, what has this taught you?"

"It has taught me that God sees our good deeds and writes them down," I said, frustrated at this point. "When someone helps us in our despair and gives us a glass of water, we should never forget, or God will forget us."

My parents always said that karma can hunt you day and night. If you do something good for your neighbor, good things will come your way. If you steal, lie, or treat people badly, karma will come around and you will be hurt. Mom told me of Margarita's sister-in-law. She competed with her mother-in-law from the first day of her marriage. She mistreated her two sisters-in-law. When her husband was away, she would tell false lies and dramatize stories to create divisiveness with the women in her husband's life. One day, the son and mother got into a horrible, controversial argument. Horrific words were exchanged between them. He said unthinkable statements to his mother. In her despair and anger and in extreme pain, the mother cursed her and his conduct. The mother and son never spoke again. Margarita said, "God, who is a forgiving God, gave her many opportunities for repentance and forgiveness.

Bold Resilient Women

But she was such an evil victim, consumed with her lies and tears that God raised his hand and punished her." Her son, a handsome, educated, tall, young man, lost his life at age twenty-four in a horrific car accident.

My grandmother and mom would say that life is a Ferris wheel. It comes around and brings you back to your starting point. When you do and say good things, you shall receive good things in your life, but when you harm others with your tongue or actions, then eventually life will hurt you.

"A tongue has no bones, but when it spreads untruthful lies, it can bend and even break steel," my mom would say.

That's why I strongly believe we are to take responsibility for our actions, our lives, and existence. We cannot condemn, blame or worry about other individual's actions. If asked for advice, tell people the truth as you see it. Never be a hypocrite and lie to someone to uplift yourself and your ego.

Dad said, "Ego is ego, meaning, all I care is about me, myself, my body and no one else. It's all about me."

True success means you have the capability and the desire to join forces and spread kindness and love to the world. The other option is to become a miserable individual who causes others around you suffering and misery. I believe what is lacking today is patience, tolerance, love, and empathy. We have all walked away from God, taking him out of our daily lives, schools, institutions, and communities.

Our children mimic the actions of their parents and protectors. They copy and feed off of our behaviors, tones, sadness, and anger. If they are unhappy, a child becomes resistant to obeying or listening to reason. They learn to tune out their own thoughts. Children are silent inspectors, analyzing their surroundings and understanding who loves them and who is there to hurt them. We must never contradict a child's feelings. It's their sixth sense that guides them from danger.

Personally, I taught my children from a young age to respect themselves. I would remind them, "I cannot always be with you. When you look in the mirror and see yourself, you must love what you see. If you don't like your image, then change your behavior. It's up to you, after all. It's the gift of free will."

Violence

When an individual is stuck in a tumultuous relationship, it is difficult to walk away and restart all over again. The abused person feels they were at fault for angering their partner and causing the abuse. Both sides feel they cannot live without each other, and they try to identify who was at fault for starting the conflict.

Domestic violence is on the rise, having increased between twenty-five and thirty percent. The World Health Organization states that one in three women has experienced physical or sexual violence by intimate partners. Young women are more prone to being abused than older women. Young men like to throw their weight around to get control of a woman. Young men from around the world have pushed, shoved, slapped, and tried to choke women in order for them to be obedient and meet their demands. Statistics say that once a young man comes to terms with the fact that a woman is not a punching bag, he matures and tries to talk things out.

Couples at a young age are possessed by each other. They feel as though, because they love an individual and cannot live without them, that they must kill them rather than walk away.

Impoverished places around the world have more violence in their homes due to economic struggles and other stresses. Iceland is the safest place in the world to live. Not only is it an economically secure country with many opportunities for all of the citizens, but they also oppose violence. They have implemented strict measurements that target safety and security.

After the pandemic, many people became angry and hostile toward their partners, colleagues, and neighbors. People are not animals; they need to be free to walk, talk, and voice their opinions in society. Many individuals I talked to have said they were angry and violent toward each other. The forced confinement made them realize they didn't have anything in common with their spouse. They were forced to work and live with each other twenty-four hours a day, seven days a week. They buried themselves in work not wanting to identify or admit their mistakes and anger. Many individuals had to be medicated to cope with anxiety and handle stress.

Many couples also found themselves overwhelmed with finances, having over-extended their spending. Many young people were being transferred or lost their jobs. Many had to downsize or move in with their parents. This caused more relationship stress.

My dad said to us, "It's a great feeling climbing the ladder of success, but when something goes wrong and you come tumbling down, you feel lost and angry. You never want to go back to your beginnings, your struggles, and suffering. Everyone loves the luxurious lifestyle. Once you taste honey, you don't want to taste vinegar."

Many couples could see the writing on the wall from the start of their relationship or marriage. But it's easy to become comfortable with people. Others think they can change someone or mold them into becoming the person they want in their arms and in their beds. It creates anger when a person is stuck in their own ways without thinking about anyone else. Confusion and animosity start in a relationship when there is a power struggle. Many individuals know how to manipulate and turn their partner against their family by taking control of their life and home. When I hear stories like this, I remember my spiritual father, Christodoulos.

"Young people see the bad and good in a person," he told me during one of our talks, as we spoke of the issues facing modern relationships. "As they walk down the aisle, they convince themselves that the person will change and express love and respect. Eleni mou, this is the biggest mistake people make. What you see is what you get. No one changes. You are born with your character. When you are kind, giving, loving, and caring from birth, you will continue until your last breath. If you are mean-spirited, a gossip, and a troublemaker, you will continue to be so. You cannot leave old tricks behind."

This is the issue couples of all ages face. Many stick it out for the sake of the children or for financial stability. The children are caught in the middle, and parents play the victim card, preying on their child's feelings. They attack each other and force the child to choose sides. When you love your child, you never get them involved in your marriage. It must be made clear that the couple started the marriage, and the children came afterward. They don't need to be brought into conflicts. Children need to be loved and protected.

"Unfortunately," Christodoulos continued, "children become the pawns in the custody battle. One is left wondering if the couple had children out of love or to secure a marriage or a financial boost."

A few years ago, a group of young women got together to fight against domestic violence. I was invited to a private meeting with the Illinois governor's wife to hear their concerns. As we were led to the family room, we saw a group of women sitting in the room, waiting to tell their stories, and next to them, there was a wall completely covered with photos of each woman and their family after being abused. All you could see were bruises and blood on their faces and bodies. In the room, standing in tears, hurt, and in agony, were fifteen women from diverse backgrounds who looked as if the world had crashed into them. One by one, they got up to share their stories of abuse and domestic violence.

One of the young women was married to a wealthy dentist who had scammed the government out of public funds—an abuser of all kinds, physically and mentally. He was arrested, locked up, and let out on bond. He had promised to take away the kids and leave her to die in the streets. This poor girl was being destroyed by this torturer, and the judicial system was failing her.

Another story was about an abusive husband and father who would go out drinking, then come home and punch everyone who stood in his way. One night, the wife told us, she stood in the middle between him and her son as the father severely punched him. As she blocked her son from the blows, he knocked her tooth out and took a cigarette and burned the young boy's arm. We were horrified. We asked her if she had any evidence, and she showed us pictures of herself and the burns on her son's hand. We couldn't believe our eyes. The system had failed her. She told us he was getting away with it because of his political connections.

Patty was married to a powerful lawyer who was the nephew of a very successful and esteemed judge. He physically, mentally, and psychologically abused her, and had many extramarital affairs. When she finally reached her breaking point, she filed for divorce. He told her to go ahead, and he promised to break her and her family. Patty would work every day for as many hours as possible while her family watched her kids. This man had her in court every day, accusing her of disobeying the arranged pickup times. This went on for years.

She said if she didn't have her children, she would have ended her life. He tormented his ex-wife and left her penniless.

Bold Resilient Women

Sheila was a strong advocate for these women. She had gone through a similar nightmare when her husband tried to kill her, and the court system didn't do anything. He got a slap on the wrist and was sent to a mental institution. He was released a few weeks later. Sheila could not understand how he got out so quickly and was allowed to be free to assault others. She said, "I don't understand why a few women judges don't defend and protect women." She gestured to the other women around her. "Most of the women in this room had women as judges." I was appalled. You would think they knew the strength of a man. I found it hard to believe women don't have compassion for another woman. Why weren't they looking at the evidence to see why these women needed to be protected?

Then there was Amelia, a tall, skinny young woman who was more influential and educated than everyone in the room. At the same time, she was mentally and psychologically destroyed. She was so fragile she could hardly stand up. My heart just ached for this young, vulnerable woman. Her husband, a very successful man, had committed her to a hospital, saying she was incompetent to take care of herself and the kids. Claiming she was delusional and crazy.

The authorities took her children away without any concrete evidence. All of their friends knew he had paid people to say things against her and make her out to be a criminal instead of a victim. She said, "I don't want to live without my children. This is called revenge. He doesn't care about the kids. He just didn't want me to walk out on our so-called perfect family life and embarrass him in front of his clients and friends. So, he decided to take away the only thing I loved in life."

Amelia said he had threatened her before, but she didn't believe he would go to the extent of plotting her destruction. Her family raised the money to hire doctors and psychologists to assess their daughter for the court hearing. They were afraid of the court system. There wasn't anything wrong with her; he had just broken her down. "Thank God," she said. "Finally, the judge saw right through him and his vindictive plotting. My children were finally handed over to me."

The governor's wife and I stayed through the night until it was 11 o'clock. We had to leave.

My heart was broken. These were all intelligent, smart, articulate, and amazing women who had thrived at one point in their lives. One day, they married a monster, and they felt and witnessed our judicial system supporting the criminals, murderers, and abusers—not them.

Today, I still question why the judicial system fails these young mothers and children. And the stories don't stop here. A young Indian nurse in her early thirties was abused and beaten up by her husband. She ran to the police station seeking help and protection, but they told her they didn't want to get involved in a domestic fight. The woman went home and continued working, caring for her child, and being abused. She attended church to pray for her and her child, along with her unborn child's safety. She was shot outside on the steps of the church.

Why didn't anyone see the violence? He continuously abused her and threatened to kill her. She was working day and night and handing over the money to him. She got pregnant with another child, thinking that by having another child, her marriage would become more solid. Why didn't someone notice the pain she was enduring when she went to church on that brutal day to pray? She walked outside and she saw him coming toward her. Before she could say anything, he shot her in the belly, killing the unborn baby. Then he shot her two more times in the face. The young mother was left on the steps practically dead.

After many months and multiple surgeries, she was still fighting for her life. Her innocent child is giving her the strength to keep going. This event has angered the entire community. Why was he not arrested when there was a complaint filed against him? All we can do is pray for this young girl and wish her a speedy recovery. I hope the judicial system will put this man behind bars for the rest of his life.

As a moral and ethical citizen, and one who has served as a human rights commissioner for the state of Illinois, I am appealing and begging the judicial system to set aside the political intentions, votes, and funding, and to see themselves in the shoes of these young, innocent women. I don't want to believe that political favors and connections should motivate anyone to defend a criminal or an abuser.

My father would say that when you are an honorable and ethical person, people and the community will give you their vote. They see your honor and integrity above all things. Integrity rises above negative comments and false accusations.

As intelligent, smart, strong, and vital women in the twenty-first century, let us be the beacon and hope for a brighter future. Let's stop domestic violence now. Let's stop failing women, mothers, and children, leaving them to be abused and brutally killed. Let's create a place where children can play and ride a bike outside, where children can be set free to see the beautiful things in life. Where women and men can raise their children without fear of indoctrination, political agendas, social media corruption, bullying, violence, and hate.

Let's end child sex trafficking by passing strict rules and laws. Look at the Middle East and their judicial system—you cannot touch anyone, or there will be truly severe consequences. We need to impose the death penalty on criminals who sell, mutilate, abuse, or destroy the innocence of a child. Children were given to us to love, defend, and protect. To make sure they are not mistreated or harmed in any way.

Let's remind our children, each other and the world, that we are all created as one under God's eyes. We are created in His image. No one is more worthy than anyone else, we are just given gifts to use wisely. God tells us that He donates everything to us and can take it away at any time. We will all leave naked from this world without any belongings, accolades, or money.

It seems like an impossible goal. But I believe if we can listen to each other, support each other, fight for what is right, and view each other without judgment, we can start down the right path to a better, brighter future.

Children Without a Choice

A family's life can be drastically changed by the birth of a child with intellectual and developmental disabilities. Being a part of the Little City Foundation Board of Directors for numerous decades has humbled me as a mother and woman to embrace these children who never had a choice in how they move and interact with the world. By being involved in their daily lives, I saw, firsthand, the suffering, acceptance, love, and compassion these families demonstrate on a daily basis.

Little City was one of the first facilities in the United States to give children with disabilities an opportunity to live a life filled with hope and acceptance. The organization empowers and motivates these people to live, work, and be productive while living independently in their communities. Little City was one of the first innovative facilities to break all barriers by demanding changes for this population. They envisioned a life on campus that was characterized by equality, dignity, respect, and freedom.

The children on the campus were treated as equal citizens. Innovative programs were created to educate them and teach them the skills to help them sustain their integrity in society. They created a farm to raise chickens and sell eggs on the corner of the campus, allowing the residents to participate in things that surrounded their campus. They built a small breakfast place for people to socialize, visit the campus, and buy their eggs and vegetables. They did not believe in isolating children with developmental disadvantages. Little City believes every child deserves a chance to belong to a community.

Bold Resilient Women

There have been many incredible and dedicated instructors, directors, and advocates throughout the years, who work hand-in-hand with parents and family members to create a safe productive environment for their loved ones. Children on campus learn to interact with others they can relate to. Many young children began to live independently with less help.

Fortunately, society had changed. Children don't have to remain institutionalized; they are treated as free citizens.

In 2009, I was the recipient of the Sidney L. Port Legacy of Distinction Award. This was one of the most distinct and monumental awards I have received. For the ceremonial event, which was to take place in the spring, I was informed that I had to be photographed on the campus for the news media and a variety of magazines. When the date was arranged, the photographers, editors, news reporters, makeup artists, and crew were beginning to set up at the grounds of Little City Foundation.

When everyone was arriving at the Little City Foundations campus, I was met at the entrance by one of our young residents. She started to call my name with her slurred and sweet voice saying, "Mrs. B. Why you here?" I responded that I came to get photographed for the magazines and the news.

Her beautiful red cheeks and face dropped, she wasn't staring at me, she was looking down at her wheelchair in silence. Her behavior left me speechless. What did I say? I was worried about her, questioning what I said or did that caused her to become upset. This was a young girl whose face would light up every time she saw me at Little City. Walking away, I kept wondering what got her so disappointed, and what triggered her behavior? I felt so sad.

I could not begin or continue the shoot. I was hurting more than she was. After replaying the moment, I realized she was upset because she wasn't going to participate in the photoshoot. Immediately, I told the journalist I could not do the shoot without her participation. I wanted her in the magazine. After a long discussion, we made a decision to include her in the shoot. I walked over to her.

"How would you feel if we took some photos to be included in the magazine?" I asked her. She broke down in tears, yelling with happiness. My heart was broken. If she could jump out of the wheelchair, she would have done it without any hesitation. Looking at her face, I noticed I had made her day. With something so simple, her morale changed very fast. Tears, smiles, and laughter lit up her face. Her life changed. The director of the facility, Mr. Jeffers, said, "Her day will be brighter with the photoshoot." One simple gesture gave her confidence and happiness.

At that moment, I realized how many simple things in life we take for granted. The freedom to walk, and enjoy the breeze on our faces, touch the flowers, hold hands with our children, swing our babies, dance, exercise, and work a job and commute with our free will. I clearly realized we have the freedom of not being isolated in a facility with limited people to see and visit. We are not confined or reside away from our loved ones and society.

From that particular day forward, I realized how difficult life is for families who are challenged by having children with intellectual and physical disabilities. It was a learning experience to understand day by day what kind of struggles and pain families are facing. Speaking with the many family members I got to know throughout the years, director Shawn, and the many employees I met through fundraising efforts, including Adam, Patty, and Phyllis, my commitment to Little City solidified. There are so many other dedicated individuals who are dedicated to making a difference in these children's lives by advocating for job skills and placements in local businesses.

Family members and employees shared many heartbreaking and horrible stories of families falling apart, parents blaming each other for the birth of this child. Siblings didn't want to be affiliated with their handicapped brother or sister. They didn't want to be stigmatized and abandoned by their friends and society.

In November of 2009, I stood in front of nine hundred attendees with tears in my eyes, accepting one of the greatest accolades of my life. I realize these children have no choice at birth, but we as a society can choose to embrace and accept them as honorable and productive citizens in our society.

Visiting the Little City campus, one realizes how blessed we are when we don't have to make difficult heartbreaking decisions. These children are faced with different environments, and parents who don't want to give up on them but have to. These parents have guilty consciences. They are handing over their child to an organization to take care and love them the way they do.

One of the mothers told me one day, "I have seen firsthand the pain and suffering of many family members who have children at the Little City Foundation campus. They might have their loved ones living in a stable, safe, and loving environment, but it still affects the entire family.

Everyone wants their child to be healthy, live in their own home, and participate in family life. It's just not possible sometimes."

Mr. Carson and Mr. Alexander, two of the founders of Little City Foundation, who both had children living on campus, said to me, "We don't know what we would have done without Little City. It has taken many challenging and difficult years to create this safe home for children with developmental and intellectual disabilities, but they have someplace to be taken care of. I don't know what we, and the many families who are facing the same predicament, would have done."

"Situations like this, my dear, tear families apart," Mr. Carson would remind me. "Everyone blames each other."

Tough Decisions

Careers and individual aspirations take many twists and turns during our lives. Although we feel angry and outraged with these detours and unexpected shifts, usually these are the moments that ultimately lead you to new opportunities.

My beloved friend, Irene Dorkofigis, was an advocate for human rights, abuse, and sex trafficking prevention—particularly for young children. She had planned on a political career, but gave it up in both the United States and Greece to support abused victims all over the world.

One day over coffee, I asked her to tell me about what she had learned while serving as an attorney in third-world countries. I wondered how she had helped so many victims by becoming a voice for justice. She stopped sipping her coffee and looked down for a moment. Around us, the coffee shop buzzed, but our table seemed surrounded by a thick silence. She looked at me with tears in her eyes and told me about her difficult and challenging experiences. She told me how the political system often failed young and innocent children who were victims of a ruthless society that did not seem to care what happened to them.

I listened to every single word. Irene is an inspiration; she ignited my zeal to fight for human rights and to become the voice of those who are silent, individuals without support for justice.

Irene was an esteemed attorney in Greece and was one of the very few women to be involved with the Red Cross in Albania. When she was there for six months during the Civil War in 1997, she saw the brutality faced by children and women who were tormented and abused. She wanted to set everyone free from this hostile environment. She helped as many as she could, smuggling people out of the country with the help of the Red Cross and many dedicated soldiers. In all, she saved more than 2,000 people.

She continued volunteering in local hospitals, teaching young children to survive by hiding and never disclosing their identity or where they lived.

She made sure children brought to her camp were kept secure and safe and were able to be transferred into other countries without any risk.

Through this turmoil, she saw the need to speak against terrorism, Communism, war, segregation, and oppression. She told me many painful stories about children being sold and abducted. She witnessed firsthand how children were being traded for sex slavery through the Mediterranean. Working closely with government representatives, she made sure she saved many young girls from being trafficked.

Of all the stories she shared, one stuck in my mind. She knew a twelve-year-old girl who was sexually, verbally, and physically abused by her brother and father. She was pawned to many foreign men for money, and kept hostage to their demonic ways and forces. At thirteen, she was raped and impregnated, and when the baby was born, she was forced to give it up. Her child was sold to strangers, who were to take the child out of the country and never be seen or heard of again.

After hearing this horrific story from one of the girl's relatives, Irene made it her mission to help her. With her political contacts, she freed the young girl and handed her to the Red Cross. She told me this was one of her greatest accomplishments. Irene never disclosed this young girl's name; all she said was that she was adopted by an amazing couple. They educated her in the most influential schools. She became a beacon of hope, working as an influential lawyer and helping many lives by being the voice for many young people.

The world needed to know that the Mediterranean is one of the primary transit regions for children being sold to sex traffickers, so I worked with Irene to publicize her work and draw attention to this inhumane practice. There is strong evidence that refugees make the journey only to be exploited; abusers, smugglers, and sex traffickers are thriving.

Irene knew so many horrific stories: people promised jobs that never materialized, so they couldn't pay to free themselves. Others had their documents confiscated and were held hostage. They were told to perform sexual services, and if they didn't abide by their wishes, they were tormented, kidnapped, and exploited by many ruthless individuals.

The rise in trafficking and exploitative practices has been well-documented by the Red Cross and many other organizations that Irene worked with undercover. She has heard horror stories of children taken from their parents, who were promised money and a good life for their children, who were then forced to perform sexual acts against their will. Many young girls were promised a good arranged marriage, but instead they were taken to unidentified locations where they were held hostage against their will and subjected to different pleasures for pedophiles.

Irene, having daughters, was angered. She would say, "This is bigger than the drug cartels. The selling of children for sex is the greatest injustice. If women really want to be proactive in being a voice for justice, then they need to start yelling at the top of their lungs for this to stop. It is the most profitable trade in the world."

Listening to her stories traumatized me and then inspired me. This was a woman who had given up everything (law, politics, family, and friendship) to fight for an incredible cause.

"If we are honorable and noble, let's rise up against children being sold for sex," she said. "We need to isolate every rapist and abuser."

The outcome of these painful and heartbreaking stories inspired me. I am committed to protecting and defending innocent victims, never allowing anyone to harm any child. I have helped safeguard many children who were involved in different situations. Young girls who had abortions, and children who had fallen victim to alcohol, drugs, and many other substance abuse issues. As a mother, it was prudent to protect not only the children I have brought into the world, but all of the other innocent human beings who cross my path.

Children in a Challenging World

The connection between a mother and child starts at the moment of conception. A mother nourishes her unborn child by making sure she eats the right things, rests, and protects her body from dangerous substances. When a child is born in this world, and as they grow, their life and survival depend on the attention and choices of the mother.

From the start, food becomes the bond between the baby and the caregiver. As my children got older, I noticed that the kitchen was the center of our connection and a meeting place. At our kitchen table we had touching and meaningful discussions and conversations; warm lovingly-made meals; and a communal workplace for school homework. We bonded through food and discussion.

My parents would say, "A good meal opens the door to conversations that one would think are impossible to discuss." They also believed that the recipe for friendship was simple. "Give someone a glass of wine and a good meal, and make them comfortable in their skin and in your sanctuary, and they will be your everlasting friend."

Today's children don't live a normal life. They live in a world of increased stress. They start competing from the day they are born. This does not reflect how parents care for or discipline a child—instead, it's a result of the world around us. What once took months or years to be taught or learned can now be retrieved within seconds. Children can sense and understand the increased pace of life. They feel tension and verbal communication from a young age. If a child senses stress, their emotions begin to change. They don't understand what is transpiring around them, leaving them wondering why things feel different and uncomfortable.

When I was young, grandparents were the center of children's lives. Multiple generations lived together in the same household or in the same neighborhood. Children had supervision all the time. Parents would work without being worried about who would pick the kids up or how they would express their feelings. They knew someone trusted was there to handle behavior changes. Children would have a warm meal on the table and be safe at home. Grandparents were hands-on caregivers, and could report what changes they saw in their grandchildren. They noted mood changes or irritable behavior in their grandchild. If they were calm and had a wonderful day at school, they would notice the calm in their behavior.

Today, both parents often have careers and have to work due to financial constraints on their family. Children are too involved in school activities, after-school tutoring, and a variety of sports. They are tired and disturbed, stressed out in their minimal free time. Their way to cope with stress is to seek out social media acceptance. When I ask many of my friends if their family has dinner together, many are honest. "No, Eleni," they say. "We're all on different schedules. It's impossible."

I believe that the lack of family dinners, a critical bonding time, has caused the separation of parents and children. Parents don't have the opportunity to see deep into the eyes of their child, to understand what their fears and problems are.

Children live in a complex and demanding world. They are caught up in thoughts of being liked and known in school, sports, and in their social climate. They are worried they won't be accepted in their environment. Children don't realize the dangers of social media and the challenges of being around the wrong crowd. They slowly integrate, worrying and confusing who they are and what their role is in today's society. Their main focus is being accepted by the cool kid on the block. Slowly, without notice, their sense of direction is deviated by the stress of wondering if they are smart enough to fit into this cool crowd. Will they persevere in getting accepted? Why are they enduring bullying from those who dislike them?

Many times, I have wondered where bullying really starts. When I was raising my children, I saw bullying happen as young as kindergarten. Children would create their own little groups of friends and play together, excluding those they didn't like. This behavior was not tolerated by the nuns. When they saw it happen, both sets of parents would be engaged in resolving this matter.

When siblings bully each other, do parents put an end to it? Or do they turn their eyes away? When my children argued and said mean things to each other, I would gather them at the kitchen counter and talk about the issues. I had them explain, and told them why bullying should not be tolerated, and told them the psychological impact on an individual's life. I was interested in hearing how the conversation had started and how it had escalated into bullying, threats, and accusations.

As a mother, when you talk about issues with your children, you understand why it happened and where it's going. Parents need to go back to the simple strategy of having time together as a family. They need to realize and recognize at the same time if their child is being attacked, bullied, or threatened in any way.

Sadly, bullying and attacks are increasingly difficult to escape. It's the responsibility of parents, educators, caregivers, and everyone in the community to recognize bullying and the aggressive behavior of a classmate. Children need to be taught how to cope and dismiss this kind of behavior.

As a society, it's our responsibility to take action and put a stop to the chaos that is taking the lives of so many young innocent children today. Schools need to assure parents that they are more proactive in their children's lives. Parents need to be held accountable and responsible if their child makes threatening comments to other students.

Ultimately, educators and parents need to work hand in hand. I was personally grateful to Judge Julie Nicholson, who presided over the Michigan school shooter trial. She saw the importance of holding parents accountable and convicted the parents as well as their son for his role in a shooting spree at Oxford High School. I wondered, *Why only ten years?* I believe they should have gotten life sentences. Maybe this could set a precedent and be a warning to parents to be more involved in their kids' lives. I believe these parents, and many others, need to be responsible for what transpires in their child's life.

I wonder if parents see signs that their kid is disoriented, angry, and out of touch with their surroundings. How can a high school student buy or steal a gun without their parents seeing any signs? Where were the parents the morning he took the gun to school? What did the parents know about their child's habits? Why would they not notice issues arising?

I believe violence starts in our backyard, our homes, and neighborhoods. It is easier to blame the person next door than to look deep and see how we have failed our children. Parents need to be arrested and condemned for their children's behavior. If parents are held accountable, I believe they will understand the intense, unending responsibility of bringing a child into this world.

My mom would say, "Once you decide to get pregnant and bring a child into this world, you will be responsible until your dying day for their life, safety, and security." She would laugh and say, "Even in your coffin, you will be twisting when you hear your children speak to you from above." As parents, we have a duty and obligation to keep them safe.

I believe parents, educators, and the government should implement strict laws against bullying and restrict social media access. Classmates should be able to take charge and help stop violence without the threat of being targeted or expelled from school.

Children are not born evil; they are innocent angels who need guidance, reassurance, and love. It's our responsibility to make them understand the meaning of the beautiful things in life. They will not appreciate the simple things unless they are taught to be satisfied with the effortless things. When you are not content with your surroundings, your environment, or your family life, you will keep searching for meaningless things. We all have failed our children by not showing them that happiness is being around those you love and the simple things we all take for granted.

Today, children can pay for everything automatically without feeling the texture of a dollar or understanding the value of money. I believe this is dangerous for a child. They don't anticipate what the value of money will be, or how to make a dollar. If you don't know how to work hard to make a dollar, it's very easy to accumulate debt in life. I believe that, before giving your child access to your credit card, you, as a parent, are obligated to teach them how to earn money. It's easy to spend your parents' money without knowledge of the larger consequences. But when you spend your own hard-earned cash, you become more likely to save more.

What you wear is meaningless. Expensive clothing should not identify you unless you are cheerful and happy. Grandma would say, "Your clothes could cost more than your paycheck, but if you are unhappy in your skin, you will feel as if you have put a sack over your body."

The car you drive should not identify you. Focus on having a car to take you wherever you want. The first car that Jimmy and I purchased at the beginning of our marriage cost $25, and we loved it. We didn't care. We had a car to take us to school and work. That $25 car died on us one summer Saturday evening on the way home after an exhausting fifteen hours of working. We stopped, laughing our hearts out, took off the license plates, and walked four miles home.

Your character, personality, intelligence, and educational skills will open many doors to achieve success and financial worth. When you build wealth and success through hard work and solid foundations, you will appreciate anything you purchase, large or small. Whether it's a car, a home, or a pair of shoes you've had your eyes on, it should give you satisfaction and gratification knowing you have worked hard to earn it. You will become energized to support and advance others to be able to gain confidence to persevere in their life. Through your success, you will instill faith and hope in other individuals.

∽

Children need to visit nature and spend time on a farm, understanding the difference between humans and animals. They need to see how they eat and interact with each other. My parents believed that when a child saw this and spent time with animals, it made them react very differently to humans. A person uses logic, intellect, and motivation to think about things. A person does not crawl; we walk on our two feet. A human being has feelings that can be affected by a person's behavior; even an animal can be affected by the kindness or rudeness of human behavior.

My parents used to say that there is nothing better in life than to see and have a conversation with an individual. They believed that you can bring a person to their senses when you are a firm and honest person. You cannot abuse or hit a person to make them obey. They would say, "Even animals have feelings; you cannot abuse them to follow your commands. But you cannot ignore the struggles and pain of humans when you accuse them of misbehaving. Their feelings consume their heart and soul.

"Children need to understand the different dynamics between people and animals. An animal only reacts. They do not talk, or outrageously kill themselves and hurt people with violence or verbal and unkind remarks. People speak and react abruptly. They can run away and shield their issues or, as many do, find an easy way out by taking their own life. It's when they understand that dynamic that they will be considerate toward everyone's feelings by identifying differences," my parents used to say. Children will grow up not only understanding nature but also appreciating all the things created by God. They will have a clear understanding that their lives should be fulfilled with the natural things that provide much for our survival.

Everyone is born with their own unique talents. We must embrace everyone's aptitudes by realizing everyone contributes to society. Children must comprehend from a young age that there will always be someone more talented, more beautiful, more intelligent, more articulate, or more gifted, and they should not see them as an obstacle to their future. We need to admire everyone's unique talents without venom, vengeance, or envy. We should embrace and support each other if we are to live in a stable and better world.

As parents, we need to teach our children the importance of being a team player. It's crucial to understand that, united, we can achieve so many remarkable and marvelous accomplishments. But divided, we will destroy ourselves, others, and our magnificent universe.

Children should not be led to believe that everyone else lives a lavish lifestyle of private airplanes, exquisite boats, expensive clothing, and luxurious furnishings. I believe this has caused more pain and grief in a child's life. The fantasy world they see is not realistic. It's an illusion. But they must know that no matter how much money you have, if you are not confident and safe in your skin, nothing will fulfill you as an individual.

When we give respect and honor to someone wonderful who has touched our lives, we start a ripple effect in praising their hard work. These people then transform themselves, becoming more confident in their daily decisions. It can make a difference in their day, year, or life.

Humans thirst for acceptance, praise, and attention. It's always better to praise an individual instead of insulting them. There is always a kind way to express your views and opinions without insulting and demeaning anyone. No one is perfect in this world, and we all make unstable and selfish decisions. It's more satisfying viewing our mistakes and misfortunes than talking negatively about someone else's oversight.

If we can become responsible for uplifting someone as they begin to fall, we have the chance of making a difference in—or saving—a life. It's only then that we will live in a loving and caring society. Let's all be empathetic to others and stop judging and condemning. Let's focus on our own areas of growth instead of speaking about someone else's misfortunes.

We were born in a beautiful world filled with so many different people who have so many precious gifts. We are given the opportunity to succeed in anything we apply our talents to achieving. We can be attentive to the needs of those around us. As creatures of this world, we can be sustainable citizens if we all start loving the creation and creator of all things, visible and invisible. We can do all these things at once because we are complex, brilliant beings. We have the power to make this world a different and better place for our children.

Today's Challenges

Many children today don't pray at the dinner table. They don't pray after waking up or when they lie their heads down at night. They don't understand that they have to thank someone for the wonderful day they had. They don't understand that they need to show appreciation and love for everything they have been given. When a child or individual gives gratitude to God, they will never have an issue in appreciating anyone's support and help. When we go out for dinner, I have the tendency to glance at the tables around us. I especially focus on tables with families and young children. I am always interested in seeing what kind of interaction and chemistry is going on between parents and children.

Having four grandchildren—two of them under the age of three—it disappoints me to see a lack of communication between family members, especially parents and young children. It always seems parents are too busy on their phone, and that they've passed a phone or tablet to their children to keep them distracted. In my personal opinion, as a mother, I believe this is a dangerous, complicated, and huge problem in raising children today.

In today's world, our children have been manipulated by what they watch. They are led by algorithms to watch the next thing, then the next thing, and continue with the next thing. They don't understand the difference between what to watch and what not to. It's the responsibility of a parent to be observant in teaching, and guiding, and observing their children.

One of the largest battles, when it comes to raising children today, is social media. It's an international problem that many families are facing. Although social media has connected us to the entire world, it has also brought divisiveness, anger, and cruelty.

You don't see the reaction on someone's face when you are bullying or disrespecting them. Therefore, you are able to hurt and anger someone without feeling remorse. When you can't look into their eyes and see firsthand the results of a confrontation, a split of a friendship will be inevitable. It is easier to write an intimidating comment to someone instead of telling them up front. You don't have to watch a reaction on social media. You can say anything you want without any precautions.

Today's society blames children for attacking other children, for bullying, or causing harmful situations for their friends or schools. We rush to blame a child and quickly judge them without looking at the parents' role in this equation.

I believe children are the innocent victims in society. They are the victims of invisible and unbearable circumstances. As a society, we have created the problem of children spinning out of control. We don't monitor our children's friends, their habits, their faces. We are disconnected from their lives.

As a mother, I think it's wise for parents to go back to the simple things in life. Teach our children what coloring books and storybooks are. We need to focus on teaching them about nature and nurture. We need to plan designated times for family to sit and have dinner together, to connect and talk to each other. We need to help them understand there are consequences to every statement and comment, and realize the ripple effect of our words and actions.

Children today are consumed with technology. They don't have time to go out and play a game, throw a ball around, or just ride their bikes down to the park. It saddens me not to see children outside on the swings and slides at local parks. When I was a child, and when my children were children, kids would spend hours at the neighborhood parks with their families and schoolmates. You heard laughter, arguments, and loud, excited voices. You saw parents, grandparents, or family members playing along, or at least sitting nearby to supervise.

Today, many of my family members and friends complain about the behavior of children. They sit in their bedrooms playing video games and scrolling through Instagram and Facebook. Children are obsessed with seeing what each friend is doing, where they are dining, where they are going on vacation, what they are buying, and what they are wearing. This constant comparison on its own causes stress for a child in coveting what his friends have. Kids don't yet understand it could all be fake. Their friends could be sitting at home and pretending they are on a holiday. It is human nature to want what your friends have. It's easier to follow someone instead of being a strong leader and having others follow you.

Suicide, I believe, has increased due to the demands of social pressure. In addition, many children are expected to follow in someone's footsteps and carry the family's legacy. This could add excruciating stress for a child, throwing fuel on an unprecedented pile of tinder. Life is already hard to manage, especially when the support systems are fragile and weak.

Children and parents need to go back to basics. Let's visit museums, libraries, parks, zoos, and farms together. When a child learns that it's the simple things in life that actually offer satisfaction and gratification, they will realize their purpose. They will be able to handle unexpected events and interact with others in a calm and serene atmosphere—no matter what's happening.

If children are to survive this fast world, they need to feel free and safe in their home, school environment, and workplace. They need to learn to be competitive and act with integrity. They need to realize that people have different talents and that everyone has weaknesses and strengths. But this does not make someone weak or a failure in life.

Last week, I was watching a special that featured a former top executive who gave up a lucrative position to go work and live on a farm in the middle of the English countryside. When he was asked by a reporter why he decided to leave everything behind and venture into farming, he said, "It's simple. My life got so complicated, I didn't realize when it was morning or night. I went to my desk and saw my bank account. I had made money, but what was different? I had not lived on my money. I was not enjoying the fruits of my labor. I came to an awakening: Everything in life I had yearned to accomplish was a means of gratification and not happiness. I never realized while working from morning to night that life outside of a big city would be so gratifying and rewarding."

He continued, his voice sounding peaceful and calm. "It's wonderful and breathtaking seeing how an animal is born and how the mother knows how to feed and nurture them. You don't realize that animals can give you the tranquility you need to live a peaceful, stress-free life."

I thought about him so much after the show. Life moves very fast with technology, glory, ego, and success. But you need to start enjoying the simple things to understand the environment, atmosphere, and the pain and sorrow of others in different parts of the world.

Children should not feel overwhelmed with our grown-up problems. They need to be children first, then adults. Often, I notice how roles are switched by the way a child addresses a parent. The child becomes the parent, the parent the child. This is why they are angry and hostile toward others. Children need to know there are boundaries that cannot be crossed. All that a child needs to know at a young age is that they are protected and loved by their parents, no matter what their home looks like compared to their friends.

When we look back, we have to be proud of the sentimental things we have taught our children. The fundamental things that bring them joy and happiness. Children need to understand that they have an obligation and responsibility to themselves and to others to be honest and caring.

Children should not be seen as objects or tools in a relationship but as something precious that God gave you to protect and defend from harm. Children mimic their parents and their reactions. When you choose to have your child witness suffering and poverty, they will think twice about disrespecting food or the person who is providing for them.

We must learn to converse with our children about everything instead of expecting them to make logical decisions. Children can pick up even the subtlest anger and animosity in a family home. It is always wise to tell them how much you love them while emphasizing the need to be a respectful responsible person.

When a child learns how to say, "I love you," "please," "forgive me," "thank you" and "I am sorry," he or she will be a humble individual who will have strong roots.

We have taken God out of our lives, homes, and families. We have become our own gods by selling our souls for money, greed, and power. Unless we teach our children that they can hide from us but cannot hide from God's eyes, they will never understand that choices have consequences. A child must have a fear not only of their parents, but a fear of God. They must know that if they do something bad, someone will see.

As my wise parents would say, "You can steal once or twice, but the third time, you will get caught, and will be punished, and held responsible."

As parents, let's give children the light, ease, and opportunity to live a normal, fulfilled life by teaching them about God, love, motivation, happiness, laughter, discipline, and strength. Let's give them the guidance to persevere in their future.

When we love each other as God has loved you and me, then we will have a world free from segregation, divisiveness, injustice, hate, and violence. We can all achieve this when we have love—and God—in our heart and soul.

Women Helping Women

Women have come a long way since my mother and grandmother were growing up. We are respected in every field and are changing the world in so many ways. We are doctors, lawyers, judges, educators, artists, and scientists, while also showing up as mothers, wives, daughters, sisters, and community members.

Bold Resilient Women

Throughout my life, I've turned to many notable women when I have needed a boost of inspiration or encouragement.

Marie Curie, the first woman to win a Nobel Prize in chemistry, discovered polonium and radium, further developing the technology for X-rays. I have always admired her intellect and curiosity, the way she kept digging for more answers.

Amelia Earhart was the first woman aviator to fly solo across the Atlantic Ocean, and was also the first person ever to accomplish the flight from Hawaii to California alone. I have always been inspired by her bravery and sense of adventure. No one thought she had the courage to fly such long and dangerous routes by herself in the 1920s and 1930s.

Rosa Parks is another heroic woman. I admired her from the moment I read about her refusal, as a Black woman, to give up her bus seat for a white passenger and move to the back. She was the catalyst for the Civil Rights Movement. I have always admired how she took a stand and fought for what was right, regardless of the consequences.

Coretta Scott King was introduced to me by Mr. Bogio. While we worked in the store together, he would tell us stories about her husband, Dr. Martin

Bold Resilient Women

Luther King, Jr., and his dream of bringing equality to all people. He held equal respect for Mrs. King.

"Mrs. King stands next to the Reverend," he would say. "She is fighting alongside him against racial discrimination and the economic disparity between Black and white people." He taught me things that were barely skimmed over by teachers and other adults in our lives. "Missy, there is no equality between the North and South, the East and West. Our children don't have the same educational material or standards of learning. It's an unfair system."

When Dr. King was assassinated, Mr. Bogio believed that Mrs. King had the power to preach peace as well. "The only way violence and rage will stop is if Mrs. King reminds the world that her husband stood for peace, equality, unity, and love," he would say. "Dr. King was not a violent man. He would condemn what's happening today in our country."

Being a young child in the 1960s, I witnessed firsthand the anger, violence, and destruction of our country. If not for this amazing and peaceful woman who came out, faced the huge crowds, and told everyone to stop the violence, I don't know what would have happened to our country and how many innocent lives would have been lost. I always admired her ability to speak out bravely, and her commitment to keep going even after she lost her husband.

I've been blessed with incredible role models in my life through my relatives and friends, but also through the bold resilient women who I have learned about and watched on a larger stage. I feel that in crafting my life and my values, they have all played a part in who I am now.

Women need to be supportive of each other's ambitions. We need to uphold our values and morals with love, empathy, and respect toward each other. We must be a collective force in the world. We must work to make a difference through compassion, resilience, positive enlightenment, and energy. We must be cautious not to engage in discriminatory behavior and comments that take people down instead of lifting them up.

In the days of the Ottoman Empire, Greek women were abducted from villages and cities and taken to Ali Pasha, the empire's leader, as tokens. He would rape them, and if they didn't abide by his rule and law, he would torture them and then throw them off a cliff or drown them in the sea. It took forty warriors to fight for independence and freedom for my mother country, Greece. The heroes of 1821 proclaimed, "Either we fight for freedom and life, or we shall die as heroes." While the men were heroes on the battlefield, the

Bold Resilient Women

women were heroes as well, keeping their allegiance to Greece and enduring many atrocities in the name of Greek independence.

In many countries today, women are still sold as slaves and kept as hostages. They still fight for their voices to be heard and to be treated equally with men. As women work to achieve independence and equality in all areas, we still have to ensure the next generation is strong, bold, and resilient. This can be achieved by teaching young women to be confident, self-sufficient, and to stand firm in their values and beliefs.

We have allowed society to take away our integrity and self-esteem by positioning women as beautiful statuettes who are only evaluated by their looks. We are only seen as sex symbols. We are seen as objects who are stripped of our free will. Young women, too, feel they have to compete with models and actresses, becoming bulimic, anorexic, and depressed while trying to exist in a society that wants only to take them down. Young girls are made to feel worthless and unworthy of their dreams. Men should see women as intellectual, intelligent, and productive individuals. They need to see women as full people. Many become stuck in self-destructive patterns, not knowing which path to follow.

We need to help young women find their inspiration. We need to show them that other women can be a life preserver when they feel lost or adrift. Whether it's by women from history, women in their own lives, or even the women in their communities, it's time to help young women lift themselves up and realize how strong and resilient they are.

Making Choices

Society manipulates us into believing we must make pivotal choices between career, children, love, education, companionship, charity, health, and faith. As a mother, wife, entrepreneur, chairman, board member, and philanthropist, I can say on a personal level that you should never face a dilemma when it comes to making choices. When an individual has stability, they can follow their heart, aspirations, and desires without analyzing things in depth. You must make choices in order to succeed in life.

Your desire to accept who you are, along with your humble family's foundation, characterizes your quest for success. Young women must feel confident in their own skin, self-worth, and self-esteem, and be resilient in their vision. You must have faith in yourself. You must be able to write your own story by engraving your own legacy. We must have confidence in creating by building our success story without depending on anyone else's approval, relying solely on ourselves and our inner instinct.

No one should have the capability and authority to make you doubt who you are and your worth in society. When you know yourself, no one can brainwash you into believing you are unattractive, brainless, or imperfect. After many doubtful moments and painful remarks, I learned to overcome what envious individuals thought. Today, in an unprecedented and unpredictable world, every young woman has to learn how to rise above negative comments. No matter how hard you try to please someone, there will always be someone to pass judgment. I have never put emphasis on someone else's looks, intelligence, talents, wealth, power, or family life. I always felt confident in praising other women for their charisma and charm.

Only by praising those around you can one facilitate empowerment in a friend and a woman. We must never forget what the Bible says: *"In His grace, God has given us different gifts."* He has given us talents to use wisely. Therefore, we should never be upset about other individuals' talents. We have to be content with our own and support everyone around us. It takes a team of talented individuals to create anything in life. No one can do it alone. Once I started gaining confidence and faith, I found a shining bright light coming from inside my heart. I felt satisfied as a whole woman. For once, I was able to admire myself, while at the same time, praise friends and other women for their talents, clothing, looks, beautiful homes, designs, and good works.

My life's success has been possible through overcoming obstacles by accepting negative criticism and spinning it into constructive highlights. I was forced to look deep into my inner world and to do a lot of soul searching to accept my flaws before I could override a friend's flaws. Forgiveness, and admitting your mistakes, are the most difficult things to accept.

The most beautiful feeling you can have as a woman, wife, mother, and friend is to be open-minded in accepting constructive criticism. As a vigorous and ambitious woman, I was never offended by someone's comments. I knew in my heart that I had fulfilled my duties and commitments to my family, friends, and the many organizations I served. I realized that the only way for people to judge anyone else was by ignoring their own faults. There isn't a human being in this world without faults; we all have our weak moments. But the beauty of free knowledge, choice, and decisions is to be able to catch yourself and correct your misconceptions.

Bold Resilient Women

As my mother used to say, "If we were all without sin, there would never be pain, suffering, competition, pride, revenge, egos, or wars." It's always encouraging to take a few steps back, analyze things, and then see situations with a clear picture and perception.

My mother would always remind me that it's easier for a needle to penetrate someone's heart than to forgive and embrace them. As humans, it's easy for us to defuse situations and not allow them to get out of control if we don't have any self-interests. However, when we have interests at stake, we turn our backs and let innocent people be condemned.

That's why you should remember that when you take a dagger and kill someone, that action penetrates much deeper into your heart, for if a dagger you give, then a dagger you shall receive in return.

Mom and Dad were not educated people, but had taught themselves how to read. I would ask my mom, "Why would someone say something so terrible about another person?"

She would say, "Honey, they have no conscience. They don't care about anything or anyone. It's the sensitive people who get hurt in life. When you love someone without wanting anything in return, there should not be any boundaries. You will love that individual today, tomorrow, and always. It's as if time has stood still. Love is not about one day. Today, I know you, and next I will forget you. We all go through arguments and misconceptions, but when people truly love each other, they can sit at the table and clarify things. This, my darling girl, is love: to look someone in the eyes and see the lie or truth. Eyes are the mirror of truth."

Mom loved the scriptures. She would say that love is simple if you follow the rule of God. Listen before you attack someone. Let them conclude their speech and their sentences. You might see things differently than what you had assumed.

"Don't ever accuse people of wrongdoing or saying things that are not true without knowing all the facts. People tend to make up stories to gain what they want. Give and support people without waiting to receive something in return. You will always feel better giving than receiving. Always remember to pray when you wake up, thank the Lord for giving you another day to see those you love and to do the things you want to achieve."

In the evening, around the table, Dad and Mom made sure we took turns saying the dinner prayer before and after eating. We had to thank God for our daily meal. Dad would say, "We have to be grateful because many people across the world will fall asleep hungry while we are full up to our ears." When we went to bed, Mom would gather us to kneel with her next to our beds and thank God for another day of health, happiness, and prosperity. This was our daily ritual. We had to be obedient to God and thankful for everything we had. Mom and Dad would say, "When someone asks you a question, answer it with truth, don't make up and fabricate stories in your mind. When you say and speak of the truth, you don't have to worry about remembering what lie you told."

She would continue. "You either care for someone or you don't. Don't ever mislead someone to think you love them and then toss them aside as if they never existed. This is a huge sin; you are playing with someone's life and feelings. People are vulnerable creatures. They react according to your treatment. As a human, you must always consider the age of a person before you make statements or comments. The younger you are, the more mistakes you make. With age comes wisdom."

She was always extremely honest about herself and her life. "I look at myself first and see the horrible mistakes I had made in my twenties, thirties, forties, fifties, sixties, seventies—even up to today in my 8eighties. I have regrets. There isn't anyone in this world who doesn't have regrets. People never stop learning to correct their mistakes, no matter how old they are."

She would add, "Enjoy every moment as if it were your last moment on this earth with your loved ones. Stop complaining and being a victim. Get up, gain strength and confidence, and look at the blessings around you. Enjoy all the wonderful things in life that were given to you and glorify God for your existence in this world. Trust God and your ability to sustain justice and integrity. Don't be envious of someone who has more than you.

"The hardest thing to do in life is to forgive someone who has caused so much pain and grief in your life. God says, 'I see everything and I write it all down. I will take revenge when I think it's the appropriate time.' You have to forgive to have peace in your heart—but don't ever forget. You must keep your guard up or else that person will continue to hurt you. When you give your promise to someone, never forget it. You never know what this promise can mean to someone at a moment of desperation."

My beautiful Grandma would say, "When you make a promise to a child and an old man, they will hold you to that promise until you come through. If you want life to go smoothly, never break a promise to a young or old person." My dad used to say, "A handshake is a promise between people, friends, and family members. We didn't believe in lawyers or documents to know what we wanted or purchased. We would seal a deal with a handshake, honesty, and integrity. Today, people draft many documents, and they are still meaningless. If you don't believe in what you want in life with honesty and respect, then you will always find a way to manipulate and scam."

Mom would say, "God knew and knows us before we were in our mother's womb. God is aware of our struggles, worries, and pain. He recognizes our emotional turmoil with our partners, family, children, and friends. He knows that we are humans who hurt emotionally when someone hurts and disappoints us. "He knows, when we don't have financial stability, to give and to support those who are less fortunate than we are. Although our heart tells us to do the right thing for others, sometimes we don't have the ability. God recognizes when our spirituality is being tested throughout life's daily challenges. He knows we try to hold on to our faith to lead us out of our problems."

Mom used to say, "God has given you, my darling girl, a good heart. He sees many people who have abused your kindness as a weakness. The devil is there testing you to see if you will curse the people who have betrayed you, but I don't want you falling in his entrapment of accusing or resenting someone. Always take the high road and let God take action.

"Many times, I, too, have felt I was caught in the middle of a storm without any place to take shelter. When you have faith, my darling daughter, God will never let you drown. He will lift you up from the storm. We all have enemies, people who envy our success and family. But don't let that stop you from following your path in life. Know you have God's—and our—protection. That's why we pray day and night for God to give you wisdom, health, and a peaceful heart to see things clearly with honesty and sincerity."

Teach Children the Meaning of Love

A child must learn so many things to be a fully actualized adult, but among the most important lessons are the meaning of love, self-respect, and respect for others. They need to learn to believe and entrust God with worries and problems, and know that their parents, family, and close friends will provide unwavering support and unconditional love. From a young age, a child must learn to keep their guard up when it comes to friends and surroundings. If a child has self-confidence and courage, they can be more of a free spirit who can do and achieve anything they want. They get this by feeling love, appreciation, and strength.

When a child understands the love and the protection their parents provide, it's less likely that they'll encounter a difficult situation without turning to their parents for support and help. In order to have a healthy relationship, your child needs to understand early on the different boundaries in life, what they consist of, and why it's important to never, ever, cross the fine line.

I believe today's roles have switched: Parents have become the outspoken, ignorant, liberated children, and the children have become the advice-giving patient parents.

My children have always known I am the person who suffered to bring them into this world, and I am the one who will love them unconditionally. They knew I was their mother first, followed by their best friend who would protect them from anyone and everything. They always knew they could never cross the line and act like the parent or try to overtake my parenting skills and responsibilities. When I said no, there was no question about anything.

It's important not to blame a child for acting out, bullying, hurting others, or themselves. We must understand the underlying problem. There isn't a child born evil; it's just that something triggers a child to be aggressive, angry, or out of control. No human being is born with bad intentions. Something in their journey caused the collapse of serenity and peace.

It's crucial for parents to monitor what children are watching, listening to, and mimicking. This makes them turn to unknown individuals and unknown substances. We must take time to follow every move they make. Society absorbs our children like a vacuum, and it's even more dangerous with social media. Social media influences their minds, leading them to believe they are not worthy to pursue their dreams. Too much outside influence, and they start to live with the perception that someone else loves them more than their parents. This makes them turn to unknown individuals.

Children become competitive from a young age. They learn to compete with everything and everyone over what they wear, where they live, who their friends are, how skinny they are, what kind of looks they have, and anything else under the sun.

Many young men and women feel they don't have the looks to date a wonderful and successful young person. They are left hopeless as they seek to be the kind of person they dream of. They try to transform themselves into something they're not. They seek out plastic and cosmetic surgery early, and it's heartbreaking to see young women living and looking like adult women instead of teenagers.

Many young adults can feel that they were born into the wrong body. Their biological sex doesn't match their gender identity, and they identify as a gender other than the one they were born into. This gender disorder can create many unanswered and challenging questions in someone's mind.

This idea of being born in a different-gendered body is a new concept in today's world. While many experts say that a child, by the age of seven, can understand the different concepts of gender, others argue there is no scientific evidence that a child can be born into the wrong body.

As a mother of a gay child, I believe we should caution each other and society against passing judgment and condemning any child who feels trapped in a different body. Feeling as though your body is wrong can lead to a child being abused physically, mentally, and psychologically. Children have their own characteristics of behavior, personality, interests, and talents, regardless of their gender. We have to allow young adults or children to express their feelings independently without obstruction. I have witnessed firsthand the pain and suffering of two friends of mine who have transgender children.

This ordeal has caused enormous pain for the parents, but above all, it has caused suffering, chaos, and turmoil in these young people's lives.

Both of these families come from influential backgrounds. They were both fearful of what their friends and family members would say. They had a difficult time expressing their feelings. They spoke quietly behind closed doors about how they would process what was happening in their child's life.

After one of the children was punched and harassed to the point where he wanted to end his life, her parents decided that no matter what, they were going to take a stand and support their daughter. I asked the father, my friend, who was a prominent doctor, if he had ever suspected a gender difference in his child, and he said, "Yes. She was always dressed in suits and wearing a hat and tie. She never showed any interest in wearing women's clothing or wearing makeup to look like a girl."

The time came, before this child was finished with high school, when she was ready for gender reassignment surgery. My friend said, "Eleni, I didn't question it. I knew my child was born in a woman's body, and it was bringing him sorrow and misery. He became depressed and didn't want to live. Therefore, I wanted to support my child instead of hurting him. I knew that if I didn't support him, it was likely that he would end his life. I love my child more than anything and accept him however he is, or identifies as being." I was in awe of his courage and compassion.

"It's not a simple discussion," he told me after I complimented him. "It's hard to accept and deal with. But with love, understanding, and patience, you can find the resolution."

The other child was born a boy but felt like he should have been born in a girl's body. In the beginning, it was very difficult. No one in the family wanted to discuss this matter, thinking the child was going through a phase. In grammar school, he was assaulted when he went to the boys' bathroom and had toilet paper and books thrown at him. The child didn't want to cause more pain for the family, so he never made the parents aware of his issues. One day, he was belittled so badly by his classmates that the next day, he told his mom he wasn't going to school because he was feeling ill.

That weekend, he didn't want to leave the house. Everyone thought he had some kind of cold or flu. When Monday morning came around, his mother knocked on the door to wake him for school. "I'm sick," he responded through the door.

"Eleni, that's when I realized something was wrong," she told me. "He loved school. Why this sudden change?" She told me that she immediately called her husband at the office and asked him to come home—they had something serious to discuss.

"When my husband arrived, he knew why I had called," she told me. "We invited my son to sit at the kitchen table with us and to open his heart. My husband, being very up front, asked him, 'How do you identify yourself, my son?' He said, 'I see myself as a girl. I hate my private parts. I don't care for them.'

"My husband was crushed, and he could not hold back his tears," she continued. "But I could not stop rubbing my child's hands, crying, and shaking. We told him, 'We will support and love you no matter how you identify yourself. We just ask that you don't make any decisions in medicating yourself until you graduate from high school.' He agreed. We also knew children who struggle with gender identity are at a greater risk of committing suicide as a result of bullying, or being victimized, or rejected by their friends and classmates."

She told me with tears in her eyes, and I could tell how deeply this fear lived in her. "I have lived a nightmare, worrying if my son is going to come home in one piece. Every day, I think about life and death. People are cruel, children above all others. They can say the most hurtful and awful things to each other."

"I can relate to your pain," I said, thinking of Evangelo.

"No, Eleni," she said firmly. "There is a huge difference between being gay and being transgender."

I started to cry and couldn't stop. I knew she was right, and that there was also a huge difference in how society perceives you and how you are treated on a daily basis.

"You cannot understand what it feels like every morning when he gets ready for school," she continued. "You can see stress, anxiety, fear, and agony in his face. When I leave him outside of school, children look at him, ready to make a statement. All the way to school, I lectured him and his two friends not to let anyone make them feel insecure. I remind them they are strong individuals and that they need to stand up for themselves. I tell them, 'Never allow anyone to bully or mistreat you in any way. I want you to love and respect yourselves so others will do the same.' I sleep and wake up with fear and stress every day."

I wish parents could understand the dangers of bullying and the effects that it has on an innocent child's life. Parents must understand the need to educate and speak to their children with love and compassion about these individuals. These young people are already marked as outsiders, and then

Bold Resilient Women

they are so crushed by people's aggressive behavior and cruel comments that they believe the world is better off without them.

Instead of creating divisiveness and anger in a child's life through our words and actions toward people who are different, we should find an opportunity to speak to our children about transgender people and that they are part of our community. That they should interact with anyone different than they are without fearing what society says. A child should not be experiencing emotional and physical abuse from their peers. We should all protect the innocence of a child from bullying and violence.

Yesterday and Today's Women

What makes women today different from our mothers and grandmothers is the ability to make choices. Women can pursue motherhood and a career at the same time without being denied their dreams. Unless a woman chooses to live on a farm, she doesn't have to wake up at the crack of dawn to be out in the fields with the hot wind blowing on her chapped face. Women today don't have to be tormented or live a life of oppression and abuse. Our grandmothers and mothers lived a life that was very physical, full of hard work that was often brutal on the body. They didn't have support or help from a husband or a caretaker. They were forced to take their children to work with them if they didn't have a parent or relative residing with them. She was limited from having any help at all.

Our mothers did not have access to a maid or even a washing machine to help them with the family laundry. They were

forced to heat water over a wooden fire to wash the clothes outside in a cradle, or in a bathtub, as my mom did. They didn't have access to electrical appliances.

Everything was done manually, leaving them very little time to sleep or take care of themselves. Somehow, they managed their time wisely. They never complained. They knew they had no choice but to keep going.

Today, we have access to so many luxuries and so much technology that simplifies our lives. We can make choices about where we will live, whether or not we want to get married, and how and where to socialize. We have choices in food, clothes, and whether or not we will have help like babysitters or housekeepers to assist us. We also have the opportunity to receive education, and financial government programs make it easy to find support through life's challenges. I think of what my mother and grandmother would have given for these opportunities. Who would they have been and how would they have lived if the world were different for them? How far could they have gone?

When I look at the women who came before me, I am reminded that women have always had the ability to be resilient. We were chosen to bear children because we can tolerate pain and suffering. We have grand ambitions, but we still stop to wipe a tear or put a Band-Aid on a scraped knee. We can be perfectionists yet are talented multitaskers. We are tigresses protecting our families. We don't need anyone for support or to provide for us. We are mothers, daughters, granddaughters, friends, cousins, entrepreneurs, philanthropists, and more. We can achieve anything our heart desires.

Today, women have unparalleled beauty, boundless dynamism, undeniable power, unwavering love, infinite kindness, and a forever youthful spirit. Women have become the beacon of stability, strength, and power. Women today have the immeasurable ability to cultivate their relationship with resistance. Women with integrity and self-esteem make extraordinary daughters, wives, mothers, and friends. Mothers of all diverse cultural backgrounds have and will continue to always shield their loved ones and others with courtesy, compassion, and love.

Bold Resilient Women

A woman today has enormous strength to love with her heart and not be consumed with fear and hatred. Women can sustain themselves through their actions by being amazing role models filled with unparalleled qualities, from the selflessness that knows no boundaries. A strong woman has the fortitude to carry and navigate her family through any storm and illuminate strength even in her darkest days.

Women, mothers, entrepreneurs, teachers, businesswomen, medical professionals, and many other professions have the unique ability to nurture, guide, and protect their loved ones without limitations.

Honorable and effective women sacrifice their own needs for the well-being of their children. A woman can motivate and inspire in ways that shatter the lives of others with her grace and resilience. A woman with aspirations teaches her constituents and friends invaluable lessons through her actions and words. Women today have learned through history and personal relationships that love is without boundaries or restrictions. Many women today fear

Bold Resilient Women

failure, love, and patience. They are apprehensive about not letting their emotions interfere in any difficult situation and circumstances. Although many women have a compassionate *agape* for everyone, many times they are deceived by their feelings, although they have a divine love for mankind.

Today's woman needs to gain a profound presence and pivotal velocity in spirituality. She needs to realize that the foundation and bond of her life, family, and relationship is based in God's hands.

A woman's strength and unwavering commitment can make the world a brighter place. Today's woman is bold and resilient. Women, today, advocate for their families, especially their children's future. Many women today are the breadwinners in their homes. They work while at the same time they take care of their responsibilities as caregivers, wives, and mothers. During difficult times, women find it in themselves to spend quality time teaching their children how to conduct themselves as citizens of a country. Faith, God, values, morals, and divine intervention are her keys to power and strength. She prays for wisdom, strength, and stability.

Women today are not expected to dress and act like model goddesses. They are respected and appreciated for their intelligence, brains, and positions in this world. Statistics today report that approximately fifty percent of the workforce is made up of women. Women are articulate, powerful, successful, and assertive; although they strive for acceptance and pursue their goals, they are still the compassionate, vulnerable, caring, and empathetic wives and mothers.

Bold Resilient Women

Women today are bold and resilient.

Acknowledgments

My book was written to rekindle the spirit of every young woman who is struggling in making life choices. Life doesn't have to be about choices, but acceptance and reality. One must prioritize their life and ambitions without overwhelming themselves and becoming captive to irrelevant and unrealistic expectations.

To my beloved husband Jimmy, for his love and support, both financially and psychologically. He has been my rock in all my endeavors.

To my dear friends, whose unconditional love, strength, and persistence gave me the power to write this book on behalf of all women and children. I deeply thank you for believing in me.

I am most grateful for the love and support of a few people who pushed me to my limits: Anna, Maria, Sandy, Stella, Soula, Marianthi, Rosa, Patty, Nicole, Charlene, Kate, Melissa, Kelly, Athena, and my sister-in-law, Vicky. I especially want to thank my beloved daughter, Victoria, and my sons, Mike, Evangelo, and George, for their drive and resilience.

It took many years of tears, observation, acceptance, inner searching, and strength to be comfortable writing about my experiences as a young girl. Being an innocent child and feeling thrown into adulthood at a very young age was both traumatizing and educational.

When I started writing my book, admitting my challenges and choices brought me anguish, tears, and deep sorrow, followed by happiness and fulfillment, followed by excruciating fear. Somehow, in becoming reacquainted with my past life, I was feeling scared and lost. I kept asking myself how it was possible at such a young age to make startling choices about marriage, family, work, education, and the future of my children.

Writing, reminiscing, and thinking made me come to terms with my existence as Eleni. A woman of hope, love, *agape*, persistence, perseverance, loyalty, empathy, compassion, faith, and philanthropy.

Through my journey and struggles, I have gained more knowledge than any school, books, lecture, or diploma could have provided me. I gained tremendous experience in all aspects of life by facing many dangerous and difficult journeys. I climbed the ladder slowly and cautiously, with vigilance and fear. I was forced to make choices quickly, as time was of the essence.

As I finished the book, I was fearful of reading it. But once I did, I realized I have no regrets about where I came from. I'm grateful for my humble orphan father and my peasant mother, innocent people who taught me simple things like love, faith, country, and generosity. They taught me to say "thank you" and "I'm sorry," and believed that knowing these words was knowing a book on life. I am proud of the child I was and the woman I have become. I am no longer a victim of circumstances, but a wise, empathetic, and robust leader of light, hope, love, and compassion. Becoming accepting of the challenges, pain, struggles, tears, and heartache of both myself and those around me has made me a stronger woman, daughter, sister, spouse, mother, friend, and philanthropist.

Looking back gave me a different perspective on my decisions, and I felt free. I realized God had a plan. I had to go through the dark tunnel to see the great light that was foreseen for me and my family.

I am thankful for all the beautiful and remarkable ups and downs. My success today is due to the long and winding road that Jimmy and I have traveled on, and when I look back, I see a humble and dedicated woman who achieved everything she dreamed of and her heart desired.

When it comes time to travel to my everlasting life, my life will be fulfilled. With humility and a humble heart, I have been a woman of faith in our Lord, Jesus Christ. I cared for my family, friends, the elderly, orphans, cancer victims, the less fortunate, the homeless, the disabled, physically and mentally abused individuals, children struggling with gender identity, and anyone else who didn't have a voice.

With love and compassion, I will leave behind an impeccable path, paving stones marked with a story of pain, suffering, happiness, joy, and love for those who worked alongside me in hopes that they, too, pave a positive path through society.

With humility, I am honored to carry the nickname "The Modern Mother Theresa." My legacy is as a faithful servant of God and a loving philanthropist.

This book is dedicated to my mom, dad, grandmothers Eleni and Georgia, Carole, Jack, Marianne, Tina, Jay, Pat, Thea Mary, Uncle Bob, and Debbie—individuals who helped me through many difficult and challenging moments. They impacted my life by being prime examples of love, faith, patience, hope, and perseverance. They gave me the strength to continue fighting without ever giving up.

Our Family

My dear Lord,

*I don't understand or know the different challenges
my friends, acquaintances, and family members have,
You, my Lord, know everything, for You knew us
before we were in our mother's womb.
I hear my family's and my friends' silence,
but You know their pain and hear their prayers.
I see their joy, happiness, and laughter,
but You, my Lord, see their suffering and tears.
I see their compassionate and giving hear, You see what they give away.
I see their empathetic heart and soul, You see the scars that they're trying to heal.
I see and experience their faith, You realize their doubts and fears.
My Lord, we all need Your loving heart.
Don't forsake us, hear our prayers.*

*In order to deserve what is given to us, we must
pay our dues and steadily work for peace and perfection.
We must savor life, and live with joy and happiness.
We must relinquish fear and seek enlightenment.
We must not dwell and focus on division but
embrace with empathy and love.
We must know our heart and soul and
seek to understand others' pain.
We must try to honor, respect, shelter, live,
create, feel, understand, grow, and love.*

Amen!

www.ingramcontent.com/pod-product-compliance
Lightning Source LLC
Chambersburg PA
CBHW030816090426
42737CB00009B/755